ASCENT

CENTER FOR TECHNICAL KNOWLEDGE

AF894493

Autodesk® Inventor® 2024 Fundamentals for CAM Users

Learning Guide

Mixed Units - 1st Edition

ASCENT - Center for Technical Knowledge®
Autodesk® Inventor® 2024
Fundamentals for CAM Users
Mixed Units - 1st Edition

Prepared and produced by:

ASCENT Center for Technical Knowledge
630 Peter Jefferson Parkway, Suite 175
Charlottesville, VA 22911

866-527-2368
www.ASCENTed.com

Lead Contributor: Jennifer MacMillan

ASCENT - Center for Technical Knowledge (a division of Rand Worldwide Inc.) is a leading developer of professional learning materials and knowledge products for engineering software applications. ASCENT specializes in designing targeted content that facilitates application-based learning with hands-on software experience. For over 25 years, ASCENT has helped users become more productive through tailored custom learning solutions.

We welcome any comments you may have regarding this guide, or any of our products. To contact us please email: feedback@ASCENTed.com.

AS-INV2401-CAM1MU-SG // IS-INV2401-CAM1MU-SG

Contents

Preface

The *Autodesk® Inventor® 2024: Fundamentals for CAM Users* is a hands-on, practice-intensive guide designed to equip CAM users with basic modeling and assembly skills in Inventor that are required prior to setting up models in Inventor CAM for manufacturing. Note that this guide does not cover any Inventor CAM functionality and is solely intended to provide introductory training in specific Inventor topics that are relevant only for CAM users. For instructions on Inventor CAM functionality, please refer to the *Autodesk® Inventor® CAM: Milling Fundamentals* guide. Also, if extensive Inventor modeling experience is required, it is recommended that you refer to the *Autodesk® Inventor® 2024: Introduction to Solid Modeling* guide.

Topics Covered

- Understanding the Autodesk Inventor software interface
- Creating, constraining, and dimensioning 2D sketches
- Creating and editing the solid base 3D feature from a sketch
- Creating and editing secondary solid features that are sketched and placed
- Manipulating the display of the model
- Duplicating geometry in the model
- Placing and constraining/connecting parts in assemblies
- Manipulating the display of components in an assembly
- Obtaining model measurements and property information
- Working with projects
- Customizing the Autodesk Inventor environment

Prerequisites

- Access to the 2024.0 version of the software, to ensure compatibility with this guide. Future software updates that are released by Autodesk may include changes that are not reflected in this guide. The practices and files included with this guide are not compatible with prior versions (e.g., 2023).
- As an introductory guide, *Autodesk® Inventor® 2024: Fundamentals for CAM Users* does not assume prior knowledge of any 3D modeling or CAD software. You need to be experienced with the Windows operating system, and having a background in drafting of 3D parts is recommended.

Note on Software Setup

This guide assumes a standard installation of the software using the default preferences during installation. Lectures and practices use the standard software templates and default options for the Content Libraries.

Lead Contributor: Jennifer MacMillan

With a dedication for engineering and education, Jennifer has spent over 25 years at ASCENT managing courseware development for various CAD products. Trained in Instructional Design, Jennifer uses her skills to develop instructor-led and web-based training products as well as knowledge profiling tools.

Jennifer has achieved the Autodesk Certified Professional certification for Inventor and is also recognized as an Autodesk Certified Instructor (ACI). She enjoys teaching the training courses that she authors and is also very skilled in providing technical support to end-users.

Jennifer holds a Bachelor of Engineering Degree as well as a Bachelor of Science in Mathematics from Dalhousie University, Nova Scotia, Canada.

Jennifer MacMillan has been the Lead Contributor for *Autodesk Inventor: Fundamentals for CAM Users* since 2007.

In This Guide

The following highlights the key features of this guide.

Feature	Description
Practice Files	The Practice Files page includes a link to the practice files and instructions on how to download and install them. The practice files are required to complete the practices in this guide.
Chapters	A chapter consists of the following: Learning Objectives, Instructional Content, Practices, Chapter Review Questions, and Command Summary. • **Learning Objectives** define the skills you can acquire by learning the content provided in the chapter. • **Instructional Content**, which begins right after Learning Objectives, refers to the descriptive and procedural information related to various topics. Each main topic introduces a product feature, discusses various aspects of that feature, and provides step-by-step procedures on how to use that feature. Where relevant, examples, figures, helpful hints, and notes are provided. • **Practice** for a topic follows the instructional content. Practices enable you to use the software to perform a hands-on review of a topic. It is required that you download the practice files (using the link found on the Practice Files page) prior to starting the first practice. • **Chapter Review Questions**, located close to the end of a chapter, enable you to test your knowledge of the key concepts discussed in the chapter. • **Command Summary** concludes a chapter. It contains a list of the software commands that are used throughout the chapter and provides information on where the command can be found in the software.
Appendices	Appendices provide additional information to the main course content. It could be in the form of instructional content, practices, tables, projects, or skills assessment.

Practice Files

1. Type the URL *exactly as shown below* into the address bar of your Internet browser to access the Course File Download page.

   Note: If you are using the ebook, you do not have to type the URL. Instead, you can access the page by clicking the URL below.

   https://www.ascented.com/getfile/id/genyorchisPF

2. On the Course File Download page, click the **DOWNLOAD NOW** button, as shown below, to download the .ZIP file that contains the practice files.

3. Once the download is complete, unzip the file and extract its contents.

   The recommended practice files folder location is:
   C:\Autodesk Inventor 2024 Intro Practice Files

   Note: It is recommended that you do not change the location of the practice files folder. Doing so may cause errors when completing the practices.

Stay Informed!

To receive information about upcoming events, promotional offers, and complimentary webcasts, visit:

www.ASCENTed.com/updates

Chapter 1

Introduction to Autodesk Inventor

Understanding how Autodesk® Inventor® models are built and how they react to change is fundamental when designing robust and intelligent models. In addition, learning the working environment is important. The environment consists of many different components, including toolbars, panels, and menus. Learning to interact with all of the components increases your modeling efficiency.

Learning Objectives

- Understand how the Part, Assembly, Presentation, and Drawing environments enable you to create and document a 3D Digital Prototype.
- Understand how the five key Inventor attributes contribute to creating robust parts and assemblies that can be easily documented.
- Load and activate a project file.
- Open existing Autodesk Inventor files.
- Navigate the software interface to locate and execute commands.
- Use the model orientation commands to pan, zoom, rotate, and look at a model.
- Assign visual styles to your models.
- Use object selection techniques to efficiently select objects in your models.

1.1 Autodesk Inventor Introduction

The Autodesk Inventor software takes you beyond 3D to Digital Prototyping by providing a comprehensive set of tools for 3D mechanical design that enables you to design, visualize, and simulate products before they are built. Digital Prototyping helps you to minimize the need for physical prototypes, design better products, reduce development costs, and get to market faster.

There are a number of tools available to design models in the Autodesk Inventor software. To begin, you must start with a foundation in solid 3D part design. Then you progress to placing the models relative to one another in an assembly, followed by creating drawings that document the 3D parts and assembly models in a 2D format.

The following are the basic environments that are commonly used for 3D model design. Parts and assemblies are often referred to collectively as components, because of the similar manner in which they are treated. For example, a drawing file might reference either a part or another assembly file.

Environment (File Extension)	**Description**
Part (.IPT)	All part modeling, sketching, and complex design takes place on individual parts.
Assembly (.IAM)	Parts are added to assemblies to position and constrain them together to form a completed design. Parts are not stored in the assembly but their data is referenced from the original part model. The only modeling data stored in the assembly is the positional data that locates each part in the assembly.
Presentation (.IPN)	Used to document disassembled views in a drawing. Additionally, it can be used to animate tasks for visualization of component movement.
Drawing (.DWG & .IDW)	Used to communicate the 3D design in a 2D format. Views and annotations are used to document the design.

The part, assembly, and drawing files shown in Figure 1–1 illustrate how the original data created in the part model is passed to the assembly and finally used in a drawing to document a 3D design in a 2D format for manufacturing.

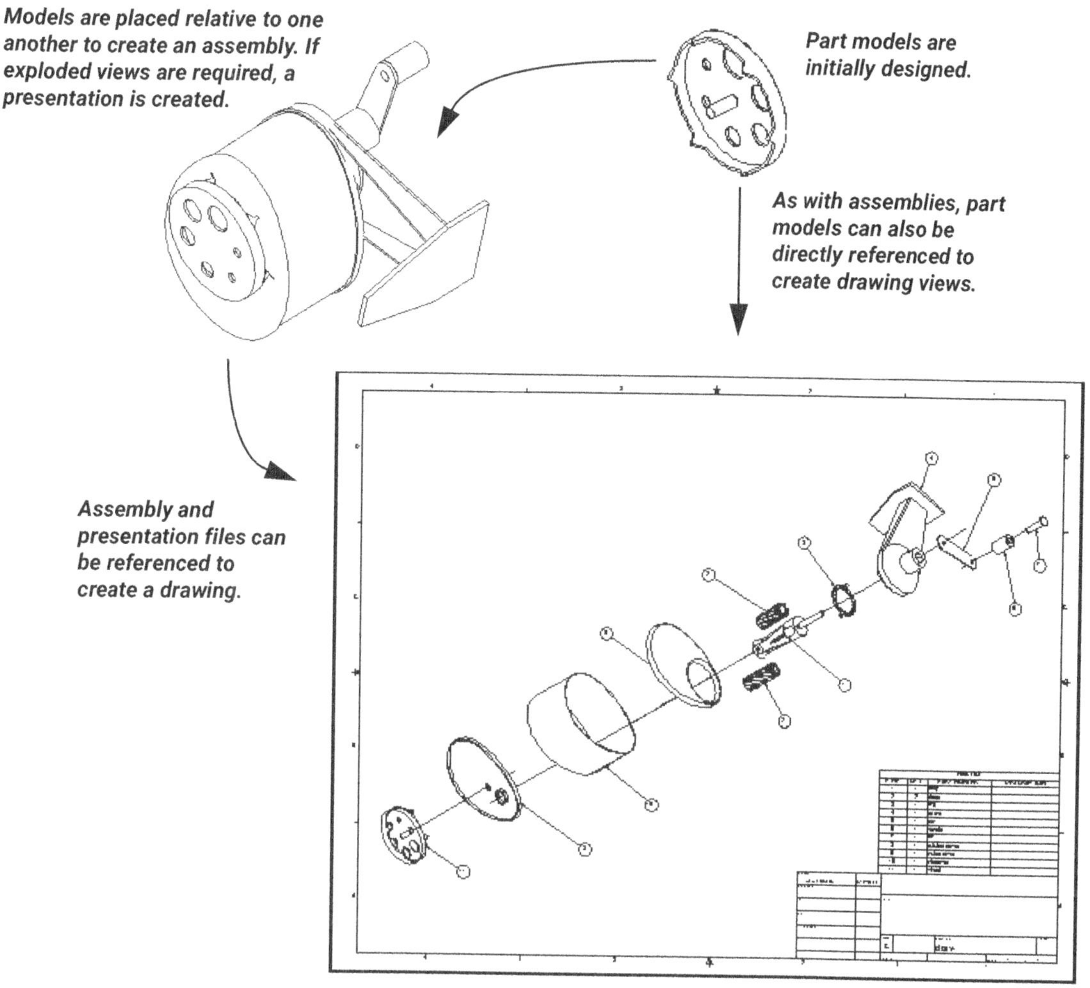

Figure 1–1

Hint: Autodesk Inventor and AutoCAD Interoperability

There are several ways to incorporate AutoCAD® DWG files in an Autodesk Inventor file. The method you use depends on your project requirements. You can open the file directly in the Autodesk Inventor software for review. You can also import and convert the AutoCAD DWG into an Inventor DWG file, where all links to the original AutoCAD DWG file are lost or you can use it as blocks in the Inventor drawing file. Alternatively, you can import and use an AutoCAD DWG as an associative underlay in an Autodesk Inventor file. These tools are discussed in detail in the *Autodesk Inventor 2024: Advanced Part Modeling* guide.

The Autodesk Inventor software has the following five key attributes:

- Feature-Based Modeling
- Parametric Features
- Associative
- Assembly Management
- Model Documentation

Feature-Based Modeling

The Autodesk Inventor software is a feature-based modeling program, which means that a part evolves by creating features one by one until it is complete. Each feature is individually recognized by the software. A part model consisting of several individual features is shown in Figure 1–2.

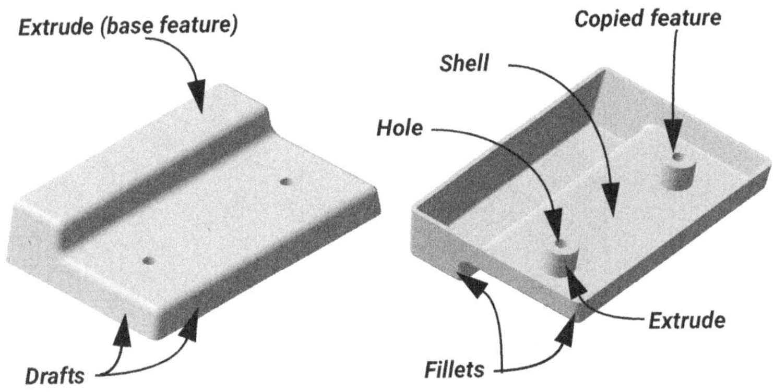

Figure 1–2

To start a design, create a simple extruded base feature that approximates the shape of the part. Continue adding features that add and remove material from the model until the part is complete, as shown in Figure 1–3.

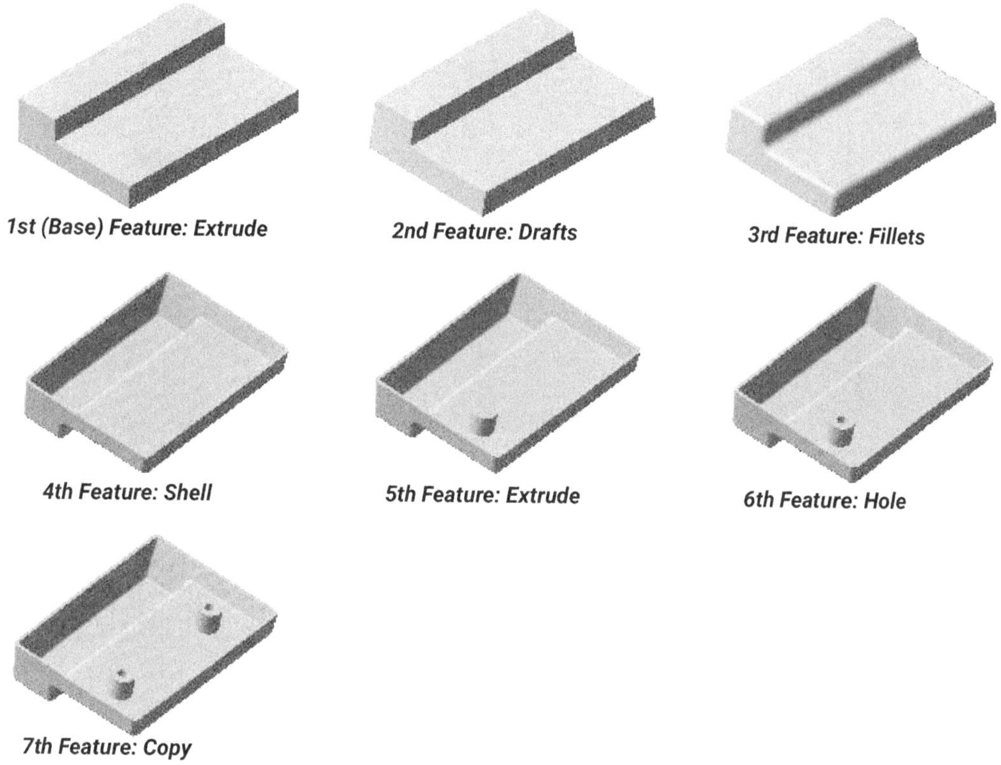

Figure 1–3

Sketched Features

A sketched feature is created by sketching and constraining a 2D cross-section on a placement plane. Then, the profile is used to create solid geometry, similar to the extrusion shown in Figure 1–4. Sketched features can either add or remove material.

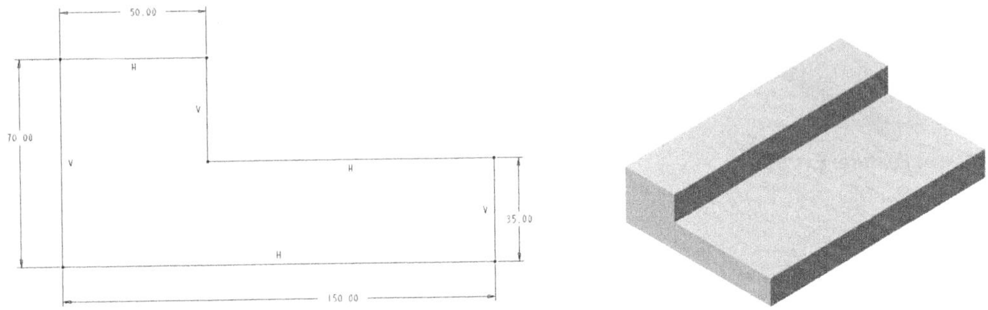

Figure 1–4

Pick and Place Features

A pick and place feature is a feature for which a shape has been predefined. For example, the cross-section of a Hole feature is a circle. To create a pick and place feature, you must define the location of the feature and the references required to locate it with respect to the existing geometry. An example of a pick and place Hole feature is shown in Figure 1–5.

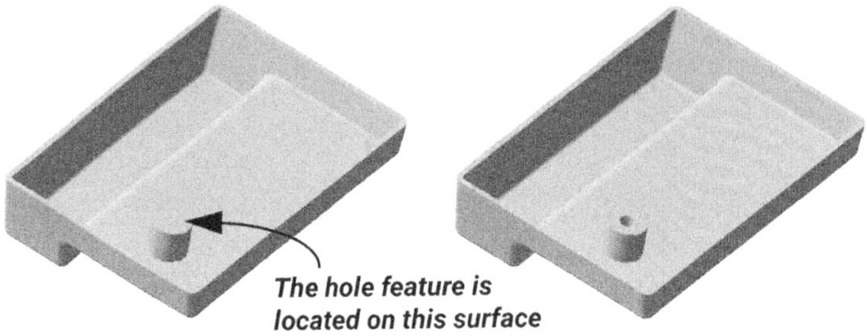

Figure 1–5

Feature Relationships

Feature-based modeling requires that features be added one by one. As a result, feature relationships are created as new features reference existing ones. For example, the hole shown in Figure 1–5 cannot exist without the cylindrical extruded feature because the hole's placement references exist in the extrusion. Feature relationships are created with all features.

Parametric Features

Parametric features are features that are created using dimensional constraints to define the feature's shape. The dimensional constraints are considered parameters: changes can be made at any time, and the features automatically update.

For example, the dimensional value that positions the cut feature shown in Figure 1–6 is changed. Therefore, the position of the feature updates to reflect the design change.

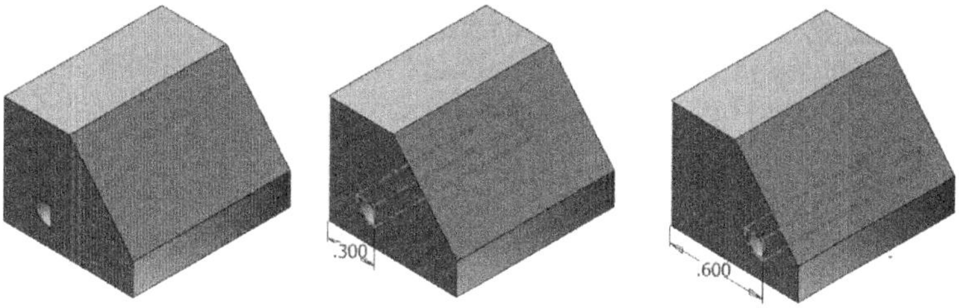

Figure 1–6

Dimensioning is an important step in the modeling process. When creating dimensions, use the following guidelines:

- Consider the dimensions that are going to be displayed in drawings and be aware of the resulting feature relationships.
- Consider changes that might need to be made to the model and how easily the dimensions facilitate these changes.
- Periodically modify dimensions to test *what if* scenarios. This is called *flexing the model* and ensures that the model behaves as expected.

Parameters and dimensions can be used in an equation to capture and control design intent. The ability to use equations in a model becomes extremely important in making a robust model.

Associative

The Autodesk Inventor software is fully associative, which means it operates in a concurrent engineering environment. You can work with the same model in different modes (e.g., Part, Assembly, or Drawing), and all modes are fully associative. Therefore, changes made to a model in any of the modes propagate to all other modes.

Assembly Management

Models built in Part mode can be used as components in an assembly. Assemblies are created by constraining components with respect to one another. The addition of constraints creates feature relationships between components and builds intelligent assemblies. Similar to features in Part mode, assembly constraints are assigned a unique internal identification number and can be used to establish relations between components.

Model Documentation

The tools available in the Drawing environment enable you to quickly create production-ready drawings for manufacturing. Drawings are created from part, assembly, or presentation models where their geometry and assembly specifications have already been defined. This information is used to create the required views in a drawing file. Adding details to your drawings enables you to communicate additional information about the design.

Drawing models are not actually contained in a drawing file. There is a link between the drawing file and the source model. If a change is made to the source model, all drawing views that reference it automatically update. The reverse, where a change made in the drawing also reflects in the model, can also be true if your workflow permits.

1.2 Getting Started with Inventor

Home Page

When you launch the Autodesk Inventor software, the *Home* page displays, as shown in Figure 1–7. This page enables you to activate a project file, create a new file, open files from the recently used list, or browse for a specific file and open it. Figure 1–7 displays the *Home* page with the Default project active. Note that it doesn't show any previously opened files; as files are opened, they will appear in this list.

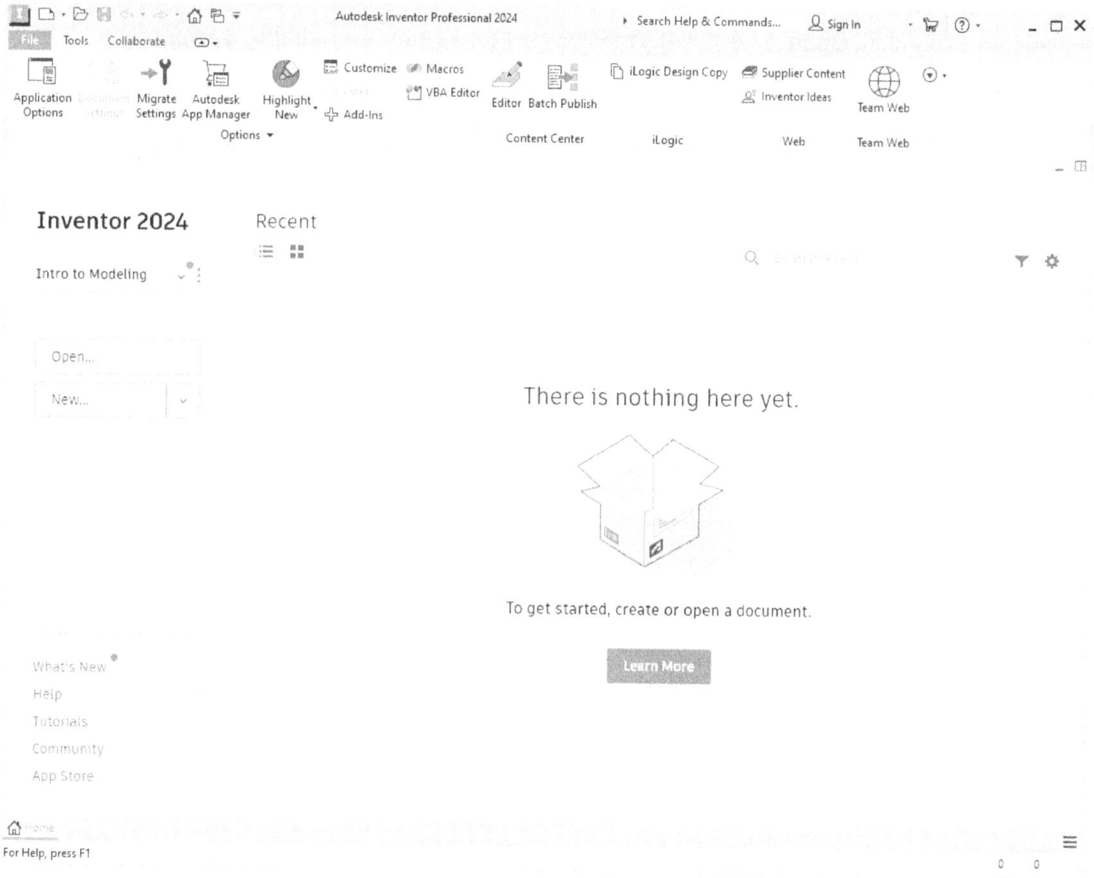

Figure 1–7

Opening Files

Files can be opened using a number of different methods in the Autodesk Inventor software. Use one of the following methods to open an existing file:

- On the *Home* page, select **Open**.
- Click (Open) in the Quick Access Toolbar at the top of the interface.
- In the **File** menu, select **Open>Open**, or select a file from the **File** menu's Recent list.

For all but the recent document methods, the Open dialog box opens. Navigate to the required file, select it, and click **Open**. The (Find Files) button in the Open dialog box can also be used to find a file to be opened.

Hint: Home Tab

The *Home* tab is available even when files are open. To return to the *Home* page, select the *Home* tab at the bottom of the Inventor graphics window, as shown in Figure 1–8.

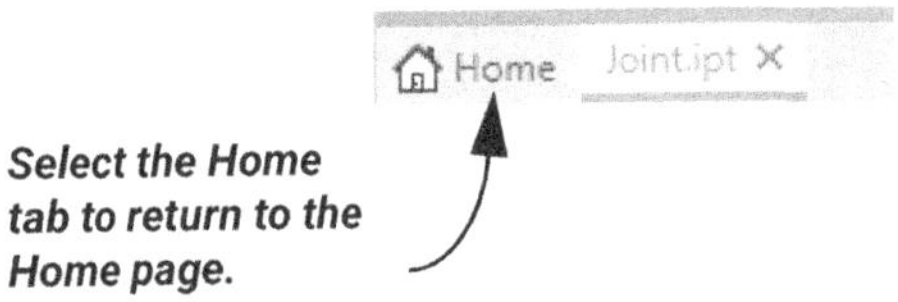

Figure 1–8

Recent List

The *Recent* area on the *Home* page lists previously opened files for the active project and enables you to open files directly from this list. List View ( ) displays the file names in a list format and Grid View ( ) displays the files as thumbnail images. Use any one of the following methods to open files in either view:

- Double-click on the files name or the thumbnail image.
- In List View, right-click on the file name and select **Open**. Alternatively, click ⋮ adjacent to the Pinned column and select **Open**.
- In Grid View, hover over the thumbnail image, select ⋮, and select **Open**.

  *Note: The **Open with options** option enables you to open specific Model State or Design View representations in the file. This will be discussed in a later topic.*

Additional tools in the Recent list include:

- Sorting files by selecting column headers in the List View or selecting the **Sort by** option in the Grid View. These enable you to sort by Name, Location, or Date Modified.
- Clicking in the Pinned column in the List View or on the thumbnail image to add a recent document to the pinned list so that it is listed at the top of the list.
- If you are using the Autodesk Vault software, a file status column displays in the *Recent* area.

Hint: Controlling the number of Listed Recent Documents

By default, a maximum of 50 recent documents are listed in the *Recent* area of the Home page. To remove a file in List View, right-click on its file name and select **Remove from Recent**. Alternatively, in Grid View, hover over the thumbnail image, select , and select **Remove from Recent**. To change the default number of files, click **Tools** > (Application Options), and on the *General* tab, change the value for the **Maximum number of recent documents**.

Project Files

If you work as part of a design team, managing access to the shared Autodesk Inventor data is crucial. Incorporating project files enables you to organize and access the files that are used. A project file is a text file that has an .IPJ format. At a fundamental level, a project file specifies the locations of the files in the project and maintains all of the required links to the files. When you open a model, the paths specified in the active project are searched to find all of the referenced files. At a more advanced level, project files can specify library locations and set many options. Project Files are discussed in more depth later in this guide.

How To: Load a Project File

1. Use one of the following methods to open the Projects dialog box to load a project:
   - On the Home page, select (Projects and Settings) > **Settings**.
   - Click (Projects) in the Quick Access Toolbar at the top of the interface.
   - In the **File** menu, select **Manage>Projects**.
   - In the New or Open dialog boxes, click **Projects**.
2. Click **Browse** and navigate to the location of the project file. Select it and click **Open**. The Projects dialog box updates and a checkmark displays next to the new project name, indicating that it is the active project.
3. Click **Done** to close the Projects dialog box.

Once a project has been loaded it remains listed as an available project. A previously loaded project can be activated by:

- Double-clicking on its name in the Projects dialog box, or
- Expanding the Projects drop-down list (⌄) on the *Home* page (as show in Figure 1–9) and selecting the project name.

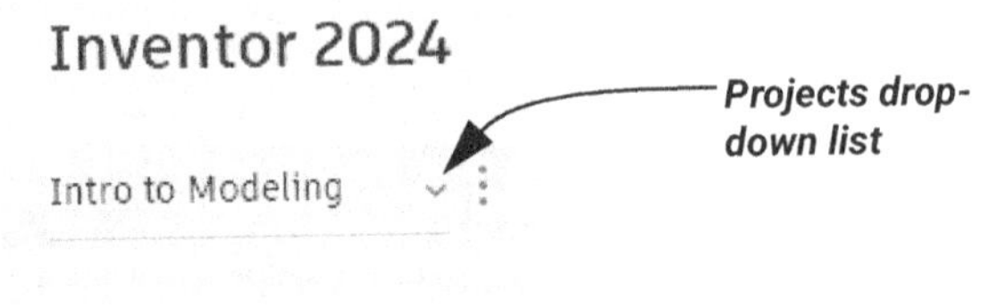

Figure 1–9

Additional options are available in the lower left corner of that Home page that enable you to review the What's New documentation for the latest software release, online Help and Tutorial documents, as well as links to the Inventor Community forum and App Store.

1.3 Autodesk Inventor Interface

Once a file has been opened, the interface updates to include additional elements. These are consistent among the various environments. The Part environment and many of the interface elements are shown in Figure 1–10.

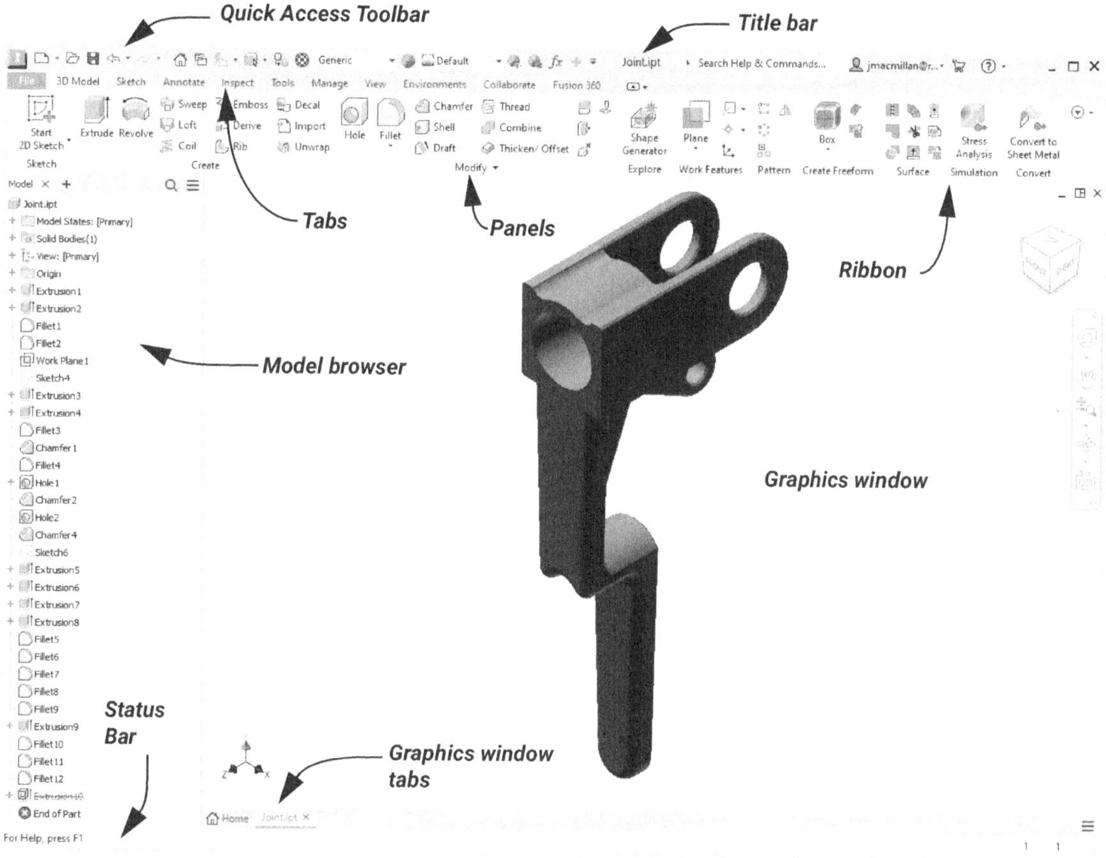

Figure 1–10

Interface

The following interface elements exist in the Part environment and the other Autodesk Inventor environments.

Title Bar

The title bar at the top of the interface displays the name of the current active file.

Ribbon/Tabs/Panels

The ribbon provides access to commands and settings. The ribbon is divided into tabs and they are further subdivided into panels. The tabs that are available vary depending on the mode that is currently active. All commands are listed in panels. Many commands can also be accessed by right-clicking on a feature in the model or in the Model browser. In Figure 1–11, the *3D Model* tab is active. Sketch, Create, and Modify are some of the panels in this tab.

Figure 1–11

- Commands can be hidden in either compressed panels or commands. To expand hidden commands, click ▾ on the panel or command name, as shown for the Modify panel and **Start 2D Sketch** command in Figure 1–12.

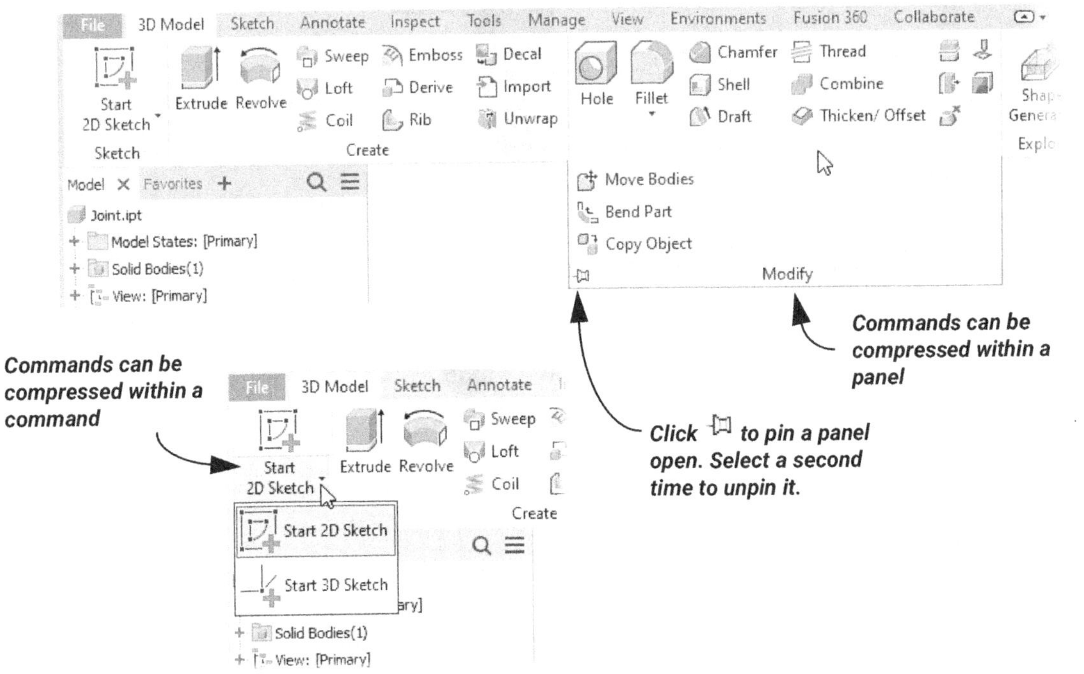

Figure 1–12

- Only commonly accessed panels display by default. To customize which panels display, expand (Show panels) at the end of each tab and select from the available list, as shown in Figure 1–13. Alternatively, you can right-click on the ribbon, expand **Show Panels**, and then select a panel.

Figure 1–13

Graphics Window

Open files are displayed and can be directly manipulated in the graphics window. As individual files are opened, they display listed as tabs along the bottom of the graphics window. Select a tab name to display it. In the example shown in Figure 1–14, a model, drawing, and *Home* tab are shown. The active model is **Joint.ipt**. Hover over the tab to access a thumbnail preview.

Figure 1–14

- Generally, maximizing each window provides the most modeling space. As required, you can minimize and resize windows, or click (Documents Menu) in the bottom right of the graphics window and use (Arrange), (Horizontal Tile), and (Vertical Tile) to customize your graphics window layout.

Quick Access Toolbar

Commonly accessed commands are available at the top of the software window in the Quick Access Toolbar, as shown in Figure 1–15.

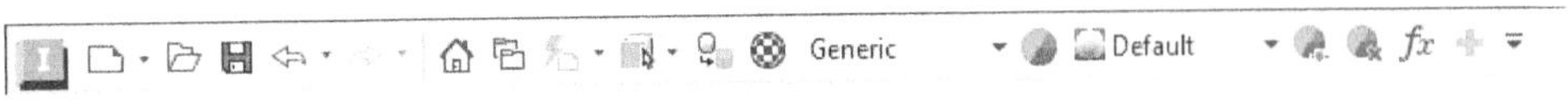

Figure 1–15

- Click on the right of the Quick Access Toolbar to customize the toolbar. Alternatively, you can right-click on any command on the ribbon and select **Add to Quick Access Toolbar**.
- The selection filter in the Quick Access Toolbar enables you to filter entities, features, or components so that you can only select that type of object.
- The (Undo) and (Redo) drop-down lists provide you with a list of previously-completed actions that were performed on the model. To jump forward or back to a point in the model's history, select it in from the drop-down list.

Model Browser

The Model browser lists all of the features or components in your models, in order of creation. The Model browser is a powerful tool that can be used to complete any of the following actions:

- Select features.
- Access commonly used options (e.g., **Delete**, or **Edit**).
- Search for features.
- Edit features.
- Display information on features.
- Change the order of features (click and drag).
- Open components in an assembly.
- Open drawings of components.
- Create drawings of parts and assemblies.
- Investigate relationships between features and components.

In the Model browser (shown in Figure 1–16), each feature is identified by its name and a symbol that identifies the feature type. Expandable nodes reveal additional information on the features.

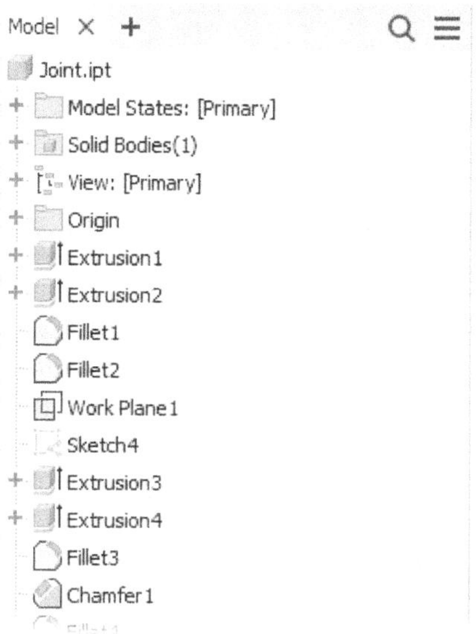

Figure 1–16

- The header of the Model browser indicates the active panel. Model is the panel that displays by default. Click + to expand the list of available panels.
  - For part models, you can activate the iLogic or Favorites panels.
  - For assemblies, you can activate the iLogic, Favorites, or Representation panels to help view model information.
  - For assemblies you can also toggle between an Assembly or Modeling view.
- Click 🔍 in the Model browser header to access the quick search panel. A search is conducted as you type in keywords. In an assembly model, the quick search also provides access to the ? and ⚡ icons, which enable you to filter unresolved and out of date data respectively.
- Click ≡ in the Model browser header to access options to expand and collapse the browser nodes, conduct an advanced search, disable the ability to edit values in the Model browser (assemblies only), set display preferences, or access help.

  Note: *The Model browser can be displayed or removed from the interface. To control its display, enable or disable the tool in the User Interface drop-down list (View tab>Windows panel).*

Status Bar

The Status Bar displays messages that are related to the active command. For example, in a sketch, the Status Bar can display information related to sketching, dimensioning, and constraining an entity.

Modeling Tools

The marking menu and feature creation controls are commonly used in the design process.

Marking Menu

The marking menu provides alternative access to commands. When you right-click in the graphics window, a radial marking menu and a vertical menu display. Both menus provide quick access to commonly used, context-sensitive commands.

- The marking menu consists of eight wedges that contain different commands. To activate a marking menu command, move the cursor in the direction of the command so that it is highlighted (as shown on the right in Figure 1–17) and select it.

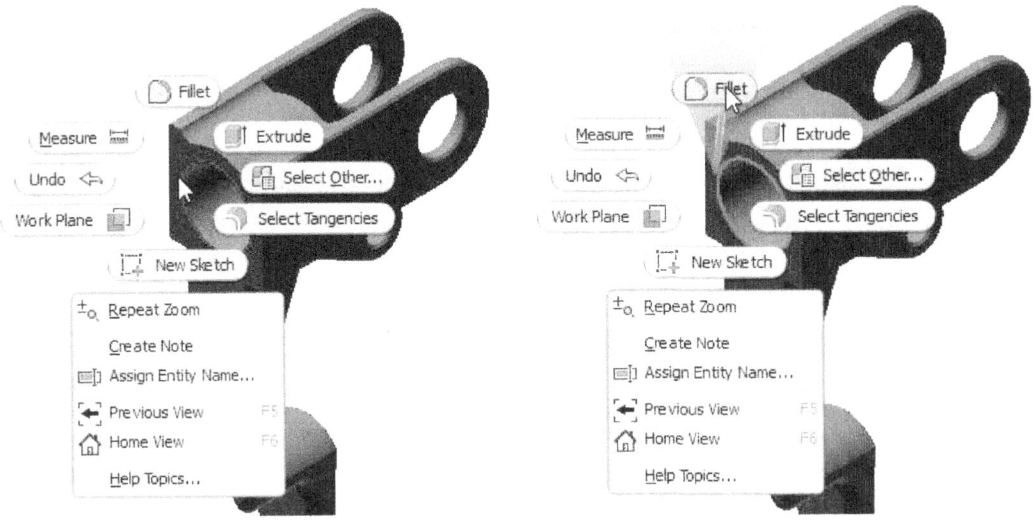

Figure 1–17

- As you become familiar with the marking menu commands, you can use gesturing behavior to initiate commands. To gesture, click and hold the right mouse button, immediately drag the cursor in the direction of the required marking menu wedge to create a trail, and release the mouse button. If these operations are completed in 250 milliseconds, the selected wedge is briefly displayed to confirm that the operation has been performed.
- To close the marking menu, you can start another command, select away from the marking menu, or press <Esc>.

***Note:** The marking menu can be customized using the **Customize** option in the Tools tab. This is covered later in this learning guide.*

Feature Creation Controls

When you create a feature, you must define a variety of properties. Depending on the feature type being created, you can define these using the Properties panel, a Feature dialog box, or the mini-toolbar.

- In the example shown in Figure 1–18, a Hole feature is being created and it uses the Properties panel to define all the hole properties. Dimensional values and references can also be defined directly on the model geometry.

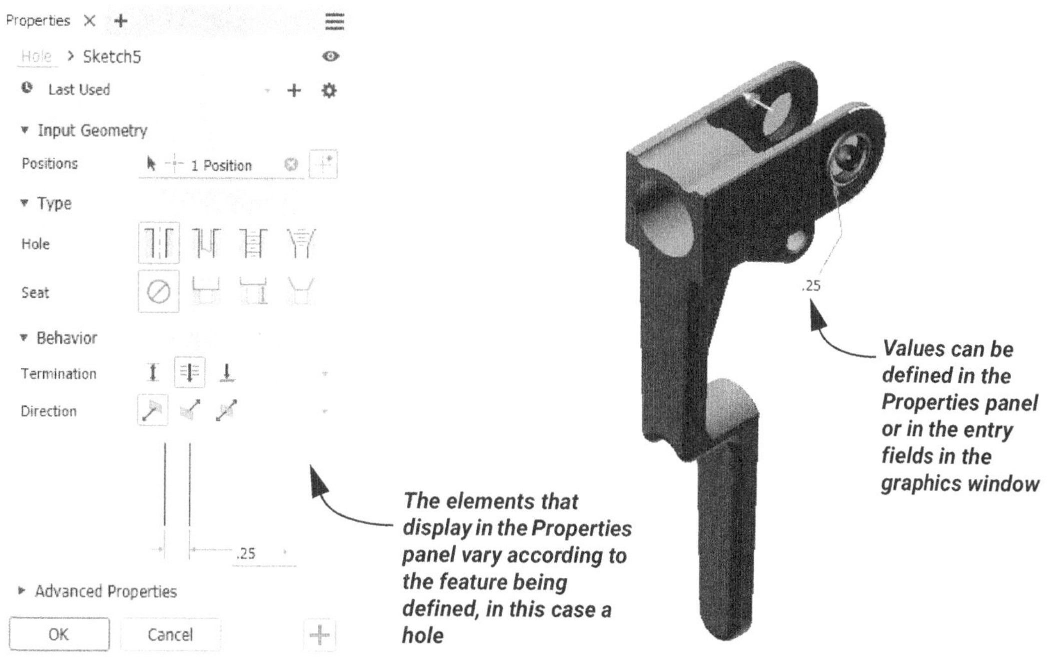

Figure 1–18

Note: *Autodesk is slowly transitioning all feature creation controls to the Properties panel interface. As of the 2024 Inventor release, this has not yet been completed.*

- In the example shown in Figure 1–19, a Chamfer feature is being created and the Chamfer dialog box and its mini-toolbar are displayed. Options can be selected in either location.

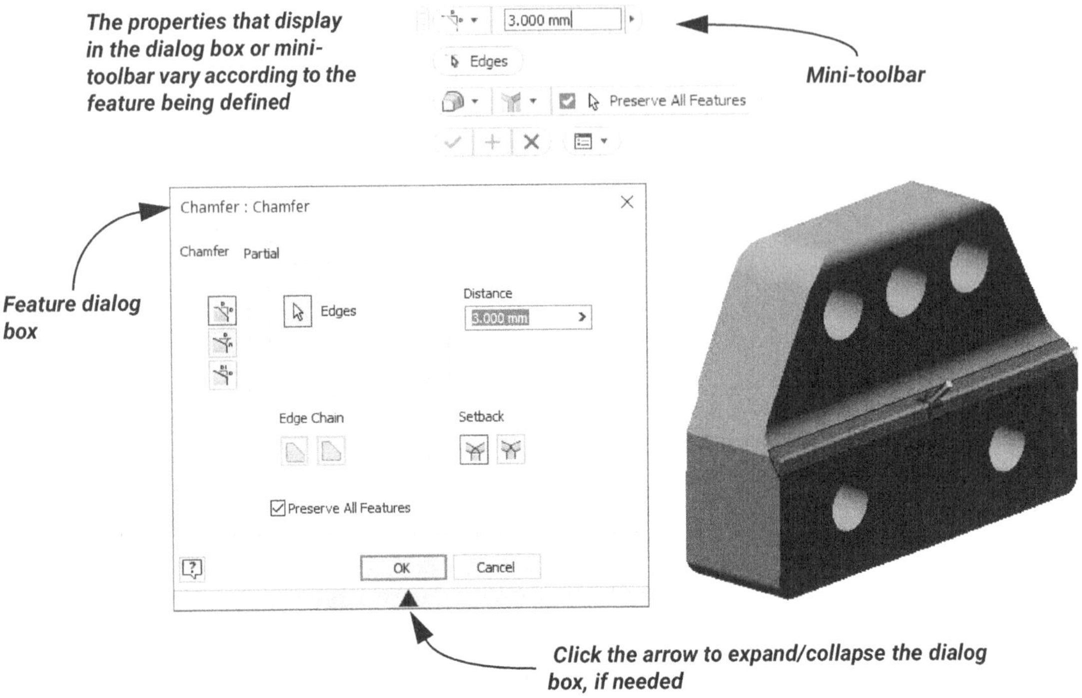

Figure 1–19

Hint: Mini-Toolbar Display

By default, the display of the mini-toolbar is toggled off. To toggle on its display, on the *View* tab, expand **User Interface** and enable the **Mini-Toolbar** option in the list of interface items. The use of the mini-toolbar is optional. In this learning guide, you will toggle it on and learn how to use it. The mini-toolbar is only available for features that use the Feature dialog box. They are not available when creating features that use the Properties panel.

Accessing Help

A number of different tools are available to get help with the software:

- To access context-sensitive help (when available), click (help icon) in any active Feature dialog box or click ☰ (Advanced Settings Menu)>**Help** in a Properties panel.
- Hover the cursor over a command name to display a tooltip, as shown in Figure 1–20. Some tooltips provide a video demonstration in place of a static image.

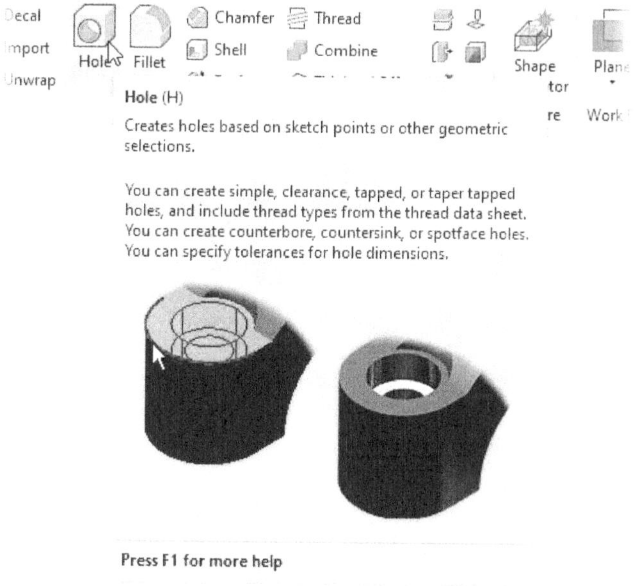

Figure 1–20

- If you are connected to the Internet, you can use Online Help. To access the Help documentation, click ⓘ (Help) in the top-right corner of the interface, click **Help** on the Home page, or press <F1>. Use the *Search* tab to enter a topic to search for or browse the available topics in the Help window.
- The Help documents can be installed locally. This installation is done in the software load point to ensure that it located when required. Once installed, in the Application Options dialog box>*General* tab, enable **Installed Local help**.
- Enter text in the *<Search Help & Commands>* field in the title bar to search for a keyword or phrase. The resulting list updates as you are typing and is divided based on the type of the result (e.g., commands, help articles, support articles, discussion groups, etc). If you press <Enter> after entering a keyword or phrase, the Help files are loaded.

1.4 Model Orientation

When working with Autodesk Inventor models, being able to manipulate their orientation and display style helps you to better visualize them. The interface elements that control this are shown in Figure 1–21.

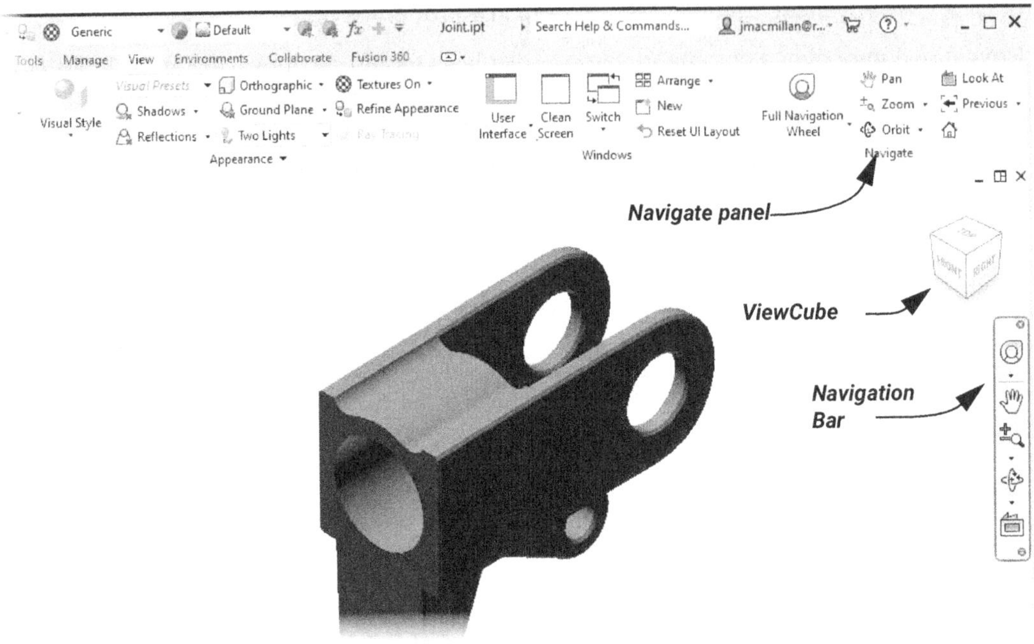

Figure 1–21

A model can be oriented using the software's pan, zoom, rotate and ViewCube controls.

Pan a Model

The **Pan** command moves a model in the graphics window in any direction planar to the screen.

How To: Pan a Model

1. Click  (Pan) in the *View* tab>Navigate panel or in the Navigation Bar.
2. Press and hold the left mouse button.
3. Move the mouse to drag the model.

   Note: *You can also pan a model by pressing and holding the middle mouse button while dragging the mouse, or by holding <F2> and panning with the left mouse button.*

Rotate a Model

The **Orbit** command rotates a model around the center of the window, free in all directions, or around the X- or Y-axis.

How To: Rotate a Model

1. Click (Orbit) in the *View* tab>Navigate panel or in the Navigation Bar. The Rotate symbol (a circle) displays on the screen. The appearance of the cursor changes based on the location of the cursor relative to this circle.
2. Drag the cursor to the required orientation.
    - To rotate freely, move the cursor inside the circle. The cursor appearance changes to . Click and hold the left mouse button and then rotate the model in any direction.
    - To rotate about the horizontal axis, move the cursor to the top or bottom handle of the circle symbol. The cursor appearance changes to . Press and hold the left mouse button and rotate the model about the Y-axis.
    - To rotate about the vertical axis, move the cursor to the left or right handle of the circle symbol. The cursor appearance changes to . Press and hold the left mouse button and drag horizontally.
    - To rotate about an axis through the center of the circle symbol (normal to the screen), move the cursor to the rim of the circle symbol. The cursor appearance changes to . Drag the mouse to rotate. To change the center of the rotation, click inside or outside the circle to set the new center.
    - To stop rotating, click again to clear it. Alternatively, while still in the orbit circle, move the cursor away from the model until displays, and click in the graphics window.

Note: *You can also press and hold <F4> to rotate using the rotate symbol.*

As an alternative to using the (Orbit) tool, you can press and hold <Shift> and use the middle mouse button to rotate the model. Using this method, the model is rotated about a pivot point that appears in the graphics window. Where the pivot point will appear on the model depends on the following:

- If the full model displays in the graphics window, the pivot point is the model geometry center.
- If the model is only partially displayed in the graphics window, the pivot point snaps to the nearest edge/face/vertex.
- If the model is fully panned outside the graphics window, the pivot point is at the cursor location.

Zoom a Model

The **Zoom** command zooms in and out on the model, on a specific entity, or on an area. The available zoom types are shown in Figure 1–22.

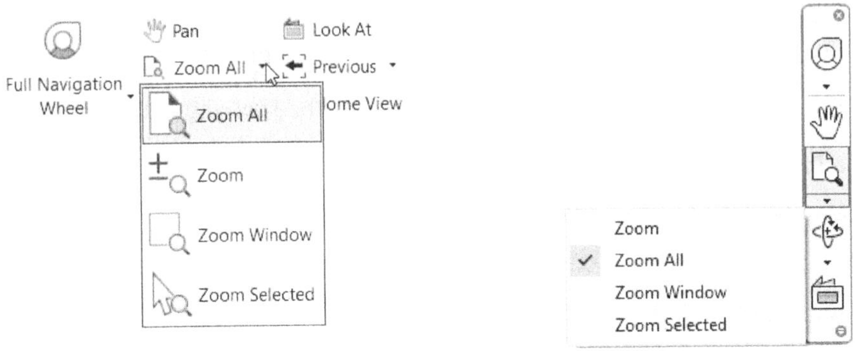

Figure 1–22

How To: Zoom in a Model

1. In the *View* tab>Navigate panel or the Navigation Bar, expand the zoom controls and click **Zoom**.
2. Press and hold the left mouse button.
3. Move the cursor down to zoom in, and up to zoom out.

   Note: *You can also press and hold <F3> to zoom.*

How To: Zoom to a Specific Entity

1. In the *View* tab>Navigate panel or the Navigation Bar, expand the zoom controls and click **Zoom Selected**.
2. Select the entity.

- When zooming to an edge or vertex (not a surface), the order in which you select the entity and toolbar icon is important. Clicking the icon, and then clicking on a point on the entity positions the entity in the center of the screen, and maintains the current zoom level. Selecting the reverse (the entity and then clicking the icon), causes the software to zoom to the selected entity. When zooming on a surface, the order of selection does not have an impact.

How To: Zoom to an Area

1. In the *View* tab>Navigate panel or the Navigation Bar, expand the zoom controls and click **Zoom Window**.
2. Select a location on the model using the left mouse button to define the corner of the bounding box zoom area.
3. Drag the mouse to draw a box over the area to zoom.
4. Press or release the left mouse button when the box has been drawn.

Refit the Model

In the *View* tab>Navigate panel or the Navigation Bar, expand the zoom controls and click **Zoom All**. The view returns to its default zoom level and the model is centered in the graphics window.

Look At

To orient a face parallel to the screen, click (Look At) in the *View* tab>Navigate panel or in the Navigation Bar, and select the face. The model reorients and displays the selected face parallel to the screen. In the example shown in Figure 1–23, a face was selected and was reoriented using this command.

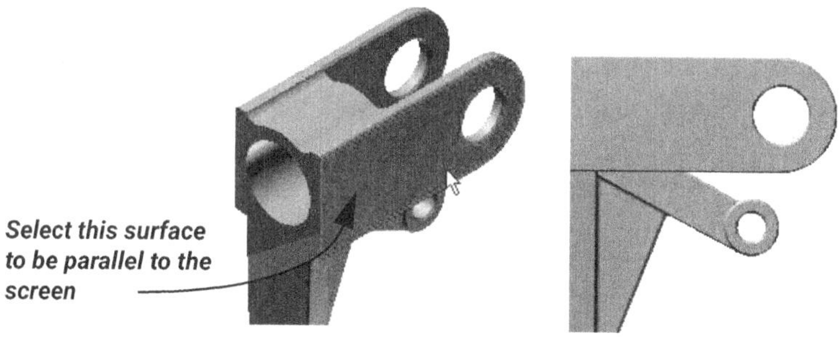

Figure 1–23

ViewCube

As an alternative to the **Look At** command, you can use ViewCube functionality to orient a model face parallel to the screen. By default, the ViewCube displays in the top-right corner of the graphics window, as shown on the left in Figure 1–24. When you hover your mouse over the ViewCube in its 2D or 3D orientation, you can return to the Home view or access additional orientation options.

Figure 1–24

The ViewCube enables the following:

- Select any of the sides of the cube to display the parallel view that is associated with it (**Front**, **Right**, **Bottom**, etc.). Edges can also be selected on the ViewCube to reorient the model.
- Set the type of view to **Orthographic**, **Perspective**, or **Perspective with Ortho Faces** by right-clicking on the ViewCube and selecting the required option.
- Return to a Home view by clicking , which displays at the top-left of the ViewCube when you hover the cursor over it. Initially the Home view is the default isometric orientation.
- Set a new Home view for your model by right-clicking on the ViewCube and selecting **Select Current View as Home**.
- Select and drag a surface on the ViewCube to rotate. If in a 2D orientation, select the rotation arrows that appear.

  Note: *To display the ViewCube settings, right-click on it and select* ***Options****. The ViewCube Options dialog box enables you to control the location, size, default ViewCube orientation, etc. The orientation enables you to select two parallel origin planes to define the orientation.*

Full Navigation Wheel

The Full Navigation Wheel (shown in Figure 1–25) provides an alternative to the *View* tab and Navigation Bar commands for zooming, panning, and rotating. The **Rewind** command on the wheel enables you to navigate through previous views.

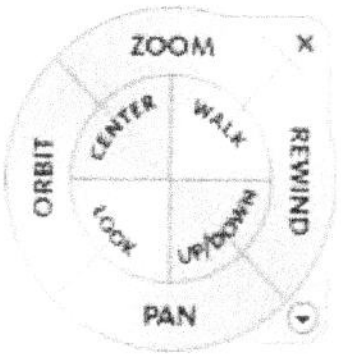

Figure 1–25

The Full Navigation Wheel moves with the cursor to provide access to the navigation tools.

How To: Use the Navigation Tool

1. Enable the tool by clicking (Full Navigation Wheel) in the *View* tab>Navigate panel or in the Navigation Bar. The Full Navigation Wheel displays attached to the mouse.
2. Press and hold the mouse on a command (e.g., **Zoom**).
3. Move the cursor to change the view as required.
4. Release the mouse button to end the navigation command.
5. Click or the **x** in the top-right corner of the tool to close the Full Navigation Wheel.

   Note: *In addition to the* ***Zoom***, ***Orbit***, ***Pan***, *and* ***Rewind*** *commands, other more advanced tools are available on the inner ring of the Full Navigation Wheel that are not covered in this guide.*

1.5 Model Display

By default, new models created using the default templates display as **Shaded with Edges**. However, other visual styles can be assigned. All visual styles are available in the *View* tab> Appearance panel as shown in Figure 1–26.

> **Note:** *The ability to use many of the styles depends on your computer's graphics hardware.*

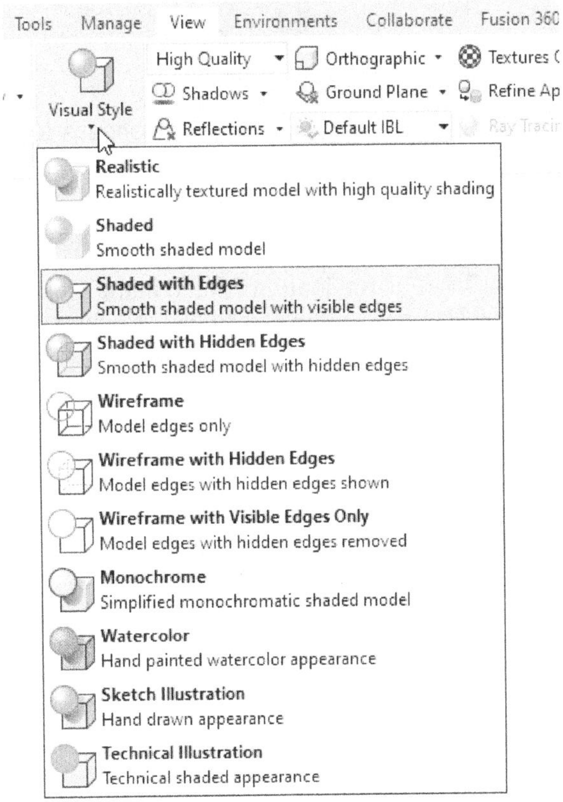

Figure 1–26

> **Note:** *The* **Realistic** *setting is dependent on the color and lighting settings that are applied in the model. When using this style you can also incorporate Ray Tracing to further enhance model display. Additionally, the watercolor and illustration settings provide artistic, hand-painted, and drawn representations of the model.*

Figure 1–27 shows some examples of the available visual styles.

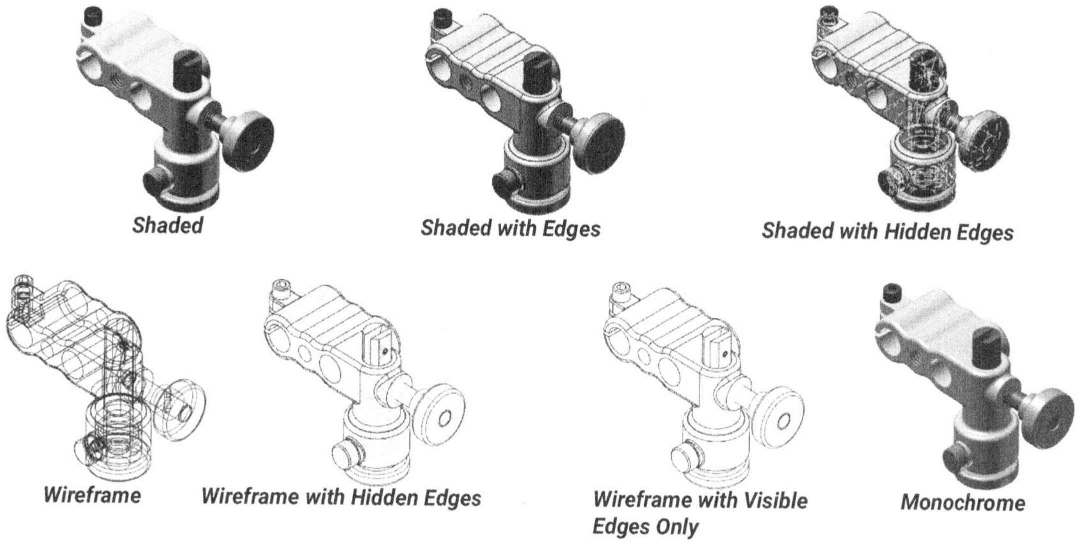

Figure 1–27

1.6 Selection Techniques

Sketched Entity Selection

There are several ways to select sketched entities for editing. Consider using any of the following:

- To select an individual object in a sketch, select it using the left mouse button.
- To add additional objects to the selection set, hold <Ctrl> or <Shift> and left-click additional objects.
- Select and drag a boundary box from left to right around objects (as shown in Figure 1–28) to select them. Only objects that are entirely enclosed in the window are selected. This is called the Window Selection technique.

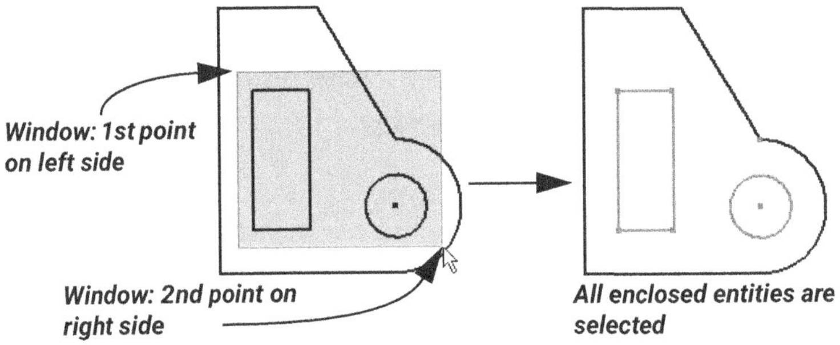

Figure 1–28

- Select and drag a boundary box from right to left around objects (as shown in Figure 1–29) to select them. Objects are selected if they are entirely enclosed in the window, or if any part of the object crosses the sketched border. This is called the Crossing Selection technique.

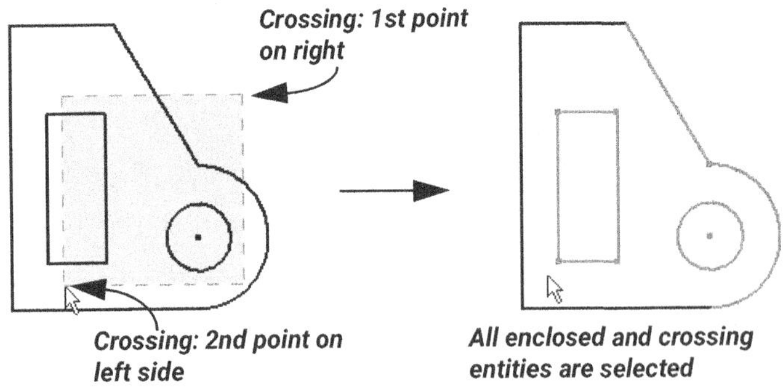

Figure 1–29

Note: *If you drag a boundary box in the wrong direction (i.e., start a window instead of a crossing), select a second point so that the sketched area is empty, and start again.*

- To clear objects, you can hold <Ctrl> or <Shift> and individually select entities, or use the window or crossing techniques to select entities. To clear all of the objects, click in a blank space in the graphics window.

Tangent Entity Selection

To quickly select tangent entities (edges or faces) in a model, right-click on an entity and select **Select Tangencies**, as shown Figure 1–30. As an alternative to using the context menu to access the command, you can also double-click on the entity to quickly select all tangent entities.

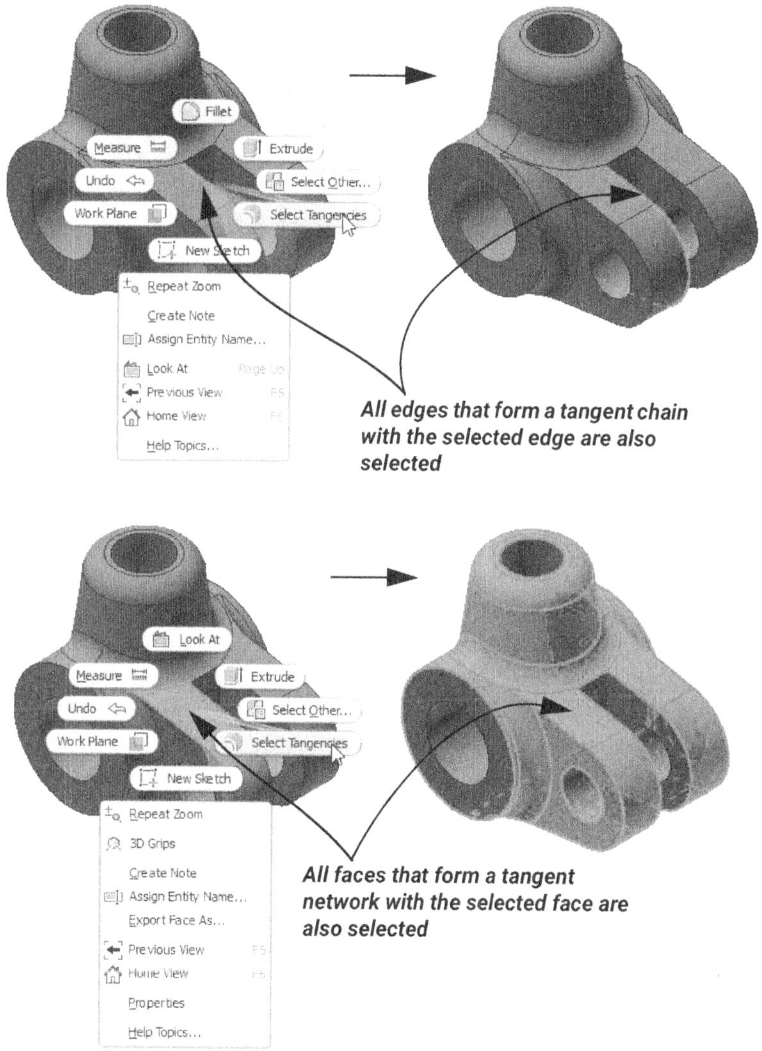

Figure 1–30

Selecting Hidden Entities or Features

To select hidden entities or features, hover the cursor over an object until a drop-down list displays, or right-click and select **Select Other** to open the drop-down list. The list displays all of the shown and hidden features and entities based on the current cursor location, as shown in Figure 1–31. Scroll through the drop-down list and select the required entity when it is highlighted. Alternatively, you can also use the middle mouse button to scroll through the shown and hidden features.

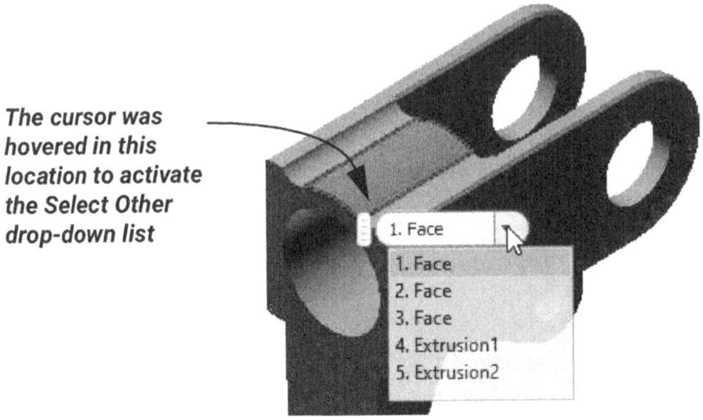

Figure 1–31

Selection Filter

The selection filter in the Quick Access Toolbar enables you to filter entities, features, or components so that you can only select that type of object. For example, if you select **Select Face and Edges**, you can only select the faces or edges on the model. The options that display in the drop-down list vary depending on the current mode. Part mode options display as shown in Figure 1–32. To quickly access the filter options without having to use the Quick Access Toolbar, press and hold <Shift> as you right-click in the main window.

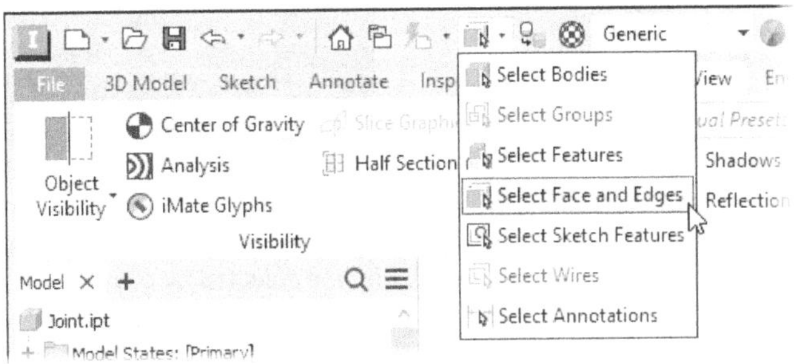

Figure 1–32

Practice 1a
Open and Manipulate a Part

Practice Objectives

- Open part and drawing files and navigate between them using the tabs at the bottom of the graphics window.
- Orient the model using the **Zoom**, **Pan**, **Rotate**, and **Look At** commands available in the ribbon, Navigation Bar, and ViewCube.
- Change the visual style of a model for improved visualization.
- Change the visibility status of features in the model.
- Modify dimension values and delete features associated with a model to verify associativity between a part and its drawing file.
- Use the Select Other drop-down list to efficiently select hidden features in a model.

In this practice, you will open and work in part and drawing files to learn the Autodesk Inventor interface. You will also manipulate the orientation of a model, delete, and modify features to learn about associativity of files between environments.

Task 1: Open a model.

1. If the Autodesk Inventor software is not already open, select **Start>All Programs>Autodesk Inventor 2024>Autodesk Inventor 2024**, or double-click on the **Autodesk Inventor 2024** icon on the desktop.
2. Project files identify the folders that contain the required models. Use one of the following methods to open the Projects dialog box to assign the project file:
   - On the Home page, select ⋮ (Projects and Settings) > **Settings**.
   - Click (Projects) in the Quick Access Toolbar at the top of the interface.
   - In the **File** menu, select **Manage>Projects**.
   - Click **Projects** in the New or Open dialog boxes.
3. Click **Browse**, navigate to *C:\Autodesk Inventor 2024 Intro Practice Files* (or the directory to which you extracted the practice files) and select **Intro to Modeling.ipj**. Click **Open**. The Projects dialog box updates and a checkmark displays next to the new project name, indicating that it is the active project. Click **Done**.

4. On the Home page, verify that the Intro to Modeling project is listed as the active projects, as shown in Figure 1–33. Once a project has been loaded, you can use this drop-down list to activate an alternate (loaded) project file.

Figure 1–33

5. Use one of the following methods to open a new file:
   - On the Home page, click **Open**.
   - In the Quick Access Toolbar, click (Open).
   - In the **File** menu, select **Open>Open**.

   Note: *If the file extensions do not display, open Windows Explorer. Select* ***View>Options>Change Folder and search options****, select the View tab, and clear the* ***Hide extensions for known file types*** *option.*

6. Select **Joint.ipt** and click **Open**. The model geometry displays and the Model browser lists all of the features in the model, as shown in Figure 1–34.

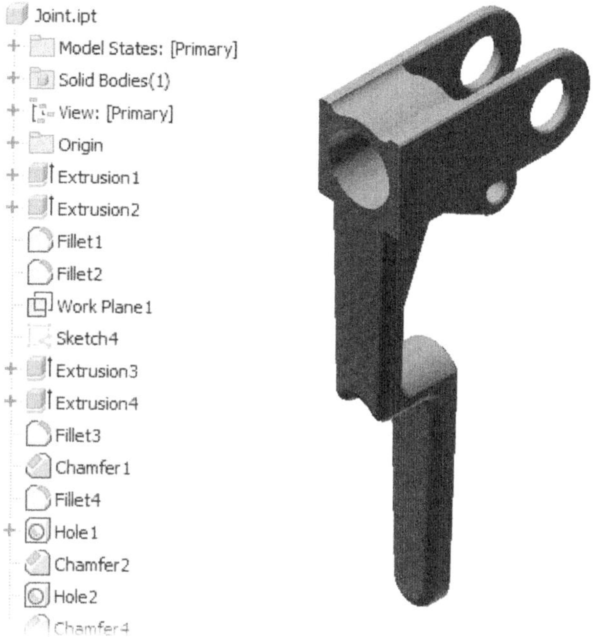

Figure 1–34

The model name displays in the header of the interface and at the top of the Model browser listing. Both names identify the model as a part (.IPT) file. The model consists of solid geometry and work features that were used as references in creating the solid geometry. In addition to the geometry and work features, there are nodes at the top of the Model browser that group the model's solid bodies, model states, and default origin features.

Task 2: Zoom in and out on the model using the Zoom command.

1. The *3D Model* tab is the active tab. Select the *View* tab at the top of the ribbon interface. The options in each tab are subdivided into panels to help you quickly find commands. Locate the Navigate panel. It contains all of the commands that you can use to manipulate the location and orientation of the model in the graphics window.

2. In the Navigate panel, click (Zoom), as shown in Figure 1–35. In some situations, similar commands are compressed in a panel and you must expand commands to access them.

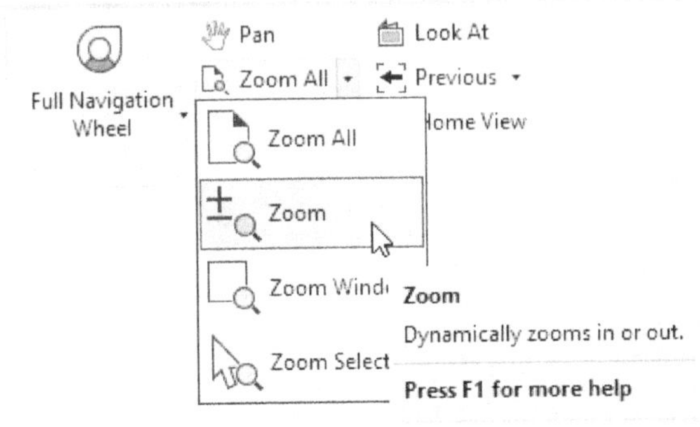

Figure 1–35

3. Move the cursor to the graphics window, click and hold the left mouse button, and move the mouse towards you to zoom in and away from you to zoom out.

4. Click (Zoom) again in the Navigate panel to toggle it off. You can also use the mouse scroll wheel to zoom in or out.

5. As an alternative to the *View* tab>Navigate panel, you can manipulate the model display using the options in the Navigation Bar on the right side of the graphics window. Similar to the Navigate panel, you need to expand the zoom options. Expand the Zoom command grouping in the Navigation Bar and click **Zoom All**, as shown in Figure 1–36.

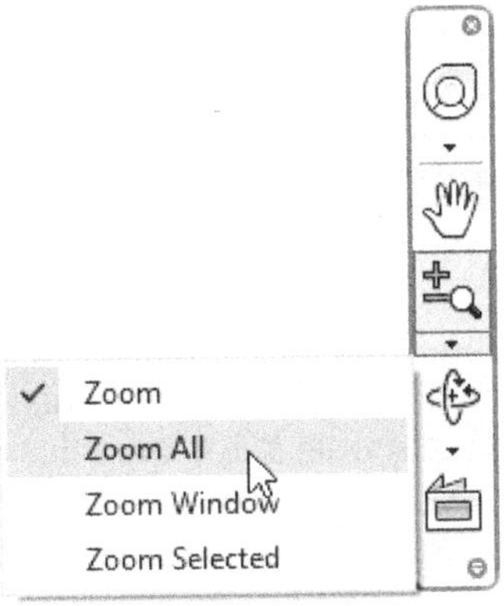

Figure 1–36

6. The model should refit to the center of the screen. If not, click (Zoom All) in the Navigation Bar.

Task 3: Zoom in on an area of the model and zoom out on the model.

1. Expand the zoom commands in the Navigation Bar and select **Zoom Window**.
2. Select a location on the model using the left mouse button to define a corner of the bounding box zoom area.
3. Drag the mouse to draw a box over the area to zoom.
4. Click or release the left mouse button again when the box is the required size. The model zooms in on the area defined by the sketched bounding box.
5. Expand the zoom commands in the Navigation Bar and **Zoom All** to refit the model in the center of the screen.
6. You can also zoom to a selected feature, face, or edge. Ensure that **Select Faces and Edges** is selected in the Filter drop-down list in the Quick Access Toolbar, as shown in Figure 1–37.

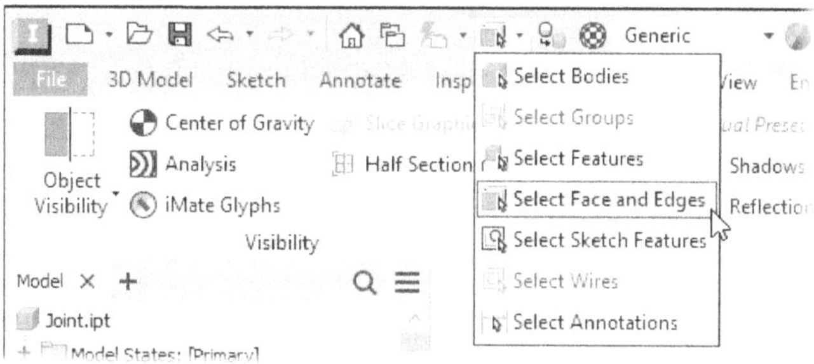

Figure 1–37

7. Expand the zoom commands in the Navigation Bar and select **Zoom Selected** to zoom in on a selected element. Select the face shown in Figure 1–38. The model is zoomed to the selected face. To zoom in on a face, you can also select the face first and then click **Zoom Selected**.

Figure 1–38

8. As an alternative to using the **Zoom All** command in the Navigation Bar, you can also double-click on the scroll wheel to zoom all.

9. When zooming in on an edge, the order in which you select the entity and the command is important. Expand the zoom commands in the Navigation Bar, select **Zoom Selected**, and select anywhere on the edge, as shown in Figure 1–39. When selected in this order, the selection point on the edge is positioned in the center of the screen and the current zoom is maintained.

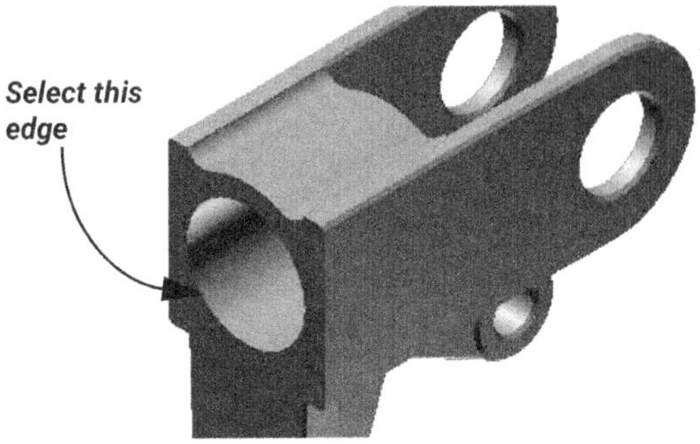

Figure 1–39

10. Use either of the **Zoom All** options to refit the model in the center of the screen.
11. Select anywhere on the same edge and then select **Zoom Selected** in the Navigation Bar to zoom to the selected entity. This time, the model zooms to the selected edge.

Task 4: Zoom in and out on the model using the Navigation Wheel.

As an alternative to using **Zoom** (not **Zoom Selected**), you can also use the Full Navigation Wheel.

1. In the Navigate panel or Navigation Bar, click (Full Navigation Wheel).
2. Click and hold the left mouse button on the **Zoom** navigation command.
3. Drag the mouse to change the view as required.
4. Release the mouse button to end the navigation command.
5. Click (Full Navigation Wheel) in the Navigate panel or Navigation Bar to close the Full Navigation Wheel. Alternatively, click the **X** icon on the Full Navigation Wheel.
6. Refit the model in the center of the screen.

   Note: *Consider trying the various zooming alternatives so that you can decide which works best for you.*

Task 5: Pan the model using the Pan command.

1. In the Navigate panel or Navigation Bar, click (Pan).
2. Click and hold the left mouse button.

3. Move the mouse to drag the model.
4. Refit the model in the center of the screen.

Task 6: Pan the model using the Navigation Wheel.

You can also pan a model using the middle mouse button or the Full Navigation Wheel.

1. Ensure that (Pan) is toggled off, and press and hold the middle mouse button to drag the model.

2. In the Navigate panel, click (Full Navigation Wheel) to enable the Full Navigation Wheel. Click and hold the left mouse button on the **Pan** navigation command. Drag the mouse to pan the view as required.

3. Click (Full Navigation Wheel) again to close the Full Navigation Wheel.

Task 7: Rotate the model using the Orbit command.

1. In the Navigate panel or Navigation Bar, click (Orbit). A circle displays on the screen. The appearance of the cursor changes depending on its location relative to the circle.

2. Move the cursor inside the circle. The cursor appearance changes to .
3. Click and hold the left mouse button and rotate the model freely in any direction.
4. Release the mouse button and move the cursor outside the circle. The cursor appearance changes to .
5. Click and hold the left mouse button to rotate about an axis through the center of the circle symbol (normal to the screen).

   Note: *To change the center of the rotation, double-click inside or outside the circle to set the new center location.*

6. Move the cursor to the line at the top of the circle. The cursor appearance changes to .
7. Click and hold the left mouse button and rotate the model about the horizontal axis.
8. Move the cursor to the line at the right or left side of the circle. The cursor appearance changes to .
9. Click and hold the left mouse button and rotate the model about the vertical axis.

   Note: *While you are still in the orbit circle, you can also disable the* ***Orbit*** *command by moving the cursor away from the model until displays and then clicking in the graphics window.*

10. Move the cursor over the ViewCube and click in the top-left corner of the ViewCube (as shown in Figure 1–40) to orient the model into its isometric Home view (3D). Alternatively, you can right-click and select **Home View** to orient the model in the same way. Note that (Zoom All) only refits the model in the center of the screen while maintaining the same orientation.

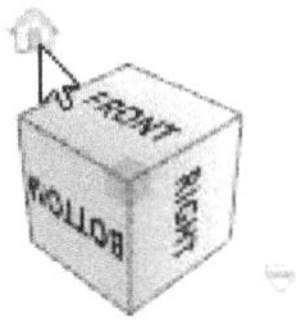

Figure 1–40

Task 8: Rotate the model using the ViewCube, keyboard, or Navigation Wheel.

As an alternative to using (Orbit), you can use the ViewCube, keyboard, or Full Navigation Wheel to rotate a model.

1. Ensure that (Orbit) is toggled off, click and hold the left mouse button anywhere on the ViewCube, and drag the mouse. Move the mouse away from the ViewCube to stop rotating.
2. Press and hold <F4>. By keeping <F4> depressed, the cursor behaves as it did when (Orbit) was active. Release <F4> to stop rotating.
3. Hold <Shift> and the middle mouse button and drag to rotate the model. Release <Shift> to stop rotating.
4. In the Navigate panel, click (Full Navigation Wheel) to enable the Full Navigation Wheel. Click and hold the left mouse button on the **Orbit** navigation command. Drag the mouse to rotate the view as required.
5. Click (Full Navigation Wheel) again to close the Full Navigation Wheel. The selection of the method to use to rotate the model is based on user preference.
6. Click in the ViewCube to orient the model into its isometric Home view, or right-click and select **Home View**.
7. Click the **X** icon in the top-right corner of the Navigation Bar to toggle off its display.
8. In the *View* tab>Windows panel, expand **User Interface**. Select the box next to **Navigation Bar** to return it to the display. The remaining options enable you to control the display of the Model browser (Model), ViewCube, Status Bar, Document Tabs, and other interface tools.

Task 9: Orient the model.

1. In the Navigate panel or Navigation Bar, click (Look At) to orient a model face parallel to the screen. Select the face as shown in Figure 1–41. The model orients into a 2D orientation.

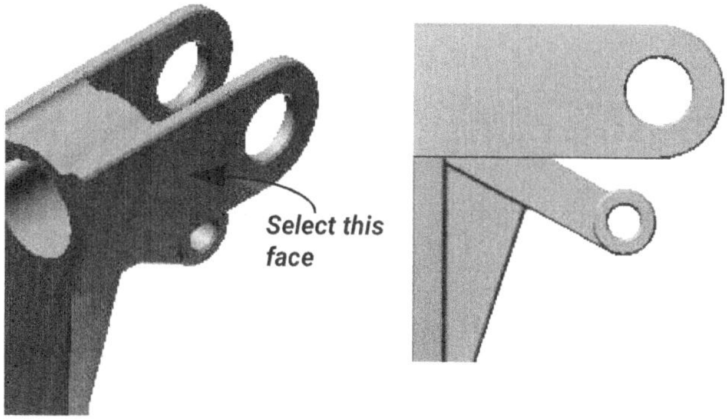

Figure 1–41

2. Note that the ViewCube has reoriented and **RIGHT** displays. Click to orient the model to its isometric Home view.

   The (Look At) command can help to orient faces that are not parallel with the origin planes. However, the ViewCube is a more efficient option for orienting into views that are parallel with the origin work planes.

3. Select the **RIGHT** face in the ViewCube as shown in Figure 1–42. The model orients as it did previously with one less step.

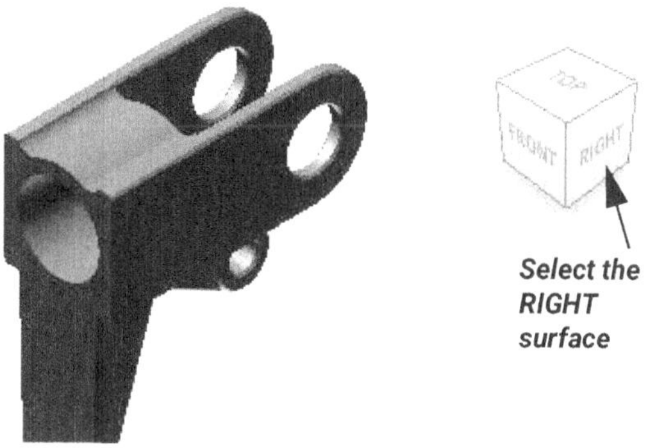

Figure 1–42

4. With the model still in a 2D orientation, move the mouse back over the ViewCube. It displays as shown in Figure 1–43. Select either of the rotating arrows to rotate the model while remaining in the RIGHT view.

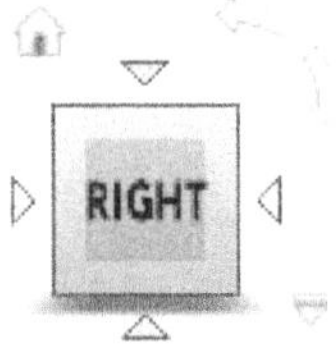

Figure 1–43

5. Click any of the four triangular icons on the ViewCube to change to a different orientation.
6. Practice orienting the model into different orientations. You can also select edges of the ViewCube for orienting.
7. Click to orient the model into its isometric Home view.

Task 10: Manipulate the visual style of the model.

The default Visual Style for models that are started with a default template is **Shaded with Edges**. In this task, you will learn to change the visual style of the model. Please note that the ability of Inventor to spin a shaded model and use all of the styles depends on the quality of its graphics hardware.

1. In the *View* tab>Appearance panel, expand **Visual Style**. Note that the model display is set to (Shaded) for this model, as shown in Figure 1–44.

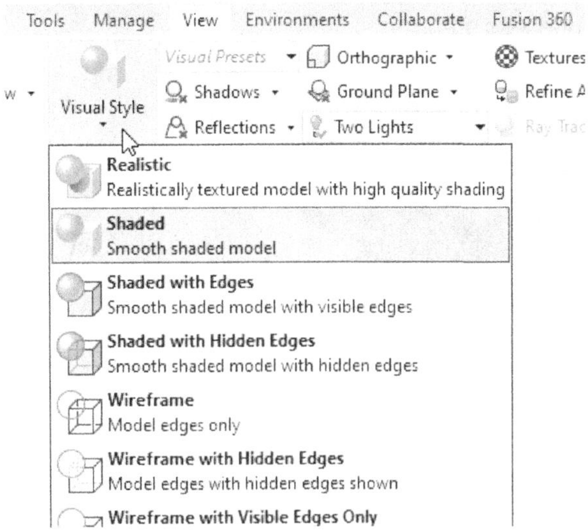

Figure 1–44

2. Click (Shaded with Hidden Edges) to set the view display so that it displays hidden edges while shaded.
3. Click + next to **Origin** to expand it in the Model browser.
4. Right-click on the **YZ Plane** in the Model browser and select **Visibility**, as shown in Figure 1–45. The YZ plane displays.

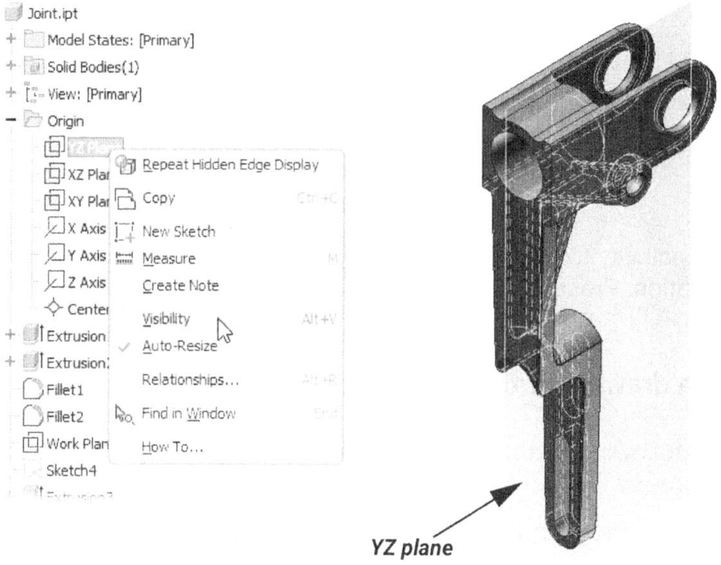

Figure 1–45

Note: *To temporarily display an origin object, hover the cursor over the feature name.*

5. Hold <Ctrl> and select the **XZ Plane** and **Y Axis**. Right-click and select **Visibility** to display both the XZ plane and Y-axis in the model.

6. Return the model to the (Shaded) display. The model displays as shown in Figure 1–46.

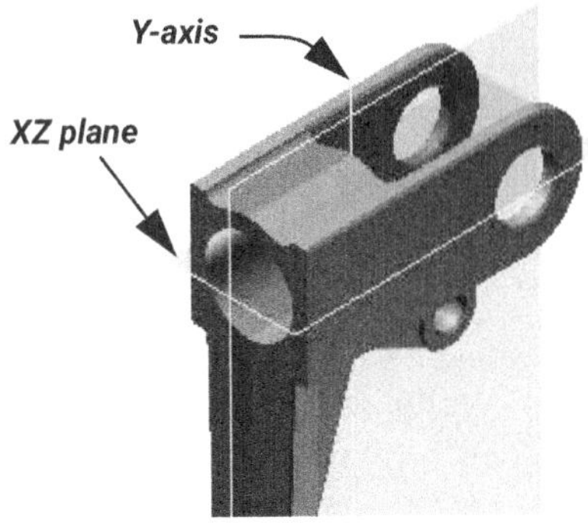

Figure 1–46

7. Toggle off the visibility for the three origin objects by selecting them again and disabling the **Visibility** option. Press and hold <Ctrl> while selecting to select all of the objects at once.

Task 11: Open a drawing of the model.

1. Use one of the following methods to open **Joint.idw**. The header in the graphics window displays the name of the drawing.
   - Select the *Home* tab and click **Open**.
   - Click (Open) in the Quick Access Toolbar at the top of the window.
   - In the **File** menu, select **Open>Open**.
   - In the Model browser, right-click on the filename (Joint.ipt) and select **Open Drawing**.
2. Note that there are now three tabs along the bottom of the graphics window. One tab is the Home page, one is the part model and one (currently active tab) is the drawing of that model.
3. Select the *Joint.ipt* tab to activate it.

Task 12: Edit feature dimensions on the model.

1. Right-click on **Fillet9** in the Model browser and select **Show Dimensions**.

   Note: *To select features directly on the model in the graphics window, you must have the selection filter in the Quick Access Toolbar set to (Select Features).*

2. Double-click on the .010 dimension in the graphics window.

3. Enter **0.05** as the new value, as shown in Figure 1–47, and press <Enter>.

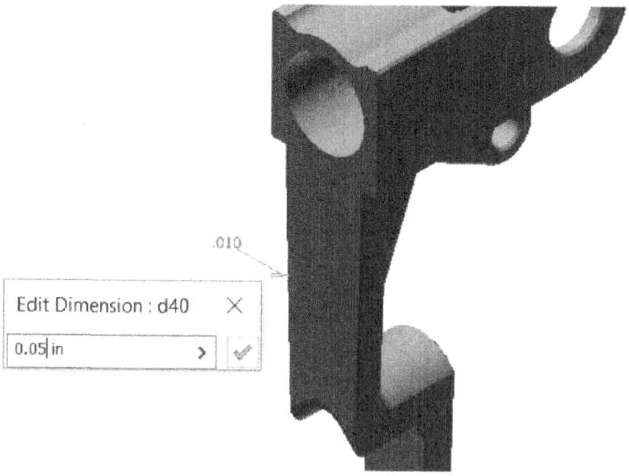

Figure 1–47

4. In the Quick Access Toolbar, click (Local Update). The radius of the fillet updates.

Note: *(Local Update) recalculates the model geometry. The length of the update time depends on the complexity of the change and the model.*

5. Double-click on **Hole1** in the Model browser or graphics window to open the Properties panel that was used to create the hole.
6. Change the 0.25 diameter to **0.15** in either the Properties panel or the on-screen entry field. Click **OK** in the Properties panel to complete the feature change. The model displays as shown in Figure 1–48.

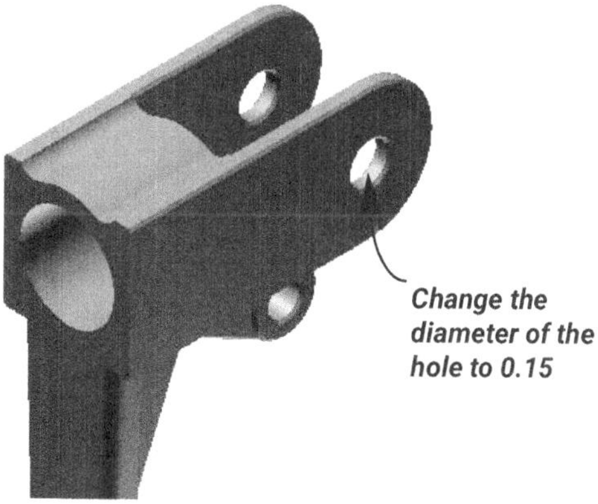

Figure 1–48

In the Hole diameter example, you edited the feature by opening the Properties panel. Alternatively, you can right-click on the feature and select **Show Dimension**. This is faster for editing multiple dimension values because the model is not updated until you explicitly click (Local Update). Using the Properties panel, the model is updated when you click **OK**. Therefore, each is updated individually. If you are making a lot of changes, the update can be more time-consuming.

7. Select the *Joint.idw* tab to activate the drawing. Note how the sizes of the fillet and hole update to reflect the changes that were made in the model.

Task 13: Delete a feature in the model.

1. Select the *Joint.ipt* tab to activate it.
2. In the Model browser, select **Extrusion11**. Right-click and select **Delete**. The Delete Features dialog box opens as shown in Figure 1–49. It prompts you to determine whether the sketch that was used to create Extrusion11 should also be deleted. You might want to delete it or you might want to retain it for use in another feature.

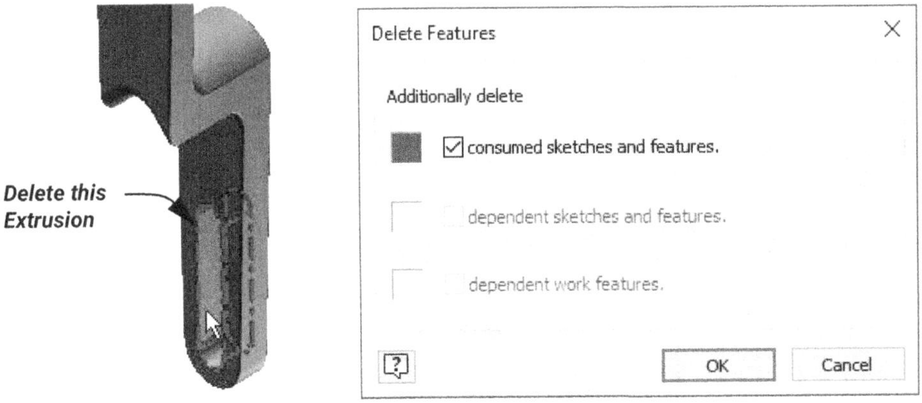

Figure 1–49

3. In this case, click **OK** to confirm the deletion of the sketches that were created as part of the extrusion (slot cut). To retain the sketch, clear the **consumed sketches and features** option.
4. Select the *Joint.idw* tab to activate the drawing. Note that the extrusion has been removed from all of the views in the drawing. If it does not update, click (Local Update).

Task 14: Edit a hole diameter in the drawing.

1. Right-click on the Ø.15 diameter dimension as shown in Figure 1–50 and select **Edit Model Dimension**.

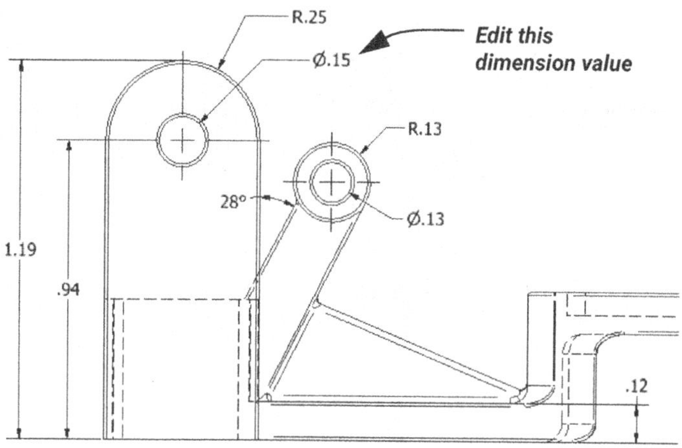

Figure 1–50

2. Enter **0.25** as the new dimension value and press <Enter>. The size of the hole updates in the drawing.
3. Activate the window containing the part to verify that the model has changed.

Task 15: Use the Select Other tool to select hidden features in the model.

1. In the part model, select the *View* tab, change the visual style to **Shaded with Hidden Edges**.
2. Hover the cursor over the extruded cut as shown in Figure 1–51. In this orientation you cannot directly select the cut geometry that lies behind this face.

Note: *The* ***Shaded with Hidden Edges*** *is only being used so you can see the hidden feature for the purpose of this practice. The Select Other tool does not require this visual setting to be used.*

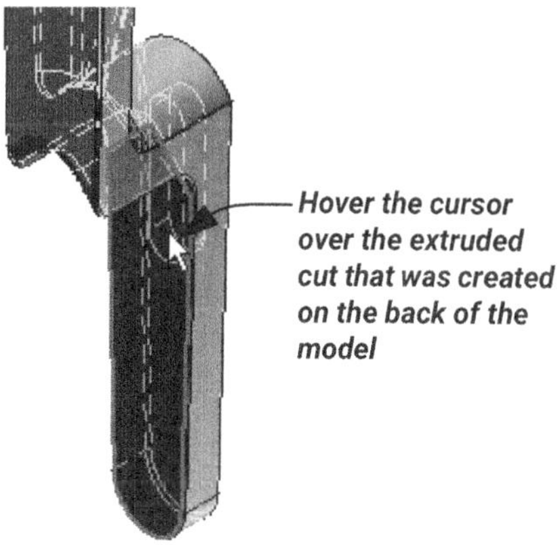

Figure 1–51

3. A drop-down list displays. Expand it as shown in Figure 1–52, and hover the cursor over each of the selections. When **Extrusion10** highlights, click to select it. The cut is highlighted in the Model browser. As an alternative to expanding the down-drop list to review the other options, use the middle mouse to scroll through the options.

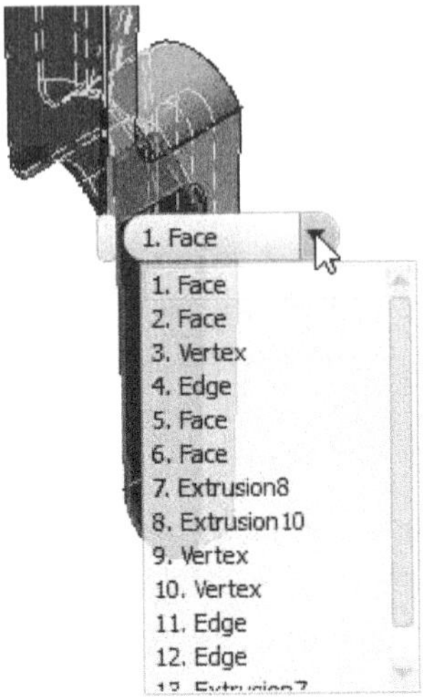

Figure 1–52

4. Right-click and select **Suppress Features**. Note that the Model browser displays **Extrusion10** in gray and is crossed out. Alternatively, you can select **Extrusion10** in the Model browser to suppress it. The previous method is more effective when you have a model with a large number of the features, and it is difficult to identify the features in the Model browser using only names.
5. Activate the window containing the drawing to verify that the drawing has changed.
6. In the Quick Access Toolbar, click 💾 to save the drawing. The Save dialog box opens indicating that changes were made to both the Model and the drawing. Click **OK** to save both files.

   Note: *The Save dialog box opens when you are saving drawings or assembly models. It indicates whether the associated files need to be saved and enables you to do so. This dialog box does not open when you are saving a part model.*

7. Close both the drawing and part file by clicking **X** in the top-right corner of the graphics window for both of the files. Alternatively, you can click **X** on the file's tab at the bottom of the graphics window or by clicking **Close** in the **File** menu.
8. On the Home page, notice that the two files that you opened in this exercise are now displayed in the Recent list for the Intro to Modeling project.

End of practice

Chapter Review Questions

1. Match the numbers shown in Figure 1–53 with the interface components listed below.

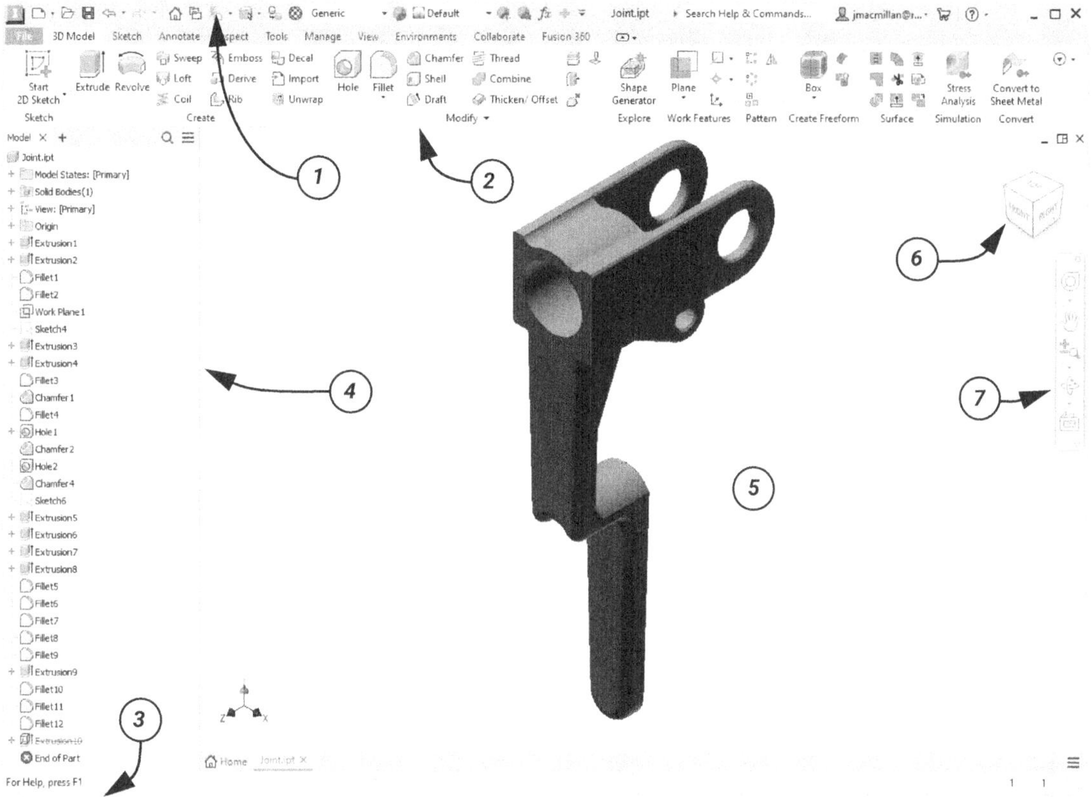

Figure 1–53

a. Navigation Bar

b. Model Browser

c. Status Bar

d. Quick Access Toolbar

e. Ribbon

f. Graphics Window

g. ViewCube

2. After editing the dimensions of a part model, you must open all drawings referencing that part to make the same dimension changes.

a. True

b. False

3. Which of the following are valid filename extensions for Autodesk Inventor files? (Select all that apply.)

a. .IPT

b. .IDW

c. .IAM

d. .INV

4. Clicking  enables you to automatically reorient the display of the model to its top view.

a. True

b. False

5. Which mouse button do you click and hold to pan the model without activating the **Pan** command?

a. Left

b. Middle

c. Right

6. Which combination of items do you select to quickly orient a model face parallel to the screen without spinning? (Select all that apply.)

a. A surface and .

b. A planar surface and .

c. A surface and .

d. A planar surface and .

e. A face on the ViewCube.

7. You can open multiple windows in one session.

a. True

b. False

8. What is the purpose of the menu shown in Figure 1–54?

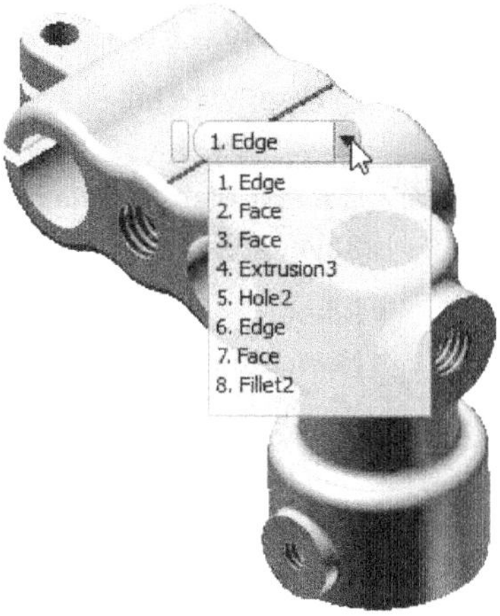

Figure 1–54

a. To switch back to a previous view or ahead to a current view.

b. To cycle through different objects for selection.

c. To pan the view left or right.

d. To zoom in or out on the selected object.

Command Summary

Button	Command	Location
	Full Navigation Wheel	• **Ribbon:** *View* tab>Navigate panel • **Navigation Bar**
	Help	• **Quick Access Toolbar** • **Keyboard:** < F1>
	Home View	• **Ribbon:** *View* tab>Navigate panel • **ViewCube** • **Context Menu: In the graphics window** • **Keyboard:** <F6>
	Look At	• **Ribbon:** *View* tab>Navigate panel • **Navigation Bar** • **ViewCube**
	Open	• **Quick Access Toolbar** • **File Menu** • **Home Page**
	Orbit (rotate)	• **Ribbon:** *View* tab>Navigate panel • **Navigation Bar** • **ViewCube**
	Pan	• **Ribbon:** *View* tab>Navigate panel • **Navigation Bar**
	Projects	• **Dialog Box:** Open and New • **Home:** Projects and Settings
	Save	• **Quick Access Toolbar** • **File Menu**
	Visual Style	• **Ribbon:** *View* tab>Appearance panel
	Zoom	• **Ribbon:** *View* tab>Navigate panel • **Navigation Bar** • **Full Navigation Wheel**
	Zoom All	• **Ribbon:** *View* tab>Navigate panel • **Navigation Bar**
	Zoom Selected	• **Ribbon:** *View* tab>Navigate panel • **Navigation Bar**
	Zoom Window	• **Ribbon:** *View* tab>Navigate panel • **Navigation Bar**

Chapter 2

Sketching Geometry

When creating sketched features, you must first sketch a 2D cross-section of the feature. The Autodesk® Inventor® Sketch environment enables you to sketch and dimension 2D geometry that is later used to create solid geometry.

Learning Objectives

- Create a new part model using a predefined template.
- Create a sketch by appropriately selecting a sketch plane.
- Project references onto a sketch plane for use in locating entities.
- Create, dimension, and constrain 2D entities in a sketch.
- Modify 2D sketch entities by trimming, extending, and splitting the sketched entities.
- Mirror or offset entities in a sketch.

2.1 Creating a New Part File

All part files are created using templates. Templates ensure the part is created with standard configurations and settings. Template files can contain features and settings, such as units, grid settings, origin planes, work features, sketches, geometry, parameters, and properties. By default, Autodesk provides template files that can be used by either selecting the template each time you start a new part or by assigning the template that should be used for all new parts.

Create a Part with a Selected Template

The following procedure explains how you can select a specific template for part creation.

How To: Create a new part with a selected template

1. Select the **New** option in any one of the following locations. Once selected, the Create New File dialog box opens as shown in Figure 2–1.
    - On the Home page, select **New**.
    - In the Quick Access Toolbar, select the  (New) option.
    - In the **File** menu, select **New**.

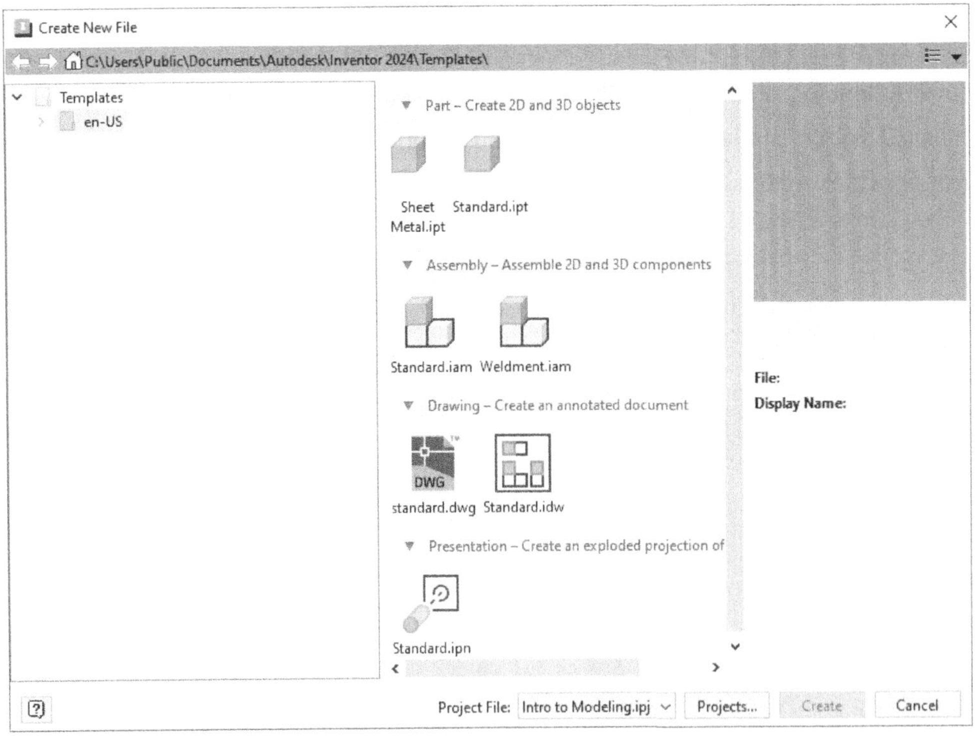

Figure 2–1

2. Expand the **Templates>en-US** folders in the left pane and select the required unit of measure (i.e., English or Metric). Notice that the right pane updates to show that the Units for the new part file is as expected.
3. In the *Part - Create 2D and 3D objects* area of the dialog box, select the standard file that is to be used to create the new part file. Note the appended letters after the word "standard" to help ensure that the correct standard is selected. The (in) indicates an English standard and (mm) is a Metric standard.
4. Click **Create**. A new part file is created and the *3D Model* tab is active.

Create a Part Using the Default Template

Using the Create New File dialog box enables you to review and ensure that the correct template is being used to create a new part file. This approach is recommended until you are comfortable that you understand the template assignment. Otherwise, you can use the following techniques to start a new part file using the default template directly, without using the Create New File dialog box:

- On the Home page, select ⌄ to expand the New menu and select **Part (.ipt)**, as shown in Figure 2–2.

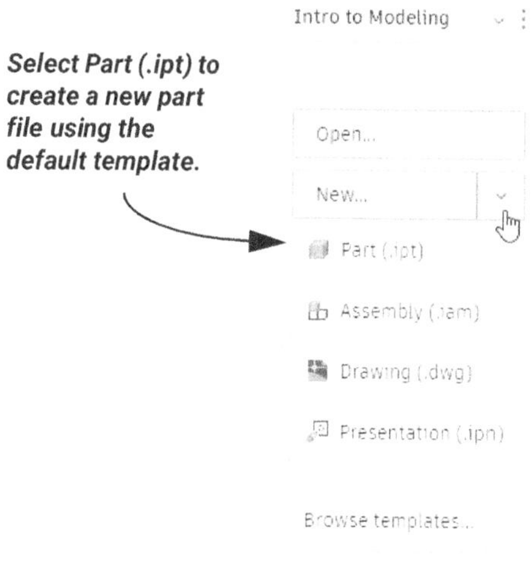

Figure 2–2

- In the Quick Access Toolbar, expand the (New) option and select **Part**. In the **File** menu, select **New** > **Part**.

*Note: If you select the (New) option directly on either the Quick Access Toolbar or in the **File** menu, the Create New File dialog box opens allowing you to select the template.*

By selecting any one of these individual options, the new part file is created and the *3D Model* tab is active. The default template that is used when creating a new part file can be customized by assigning the template in the Inventor **Application Options**.

How To: Set the default template for new files

1. In the Tools menu, click  (Application Options). Select the *File* tab in the Application Options dialog box and click **Configure Default Template**. The Configure Default Template dialog box appears showing you the current units and standard for the currently assigned default template. For example, Figure 2–3 shows that the currently assigned default template is in Inches with the ANSI drawing standard.

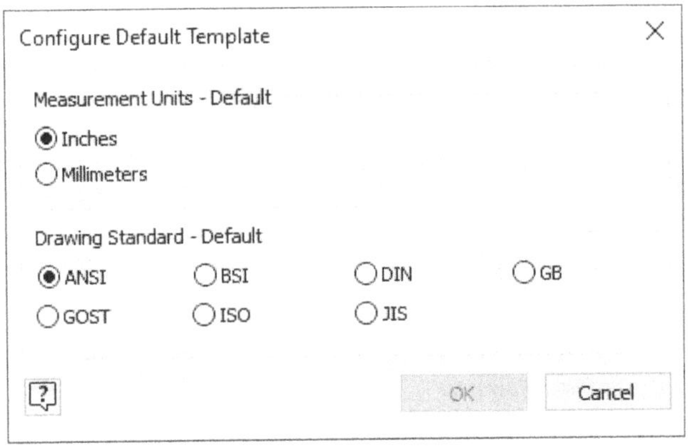

Figure 2–3

2. Select the required measurement units and drawing standard that should be used as default. Click **OK** and confirm to **Overwrite** the default template.
3. This sets the default template that is presented when you create a new part file; however, it does not prevent you from creating a model in inches by selecting New on the Home page as was shown in the previous exercise.
4. Click **OK** to close the Application Options dialog box.

Origin Features

Origin planes are non-solid features that only exist in space. They do not have a thickness or mass.The default part templates contain the following Origin features:

- Three orthogonal planes: YZ Plane, XZ Plane, and XY Plane.
- Three axes: X Axis, Y Axis, and Z Axis.
- A Center Point at the default (0,0,0) point.

These Origin features can never be moved or deleted. Figure 2–4 shows the default Origin features and how they are listed in the **Origin** node of the Model browser. When an origin plane is selected, it highlights in blue and its name appears in the graphics window to help identify it.

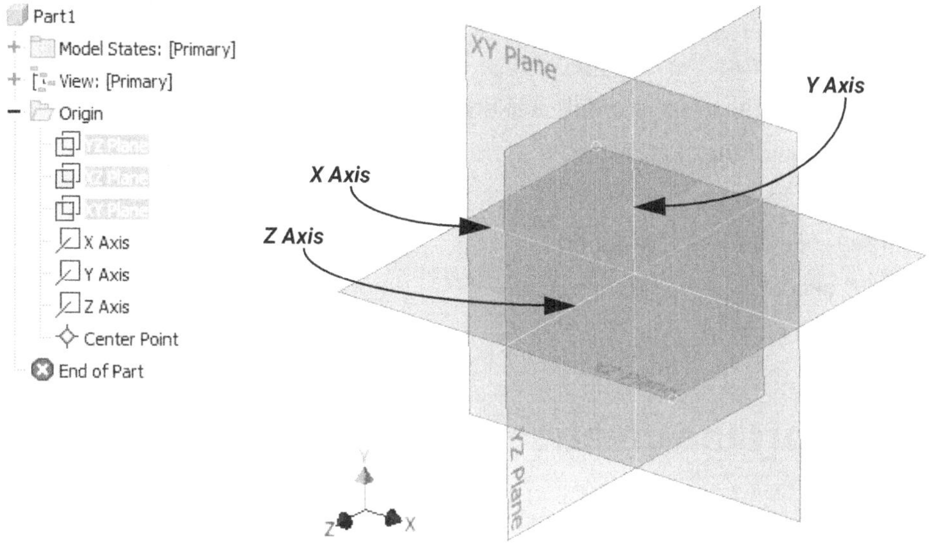

Figure 2–4

When you create a new part, the Origin features are not displayed. They can be displayed in any of the following ways:

- To toggle on origin feature visibility, expand the **Origin** node in the Model browser, right-click on the feature (e.g., YZ plane), and select **Visibility**. Alternatively, select the features in the Model browser and press <Alt> + V on your keyboard. This shortcut enables you to toggle an origin feature's visibility on and off.
- To temporarily display an Origin feature, hover the cursor over the feature in the Model browser to display it in the graphics window.

2.2 Creating a Sketch

Sketches are used in the creation of many different solid geometry creation tools. It is recommended that you use the following workflow to create a sketch whether it is to create the base feature (first solid feature in a new part) or secondary sketched geometry (that adds or removes geometry to/from the base geometry).

Use the following general steps to create a sketch:

1. Start the creation of the sketch.
2. Define the sketch plane.
3. Project reference entities, if required.
4. Create a 2D sketch.
5. Complete the sketch.

Step 1 - Start the creation of the sketch.

To create a sketched base feature, you must start with a sketch. A sketch is a 2D representation of the section that is used to create the solid geometry in the model. To start the creation of a sketch in the model, use one of the following methods:

- In the *3D Model* tab>Sketch panel, click (Start 2D Sketch).
- Right-click in the graphics window and select **New Sketch**.

Step 2 - Define the sketch plane.

Before sketching you must define the 2D plane on which to sketch the entities. During base feature creation, any one of the default origin planes (YZ, XZ, and XY) can be selected. Once the new sketch command has been initiated, the origin planes are temporarily displayed in the graphics window and can be selected, as shown in Figure 2–5. You can hover the cursor over any of the displayed planes to display the plane's name. Select any of the planes to define the plane on which the sketch is going to be created.

> ***Note:*** *As you create geometry in your models, refer to the Origin indicator ( ) in the bottom-left corner of the graphics window to ensure that you understand the X-, Y-, and Z-orientations when selecting origin planes.*

Alternatively, in the Model browser, next to the Origin, click + to expand it and select any of the origin planes, as shown in Figure 2–5.

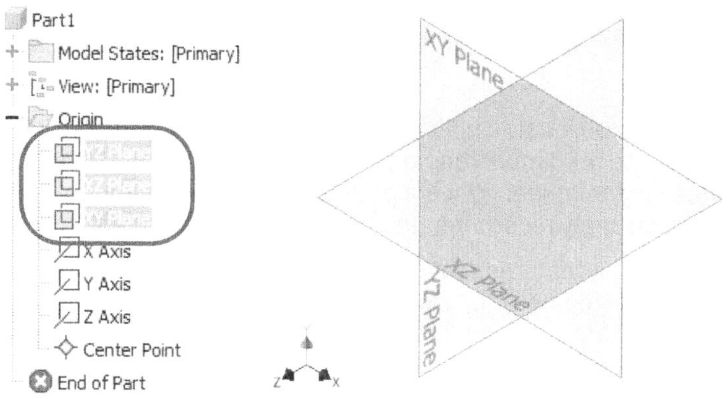

Figure 2–5

Once the sketch plane has been selected, it is reoriented parallel to the screen. The origin (0,0,0) of the sketch is positioned at the center of the graphics window. You are now in the Sketch environment and the *Sketch* tab is active.

Hint: Creating the Sketch

As an alternative to initiating a new sketch command and then selecting the sketch plane, you can select the sketch plane first and then initiate the command, using any of the following methods:

- Right-click on the origin plane name in the Model browser and select **New Sketch**.
- Select the origin plane name in the Model browser, and in the *3D Model* tab>Sketch panel, click (Start 2D Sketch).
- Select the origin plane name in the Model browser and click (Create Sketch) in the graphics window.

Hint: Setting an Origin Plan as Default

When you consistently create base features on the same Origin plane, you can set an option so that when a new part is created you are immediately placed in the Sketch environment, ready to sketch on a specified Origin plane. In the *Tools* tab>Options panel, select **Application Options**.

1. In the Application Options dialog box, in the *Part* tab, select a sketch plane in the *Sketch on new part creation* area.
2. Click **OK**. All of the new parts are launched and sketch creation is started on the specified plane.

Step 3 - Project reference entities, if required.

Sketched geometry should be located with respect to existing reference entities. Reference entities provide a reference for dimensioning and constraining sketched entities so that their location is fully defined in the model. While a part can be created without referencing Origin features, using them is strongly recommended to create a robust model that is easy to modify.

For a base feature, the Origin features that exist in the template can be used. By default, the Origin Center Point is projected onto the sketch plane. You must explicitly project any of the origin planes (or axes) as further references. As you progress in a design, previously sketched or solid entities can also be selected and projected as reference entities for new sketches.

How To: Project a Reference Entity

1. In the Create panel, click (Project Geometry) or right-click and select **Project Geometry**.
2. Select any of the origin planes or axes to be projected onto the sketch plane. The references are represented as yellow lines on the sketch plane.
3. Right-click and select **OK** to complete the selection or press <Esc> to cancel the command.

Step 4 - Create a 2D sketch.

Once the reference entities have been projected, you can begin to create the 2D sketched entities using the options in the Create panel of the *Sketch* tab. The *Sketch* tab is shown in Figure 2–6.

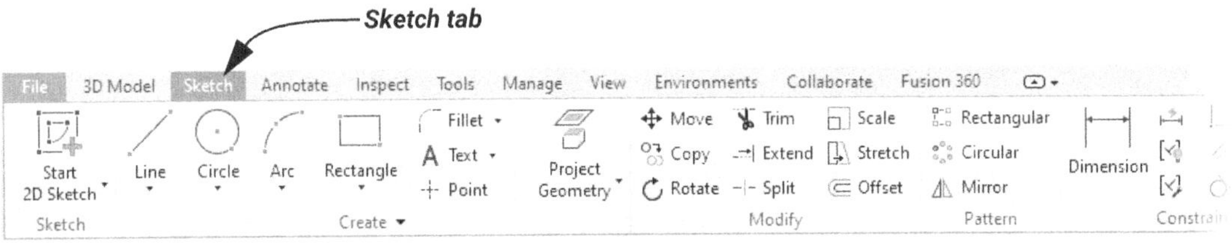

Figure 2–6

Grid and Axis Display

By default, grid lines are not displayed in a sketch. You can control the display of the grid lines in the *Sketch* tab in the Application Options dialog box (*Tools* tab>Options panel, click (Application Options) using the options in the *Display* area as shown in Figure 2–7. You can also toggle the coordinate system indicator on and off. To control grid snapping which causes the cursor to move in increments, toggle on the **Snap to grid** option on the *Sketch* tab.

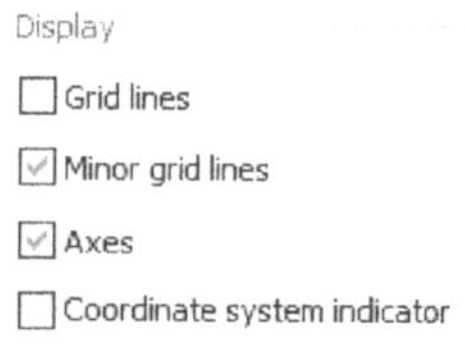

Figure 2–7

Note: *The Application options are global and affect all files that you open. For individual files, snap and grid spacing can be set in Document Settings.*

Slice Graphics

- When the sketch plane is located in or behind other geometry, you can temporarily remove the portion of the model that is in front of the sketch plane using the **Slice Graphics** option. To use this option, orient the model so that the portion you want to remove is in front of the sketching plane and then right-click on the graphics window and select **Slice Graphics**, as shown in Figure 2–8. Alternatively, you can click  (Slice Graphics) in the Status Bar.

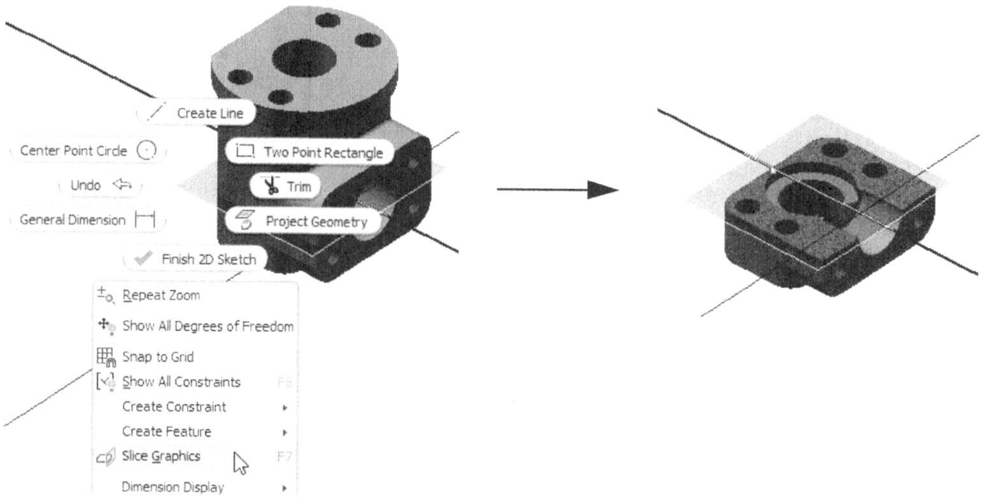

Figure 2–8

Step 5 - Complete the sketch..

When you are satisfied with the geometry, dimensions, and constraints, click  (Finish Sketch) in the Exit panel, or right-click and select **Finish 2D Sketch** to complete the sketch.

2.3 Sketch Geometry

To create a solid base feature or any solid secondary geometry, the sketched entities must form a closed section. If the sketch's section is not closed, you can only create surface geometry. The available entities are all located on the *Sketch* tab>Create panel, as shown in Figure 2–9.

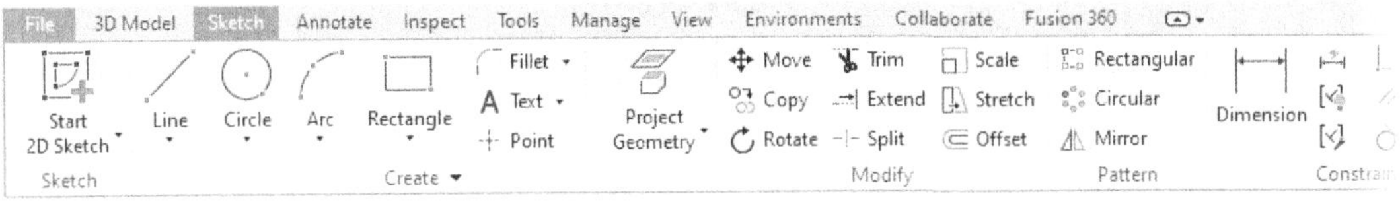

Figure 2–9

Use the following general steps to create sketched entities:

1. Select the command.
2. Locate the entity.
3. Complete the command.

Step 1 - Select the command.

To create a sketched entity, you must select a command in the Create panel or right-click and select a command. For example, in the Create panel, click  (Line), or right-click and select **Create Line**, to sketch a geometry line. The commands are discussed at the end of this topic.

Step 2 - Locate the entity.

Read the Status Bar to determine what you need to select. Move the crosshairs to the start point of the entity and click the left mouse button (do not press and drag). Continue selecting points as required using the left mouse button.

Dynamic Input and Dimensioning for Sketching

When creating a Line, Rectangle, Circle, Arc, Slot, or Point entity, a dynamic input line displays as soon as you drag the cursor onto the graphics window. This line provides input fields to define the start location of an entity (relative to 0,0,0), values to extend the entity, and angular values to position the entity, as shown in Figure 2–10. The field highlighted in blue is the active value. To toggle to alternate fields, press <Tab>.

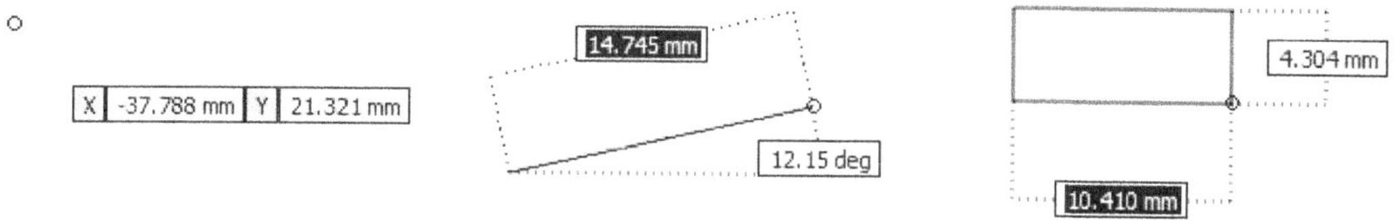

Figure 2–10

> ***Note:*** *When sketching entities using dynamic input, the dimensions default to using polar coordinates while measuring relative. To change the coordinate type, right-click and expand the Coordinate Type options.*

As soon as you enter a value into a dynamic input field and press <Enter>, the entity is placed and a dimension is automatically created. If multiple values must be entered in various fields, enter a value, press <Tab> to toggle to the next field, and enter its value. Only press <Enter> once all values are defined. Note that any entities located with the cursor must be explicitly dimensioned.

- When creating a Primitive as the base feature, you must use the Dynamic Input method to create dimensions that are associated with the feature.
- To disable dynamic input, in the Application Options dialog box (*Tools* tab>Options panel> (Application Options)), in the *Sketch* tab, clear the **Enable Heads-Up Display (HUD)** option. Additionally, you can select **Settings** and specify whether Cartesian or Polar Coordinates are used for pointer and dimension input.
- To disable the automatic creation of dimensions when entities are created using dynamic input, in the Constraint Settings dialog box, in the *General* tab, clear the **Create dimensions from input values** option.

Automatic Constraining

As you sketch entities, constraints are automatically assumed by the software.

- The assumed constraints are temporarily displayed in the model to help identify which constraint is being assigned based on how the entities are being located.
- Once the entity command has been completed the temporary display of the constraints is cleared. To redisplay them you can select the entity or use the constraint display tools.

Figure 2–11 displays the sketched entities as they progress from the first vertical entity into the perpendicular entity (shown on the left) and then onto the tangent arc entity (shown on the right). As you are sketching the constraint icons display temporarily to help in sketching.

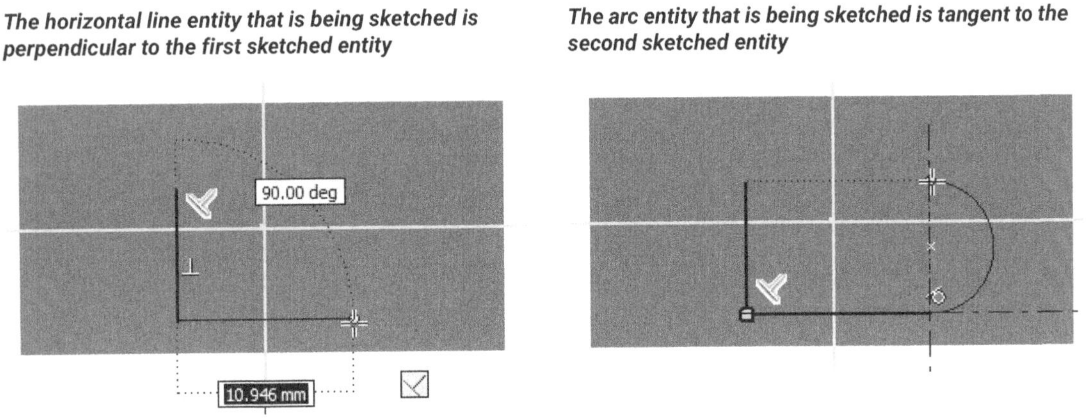

Figure 2–11

Figure 2–12 displays the completed sketch that has been added to the top face of the base feature.

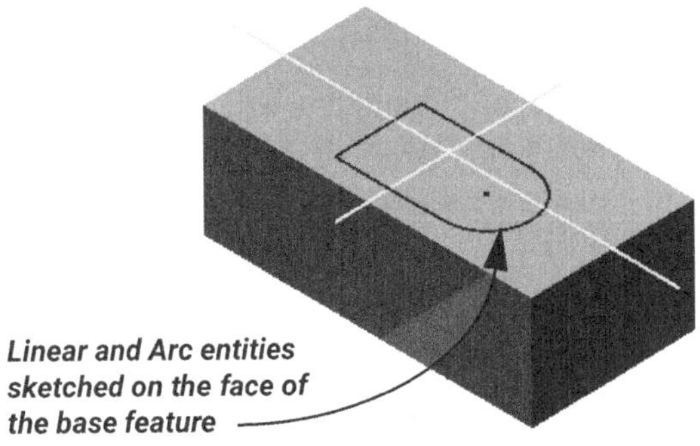

Figure 2–12

Step 3 - Complete the command.

To finish sketching, use any one of the following:

- Press <Esc>.
- Right-click and select **OK**.
- Activate a new sketching tool.

Sketching Tools

The sketching tools are available in the Create panel and are divided into four entity groupings (linear, circular, arc, and rectangular). The commonly used commands are described in more detail and the remaining commands are described in lists at the end of the topic.

Line

In the Create panel, click (Line), or right-click and select **Create Line**, to sketch a geometry line. Move the crosshairs to the start point of the line and click the left mouse button (do not press and drag). Move the crosshairs to the end point and click the left mouse button to locate the line. Continue selecting points to add more lines. To finish sketching, use any one of the following:

- Press <Esc>.
- Right-click and select **OK**.
- Press <Enter>. (The **Create** Line command remains active.)
- Activate a new sketcher tool.

Line Close

After two or more line segments have been drawn consecutively, you can right-click and select **Close** to automatically add a final line segment between the first and last points entered.

Rectangle

In the Create panel, click (Rectangle) or right-click and select **Two Point Rectangle** to sketch a rectangle. Move the crosshairs to the point at which the rectangle begins and click the left mouse button. Move the crosshairs to the point at which the rectangle ends and click the left mouse button. Use any of the methods listed above to finish sketching.

Circle

In the Create panel, click (Circle) or right-click and select **Center Point Circle** to sketch a circle. Select the center point and a point on the outer extent of the circle.

Slot

In the Create panel, expand Rectangle, and click (Slot Center to Center) to sketch a slot. The marking menu does not contain a **Slot** option. Move the crosshairs to the start point of the arc-center on one end of the slot and click the left mouse button. Move the crosshairs to locate the arc-center on the other end of the slot and click the left mouse button to locate the center-line. Move the cursor away from the center-line to the required size of the slot and click the left mouse button. Other **Slot** options are available in the drop-down list. The selections required to create each type vary slightly. Refer to the Status Bar for guidance with entity placement.

> ***Note:*** *When sketching, you will often need to delete and undo/redo. To delete a sketch entity, select the entity and press <Delete>. You can also right-click on the entity and select* ***Delete****. To undo or redo sketching actions, click and in the Quick Access Toolbar, respectively. The* ***Undo*** *command is also available in the marking menu.*

Additional Sketching Commands

Figure 2–13 shows the drop-down lists for each entity in the Create panel.

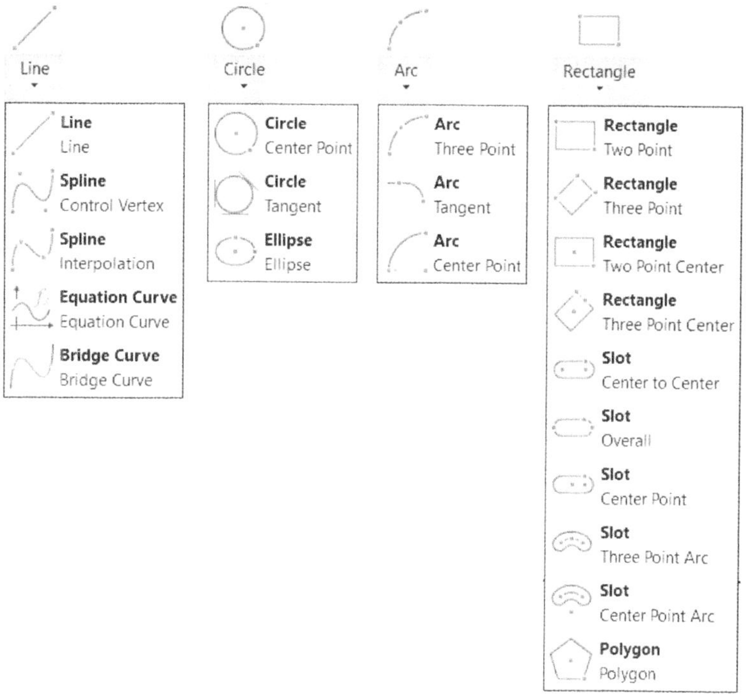

Figure 2–13

Note: Line, Circle, Arc, and Rectangle are the default entity options that display in the Create panel. These defaults are replaced by the most recently selected entity from each drop-down list as they are used.

Line Drop-Down List

- **(Spline (Control Vertex)):** Enables you to sketch a free-form curve. Select multiple points to create the spline. Each point that is placed defines the vertices of the control frame.
- **(Spline (Interpolation)):** Enables you to sketch a free-form curve. Select multiple points to create the spline. The spline is drawn through each point.
- **(Equation Curve):** Draws a curve based on the entry of an equation.
- **(Bridge Curve):** Draws a smooth (G2) continuous curve between two curves.

Circle Drop-Down List

- **(Tangent Circle):** Draws a circle tangent to three selected lines.
- **(Ellipse):** Creates an ellipse. Select the first point to define the center. Select the second point to define its major or minor axes. Select the third point to finalize the size of the ellipse.

Arc Drop-Down List

- **(Tangent Arc):** Draws an arc tangent to an existing line or arc. Select the end of the line or arc as the first point and move the cursor to define the end of the arc.
- **(Three Point Arc):** Draws an arc at three selected points. Select the two end points, and then select a point on the arc. The last point determines the center and radius.
- **(Center Point Arc):** Draws an arc at three selected points. The first point determines the center of the arc and the other two determine the ends of the arc.

Rectangle Drop-Down List

- **(Three Point Rectangle):** Draws a rectangle at any angle. Select three points to create the rectangle. The first two points define one side and the third point locates the opposite side.
- **(Two Point Center):** Draws a rectangle along the X- and Y-axes. Select two points to create the rectangle. The first point defines the center of the rectangle and the second point defines an outer corner.
- **(Three Point Center):** Draws a rectangle at any angle. Select three points to create the rectangle. The first point defines the center of the rectangle, the second defines the first side, and the third point defines the second side.
- **(Overall):** Draws a slot by selecting three points. The first two points define the entire length of the slot and the third selection defines the slot's thickness.
- **(Center Point):** Draws a slot by selecting three points. Select the center point of the slot, followed by the center point of one arc and finally select a point to define the slot's thickness.
- **(Three Point Arc):** Draws a slot by selecting four points. The first three points define the arc length and radius of the slot and the fourth selection defines the slot's thickness.

- (Center Point Arc): Draws a slot by selecting four points. The first three points define the center point of the arc, its arc length, and the radius of the slot. The fourth selection defines the slot's thickness.
- (Polygon): As with rectangles, polygons can be drawn with a series of lines. However, it is easier to use this command so that all of the sides and angles are equal. You can the draw polygons as:
  - **(Inscribed):** Uses the vertex between two edges to determine size and orientation.
  - **(Circumscribed):** Uses the midpoint of an edge to determine the size and orientation.

The following additional sketching tools are also useful when using the entity types to create a sketch.

Tangent Arc Using a Line

The **Line** command also enables you to sketch tangent or perpendicular arcs. These types of arcs must start at the end of an existing line or arc.

How To: Draw an Arc Tangent to or Perpendicular to a Line

1. With (Line) enabled, place the cursor at the end point of the line/arc. The yellow dot at the center of the crosshairs displays in green if you are drawing a new object or gray if you are continuing an object.
2. Press and hold the left mouse button and drag in the required direction (i.e., tangent or perpendicular).
3. Release the left mouse button to select the end point for the arc.

Tangent Line Between Two Circles/Arcs

The **Line** command can be used to sketch a line that is immediately tangent to a circle or arc. It can also be used to ensure tangency between two existing circles or arcs.

How To: Sketch a Line That Is Tangent to Two Circles/Arcs

1. Start the **Line** command.
2. Select and hold the cursor over one of the two circles.
3. While continuing to hold the left mouse button, drag it to the next circle and position the cursor so that the Tangent constraint is visible.

4. Release the mouse button to locate the tangent line, as shown in Figure 2–14.

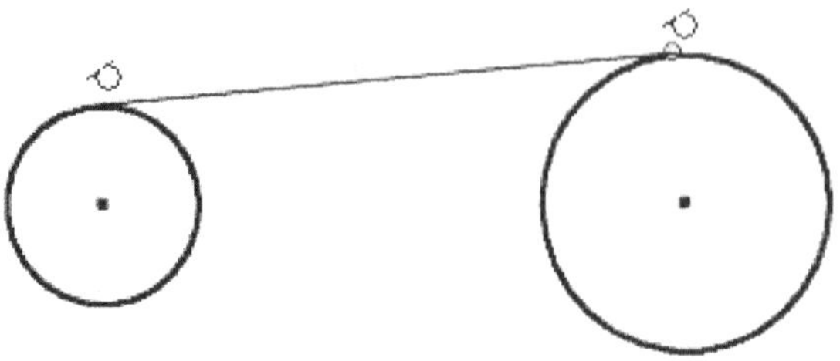

Figure 2–14

Sketched Fillets and Chamfers

The **Fillet** and **Chamfer** commands in the Sketch environment enable you to modify the intersection of two lines in a 2D sketch, as shown in Figure 2–15. Fillets and chamfers can also be created as their own independent feature types. This is discussed later in this guide.

- The fillet rounds corners in a sketch by placing an arc at the intersection of two lines. The fillet arc is always tangent to the intersecting entities.
- A chamfer is an angled corner. Its size is determined by distances along each line from their intersection, or by a distance and an angle.

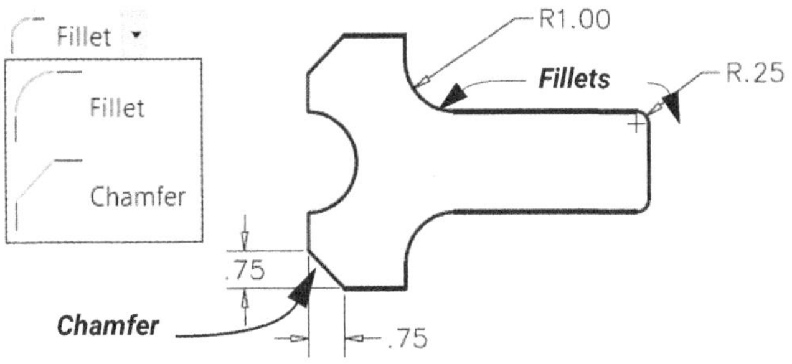

Figure 2–15

How To: Create a Sketched Fillet

1. In the Create panel, click (Fillet).
2. Enter a dimension value in the 2D Fillet dialog box, but do not press <Enter>.
3. Select the intersected entities or directly at the intersection point to create the fillet. The dimension is added to the fillet arc.
   - By default, the first fillet added includes a dimension value. Any additional fillets are driven by this value and no dimension is added. To place a fillet that has independent dimensions for each fillet, click prior to creating the fillet.

4. Continue to select entities to add additional fillets.
5. Press <Esc> or close the 2D Fillet dialog box to end the command.

How To: Create a Sketched Chamfer

1. In the Create panel, click (Chamfer). The 2D Chamfer dialog box opens, as shown in Figure 2–16.

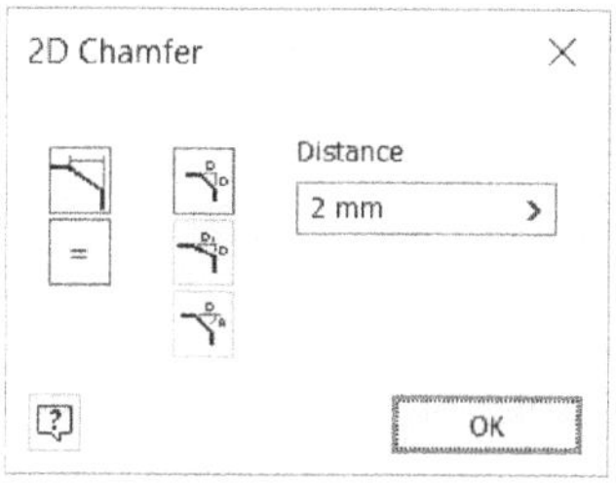

Figure 2–16

2. Select the chamfer option and dimensioning scheme.
3. Enter a dimension value(s) in the 2D Chamfer dialog box. Do not press <Enter>.
4. Select the intersected entities to create a chamfer. The dimension is added to the chamfer.

The options in the 2D Chamfer dialog box are described as follows:

(Create dimension)	Enable this option to create a chamfer without any dimensions.
(Linked values)	Links the values for second and subsequent chamfers to the first chamfer.
(Equal distances) 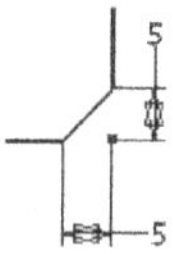	Creates a line at equal distances from the corner on each side. Enter the distance in the *Distance* field.
(Two distance) 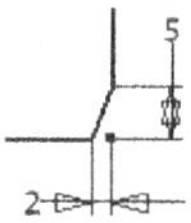	Creates a line at Distance1 along the first selected line and at Distance2 along the second selected line.
(Distance & angle) 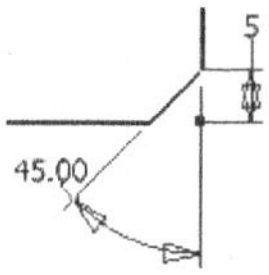	The line created is defined by a distance and an angle. The angle is between the first line you select and the new line that you create.

Hint: Part Features Versus 2D Sketched Entities

When designing a model, you can include fillets and chamfers in your 2D sketches or create them as separate fillet and chamfer part features. Consider the following:

- Chamfer and fillet features can be deleted, modified, and suppressed without needing to access the original sketch.
- If you need to change the edges selected for fillets or chamfers, you can easily edit the feature and select the edges you want to add or remove from the feature.
- The model is more robust and easier to modify if fillets and chamfers are created as features, rather than in the sketch.

Point Snaps

When sketching entities, consider right-clicking and using the **Point Snaps** options in the context menu. Snaps enable you to locate the entity points by snapping to the following points of existing entities in a sketch:

- Endpoints
- Midpoints
- Intersections
- Centers
- Quadrants
- Tangencies
- Apparent intersection points of existing entities
- The middle of two selected points

Construction Entities

Construction entities are used as references and aids in sketching. They do not create solid geometry. It is common to use construction lines when sketching to indicate that arcs or circles lie along the same line or to indicate the midpoint of a line.

In the Format panel, click ⦣ (Construction) to sketch a construction entity (e.g., line, arc, etc.). Construction entities display as dashed lines and you can add dimensions and constraints to them. An example of circular construction entities is shown in Figure 2–17. To change a construction entity to solid geometry, select the entity and click ⦣ (Construction) in the Format panel.

The circular construction entities were used here to create squares centered about the center point. The dimensions of each square are driven by the diameter of the construction circle.

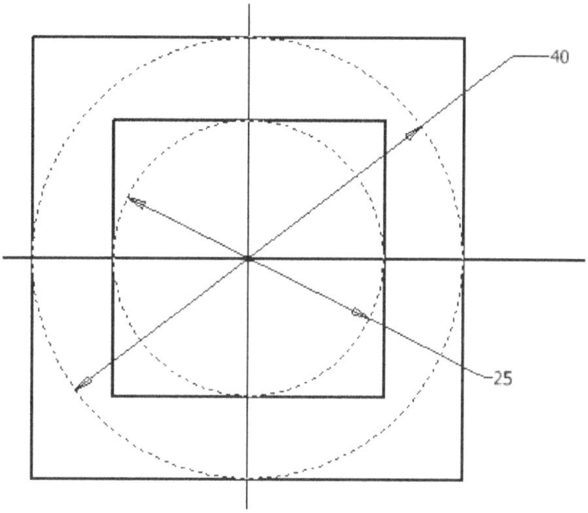

Figure 2–17

2.4 Constraints

Constraints are relationships between:

- Two entities,
- An entity and the coordinate system, or
- An entity and projected reference entities.

A sketch does not need to be dimensioned or constrained to create 3D geometry. However, it is recommended that you ensure the correct design intent.

Constraints can be implied in a sketch or they can be explicitly assigned. By default, the software automatically infers constraints as entities are sketched. For example, constraint indicators are displayed as you sketch an entity that is horizontal/vertical, or parallel/ perpendicular with a reference. Once located, the constraint is applied.

Hint: Changing the Inferred Constraint Reference

The software automatically determines which existing reference and inferred constraint type is assigned to an entity as it is being sketched. If the inferred constraint is not as required, hover the cursor over a different entity in the sketch to infer a different constraint type and then place the entity.

To control which constraints are inferred while sketching, in the *Sketch* tab>Constrain panel, click (Constraint Settings). Select the *Inference* tab in the Constraint Settings dialog box and enable/disable the constraints that are to be inferred, as required.

Although constraints are automatically assumed and created as you sketch, you can also apply your own constraints to further capture your design intent.

Use the following general steps to assign sketched constraints:

1. Review constraints and degrees of freedom.
2. Assign constraints.
3. Remove and control constraints, as required.

Step 1 - Review constraints and degrees of freedom.

Reviewing Existing Constraints

To display the constraints applied to your sketch, use one of the following techniques:

- Select the entity in the sketch to temporarily display the constraint.
- To display of the all constraints in the sketch, in the Status Bar, click (Show All Constraints), or press <F8>.
- To only display the constraints applied to the selected entities, click (Show Constraints) in the Constrain panel. Showing the constraint using this method keeps the constraint on the screen until it is cleared.

When a constraint displays, you can select and drag it as required. Consider the following:

- Hover the cursor over a constraint symbol to highlight the entities affected.
- To hide all of the constraints from the sketch, in the Status Bar, click (Hide All Constraints) to toggle their display off or press <F9>.

The sketch shown in Figure 2–18 displays constraints displayed with the sketched entities.

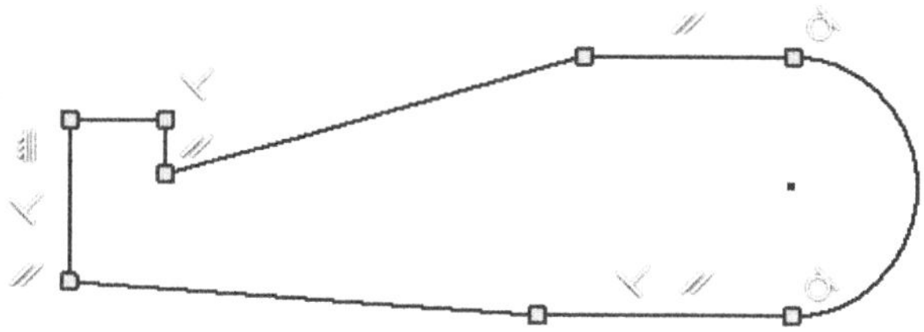

Figure 2–18

Reviewing Degrees of Freedom

As you sketch entities, constraints are automatically assumed and assigned for you. However, further dimensions and constraints are generally always required. The lower right corner of the Status Bar (as shown in Figure 2–19) indicates the number of missing dimensions to fully locate the sketch.

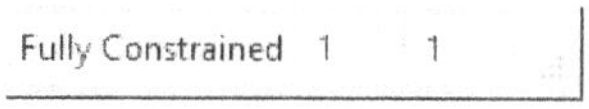

Figure 2–19

Reviewing the remaining degrees of freedom can help you to determine where additional constraints and dimensions are required. To display the degrees of freedom in a sketch, click (Show Degrees of Freedom) in the Status Bar.

Step 2 - Assign constraints.

Once entities have been sketched, you can manually add additional constraints using the Constrain panel, shown in Figure 2–20. Select the required constraint icon and select the entities that you want to constrain.

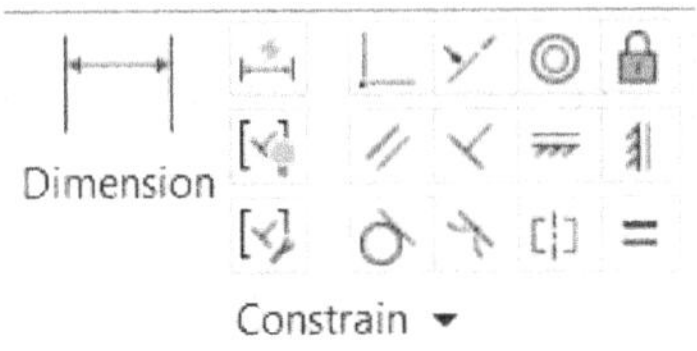

Figure 2–20

Note: *When assigning constraints, the order in which they are selected does not determine how they update. The driving entity is the first drawn in the sketch, unless there are other constraints or dimensions assigned that prevent updating.*

Parallel and Perpendicular

 (Parallel) and  (Perpendicular) ensure that lines are parallel or perpendicular, respectively. The lines shown in Figure 2–21 are constrained to be parallel and perpendicular.

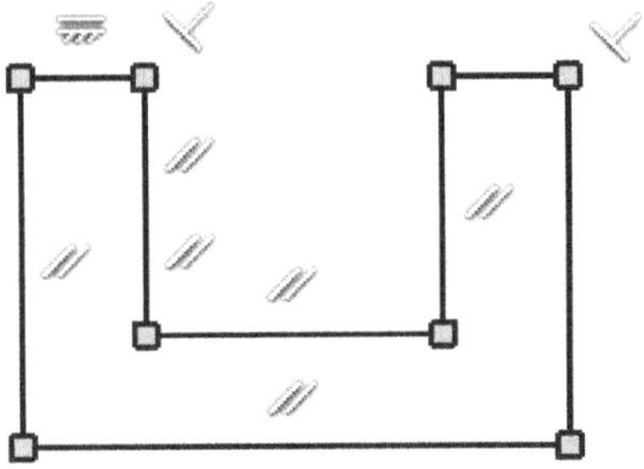

Figure 2–21

Tangent

 (Tangent) ensures that the selected items are tangent. The objects do not need to touch to be tangent. The arc shown in Figure 2–22 is constrained to be tangent to the geometry lines at its end point.

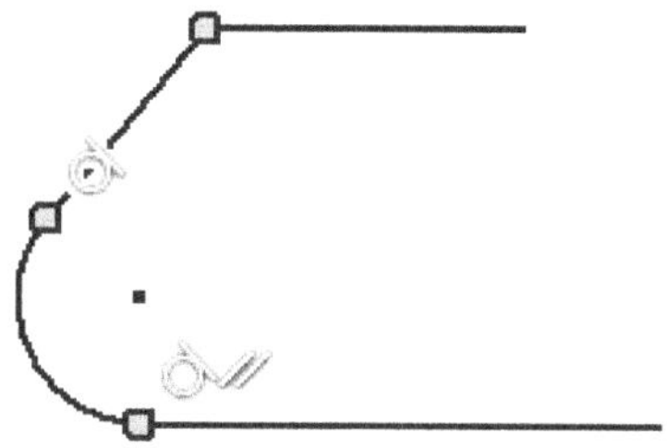

Figure 2–22

Smooth (G2)

 (Smooth) ensures that the selected entities continue the same curvature values between the entities (curvature continuous). The spline shown in Figure 2–23 is constrained to be curvature continuous to the geometry line at its end point.

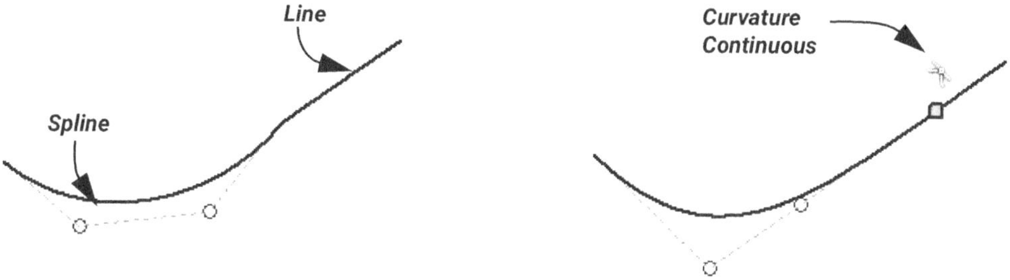

Figure 2–23

Collinear

 (Collinear) ensures that selected objects lie on the same line. The constraints can be applied between lines and ellipse axes. The lines shown on the right in Figure 2–24 are constrained to be collinear.

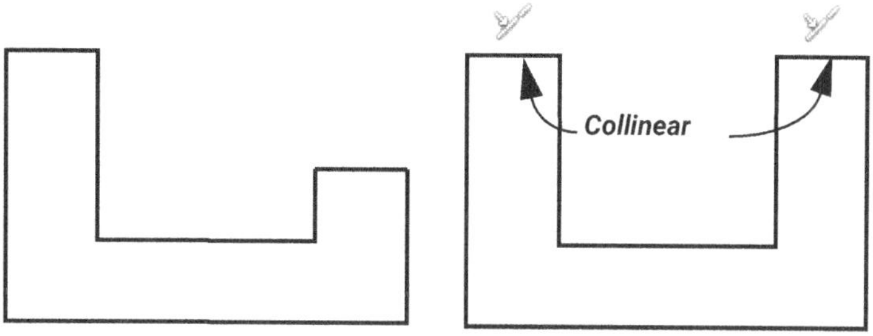

Figure 2–24

Coincident

 (Coincident) ensures that two selected points are coincident. If a point and an entity are selected, the point lies on the entity or along the extension of the entity. As shown in Figure 2–25, two Coincident constraints were automatically created when the arc was sketched. They indicate that the end points of the arc lie on the horizontal line. One additional Coincident constraint was added manually (as shown on the right), so that the center of the circle lies on the center of the horizontal line. With Coincident constraints, only small yellow boxes display in a sketch when **Show Constraints** is used.

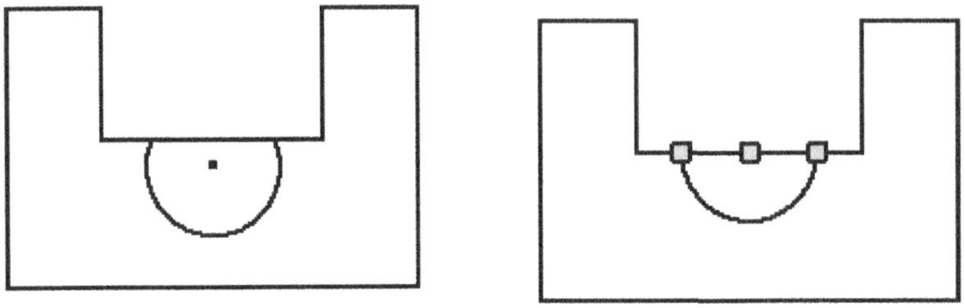

Figure 2–25

Concentric

 (Concentric) ensures that the selected arcs, circles, or ellipses have the same center point. The circles shown on the right in Figure 2–26 are constrained to be concentric with one another.

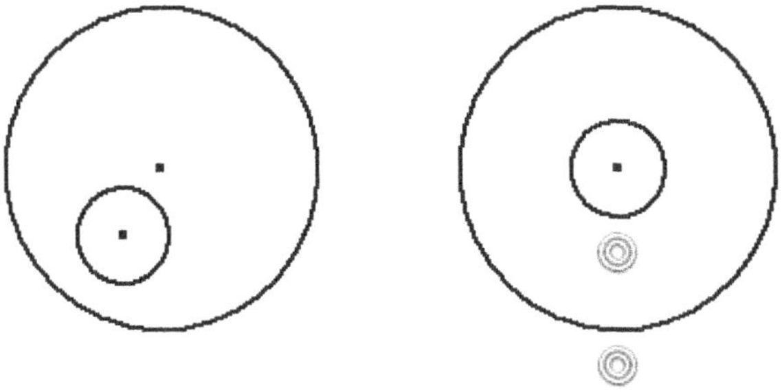

Figure 2–26

Equal

(Equal) ensures that all selected lines have the same length or that all selected circles and arcs have the same radius. The lines shown on the right in Figure 2–27 are constrained to be equal in length. The = keyboard key can be used as a shortcut to activate the Equal constraint.

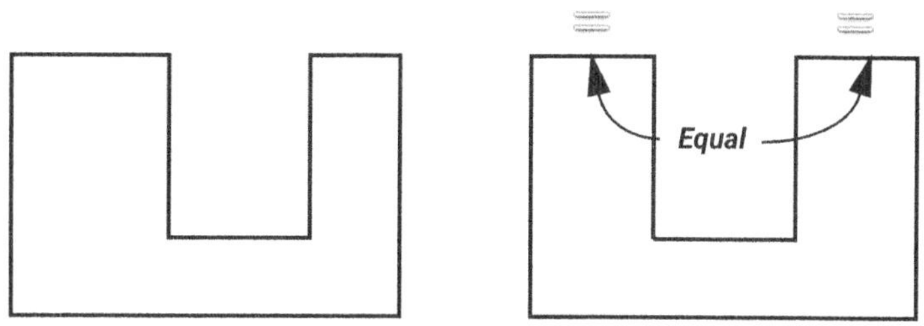

Figure 2–27

When assigning the Equal constraint, the result depends on if dimensions are present on the entities:

If...	Then...
No dimensions are present on either selected entity	The resulting entities are resized as the average size.
One dimension is present	The values of the resulting constrained entities are those of the dimension.
Dimensions are present on both entities	A prompt displays noting that the sketch is over-constrained.

Horizontal and Vertical

(Horizontal) and (Vertical) ensure that a line is horizontal or vertical, respectively. The lines shown on the right in Figure 2–28 are constrained to be horizontal and vertical. The - keyboard key can be used as a shortcut to activate the Horizontal constraint.

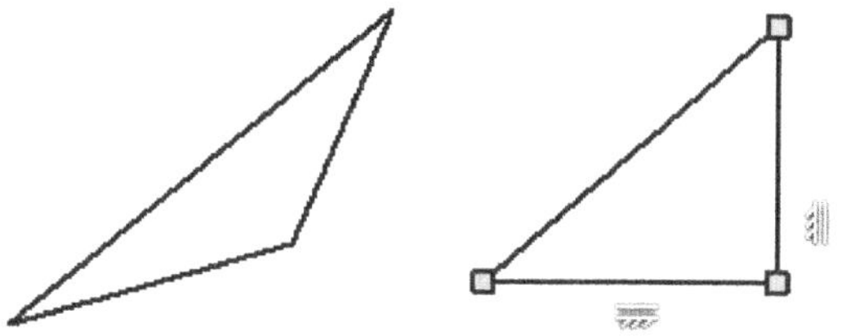

Figure 2–28

Horizontal can also be used to align two circle center points horizontally and Vertical can be used to align two circle center points vertically. The circle center points shown on the left in Figure 2–29 are constrained to line up horizontally and vertically, as shown on the right.

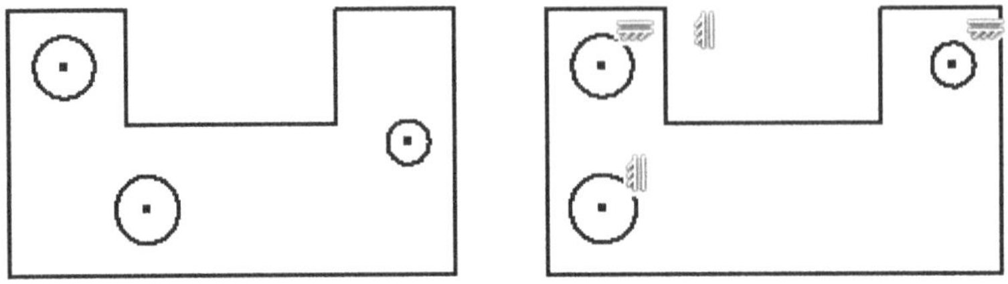

Figure 2–29

Fix

(Fix) fixes a selected point or object relative to the default coordinate system (Sketch environment 0,0,0). The vertex shown in Figure 2–30 is fixed relative to the default coordinate system.

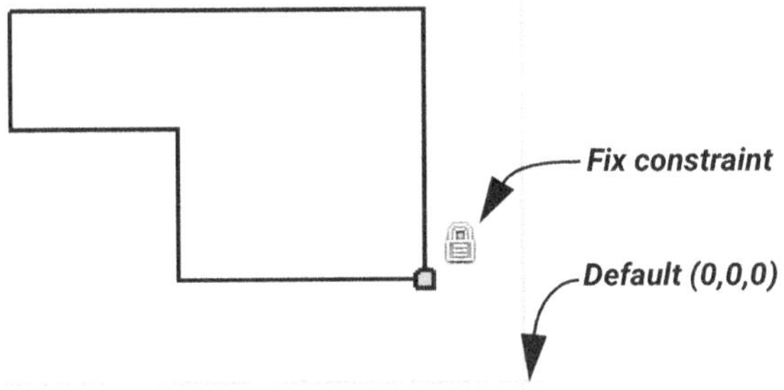

Figure 2–30

Symmetric

(Symmetric) ensures that the selected lines or points are symmetric about a selected line. To apply this constraint, select the first line or point, select the second line or point, and then select the line of symmetry. The vertical lines in Figure 2–31 are constrained to be symmetric about the center line.

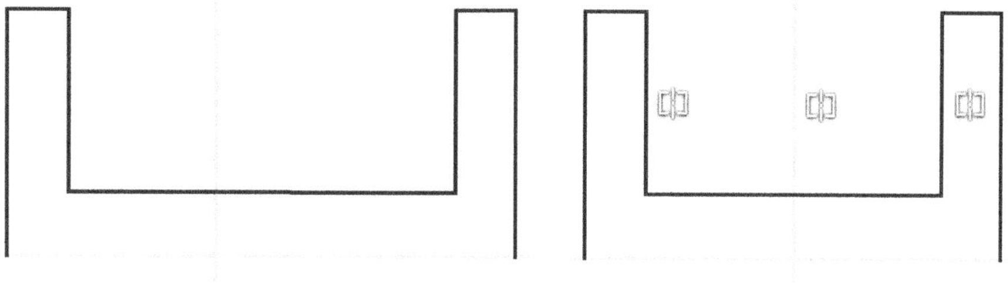

Figure 2–31

Reference

A Reference constraint is automatically added to sketches when you use the **Project Geometry** option, as shown in . This constraint cannot be explicitly set using a constraint in the Constrain panel.

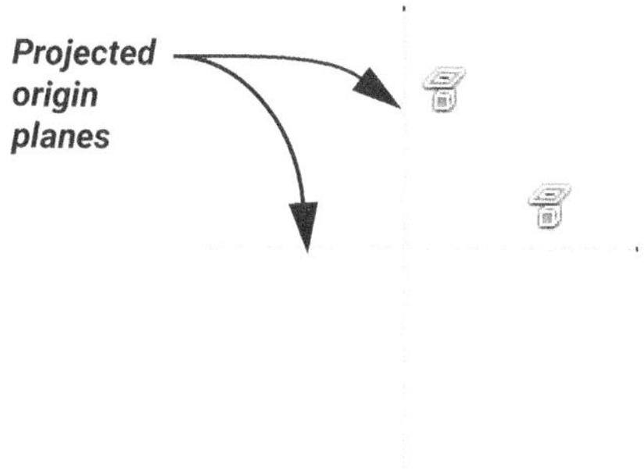

Figure 2–32

Step 3 - Remove and control constraints, as required.

Over Constraining Entities

It is not possible to over constrain a sketch. If you try to place a constraint that over-constrains it, an Error dialog box opens, as shown in Figure 2–33. You must click **Cancel** to continue.

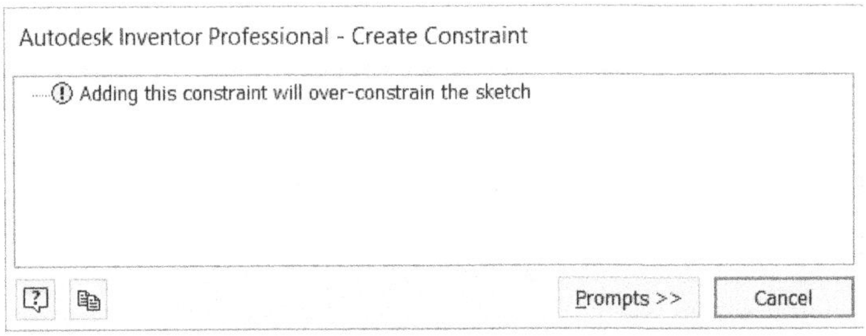

Figure 2–33

If you encounter an over-constrained sketch, keep the dimension that best suits the design intent.

Constraint Settings

Using constraint settings enables you to customize how constraints are inferred and displayed in a sketch. To open the Constraint Settings dialog box, in the *Sketch* tab>Constrain panel, click (Constraint Settings). The Constraint Setting dialog box is shown in Figure 2–34.

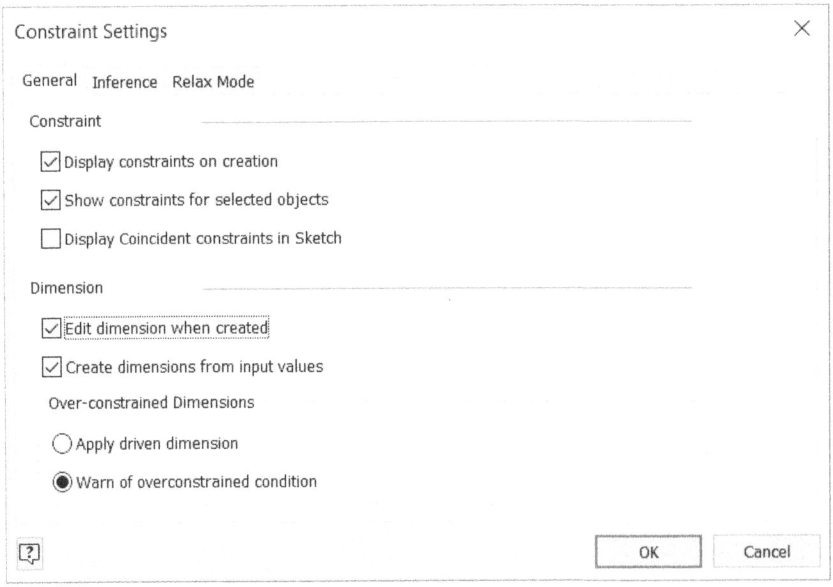

Figure 2–34

Using the *General* and *Inference* tabs in the Constraint Settings dialog box you can do the following:

Control Constraint Display

In the *General* tab you can use the following constraint options to control how constraints display when creating a sketch.

- **Display constraints on creation:** Enables you to display the constraint symbols for the constraints that are being assumed as you sketch.
- **Show constraints for selected objects:** Enables you to display the constraints associated with a selected entity. If disabled, the only way to display an entity's constraint symbols is to click (Show All Constraints) in the Status Bar.
- **Display Coincident constraints in Sketch:** Enables you to control whether the coincident constraint symbol displays when entities are sketched.

Control Constraint Inference

The *Inference* tab (shown in Figure 2–35) in the Constraint Settings dialog box controls how the software assumes constraints as entities are sketched.

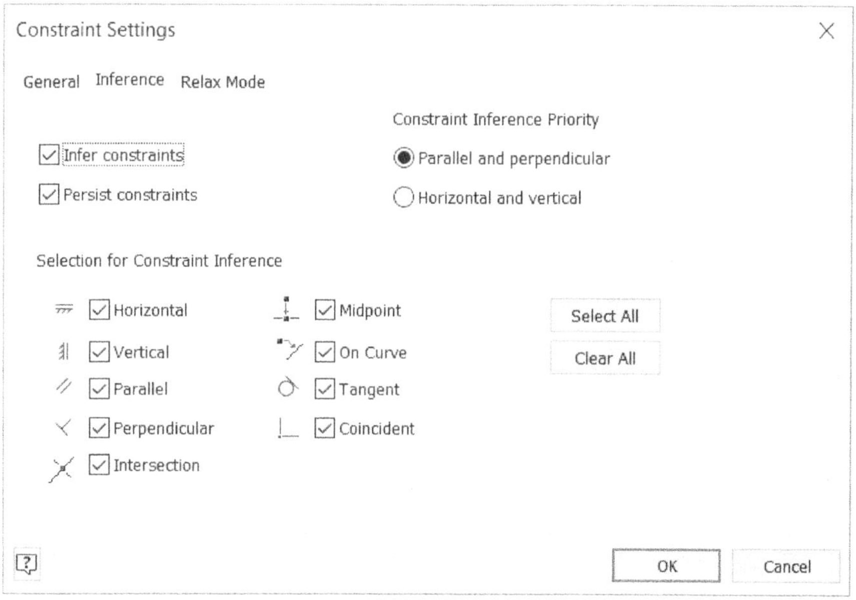

Figure 2–35

- The automatic assignment of constraints is called *constraint inference*. By default, constraint inference is enabled in a sketch. To disable it, clear the **Infer constraints** option.

- With **Infer constraints** toggled on, the additional **Persist constraints** option is also available. It controls whether the inferred constraint is permanently assigned once the entity has been placed. By default, this option is enabled in a new sketch.

  Note: *Toggling off* ***Infer constraints*** *or* ***Persist constraints*** *does not affect the creation of the Coincident constraint. This helps in preventing open profile sketches.*

- If **Infer constraints** is disabled, **Persist constraints** is automatically disabled. When enabling **Infer constraints**, ensure that **Persist constraints** is set as required.

Hint: Temporarily Controlling Constraint Inference and Persistence

When sketching geometry, you can manually enable and disable the inference and persistence options in the Constraint Settings dialog box. However, you can also press and hold <Ctrl> to disable them during the sketching process.

- The *Selection for Constraint Inference* area enables you to select the constraints that the software can infer during sketch creation. Select the constraint options as required. Although a constraint inference might be disabled for a specific constraint, you can still apply it manually if required.
- The *Constraint Inference Priority* area enables you to determine the priority of whether the Parallel/Perpendicular or Horizontal/Vertical constraints are inferred over one another when the sketch is created.

Constraint Inference Scope

To control the inference scope, in the expanded Constrain panel, click (Constraint Inference Scope). The Constraint Inference Scope dialog box opens and enables you to specify the geometry that can be used to infer constraints. The options include:

- **Geometry in Current Command:** Constraints are inferred to the geometry created in the current command.
- **All Geometry:** Constraints are inferred to in all of the active sketch geometry.
- **Select:** Constraints should be inferred to only selected geometry.

Deleting Constraints

To delete constraints, use one of the following:

- Display the constraint symbol that is to be deleted, select it, right-click, and select **Delete**, as shown in Figure 2–36. To display a coincident constraint symbol, hover over its yellow square icon.
- Select the required constraint symbol, and press <Delete>.

- Select entities in the sketch, right-click and select **Delete Constraints**. To delete coincident constraints, select the entities, right-click and select **Delete Coincident Constraints**. The delete options in the context menu are shown in Figure 2–36.

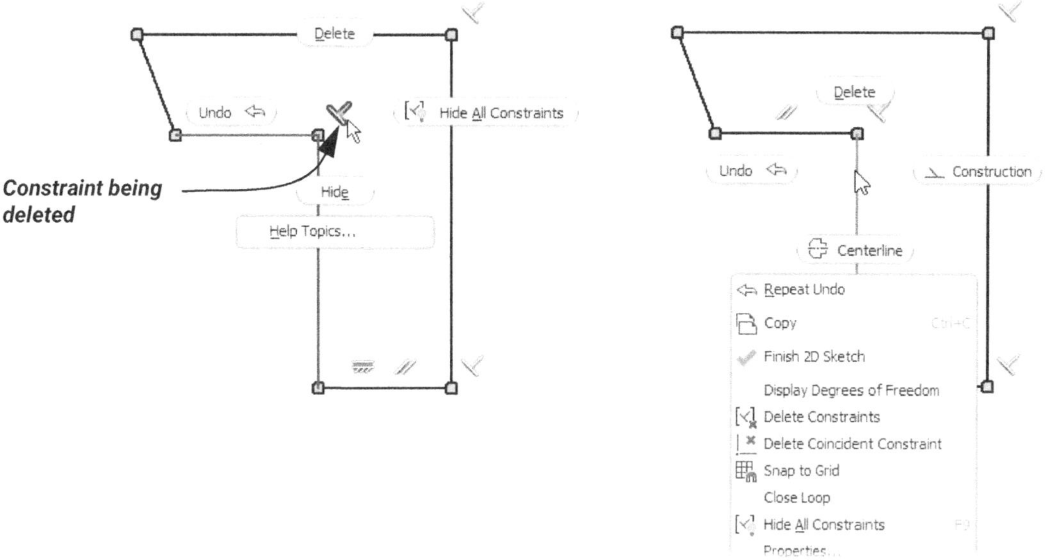

Figure 2–36

Relax Mode

Constraints can prevent entities from moving when changes are required. When enabled, Relax Mode enables you to make changes to the geometry and to apply new constraints that would otherwise not be possible without deleting constraints. Figure 2–37 shows an example of how Relax Mode can be used. Once relaxed and a sketched entity is moved, constraints are assigned based on the new placement location of the entity.

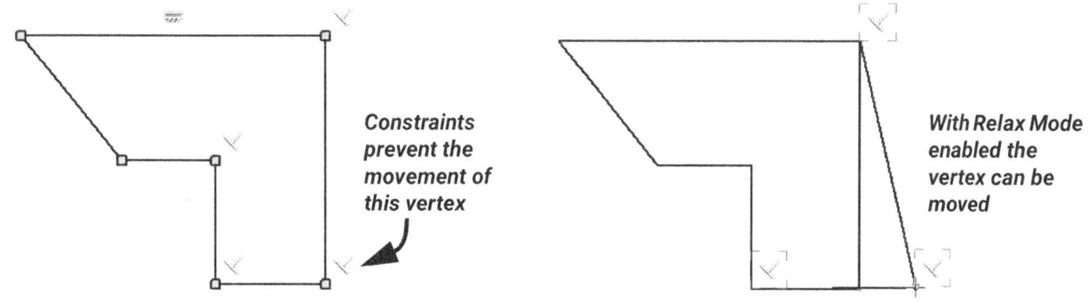

Figure 2–37

By default, Relax Mode is disabled. To enable it, use one of the following techniques:

- In the Status Bar, click (Relax Mode) to toggle it on/off.
- In the *Sketch* tab>Constraint panel, click (Constraint Settings), and select the *Relax Mode* tab. Select **Enable Relax Mode** to toggle it on.

The Constraint Settings dialog box contains added configuration options for Relax Mode. Once enabled, the *Constraints to remove in relax dragging* area becomes available, as shown in Figure 2–38. You can enable or disable specific constraints to define which constraint types are to be relaxed during dragging.

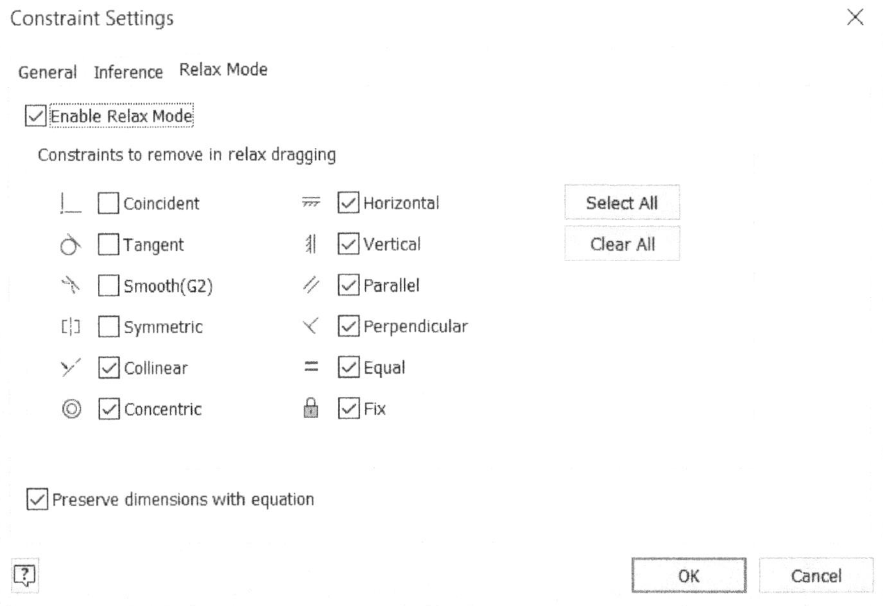

Figure 2–38

2.5 Dimensions

Dimensions define the size and locations of the objects in the sketch. A sketch does not need to be dimensioned or constrained to create 3D geometry. However, it is recommended to verify the correct design intent in your model. Once entities are added, the number of dimensions required to fully constrain the sketch displays in a field in the bottom-right corner of the main window.

How To: Create a Dimension

1. In the Constrain panel, click (Dimension) or right-click and select **General Dimension**.
2. Select the entity or entities with your left mouse button.
3. Move the cursor to the dimension's placement location and press the left mouse button to place the dimension.

The dimension type created depends on whether you select an entity or its endpoints. For example, selecting two non-parallel lines creates an angular dimension, while selecting two end points creates a linear dimension. A constrained sketch is shown in Figure 2–39.

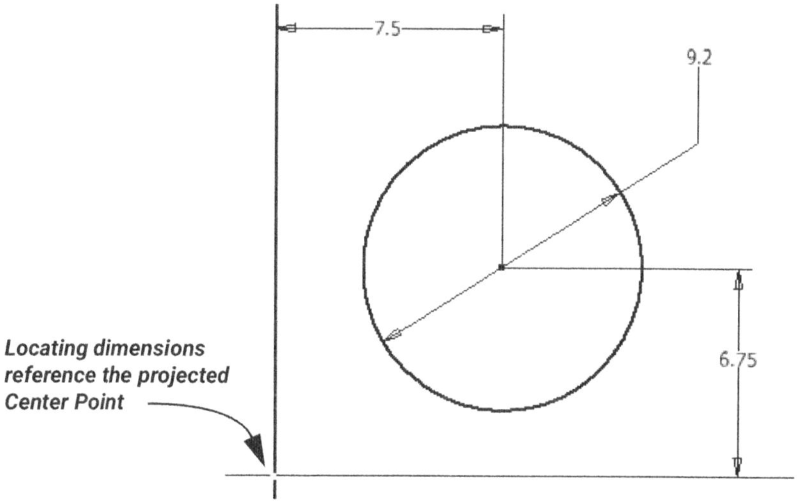

Figure 2–39

The first General dimension (not automatic) that is added to a sketch and then subsequently modified determines the sketch's scale. All of the other sketch entities scale to reflect the value used. As soon as a second dimension is added, automatic scaling is disabled.

Hint: Disabling Entity Scaling Based on Modification

To disable entity scaling , complete the following:

1. In the *Tools* tab>Options panel, select **Application Options**.
2. In the Application Options dialog box, in the *Sketch* tab, clear the **Auto-scale sketch geometries on initial dimension** option.
3. Click **OK**.

Automatic Dimensions

In the Constrain panel, click (Automatic Dimensions and Constraints) and click **Apply** to place all of the dimensions and/or constraints required to fully constrain the sketch. This command dimensions to existing sketched or projected geometry. The Auto Dimension dialog box is shown in Figure 2–40.

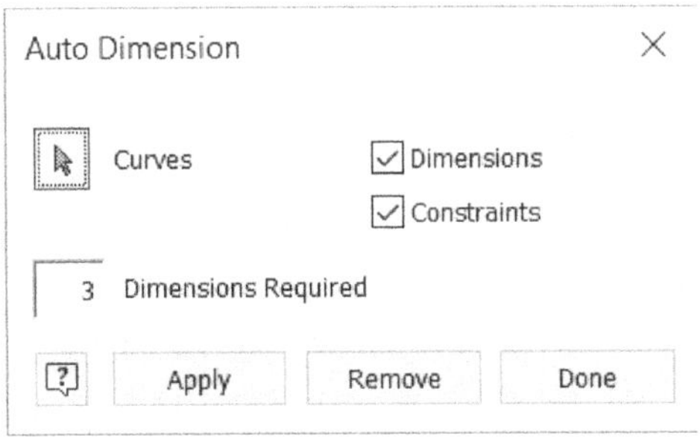

Figure 2–40

The **Automatic Dimensions and Constraints** command automatically assigns dimensions. However, it might not create them to suit your design intent. Consider using this option to determine how many additional dimensions and constraints are required and where. Once added, if they don't meet your design intent, consider using **Remove** to quickly remove dimensions and constraints from selected objects. The options in the Auto Dimension dialog box are described as follows:

Curves	Enables you to select the objects to be dimensioned.
Dimensions Required	Lists the number of dimensions and constraints required to fully dimension the sketch.
Dimensions	Enables you to apply dimensions to the selected objects.
Constraints	Enables you to apply constraints to the selected objects.

The following additional dimension types can be created using the General dimension type.

Center Dimensions

To create center dimensions, select the two entities to dimension the distance between circles and arcs. Move the cursor to the required location and place the dimension using the left mouse button. The different methods for dimensioning the linear entities shown in Figure 2–41 are as follows:

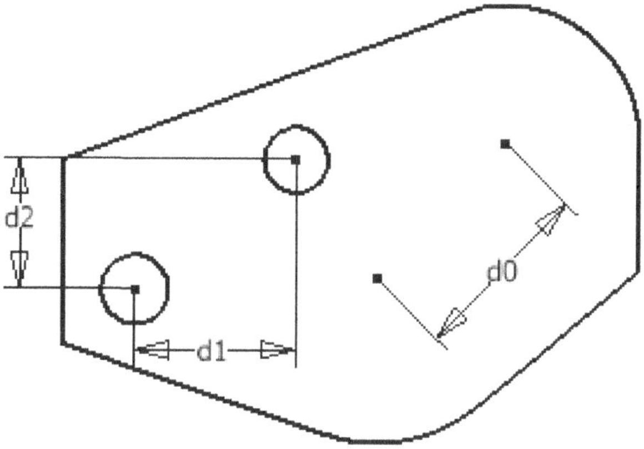

Figure 2–41

To place dimension d0	Select the centers of the arcs. Position the cursor in the location in which you want to place the dimension, right-click, and select **Aligned**. Alternatively, place the dimension at a point along a line that joins the two centers. When it displays, click the left mouse button. Move the cursor to the required location and click to locate the dimension.
To place dimensions d1 and d2	Select the centers of the circles or circular entities. Position the cursor in the location at which you want to place the dimension and click the left mouse button.

Radius/ Diameter Dimensions

To create radius or diameter dimensions, select an arc or circle to create a radius dimension. Position the cursor at the location in which you want to place the dimension and press the left mouse button. By default, the dimension type for arcs is radius and the dimension type for circles is diameter, as shown in Figure 2–42.

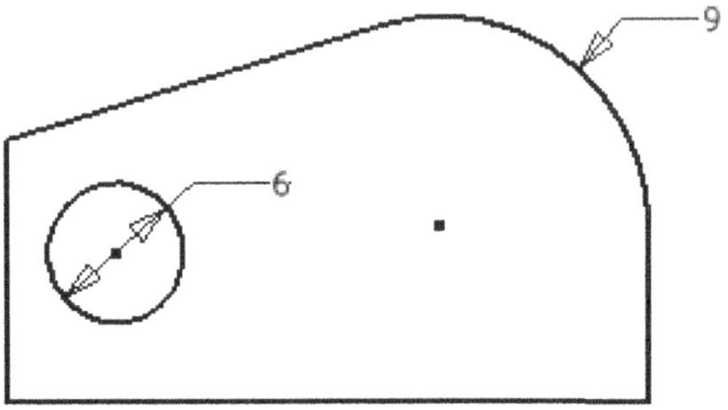

Figure 2–42

To change the type of dimensions, right-click and select **Radius** or **Diameter** from the **Dimension Type** menu before placing the dimension. Position the cursor at the location at which you want to place the dimension and click the left mouse button.

Angular Dimensions

To create angular dimensions, select lines A and B and place the angular dimension using the left mouse button. The resulting angle is dependent on the placement location of the dimension, as shown in Figure 2–43. Alternatively, you can create an angular dimension by selecting three points.

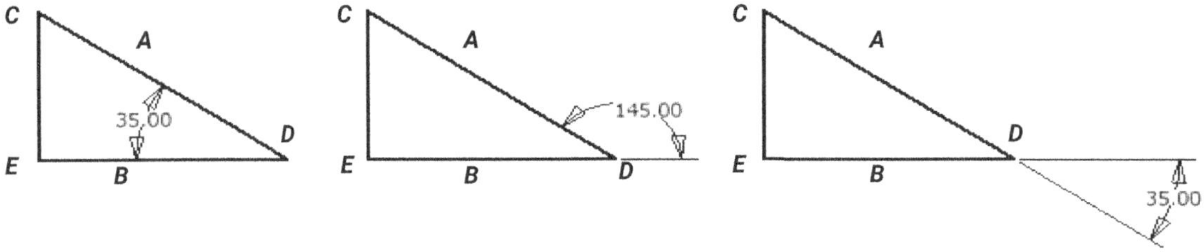

Figure 2–43

Tangent Dimensions

To create a tangent dimension, select the first arc, and move the cursor over the second arc. When displays, select the second arc and place the dimension, as shown in Figure 2–44.

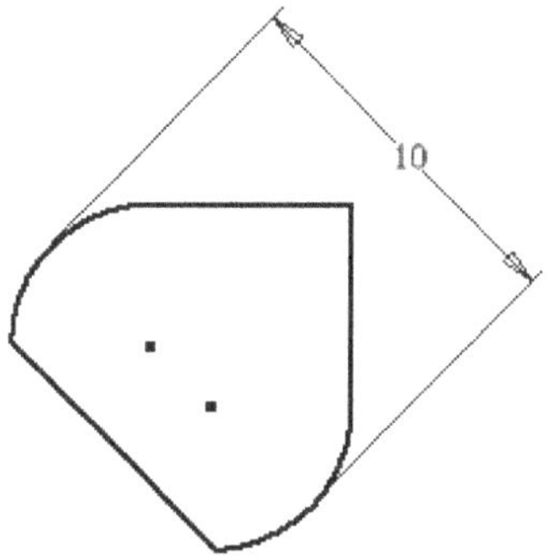

Figure 2–44

Revolved Sketch Dimensions

When sketching a cross-section of a revolved feature, only half of the section needs to be sketched. The cross-section is then revolved about the center line at a specified angle.

To create a diameter dimension on the section of a revolved feature, select the center line of the revolved cross-section and then the geometry, right-click, and select **Linear Diameter**. Figure 2–45 shows a revolved diameter dimension. This dimensioning scheme can also be used to dimension symmetrical entities.

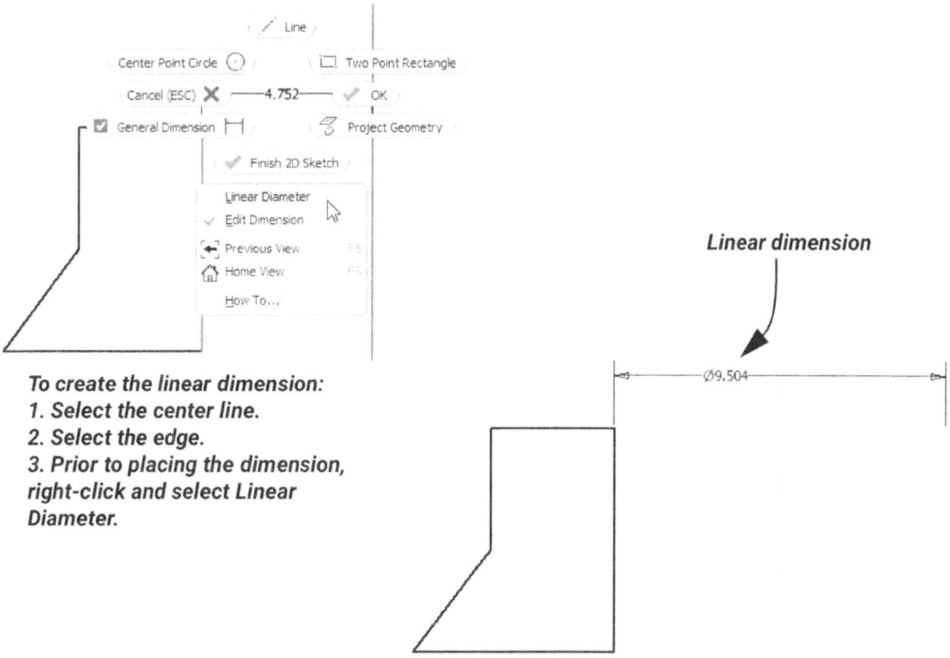

Figure 2–45

Arc Length Dimensions

To create an Arc Length dimension, select the arc, right-click, and select **Dimension Type>Arc Length**, then place the dimension, as shown in Figure 2–46.

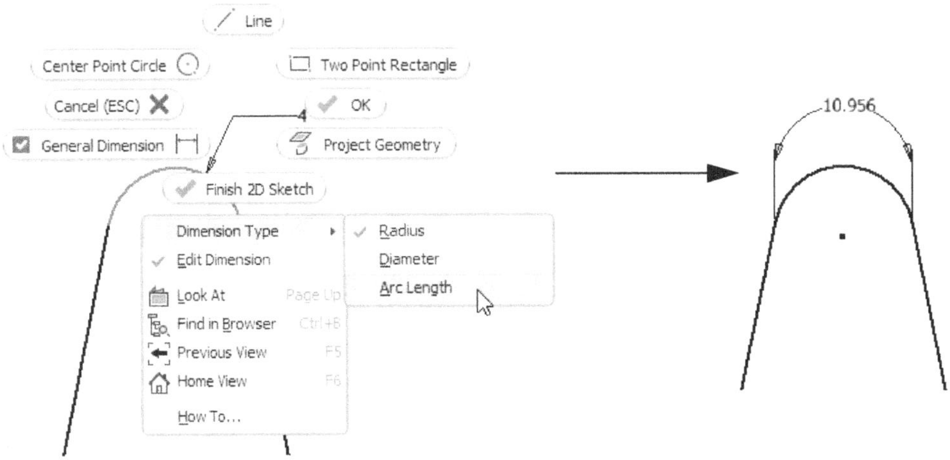

Figure 2–46

Dimension Types

When you are working in an Imperial template, you have the flexibility to change the dimension style from **Decimal** to **Fractional** or **Architectural**. This is done by editing the dimension value, expanding the menu in the *Dimension* field, and selecting a new option, as shown in Figure 2–47.

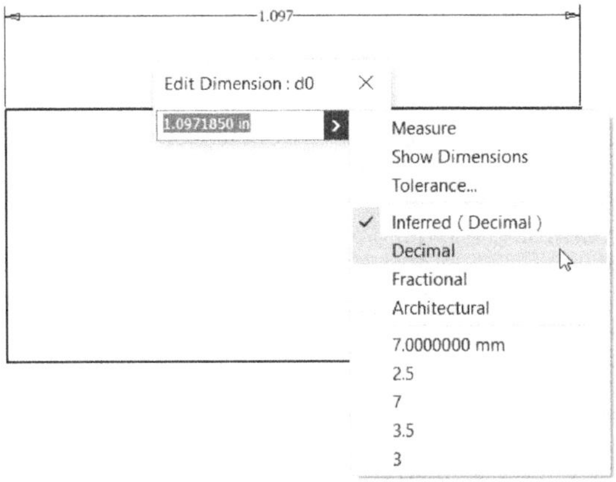

Figure 2–47

Over Dimensioned Entities

If you try to apply a dimension that is going to over-dimension the sketch, the dialog box shown in Figure 2–48 displays. You can cancel the command or place as a driven dimension. Driven dimensions display in parentheses, as shown in Figure 2–48. You cannot modify them, but they update if other dimensions are changed.

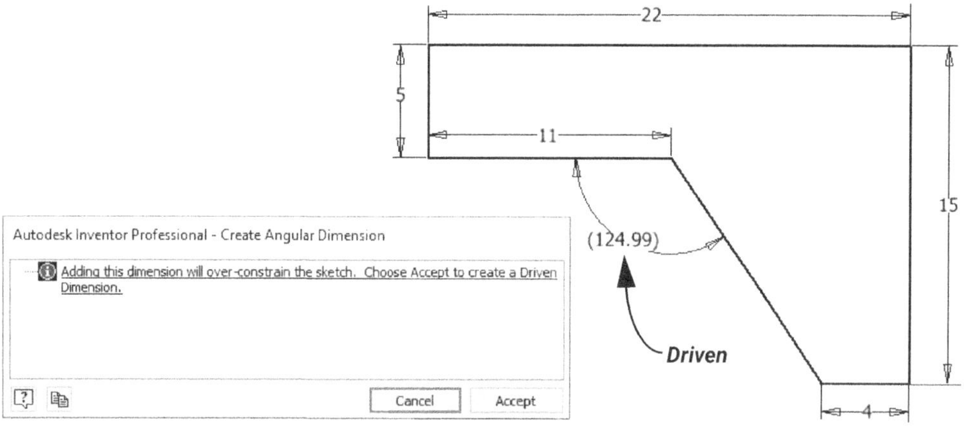

Figure 2–48

If you encounter an over-dimensioned sketch, keep the dimension that best suits the design intent.

Modifying Dimensions

Sketch dimensions control the size of the geometry and therefore are parametric. By default, a dimension is immediately modifiable as soon as it is placed in the sketch. To disable this functionality so you can first place all of the dimensions and then modify them later, right-click in the graphics window and clear the **Edit Dimension** option before placing the dimension. Alternatively, in the Constraint Settings, clear the **Edit dimension when created** option.

How To: Edit a Value of a Dimension

1. Double-click on the dimension. If the **Dimension** command is already active, only a single-click is required.
2. Enter a new value in the Edit Dimension dialog box.
3. Click  or press <Enter>.

Deleting Dimensions

To delete a dimension, select the dimension, right-click, and select **Delete** or press <Delete>.

2.6 Basic Sketch Editing Tools

The *Sketch* tab provides additional editing tools that can be used to modify sketch entities.

Trim

Trim removes the segment of the entity to the nearest intersection in each direction from the selected point. The selected portion of an object (e.g., lines or arcs) is removed, as shown in Figure 2–49. Selecting an object without an intersection deletes the object. If the intersections contain multiple possibilities for trimming, move the cursor over each segment. If it can be trimmed, it displays as a red dashed entity.

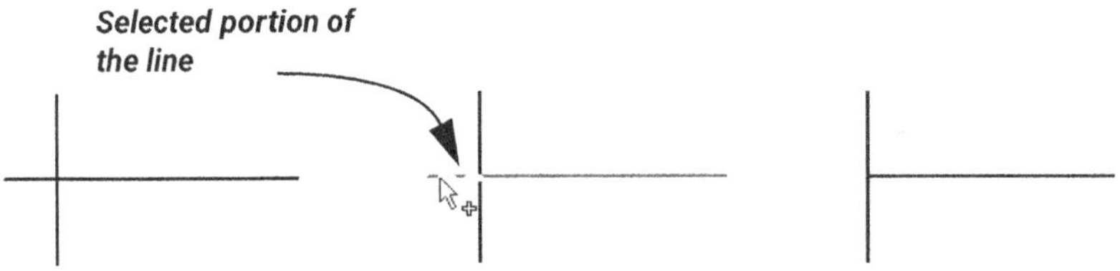

Figure 2–49

How To: Trim Sketched Entities

1. In the Modify panel, click (Trim) or right-click and select **Trim.**
2. Move the cursor over the portion of the entity that you want to trim. A preview of the trim displays.
3. Click the left mouse button to remove the portion.

Trimming can also be done dynamically once the command is initiated. Drag the freehand line over the required entities that are to be removed. Release the mouse button to remove the entities from the sketch.

Extend

Extend continues an entity to meet the next entity in its path or to close an open sketch, as shown in Figure 2–50.

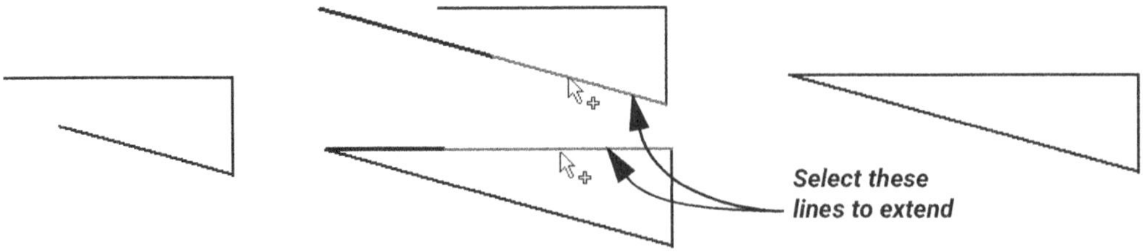

Figure 2–50

How To: Extend Sketched Entities

1. In the Modify panel, click (Extend) or if the **Trim** command is already active, right-click and select **Extend.**
2. Move the cursor over the portion of the entity that you want to extend. A preview of the extend displays.
3. Click the left mouse button to extend the entity.

Extending can also be done dynamically once the command is initiated. Drag the freehand line over the required entities that are to be extended. Release the mouse button to extend the entities from the sketch.

> ***Note:** To toggle between **Trim** and **Extend** (or vice-versa) when a command is active, press and hold <Shift>.*

Mirror

Entities can be mirrored in a sketch. The sketch shown in Figure 2–51 is created using the **Mirror** sketch tool and a construction line as the mirror line.

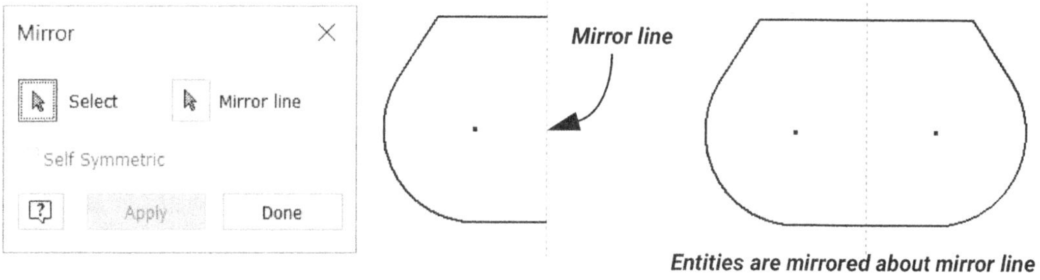

Figure 2–51

How To: Mirror a Selected Object About a Mirror Line

1. In the Pattern panel, click (Mirror). The Mirror dialog box displays.
2. Select the sketch entities that you want to mirror.
3. In the Mirror dialog box, click (Mirror line). The mirror line can be:
   - Entities within the geometry that are selected to mirror
   - Projected Origin feature
   - Projected model edge
   - Straight sketched or construction lines
4. Select a mirror line, and click **Apply**.

Split

The **Split** command enables you to split an entity (e.g., line, arc, or spline) based on an intersecting entity (e.g., entity, workplane, or surface). To split an entity, click (Split) in the Modify panel and select the entity to split. Before selecting the entity to split, hover the cursor over the entity to preview a cross mark that indicates the split location. In cases where multiple solutions are possible, the nearest one is assigned. Once split, the segments maintain all constraints, except for **Equal** and **Symmetric**, if they apply. Dimensions are also maintained when entities are split.

Offset

The **Offset** command enables you to create new entities by offsetting existing feature edges. Rather than sketching each set of entities separately, offsetting enables you to create a copy of the projected geometry and positions it at an offset distance from the original. An example of a sketch created by offsetting feature edges is shown in Figure 2–52.

> ***Note:*** *Projected geometry can be offset as well as sketch geometry.*

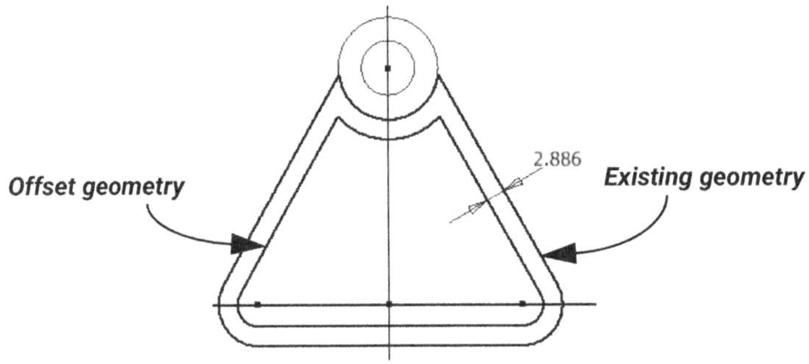

Figure 2–52

How To: Offset Entities

> ***Note:*** *The option settings are maintained the next time the Offset command is used.*

1. Sketch or project the geometry that is to be offset.
2. In the Modify panel, click (Offset).

3. Right-click in the graphics window and select one of the options shown in Figure 2–53.

__Loop Select:__ Enables you to select one or more entities to offset loops or continuous curves. To offset individual edges, clear this option.

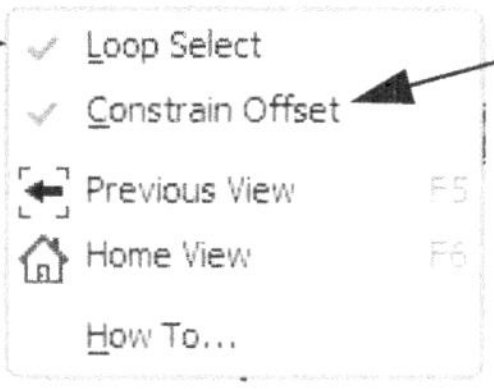

***Constrain Offset:* Applies an Equal constraint to the distance between the offset geometry and the original geometry, requiring only a single dimension. To control each offset entity with its own dimension, clear this option.**

Figure 2–53

4. Select the entities or projected geometry to offset.
5. Drag the entities to the offset location and click to place them. As the entities are dragged and reach zero length, they are removed from the offset geometry set.
6. To complete the offset, right-click and select **OK,** press <Esc>, or select a new command.
7. Dimension and constrain the offset geometry as required to fully locate it in the sketch. Offset geometry only needs one offset dimension to fully locate it relative to its parent entities.

Move, Copy, Rotate, Scale, and Stretch

The following describes some of the more advanced tools that can be used to edit a sketch. All of the editing tools described are located in the *Sketch* tab>Modify panel.

(Move)	Moves original 2D sketch geometry or copies and moves it.
(Copy)	Copies the source entities to one or more locations in the sketch or to another sketch. No relationship is established between the new and source entities. Copying entities can also be done using **Move** and **Rotate**. However, **Copy** enables you to create multiple instances at once.
(Rotate)	Rotates sketch entities about a center point.
(Scale)	Enlarges or reduces the size of sketched entities by entering a scale factor.
(Stretch)	Stretches entities versus simply selecting and dragging them. Unlike using the select-and-drag technique, which does not enable you to manipulate constrained geometry, the **Stretch** command enables you to stretch constrained geometry while maintaining its constraints.

The workflow for these sketch editing tools are similar.

How To: Edit Sketched Geometry Using These Tools

1. Select the required editing command. The associated dialog box opens, as shown in Figure 2–54.

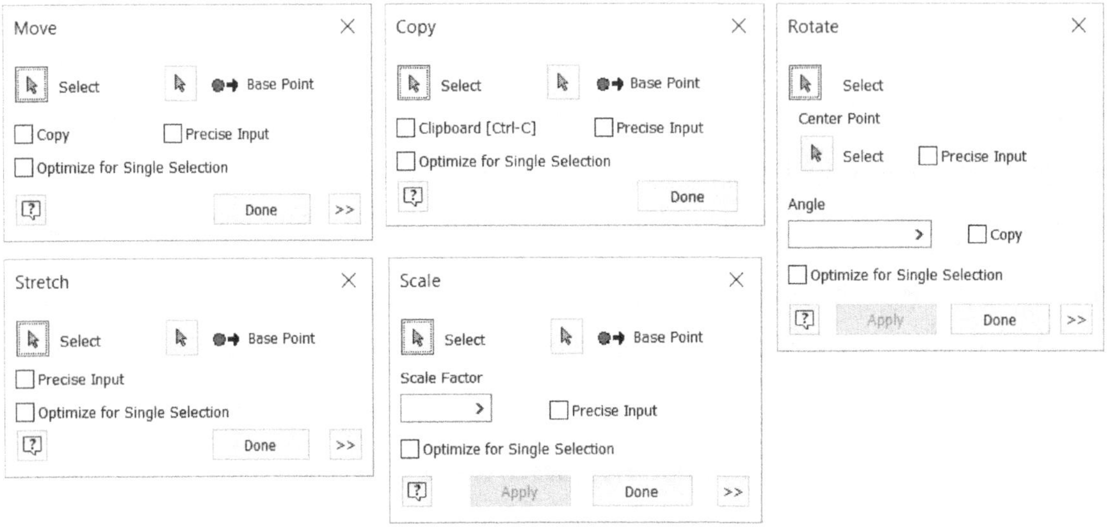

Figure 2–54

2. Select the entities to edit using  (Select). To select multiple entities, press and hold <Ctrl>, right-click and select **Select All**, or use one of the two window selection techniques shown in Figure 2–55.

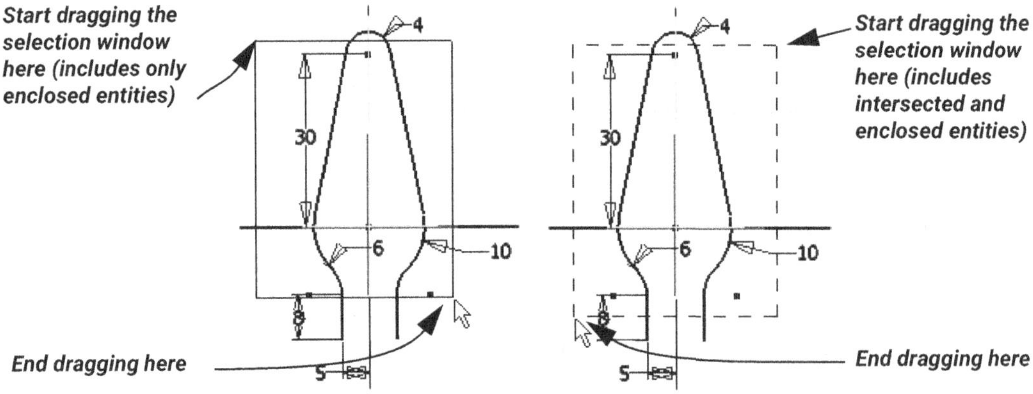

Figure 2–55

Note: *The* ***Optimize for Single Selection*** *option can be used to automatically advance to*  *(Base/Center Point) selection once a single entity has been selected for editing.*

Hint: Selection Tools

- For the **Copy** command, once entities are selected, you can use **Clipboard** to place the entities on the clipboard for pasting into the same or another sketch.
- For the **Stretch** command, entity selection (lines, points, arcs) is important, otherwise the command functions similar to the **Move** command.

3. For the **Move** and **Rotate** editing commands, you can select **Copy** in the dialog box to make a copy of the entities as you move or rotate them.
4. For the **Move**, **Copy**, **Scale**, and **Stretch**, click (Base Point) and for **Rotate**, click (Center Point). In both situations, select a point on the original geometry as the reference/pivot point for the operation. Alternatively, you can select **Precise Input** to enter a location for the reference.
5. Select a point to which to move, copy, scale, rotate, or stretch. As you drag the cursor, the edited sketch displays. When rotating or scaling, you can also manually enter a rotation or scale value.
6. Click **Done** to complete the operation.

Depending on the dimensional and geometric constraints, the dialog box shown in Figure 2–56 (or a similar dialog box) might open, prompting you to remove constraints or relax dimensions. Click **Yes** to remove any existing constraints; however, consider that you might want to add them again later to ensure that the design intent is maintained. You can also click Prompts to set how the software handles dimension/constraint conflicts in the future.

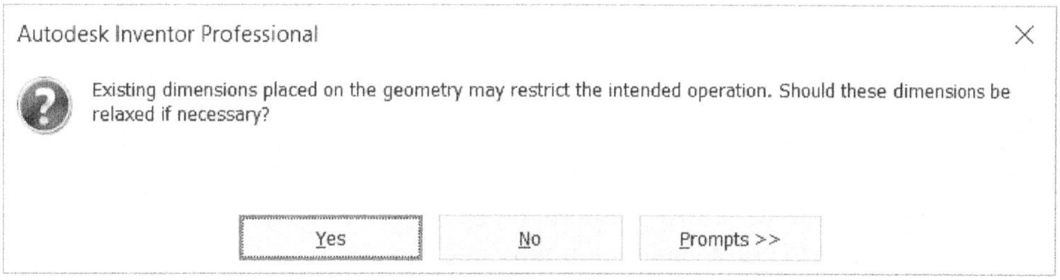

Figure 2–56

Copy and Paste

As an alternative to using the **Copy** command in the Modify panel, you can use the standard keyboard driven **Copy** (right-click and select **Copy** or <Ctrl>+<C>) and **Paste** (right-click and select **Paste** or <Ctrl>+<V>) functionality in a sketch. You can copy in the same sketch, to another sketch in the same model, or a sketch in a different model. Regardless of the target location, select the source entities and initiate the copy functionality. Once the entities are saved to the clipboard, you can paste using any of the following techniques.

- Right-click and select **Paste** in the same sketch. Use the right-click **Paste** option on a Model browser Sketch node or in the graphics window if the sketch is active.
- Finish the current sketch, in the Model browser locate the target sketch in the same model, right-click and select **Paste**.
- Open a new part to copy into, locate the target sketch in the Model browser, right-click, and select **Paste**. If the sketch does not exist, create it, right-click in the graphics window, and select **Paste** while in the Sketch environment.

Using AutoCAD Data in Inventor

There are two workflows that can be used to incorporate AutoCAD® .DWG data into the Autodesk® Inventor® software for use in creating 3D geometry. The choice of whether to use either workflow is dependent on whether you require an associative link to be maintained with the AutoCAD .DWG data.

- When creating a sketch, the (Insert ACAD File) option on the Insert panel enables you to select and import an AutoCAD .DWG file into a sketch to create 3D geometry.
  - During import you can select which layers and selectively choose entities that are to be imported onto the active sketch. The data is imported as native Autodesk Inventor data and no associative link is maintained to the .DWG file.
  - You can add dimensions and/or constraints as required to capture your design intent and use the sketch to create solid geometry.
- An AutoCAD .DWG file can also be inserted directly into a part file and used to create 3D geometry or placed in an assembly file and used to constrain geometry. This option enables you to maintain an associative link between the AutoCAD .DWG and the part file, so that any changes to the .DWG data updates in the part file.
  - The general workflow for inserting an AutoCAD part file includes inserting the file (*Manage* tab>Insert panel, click (Import)) on a selected planar face or work plane and then projecting the data onto a sketch using the **Project DWG Geometry** option in the sketch.

- The general workflow for placing an AutoCAD part file in an assembly involves using the **Place** option, selecting the file, and selecting a reference plane and point to locate the .DWG file. The **Place** option can be used to create or locate geometry in an assembly.
- Multiple AutoCAD .DWG files can be inserted on different planes to create the required 3D geometry.

Note: *More information on this workflow is covered in the Advanced guide, or you can search for Associative DWG or DWG Underlay in the Help documentation.*

Practice 2a
LBracket

Practice Objectives

- Create a new part model using a pre-defined template.
- Create an L-shaped sketch using the appropriate tools in the *Sketch* tab.

In this practice, you will create a new model using a standard template file. The geometry, shown in Figure 2–57, is created using the tools in the *Sketch* tab. It is created by referencing the projected center point to dimension and constrain the sketched line entities.

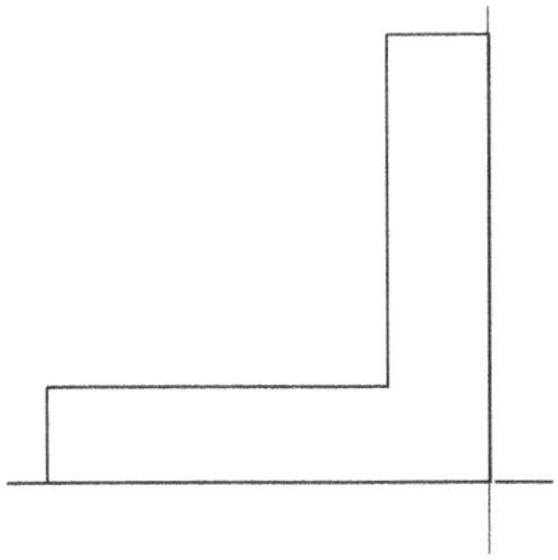

Figure 2–57

Task 1: Create a new model using the default part template.

1. In the Tools menu, click (Application Options). Select the *File* tab in the Application Options dialog box and click **Configure Default Template**. The dialog box appears showing you the current units and standard for the default template. For example, Figure 2–58 shows the default templates currently assigned for Inventor are in Inches and will use the ANSI drawing standard.

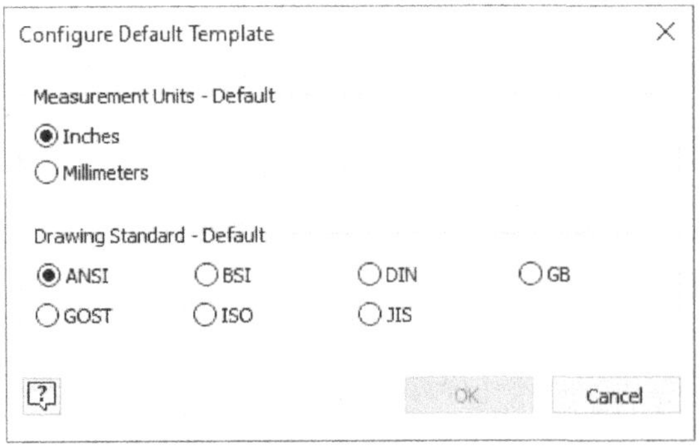

Figure 2–58

2. Select **Millimeters** and **ANSI**, if not already set. Click **OK** and confirm to **Overwrite** the default template. This sets the default template that is presented when you create a new part file; however, it does not prevent you from creating a model in inches by selecting **New** on the Home page as was shown in the previous practice.
3. Click **OK** to close the Application Options dialog box.
4. On the Home page, select ⌄ to expand the New menu as shown in Figure 2–59.

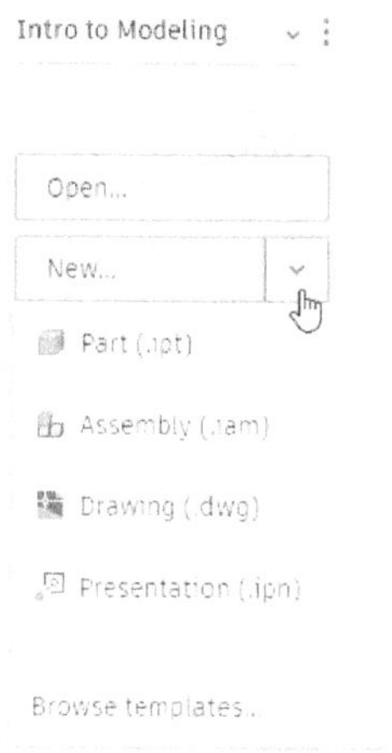

Figure 2–59

5. Select **Part (.ipt)**. This creates a new part file using the default template (which was just set to millimeter/ANSI) without having to use the Create New File dialog box.

Hint: Creating New Files

As an alternative to expanding the New menu and selecting **Part (.ipt)**, you can select **New** to open the Create New File dialog box and manually select the template to use for the part. Alternatively, you can also use the following techniques to select a new template as the basis of a new file:

- In the Quick Access Toolbar, click 🗋 (New).
- In the **File** menu, select **New** and the file type.

Task 2: Create a sketch.

1. In the Model browser, next to the Origin, click + to expand it.
2. In the top right-hand corner of the graphics window, hover the mouse over the ViewCube and select ⌂ to reorient the model into a 3D orientation.

3. In the Model browser, select the **XY Plane**. In the *3D Model* tab>Sketch panel, click (Start 2D Sketch) or click (Create Sketch) in the graphics window to start a new sketch. You are placed in the Sketch environment, the XY plane is the current sketch plane, and the *Sketch* tab is active.

   ***Note:** Alternatively, you can right-click on the plane name in the Model browser, or in the graphics window (if displayed), right-click and select **New Sketch**. Or you could have initiated the command first and then selected the XY plane as the sketching plane.*

Task 3: Sketch the base feature section.

1. In the Create panel, click (Line) or right-click and select **Create Line**.
2. Hover the cursor over the projected center point at the center of the sketch. The cursor should snap to this reference. Start the sketch by pressing the left mouse button at the projected center point, as shown in Figure 2–60.

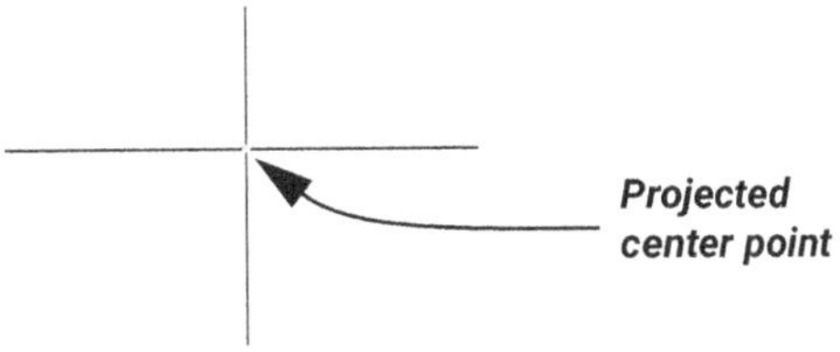

Figure 2–60

3. Sketch the six lines shown in Figure 2–61. Use the left mouse button to start and end each line segment. When drawing the lines, do not worry about their lengths, and draw the lines horizontally and vertically in a similar scale to that shown in Figure 2–61. When drawing the last line segment, which returns to the projected Center Point, ensure that the cursor snaps to this reference before selecting.

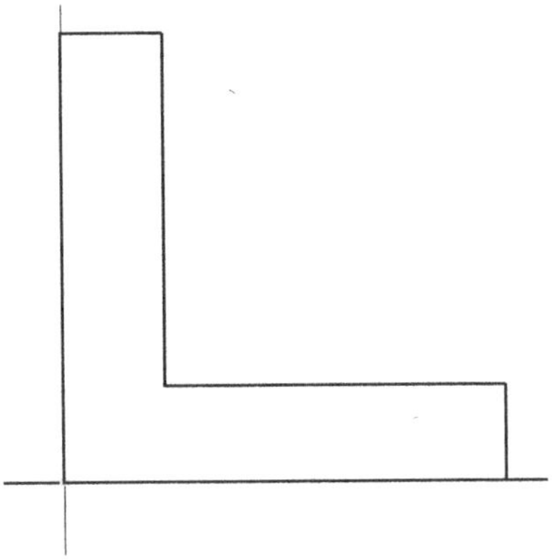

Figure 2–61

4. Press the <Esc> key to quit the line command. The bottom right corner of the main window also indicates that four dimensions are required.

   Note: *If required, you can quickly restart a command by pressing <Spacebar> or <Enter>, or by right-clicking and selecting the command again from the top of the list.*

5. In the Constrain panel, click (Automatic Dimensions and Constraints) to also reveal the number of required dimensions, as shown in Figure 2–62.

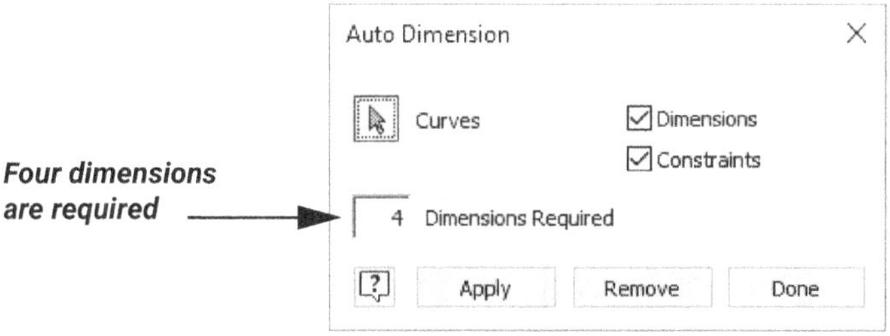

Figure 2–62

   Note: *Automatically dimensioning a sketch is helpful when determining a missing dimension. However, it is not recommended for use in dimensioning a full sketch, as it does not assume the design intent of the sketch.*

6. Click **Apply** to apply the dimensions automatically.
7. Click **Done** to close the Auto Dimension dialog box.

8. If required, delete, recreate, and modify the dimensions to match those shown in Figure 2–63.

- To reposition a dimension, select it using the left mouse button, drag it and release the mouse button in the required location.
- To edit a dimension value, double-click on the value, enter a new value, and then press Enter.
- To create a new dimension, in the Constrain panel, click (Dimension) and select entities on the sketch. Once the dimension displays attached to the cursor, drag to locate the dimension, and click to place it.

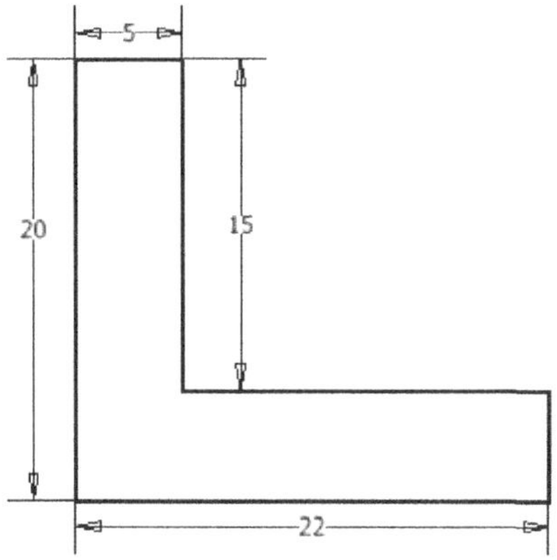

Figure 2–63

9. In the Exit panel, click (Finish Sketch), or right-click and select **Finish 2D Sketch**.

10. Hover the cursor over the ViewCube and click (Home) to return to the model to its default 3D orientation, if it does not automatically return to its default orientation.

Task 4: Save the model and close the file.

1. In the Quick Access Toolbar, click (Save) to save the model.

2. Enter **L_shape** in the *File name* field and click **Save**. This file will be used to create solid geometry in a later practice.

3. In the graphics window, click (Close) to close the window.

End of practice

Practice 2b
Sketched Geometry

Practice Objectives

- Use existing surfaces to create 2D sketches.
- Project existing geometry and use the ***Sketch*** tab to create sketched geometry.

In this practice, you will create 2D sketches on existing surfaces using tools in the *Sketch* tab. The basic sketches that you will create are shown in Figure 2–64.

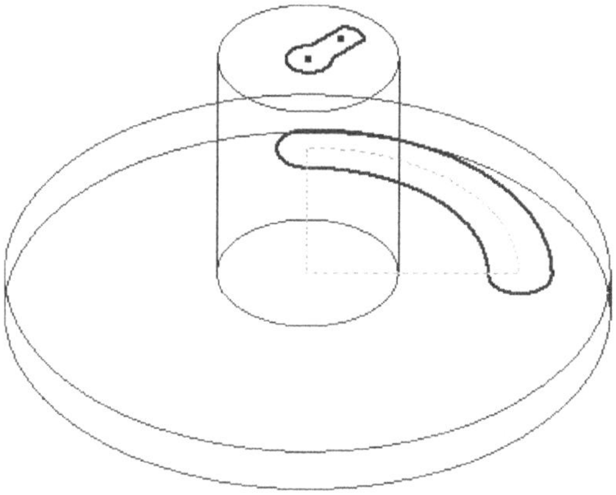

Figure 2–64

Task 1: Open an existing file.

1. Open **Flange.ipt.** The part displays as shown in Figure 2–65.

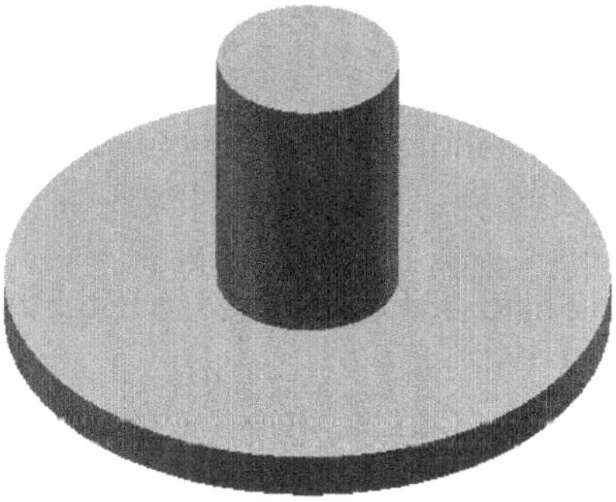

Figure 2–65

Task 2: Create a 2D sketch.

1. Click (Start 2D Sketch) and select the face shown in Figure 2–66. The part orients so that the selected plane faces parallel to the screen.

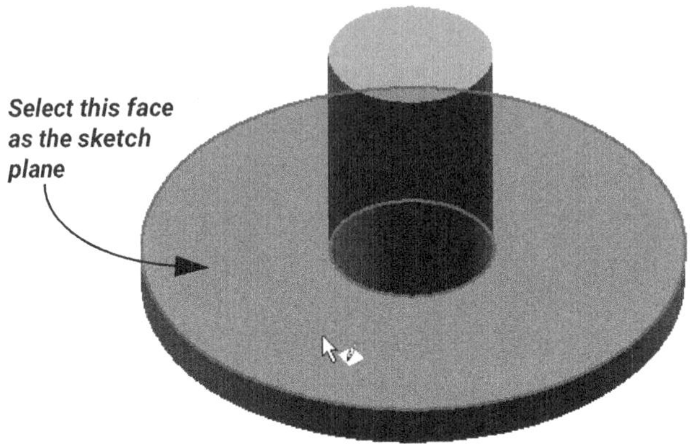

Figure 2–66

2. Display the model as wireframe (*View* tab>Appearance panel, Visual Styles drop-down list).
3. In the Status Bar in the graphics window, click (Slice Graphics). All of the geometry that lies in front of the sketch plane is temporarily removed from the display. Note that the origin center point has been projected automatically.
4. Ensure that the *Sketch* tab is selected. Click (Project Geometry) or right-click and select **Project Geometry**.
5. Select the Y Axis in the Model browser. It displays in yellow to indicate that it has been projected.
6. Click (Slot Center Point Arc) from the expanded Rectangle drop-down list.
7. Select the projected origin center point as the center point of the slot.
8. Drag the cursor into the top left-hand quadrant. The placement of the mouse defines the direction in which the slot is created. The measurements are based from the left side of the slot.
9. Enter **14** in the dynamic input field when prompted to enter the location of the start point of the center of the arc. Press <Enter>.
10. Drag the cursor to the right. Enter **90** in the dynamic input field when prompted to enter the end point of the center of the arc. Press <Enter>.
11. Enter **5mm** in the dynamic input field when prompted to select a point on the slot to define its size. Press <Enter>.

12. In the Constrain panel, click (Symmetry). Select the two center points of the slot as the sketch elements and then select the projected Y-axis as the symmetry line.
13. The slot was created with dimensions because the dynamic entry value fields were used. If they had not been, you would have to dimension the entities using (Dimension). The sketch should display similar to that shown in Figure 2–67.

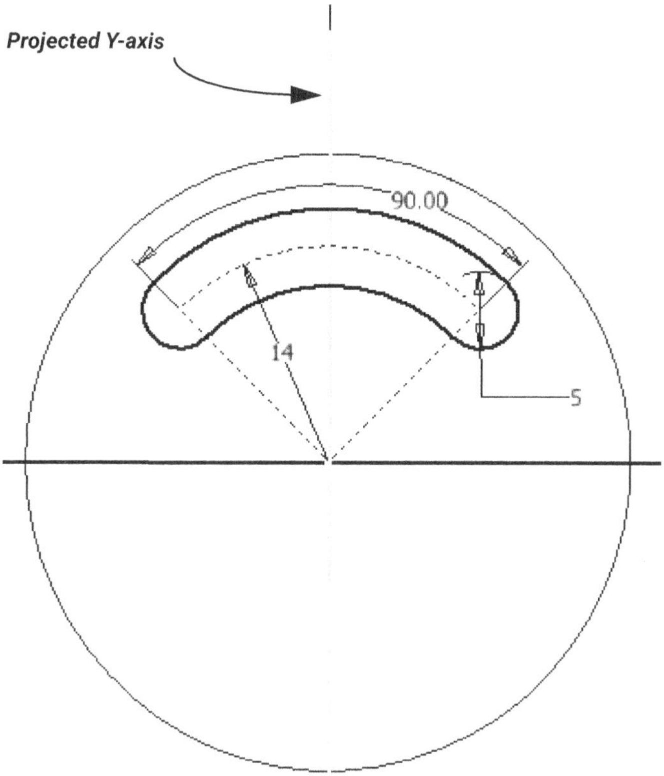

Figure 2–67

14. In the Status Bar, click (Show All Constraints) to display the constraints applied in the sketch, if not already displayed. Review the constraints placed on the sketch.

Note: *You can also press <F8> to display all of the constraints. You can also press <F9> to hide all of the constraints.*

15. Click (Hide All Constraints) to toggle off the display of constraints.

16. In the Exit panel, click (Finish Sketch) or right-click and select **Finish 2D Sketch** to finish the sketch.

17. Select the newly created sketch in the Model browser, right-click and select **Visibility** to hide the sketch.

Task 3: Create a 2D sketch.

1. Click (Start 2D Sketch) and select the face shown in Figure 2–68. The part orients so that the selected plane faces parallel to the screen.

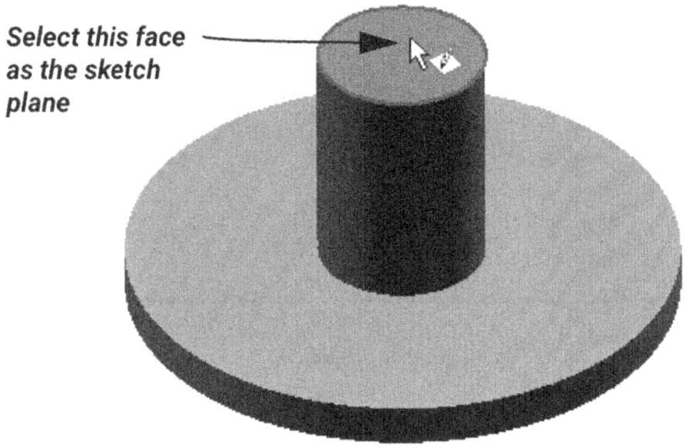

Figure 2–68

2. Project the Y-axis and the circular edge of the sketch plane (if not already projected).
3. Use the tools in the *Sketch* tab to create the sketch entities shown in Figure 2–69.
4. In the Constrain panel, click (Symmetry). Select the two vertical linear entities and then select the projected Y-axis as the symmetry line.
5. In the Constrain panel, click (Dimension). Select the two vertical entities using the left mouse button and place the dimension value as shown in Figure 2–69 using the left mouse button. Enter **2** as its value.
6. Select the circle entity using the left mouse button and place the dimension as shown in Figure 2–69 using the left mouse button. Enter **3** as its value.

   Note: *Alternatively, if you had entered values using the dynamic input fields as you were sketching the entities you would not need to create the dimensions, other than to position the entities in the sketch relative to the projected references.*

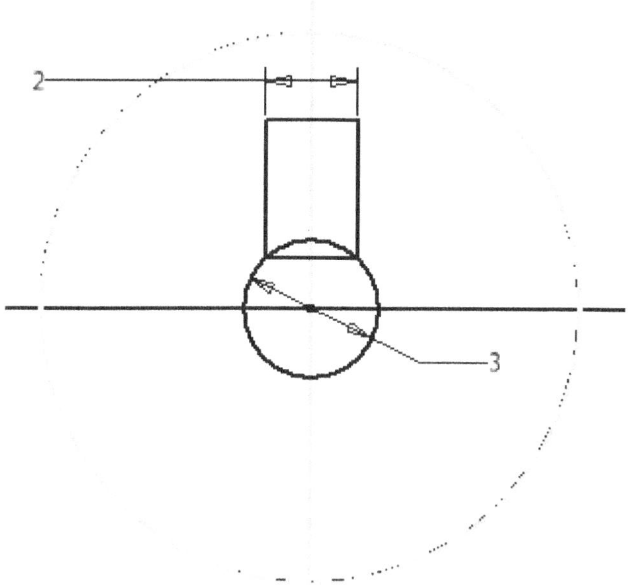

Figure 2–69

7. Click (Trim) to remove the overlapping entities so that the sketch displays as shown in Figure 2–70.
8. Add the additional dimension to fully constrain the sketch to the projected origin center point, as shown in Figure 2–70.

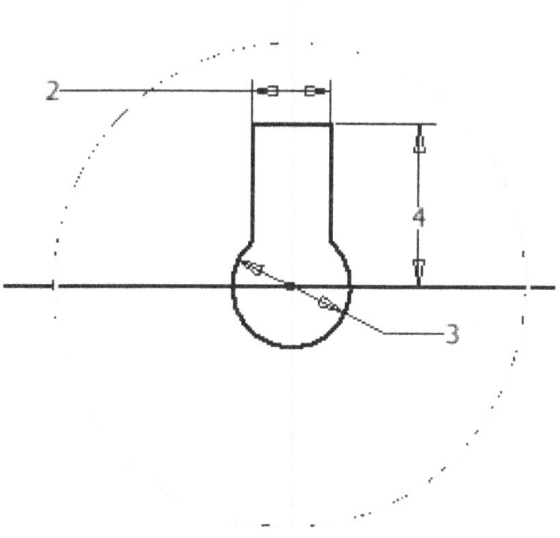

Figure 2–70

9. With the removal of the entities, it is possible that the sketch can no longer resolve the location of the two entities on the circle, relative to each other. If so, the status bar indicates that one dimension is still required to fully constrain the sketch. Whether this occurs depends on how you sketched the geometry.

10. In the Constrain panel, click (Horizontal). Select the top horizontal line to ensure that it is horizontal, as shown in Figure 2–71.

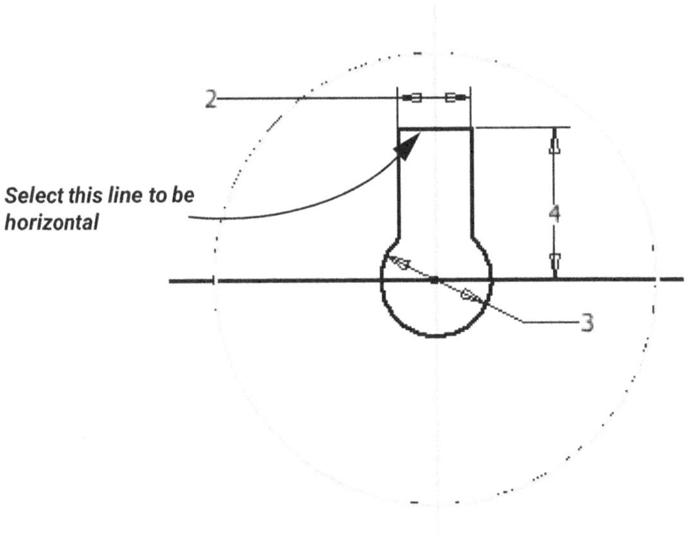

Figure 2–71

11. In the Exit panel, click (Finish Sketch) or right-click and select **Finish 2D Sketch** to finish the sketch.

12. In the Model browser, select the newly created sketch and then select it again, and rename it as **Keyhole**.

Task 4: Modify the sketch and sketch values.

1. Double-click on the Keyhole sketch.

2. Modify the sketch as shown in Figure 2–72. Create an arc and remove the appropriate dimensions and entities.

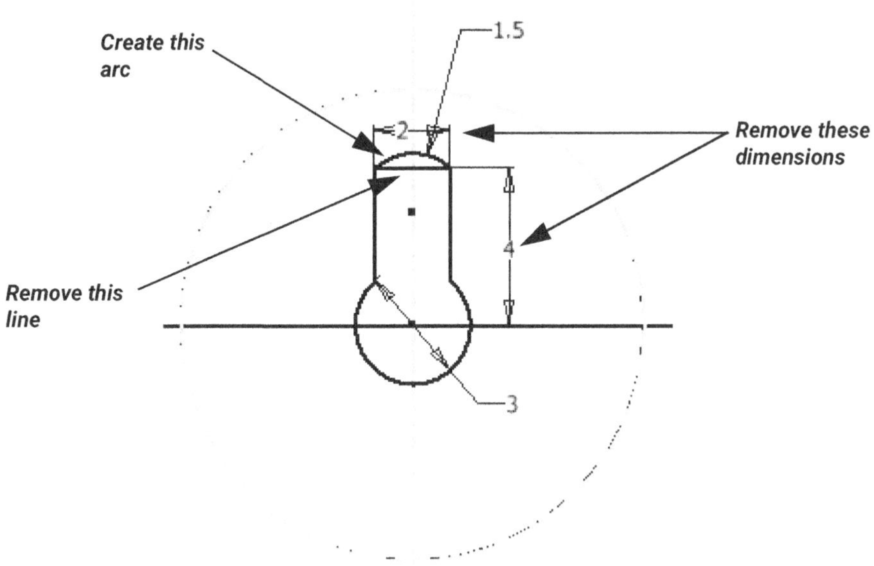

Figure 2–72

3. Create the dimensions as shown in Figure 2–73. Ensure that the sketch is fully constrained. You might need to add a coincident constraint to the center point of the arc and Y-axis.

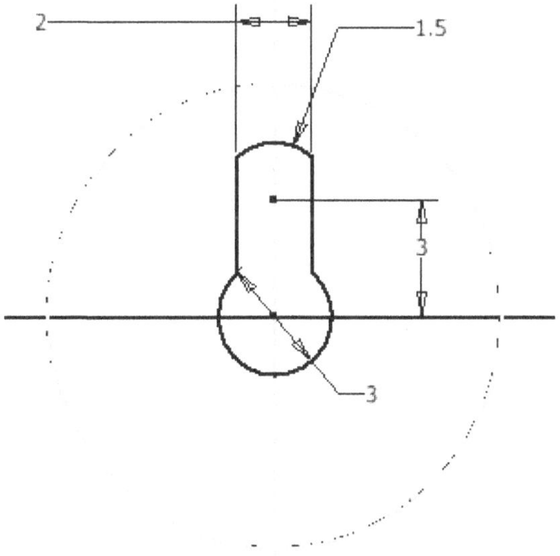

Figure 2–73

4. In the Exit panel, click (Finish Sketch) or right-click and select **Finish 2D Sketch** to finish the sketch.
5. Toggle on the visibility of the initial sketch. Select each sketch in the Model browser, right-click and select **Dimension Visibility** to hide the sketched dimensions.
6. Save the file and close the window. In the next chapter, you will learn how to use these sketches to remove material from the model.

End of practice

Chapter Review Questions

1. Which of the following statements is true when creating the initial base feature in a new part using the **Standard.ipt** template, as shown in Figure 2–74? (Select all that apply.)

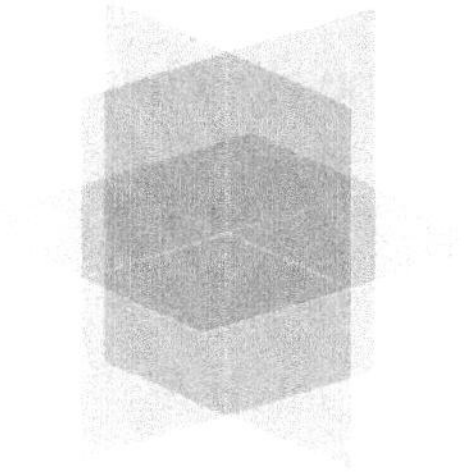

Figure 2–74

   a. Select any one of the origin planes that are displayed in the graphics window to define the sketch plane.
   b. Select any one of the origin planes that are listed in the Model browser to define the sketch plane.
   c. Select any existing solid geometry face to define the sketch plane.

2. Construction entities can be used directly to create solid geometry.
   a. True
   b. False

3. Which tool temporarily hides the portion of a part that is above the sketch plane to display the plane more clearly for sketching?
   a. Slice Graphics
   b. Relax Mode
   c. Look At
   d. Hidden Edge Display

4. Which of the following statements describes trimming sketch entities?

a. Continues an entity to meet the next entity in its path or to close an open sketch.

b. Removes the segment of the entity to the nearest intersection in each direction from the point selected.

c. Duplicates a source entity to one or more locations in the sketch or to another sketch.

d. Provides a specific tool for stretching sketched entities versus simply selecting and dragging them in the sketch.

5. Which of the following can be made equal using (Equal Constraint)? (Select all that apply.)

a. Angles between lines

b. Line Lengths

c. Arc Radii

d. Circle Diameters

6. How can you control the visibility of constraint symbols in the graphics window display? (Select all that apply.)

a. To show or hide all of the constraints on a sketch, toggle (Show All Constraints) and (Hide All Constraints) in the Status Bar.

b. Select the entity to which it is associated.

c. Use <F8> to show all of the constraints and <F9> to hide them.

d. Select the symbol and press <Delete>.

7. The sketched entities shown on the left in Figure 2–75 are fully constrained. Which of the following statements best describes the (113.91) dimension value, as shown on the right in Figure 2–75?

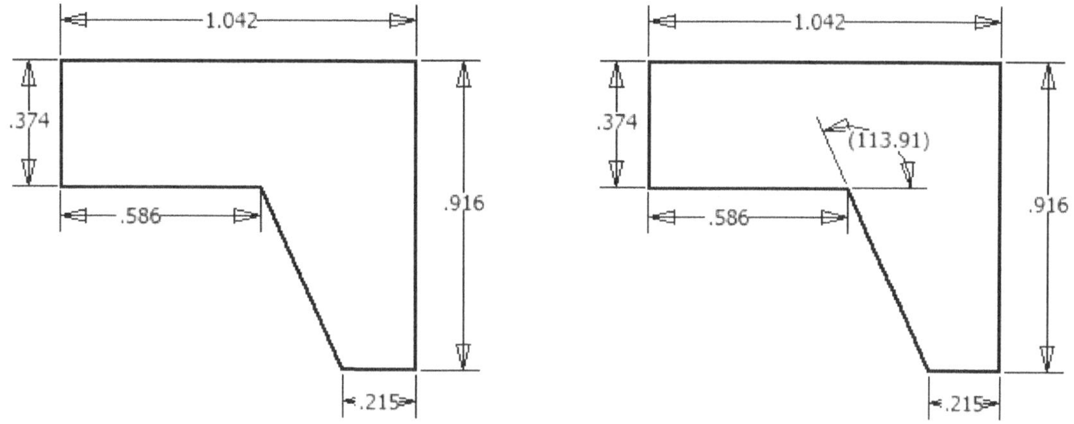

Figure 2–75

a. The (113.91) dimension is a Driven Angular Dimension and cannot be modified to change the size of the sketch.

b. The (113.91) dimension is a General Angular Dimension and cannot be modified to change the size of the sketch.

c. The (113.91) dimension is a Driven Angular Dimension and can be modified to change the size of the sketch.

d. The (113.91) dimension is a General Angular Dimension and can be modified to change the size of the sketch.

8. Which of the following sets of constraints is used to manipulate the geometry on the left to that on the right in Figure 2–76?

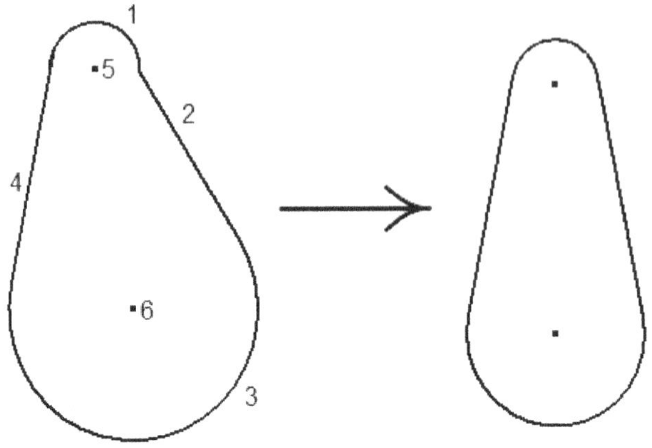

Figure 2–76

a. 1 tangent with 2, 1 tangent with 4, 5 coincident with 6.

b. 1 tangent with 2, 1 tangent with 4, 5 concentric with 6.

c. 1 tangent with 2, 1 tangent with 4, 5 collinear with 6.

d. 1 tangent with 2, 1 tangent with 4, 5 vertical with 6.

9. Based on the constraint symbols shown in Figure 2–77, which constraint types are applied to the bottom horizontal entity? (Select all that apply.)

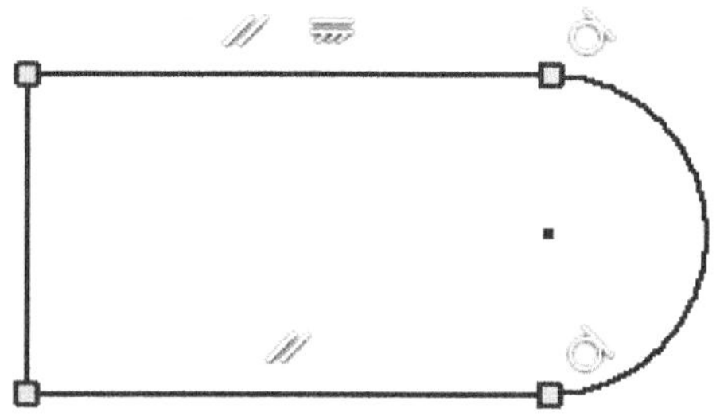

Figure 2–77

a. Symmetric
b. Parallel
c. Perpendicular
d. Tangent
e. Collinear
f. Coincident

10. Fillets and chamfers that are added in the sketch become separate Fillet and Chamfer features in the Model browser once the sketch has been completed. They can be selected and deleted independent of the sketch.

a. True
b. False

11. What types of sketch entities can you use as the mirror line when mirroring geometry? (Select all that apply.)

a. Construction line
b. Solid line
c. Projected part edge
d. Projected work plane

12. The **Offset** option is commonly used to create sketched entities offset from projected geometry. In the sketch shown in Figure 2–78, how many dimensions are required to fully constrain the sketch? Assume **Constrain Offset** and **Loop Select** are toggled on.

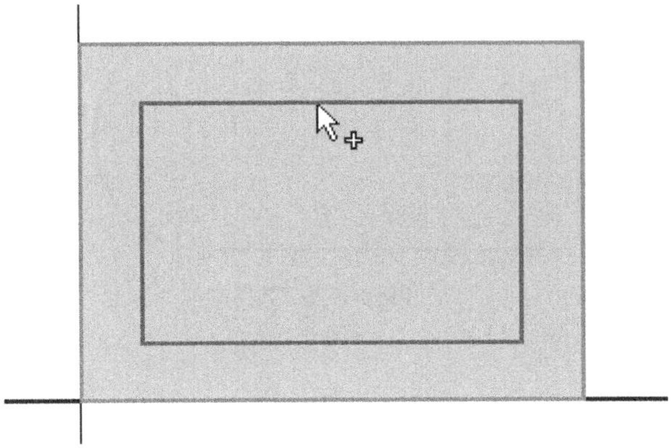

Figure 2–78

a. 1
b. 2
c. 3
d. 4
e. More than 4

Command Summary

Button	Command	Location
	Application Options	• **Ribbon:** *Tools* tab>Options panel • **File** menu>Options
	Automatic Dimensions	• **Ribbon:** *Sketch* tab>Constrain panel
	Bridge Curve	• **Ribbon:** *Sketch* tab>Create panel
	Center Point Arc	• **Ribbon:** *Sketch* tab>Create panel
	Center Point Arc Slot	• **Ribbon:** *Sketch* tab>Create panel
	Center Point Slot	• **Ribbon:** *Sketch* tab>Create panel
	Chamfer (sketch)	• **Ribbon:** *Sketch* tab>Create panel
	Circle	• **Ribbon:** *Sketch* tab>Create panel • **Context Menu:** In the graphics window
	Coincident	• **Ribbon:** *Sketch* tab>Constrain panel
	Collinear	• **Ribbon:** *Sketch* tab>Constrain panel
	Concentric	• **Ribbon:** *Sketch* tab>Constrain panel
	Constraint Settings	• **Ribbon:** *Sketch* tab>Constrain panel
	Construction	• **Ribbon:** *Sketch* tab>Format panel
	Dimension	• **Ribbon:** *Sketch* tab>Constrain panel • **Context Menu:** In the graphics window
N/A	**Dimension Visibility** (of sketch)	• **Context Menu:** In the Model browser • **Ribbon:** *View* tab>Visibility panel
	Document Settings	• **Ribbon:** *Tools* tab>Options panel
	Ellipse	• **Ribbon:** *Sketch* tab>Create panel
	Equal	• **Ribbon:** *Sketch* tab>Constrain panel

Button	Command	Location
	**Equation Curve**	• **Ribbon:** *Sketch* tab>Create panel
	**Extend**	• **Ribbon:** *Sketch* tab>Modify panel • *(toggle between* ***Trim*** *and* ***Extend*** *using <Shift>)*
	**Fillet** *(sketch)*	• **Ribbon:** *Sketch* tab>Create panel
	**Fix**	• **Ribbon:** *Sketch* tab>Constrain panel
	**Horizontal**	• **Ribbon:** *Sketch* tab>Constrain panel
	**Line**	• **Ribbon:** *Sketch* tab>Create panel • **Context Menu:** In the graphics window
	**Mirror**	• **Ribbon:** *Sketch* tab>Pattern panel
	**Offset**	• **Ribbon:** *Sketch* tab>Modify panel
	**Overall Slot**	• **Ribbon:** *Sketch* tab>Create panel
	**Parallel**	• **Ribbon:** *Sketch* tab>Constrain panel
	**Perpendicular**	• **Ribbon:** *Sketch* tab>Constrain panel
	**Polygon**	• **Ribbon:** *Sketch* tab>Create panel
	**Project Geometry**	• **Ribbon:** *Sketch* tab>Create panel • **Context Menu:** In the graphics window
	**Rectangle**	• **Ribbon:** *Sketch* tab>Create panel • **Context Menu:** In the graphics window
	**Relax Mode**	• **Status Bar**
	**Show All Constraints**	• **Context Menu:** In the graphics window • **Status Bar**
	**Show Degrees of Freedom**	• **Status Bar**
	**Show Selected Constraints**	• **Ribbon:** *Sketch* tab>Constrain panel
	**Slice Graphics**	• **Context Menu** • **Status Bar**

Button	Command	Location
	Slot	• **Ribbon:** *Sketch* tab>Create panel
	Smooth (G2)	• **Ribbon:** *Sketch* tab>Constrain panel
	Spline (Control Vertex)	• **Ribbon:** *Sketch* tab>Create panel
	Spline (Interpolation)	• **Ribbon:** *Sketch* tab>Create panel
	Split	• **Ribbon:** *Sketch* tab>Modify panel
/	**Start 2D Sketch**	• **Ribbon:** *3D Model* tab>Sketch panel • **Marking Menu** • **Heads-up Display**
	Symmetric	• **Ribbon:** *Sketch* tab>Constrain panel
	Tangent	• **Ribbon:** *Sketch* tab>Constrain panel
	Tangent Arc	• **Ribbon:** *Sketch* tab>Create panel
	Tangent Circle	• **Ribbon:** *Sketch* tab>Create panel
	Three Point Arc	• **Ribbon:** *Sketch* tab>Create panel
	Three Point Arc Slot	• **Ribbon:** *Sketch* tab>Create panel
	Three Point Center Rectangle	• **Ribbon:** *Sketch* tab>Create panel
	Three Point Rectangle	• **Ribbon:** *Sketch* tab>Create panel
	Trim	• **Ribbon:** *Sketch* tab>Modify panel • **Context Menu:** In the graphics window • *(toggle between **Trim** and **Extend** using <Shift>)*
	Two Point Center Rectangle	• **Ribbon:** *Sketch* tab>Create panel
	Vertical	• **Ribbon:** *Sketch* tab>Constrain panel

Chapter 3

Creating Sketched Features

Sketched features can add or remove material from a model. To create any of these sketched features, a sketch is required prior to creating the feature types. As features and design intent become more complex, additional options are available to help you create more advanced secondary features.

Learning Objectives

- Create an extruded feature and define its material removal option, extent, and direction.
- Create a revolved secondary feature and define the material removal option, extent, and direction.
- Make changes to a sketched feature.

3.1 Extrude and Revolve Features

Extruded and revolved features are created by selecting a 2D sketch and defining an extrusion depth. In the case of a revolve, you must also select an axis of revolution. These features can either add or remove material.

Use the following general steps to create an extruded or revolved feature:

1. Create or select the sketch references.
2. Start the creation of the feature.
3. Add or remove material.
4. Specify the direction and distance.
5. Complete the feature.

Step 1 - Create or select the sketch references.

To create an extrude or revolve, you must define the profile of the shape that will be either extruded or revolved. You can either select an existing sketch or create a new sketch.

To create a new sketch, use one of the following methods. The sketching plane can be a work plane or the planar face of an existing feature. When you select the planar face of an existing feature as a sketching plane, the origin center point is automatically projected onto the sketch plane.

- Select a sketching plane and click  (Start 2D Sketch) (*3D Model* tab>Sketch panel).
- Select a sketching plane and click  in the heads-up display.
- Select a sketching plane, right-click, and select **New Sketch**.

An existing sketch can also be reused to create additional features. To share a sketch, right-click on the sketch in the Model browser and select **Share Sketch** or drag a sketch outside of its feature and drop it. The sketch displays (with the same name) in the Model browser before the feature that originally used the sketch.

Once the sketch plane is active, you can use sketching tools in the *Create* panel to create the profile for either the extrude of the revolve. In both cases, the profile must be a closed sketch to create solid geometry. For revolved features, the reference axis that will be used as the axis of revolution must also exist prior to creating the feature. This must be a linear reference (i.e., edge, work axis).

Hint: Using Projected Geometry

You can also project part edges onto the sketch plane to be used as sketch geometry, or as targets for constraints and dimensions. As you reference edges while sketching, these edges/vertices are also automatically projected. Using projected edges in the sketched geometry creates a feature relationship. If the referenced geometry (projected geometry) changes, the sketched geometry updates.

- To project a feature edge onto a sketch plane, on the *Sketch* tab>Create panel, click  (Project Geometry) and select the edge to project onto the sketch plane.

It is recommended that sketched geometry be located with respect to existing features. Ideally, you should locate sketched geometry to Origin features whenever possible. Origin features are more stable than feature edges.

Step 2 - Start the creation of the feature.

Once the sketch has been fully dimensioned and constrained, you can add thickness or depth to the sketch. The simplest way to add depth is to extrude or revolve the sketch. Extruding the sketch means adding or removing material perpendicular to the sketch plane. Revolving the sketch means adding or removing material radially around an axis of revolution. Examples of adding geometry using an extrude or revolve are shown in Figure 3–1 and Figure 3–2, respectively.

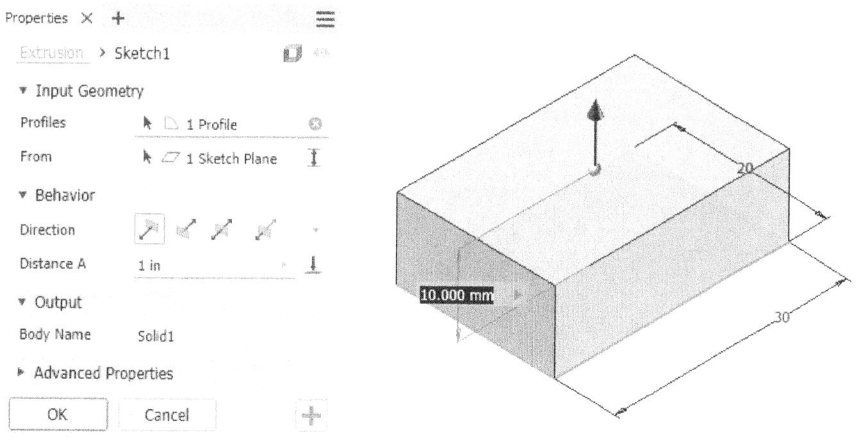

Figure 3–1

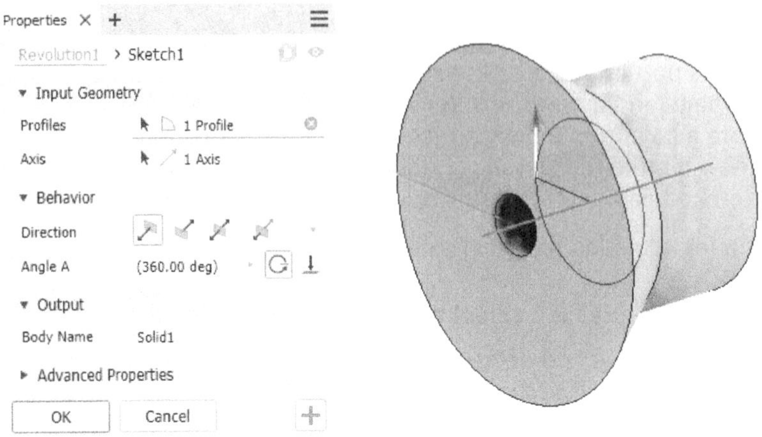

Figure 3–2

The following three methods can be used to create a new extrusion in a model:

- In the *3D Model* tab>Create panel, click 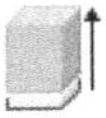 (Extrude) or  (Revolve).
- Select the sketch and click  or  in the heads-up display.
- Right-click in the graphics window and select **Extrude** or **Revolve**.

The *Profiles* field is active by default when you start the commands. If a single closed sketch exists in the model, it is automatically selected as the profile. The Profiles field lists for the feature and a preview of the feature displays. If multiple sketches exist, the *Profiles* field displays active (blue underline) and prompts to "Select Profiles", as shown in Figure 3–3. This indicates that you must select a profile.

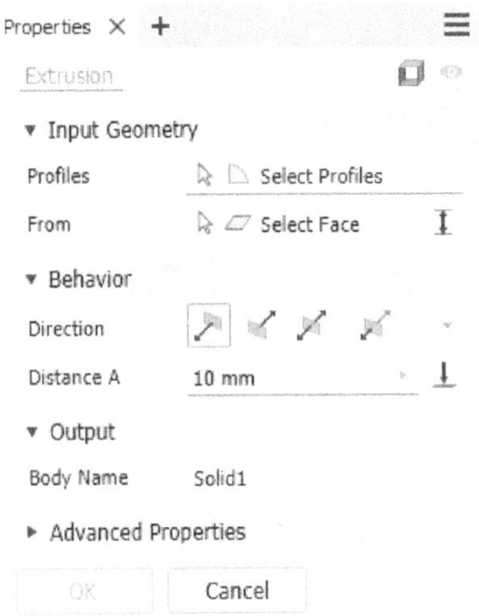

Figure 3–3

- By default, the *From* field is set to the sketch plane or parent face of a selected profile. This identifies the plane from which the extrusion will start. If required, activate this field and select a different From reference.
- For a Revolve feature, an *Axis* field is also available in the Input Geometry area. This will not populate by default, you must activate it and select a linear reference.

Step 3 - Add or remove material.

When creating the base feature (first solid feature in the model), the solid geometry is automatically added to the model as the first Solid Body. When creating secondary extruded or revolved geometry, you can define how it will interact with the existing geometry. This is defined using the *Boolean* options in the *Output* area.

- when creating a secondary extrude or revolve feature, the (Join), (Cut), and (Intersect) options are all available. These options enable you to specify whether the feature will add material (Join), remove material (Cut), or create the feature as an intersection (Intersect), as shown in Figure 3–4. The **Intersect** option creates geometry from the shared volume of the new and existing features and removes material outside the shared volume.

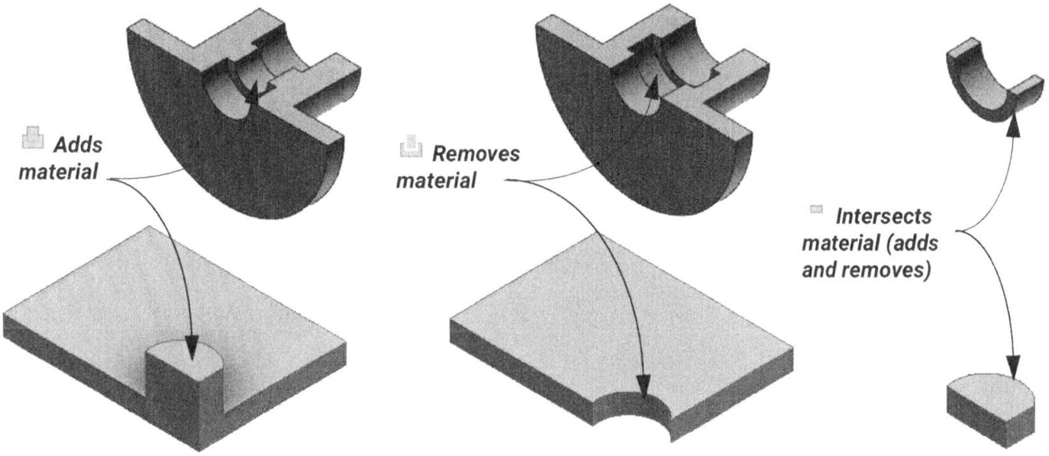

Figure 3–4

- The (New Solid) option creates the new feature as a new solid body. This is required when modeling using the multi-body modeling technique. This is discussed in advanced level guides.

Step 4 - Specify the direction and distance.

There are a number of options provided for defining the direction and depth of extruded features. These options are set in the *Behavior* area of the Properties panel.

> ***Note:*** *Hover the cursor over the icon to display its tooltip information.*

Direction

Direction icons (, , , and) set the direction to extrude/revolve from the sketch plane or how it extrudes on both sides of the sketch plane. Extrude directions are shown in Figure 3–5 to Figure 3–8. You can select the direction using the icons in the Properties panel. These options are also available for a revolve feature.

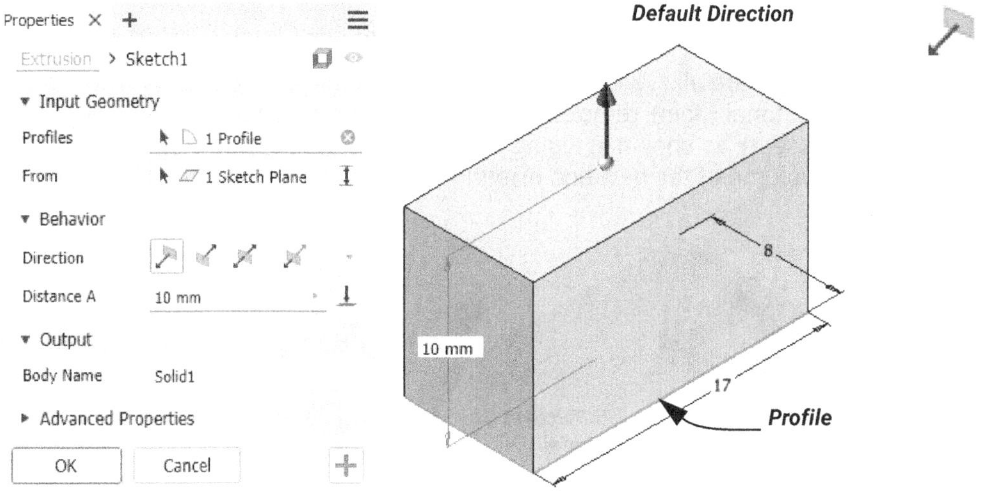

Figure 3–5

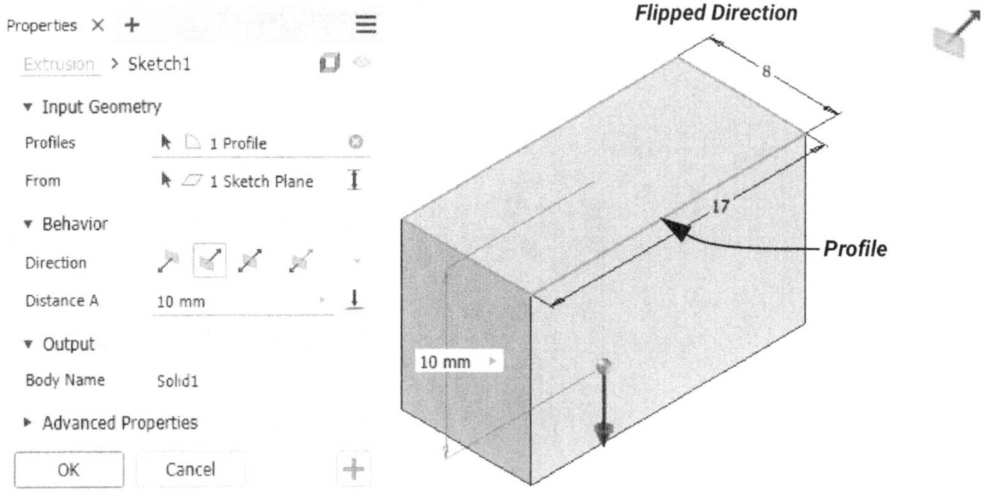

Figure 3–6

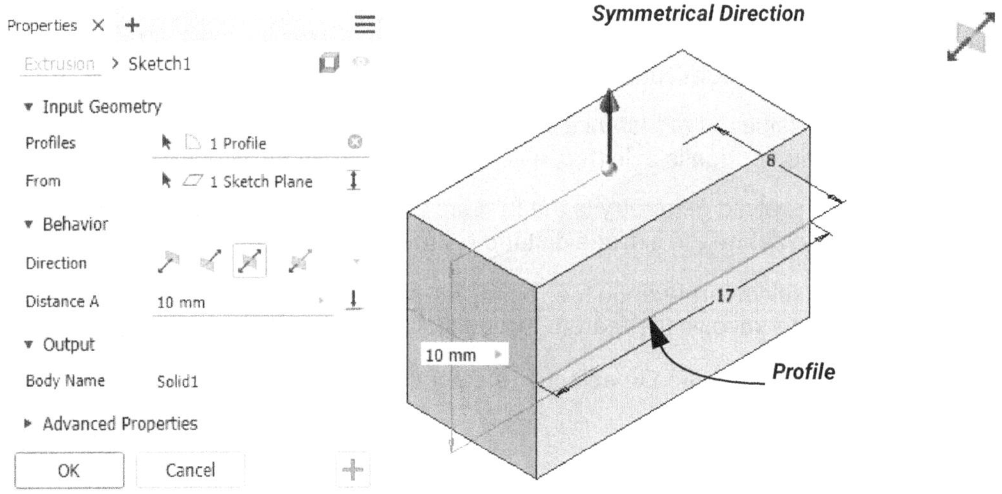

Figure 3–7

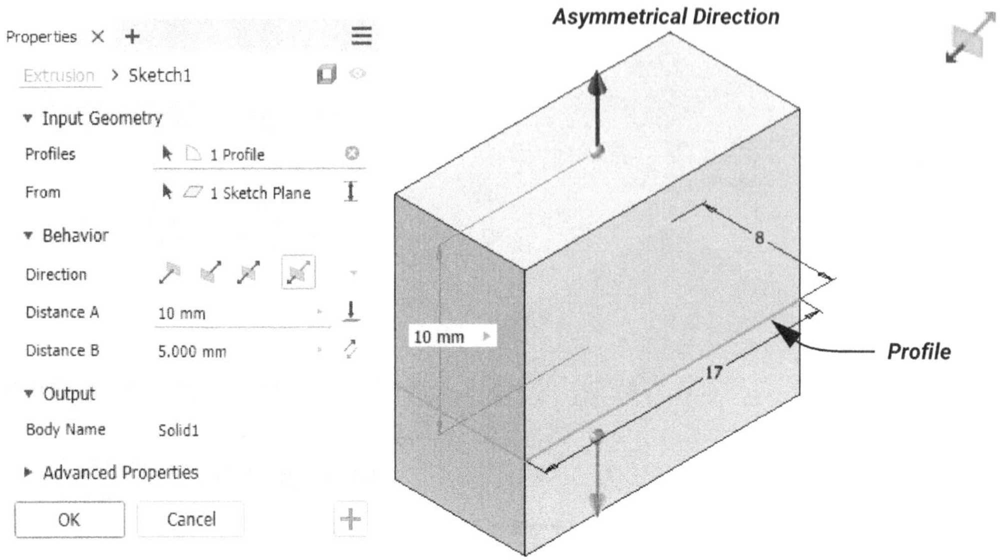

Figure 3–8

Distance

There are several options for defining the *Distance*. The choice of option depends on your intent and whether it is the first or subsequent solid geometry in the model.

- Enter an extrusion value in the *Distance A* field to assign a specified depth value. If the asymmetric Direction option is selected, a second *Distance B* field is added.
- If the extruded or revolved geometry is the first solid geometry in the model, the only two options available to define the extrude distance is to enter a dimensional value or use the (To) option to select a reference (i.e., point, vertex, face, or plane) to extrude to. For a revolve, you can enter revolve the feature through a full 360 degrees, enter a angle rotation value or use the (To) option to select a reference.

- Enabling the (Between) option adjacent to the *From* field can be used to customize a start and end plane for the geometry. You can define the start plane as something other than the profile's sketch plane. For a base feature, it enables you to extrude between two work planes, as shown at the top of Figure 3–9, or between two planes as shown at the bottom of Figure 3–9. When used, the *Distance A* field populates with a reference dimension shown in brackets (e.g., (7.000 in) or (4.090 in)).

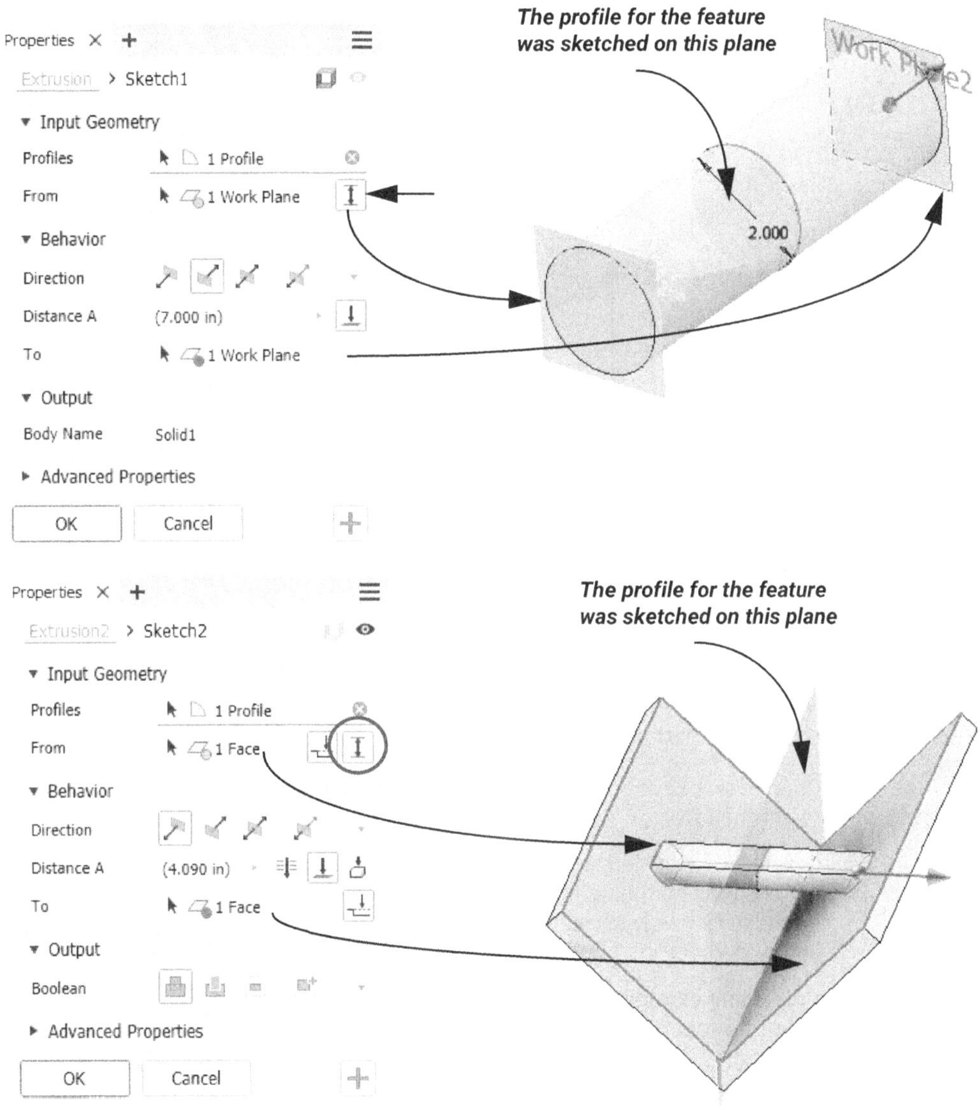

Figure 3–9

- When creating a secondary extrude or revolve feature, a number of additional options are provided for defining the depth and direction. Many of these options enable you to reference other geometry to control the depth. The depth options are shown in Figure 3–10.

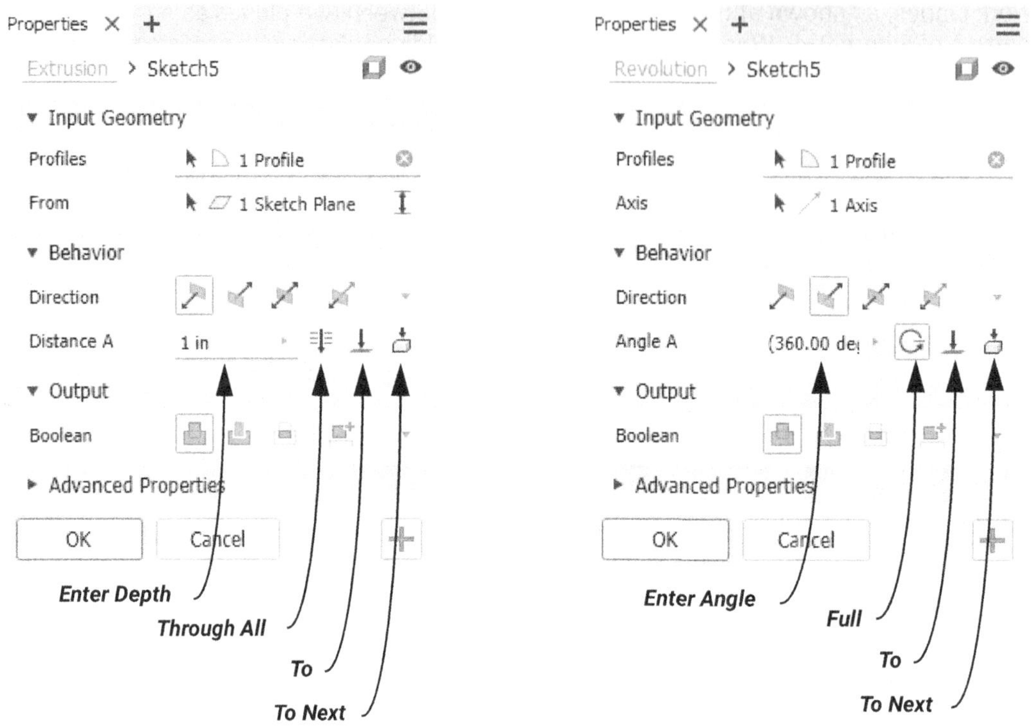

Figure 3–10

The additional **Distance** and **Angle** options that are available when creating secondary sketched features are defined as follows:

To	Creates an extruded or revolved feature so that it extends to a selected reference face.
To Next	Creates an extruded or revolved feature so that it extends to the next possible face or plane that it fully encounters. The sketch that is being extruded or revolved must fully intersect the face or body that it encounters for the feature to be created.
Through All / Full	Creates an extruded or revolved feature through all of the geometry in a defined direction.

Alternate Solution

There may be situations when an irregular surface or a cylinder is selected as a termination surface. In these situations, the extend location on the face might not be clear (e.g., it could be on either side of the cylinder), or there might be multiple intersection locations. The (Alternate Solution) option in the Properties panel can be selected to toggle through the available options.

Figure 3–11 shows how this option can be used when the extrude reference has two possible solutions.

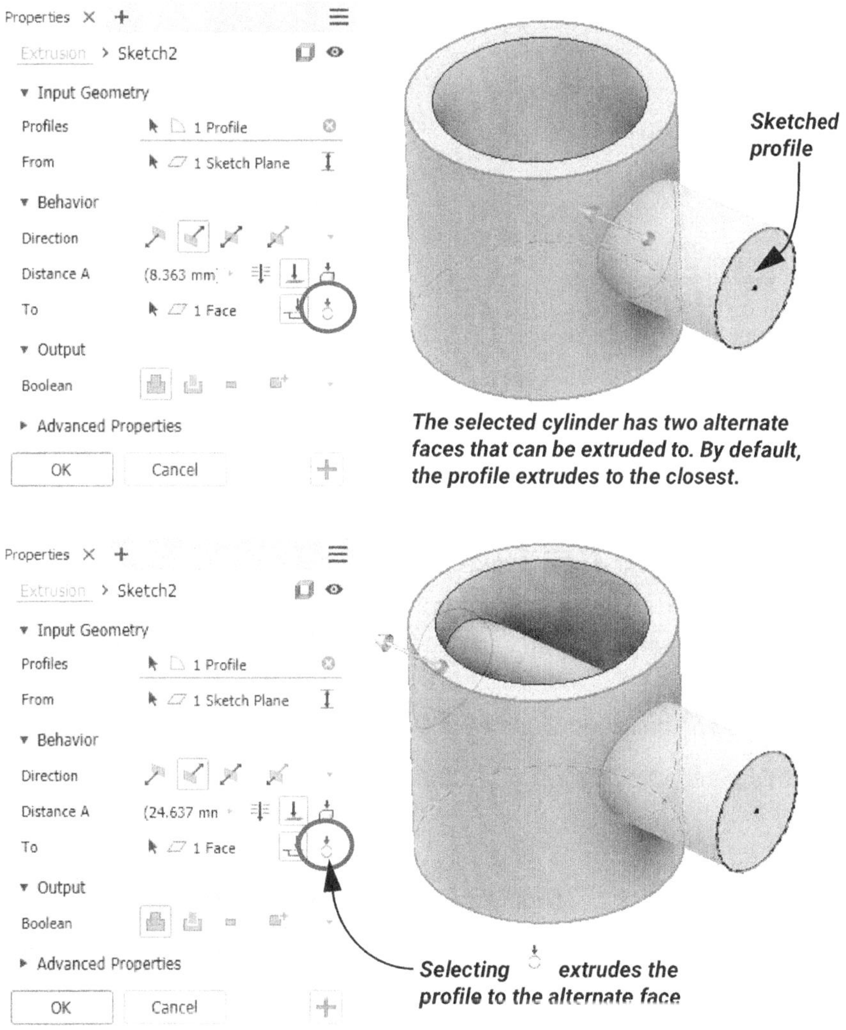

Figure 3–11

Taper

Tapering enables you to specify an angle for an extruded feature. A positive taper angle increases the cross-section, while a negative taper angle decreases the cross-section. To taper, expand the *Advanced* area in the Properties panel and enter a taper angle, as shown in Figure 3–12.

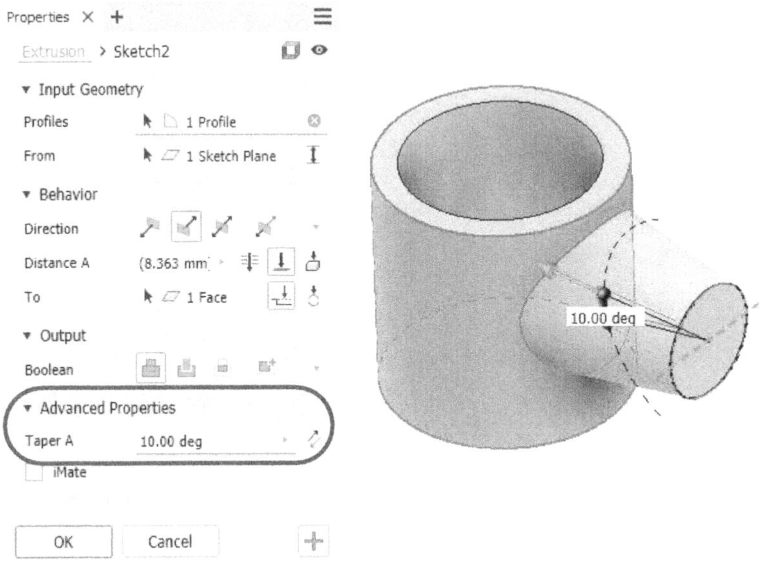

Figure 3–12

Step 5 - Complete the feature.

Once all options have been defined, you can complete the feature using any of the following methods:

- Right-click in the graphics window and click **OK**.
- In the Properties panel, click **OK**.
- Press <Enter>.
- In the Properties panel, click  (Apply and create new) to apply and create a new extrude feature.

By default, a sketch used to create a feature is not displayed in the model and becomes embedded within the feature node. To display the sketch, expand the feature and right-click on it in the Model browser and select **Visibility**. The sketch and its dimensions display on the part. To hide the sketch dimensions while displaying the sketch, right-click on the sketch in the Model browser and select **Dimension Visibility**.

3.2 Editing Sketched Features

To make modifications to a feature, right-click on the feature in the Model browser and select the required option, as shown in Figure 3–13. Additional options are also available to edit a sketched feature.

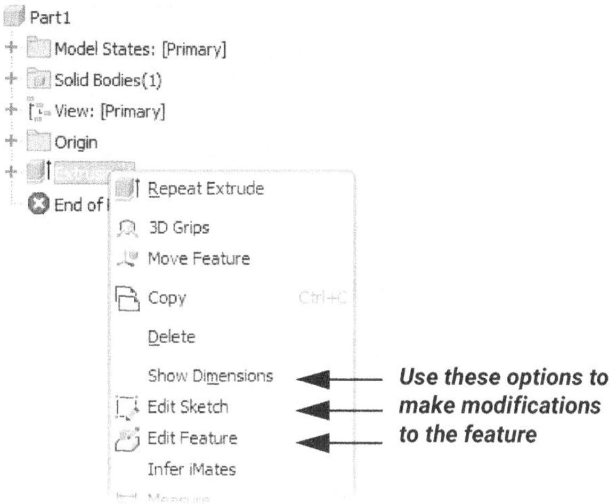

Figure 3–13

Show Dimensions

If you are only making changes to dimension values for a feature or its sketch, right-click and select **Show Dimensions** to display the dimensions for the selected feature, as shown in Figure 3–14. This enables you to change the values by double-clicking the dimension and entering a new value in the field that displays. The dimensional changes are not automatically reflected until you click (Local Update) in the Quick Access Toolbar to update the model.

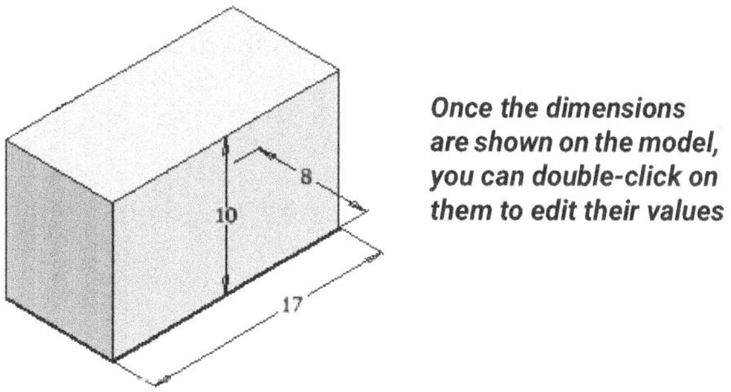

Figure 3–14

Note: *Feature dimensions that display using **Show Dimensions** display only until another feature is selected in the Model browser or in the graphics window.*

Sketch Visibility

Once a sketch is used to create solid geometry, it is consumed within its new parent feature. By default, this sketch is not visible on the model. To make the sketch visible, expand its parent feature in the Model browser, right-click on it, and select **Visibility**. Alternatively, you can select a face to which the feature belongs and click . The sketch and its dimensions display on the part, as shown in Figure 3–15. Double-click on any dimension to edit its value.

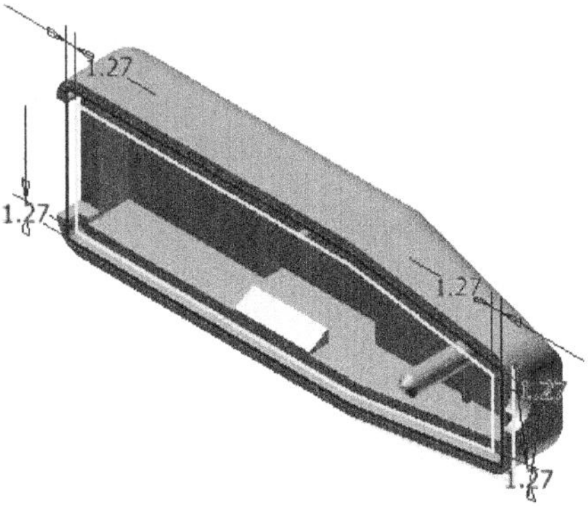

Figure 3–15

- If the screen becomes too cluttered after displaying a number of sketches, you can hide the dimensions of a selected sketch by right-clicking on the sketch in the Model browser and selecting **Dimension Visibility**. Alternatively, select the sketch in the Model browser and press <Alt> + V on your keyboard. This shortcut enables you to toggle a sketch's visibility on and off.
- You can clear the display of dimensions from all sketches in the model at once by selecting the **Sketch Dimensions** Object visibility setting (*View* tab>Visibility panel),

Edit Sketch

To make changes to the sketch, use one of the following methods to activate the Sketch environment:

- Double-click on the sketch in the Model browser.
- In the Model browser or the graphics window, select the sketch, right-click, and select **Edit Sketch**.
- Select an entity in the sketch or in the solid feature, and click  in the heads-up display on the sketch.

Edit Feature

To make changes to the options and elements that were available when a feature (e.g., extrusion) was originally created, use one of the following methods:

- Double-click on the feature in the Model browser.
- In the Model browser or the graphics window, select the feature, right-click, and select **Edit Feature**.
- Select a face on the feature and click in the heads-up display on the model.
- Double-click on the feature in the graphics window.

Show Input

To display the source sketch plane for a sketch, right-click on the sketch and select **Show Input**.

Change the Sketch Plane

The sketch plane for a base feature is defined when the sketch is created and the base feature becomes a child of that plane. The sketch plane can be changed after a sketch is created; however, keep in mind that references made to any existing entities or work features will be lost.

How To: Change the Sketch Plane

1. In the Model browser, right-click on the sketch and select **Redefine**. If the sketch is consumed by a solid feature, expand the solid feature name and then select the sketch plane.
2. Select another sketch plane (e.g., YZ plane) in the Model browser.

Hint: Naming a Sketch

Assigning custom names to features can help you to locate and identify features in the Model browser. To assign a custom name for the base feature you can use either of the following methods:

- At the top of the Properties panel, select Extrusion and enter a name for the sketch.
- Select the feature in the Model browser twice (do not double-click) and enter a new name.

Practice 3a
Extruded Base Feature

Practice Objectives

- Create an extruded base feature using an existing sketch.
- Modify the extruded base feature to incorporate dimensional and feature direction changes.

In this practice, you will open a model and use an existing sketch in the model to create an extruded base feature, as shown in Figure 3–16.

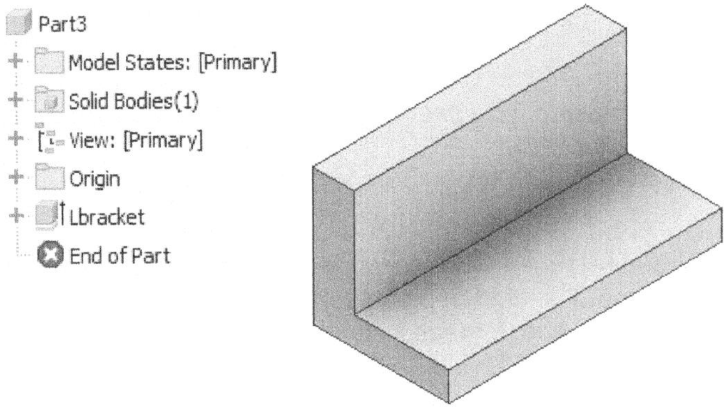

Figure 3–16

Task 1: Select the feature type and define the depth.

1. Open **L_shape.ipt**. If you did not complete the previous practices, open **L_shape_extrude.ipt**.
2. Use any of the following methods to activate the **Extrude** option:
   - In the *3D Model* tab>Create panel, click  (Extrude).
   - Right-click in the graphics window and select **Extrude**.
   - In the Model browser, left-click on the Sketch name and click  in the graphics window's Heads-up display.
   - Press <E>.

3. The Properties panel and a preview of the extruded model are displayed. The section is identified as the *Profiles* reference and it has been extruded to a default depth. You will work in the Properties panel to further define the feature. Enter **30** as the *Distance A* value. Do not press <Enter> after typing the depth value. After typing the value, pause for a few seconds and the model updates with your changes. Once a value has been entered, right-click and select **OK (Enter)**, or click **OK** in the Properties panel. The model displays as shown in Figure 3–17.

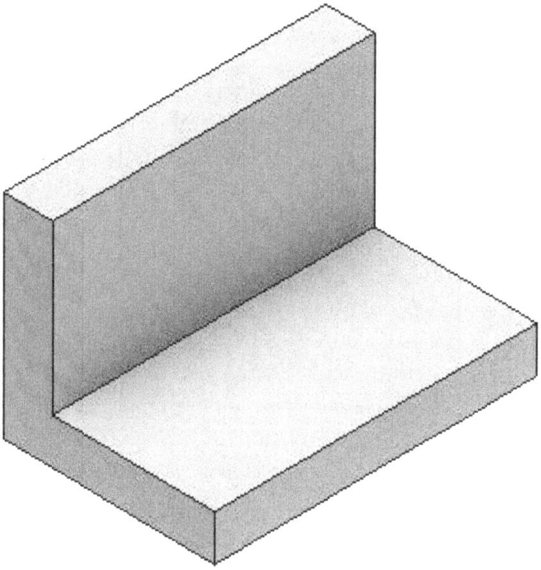

Figure 3–17

Task 2: Modify dimension values associated with the extrusion.

1. Right-click on **Extrusion1** in the Model browser and select **Show Dimensions**. The extrusion dimensions display on the model.

   Note: *If you double-click on* ***Extrusion1*** *in the Model browser, the Properties panel opens, enabling you to modify the extrusion details.*

2. Double-click on the dimension that represents the thickness of the feature (in Figure 3–18, this is the dimension with the value of 4.545). Enter **6** as the new dimension value and press <Enter>.
3. Double-click on the dimension that represents the depth of the feature (in Figure 3–18, this is the dimension with the value of 30). Enter **40** as the new dimension value and press <Enter>.

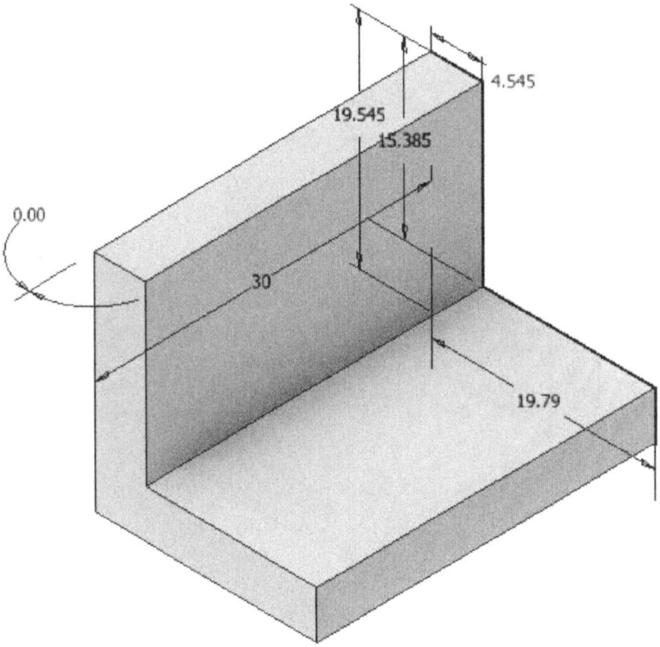

Figure 3–18

4. In the Quick Access Toolbar, click (Local Update) to update the feature.

Task 3: Redefine the extrusion direction.

1. Double-click on **Extrusion1** in the Model browser. The Properties panel displays. Alternatively, you can right-click on **Extrusion1** in the Model browser and select **Edit Feature** to open the Properties panel.
2. Click (Flipped) to flip the direction of the extrusion. Note that the preview of the extrusion flips to the opposite side of the sketch plane.
3. Click (Asymmetric) as the extent direction. The Properties panel updates for you to specify *Distance A* and *Distance B* values for both sides of the sketch plane. Note the preview of the extrusion.

4. Click (Symmetric) to extrude the feature equidistant from the sketch plane. Note the preview of the extrusion.
5. To assign a custom name for the base feature, select **Extrusion1** at the top of the Properties panel and enter **Lbracket** as the new name.
6. Click **OK**. The model and Model browser display as shown in Figure 3–19.

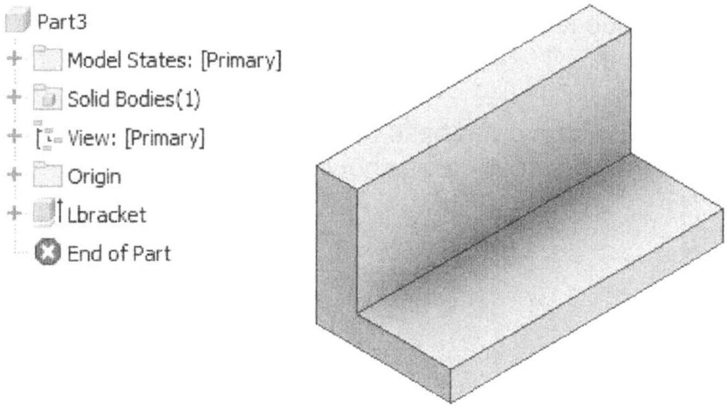

Figure 3–19

Task 4: Save the model and close the file.

1. In the Quick Access Toolbar, click (Save) to save the model.
2. In the graphics window, click (Close) to close the window.

End of practice

Practice 3b
Create a Sketched Revolve

Practice Objectives

- Create a revolved base feature using a provided sketch.
- Create a secondary extrude feature that references a face and entities in the base feature to fully constrain it.

In this practice, you will create a revolved base feature from an existing sketch and create an extruded cut on a face of the base feature, as shown in Figure 3–20.

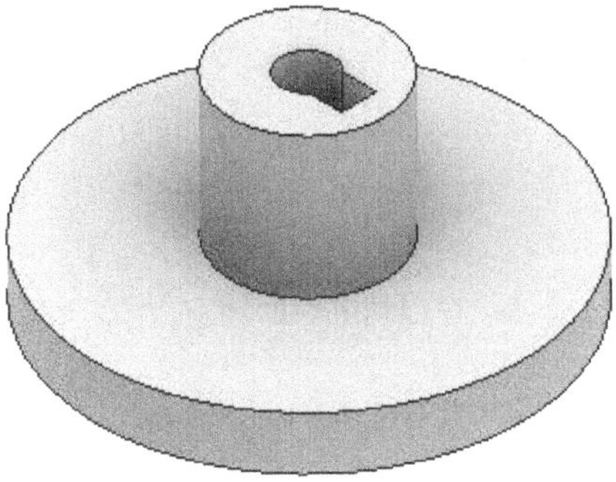

Figure 3–20

Task 1: Open a part file and create a revolved base feature.

1. Open **rev_flange_1.ipt**.
2. In the Create panel, click  (Revolve).

3. The sketch is automatically selected as the Profile. Select the line (projected XZ Plane) shown in Figure 3–21 as the axis of rotation.

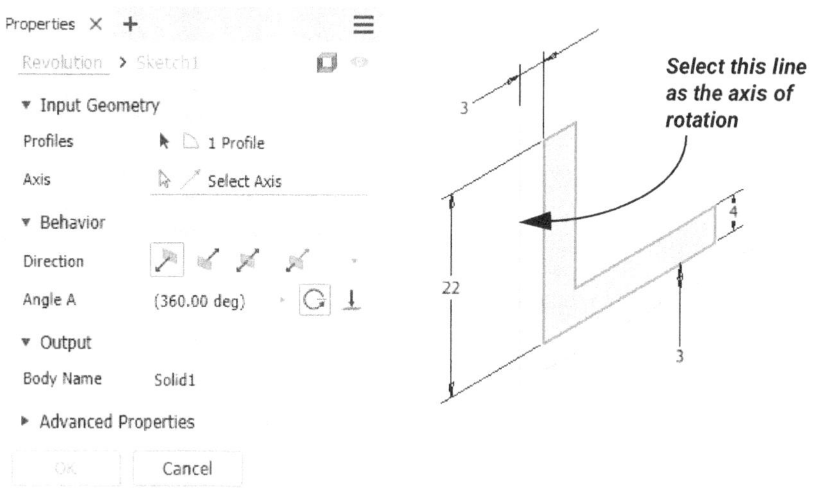

Figure 3–21

4. The revolved feature is automatically revolved 360 degrees ((Full)), as shown in Figure 3–22.

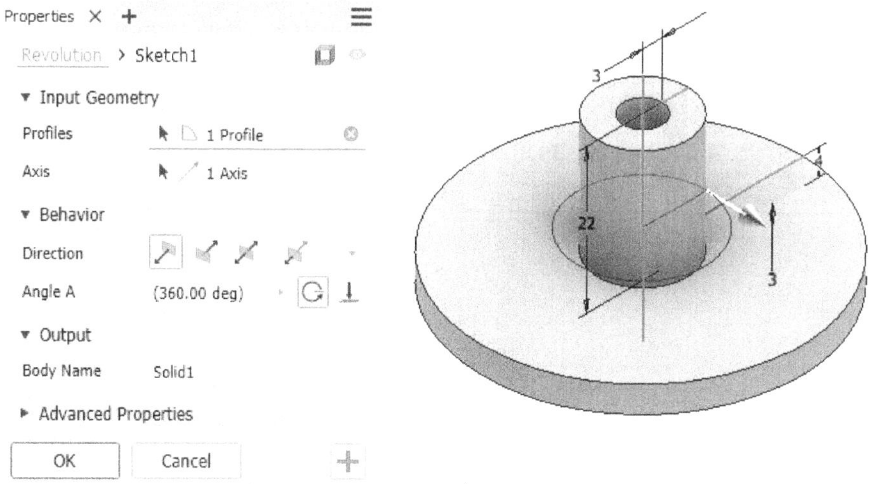

Figure 3–22

5. To change the value of the revolved angle, click in the *Angle* field and enter **220**.

6. Click to change the direction of the feature creation. The revolved feature displays as shown in Figure 3–23.

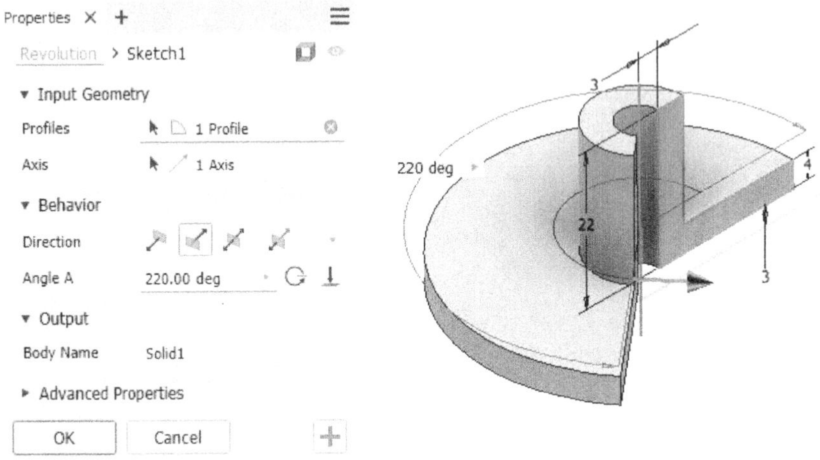

Figure 3–23

7. Complete the feature.

Task 2: Modify the feature.

1. Right-click on **Revolution1** in the Model browser and select **Show Dimensions**.
2. Double-click on the 220 degrees dimension, as shown in Figure 3–24, and change the angle value to **360** degrees.
3. Double-click on the 4 dimension, as shown in Figure 3–24, and change the value to **6**.

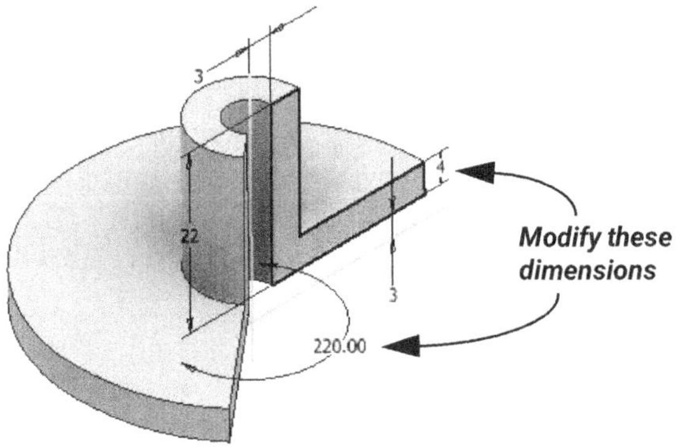

Figure 3–24

4. In the Quick Access Toolbar, click (Local Update) to update the model.

Task 3: Create an extruded cut by sketching the section.

1. Select the top circular face of the model and click  to create a new sketch, as shown in Figure 3–25. Alternatively, you can right-click on the top circular face of the model and select **New Sketch** to create a new sketch on the plane.

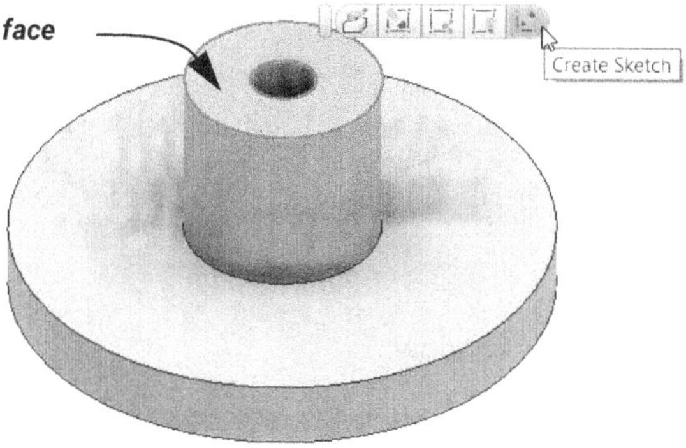

Figure 3–25

2. Sketch and dimension three lines with respect to the center point of the circular edge, as shown in Figure 3–26. Project the XZ Plane and apply the Symmetric constraint to the two parallel horizontal lines to fully constrain the sketch.

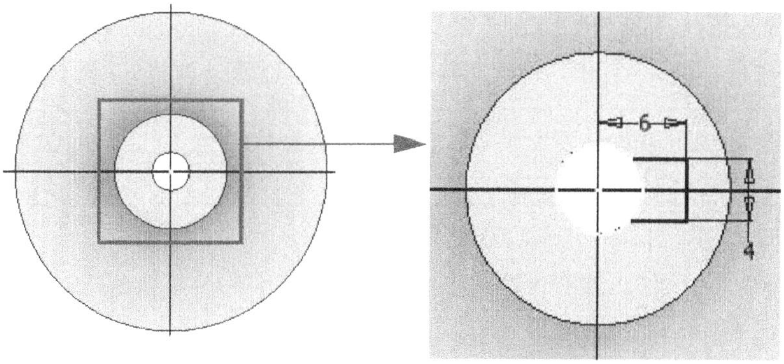

Figure 3–26

3. Finish the sketch.

4. In the *3D Model* tab>Create panel, click  (Extrude) to create a cut using this sketch.
5. Select the new sketched profile. It is not automatically selected because there are now two closed sections in the part. Both of the sections exist in the newly created sketch.

6. Click  (Cut) to remove material, if not already set.
7. Enter **16** in the *Distance A* field.

8. Ensure that the cut is extruded inside the part. If required, change its direction.
9. Complete the feature. The model displays as shown in Figure 3–27.

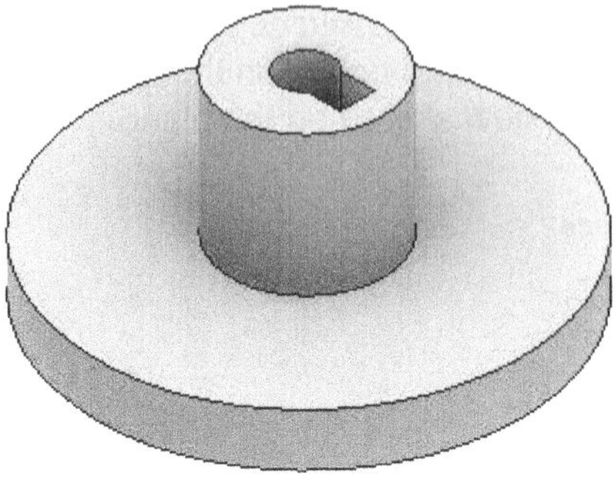

Figure 3–27

10. Save the part and close the window.

End of practice

Chapter Review Questions

1. Which command is used to create an extrusion that adds material to existing solid geometry?
   a. (Join)
   b. (Intersect)
   c. (Cut)
   d. (Solid)

2. The **Alternate Solution** option displays in the Properties panel if the termination face is not clear. Which of the following extent options is being used if this option displays?
   a. Distance
   b. To Next
   c. To
   d. All

3. Which option do you use to open a feature's Properties panel to enable you to make a change to the feature (such as flipping the extrusion direction)?
   a. Edit Sketch
   b. Show Dimensions
   c. Edit Feature
   d. Properties

4. What option enables you to change the sketch plane of a feature?
   a. Show Dimension
   b. Edit Feature
   c. Edit Sketch
   d. Redefine

Command Summary

Button	Command	Location
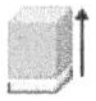	**Extrude**	• **Ribbon:** *3D Model* tab>Create panel • **Heads-up Display:** In the graphics window with a sketch selected • **Context Menu:** In the graphics window • **Keyboard:** <E>
	**Revolve**	• **Ribbon:** *3D Model* tab>Create panel • **Heads-up Display:** In the graphics window with a sketch selected • **Keyboard:** <R>

Chapter

4

Creating Pick and Place Features

Chamfers, fillets, and holes are known as pick and place features. This means that the shape of the feature is implied; therefore, you are not required to sketch the section. Pick and place features can be added once the model's base feature has been created.

Learning Objectives

- Create a chamfer by defining its dimension scheme and placement references.
- Create constant and variable fillets by defining placement references, dimensions, and shape settings.
- Create a hole by defining its type, placement reference, dimensions, and depth options.

4.1 Edge Chamfers

A chamfer adds a beveled edge between two adjacent surfaces, as shown in Figure 4–1. An edge chamfer can add or remove material.

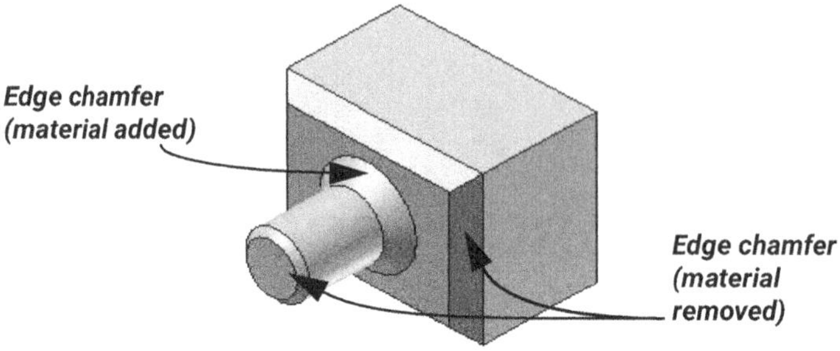

Figure 4–1

Use the following general steps to create an edge chamfer along the entire length of an edge:

1. Start the creation of the feature.
2. Define the dimensioning scheme.
3. Select the placement references and enter distances.
4. Select additional options, as required.
5. Select references to create a partial chamfer, as required.
6. Complete the feature.

Step 1 - Start the creation of the feature.

Use one of the following methods to create an edge chamfer:

- Select the edge(s) to be chamfered and click  in the heads-up display on the model.
- In the *3D Model* tab>Modify panel, click  (Chamfer) to start the creation of an edge chamfer.

Once the command is selected, the Chamfer dialog box opens. By default, the display of the mini-toolbar is toggled off. On the *View* tab, expand **User Interface** and enable the **Mini-Toolbar** option to display it. To collapse the dialog box, click the up arrow at the bottom of the dialog box.

Step 2 - Define the dimensioning scheme.

Edge chamfers have three alternative dimension types that can be used. Select the type from the lists shown in Figure 4–2. Changing dimension types clears the reference edge selection. It is recommended that you define the dimension type before selecting a placement reference.

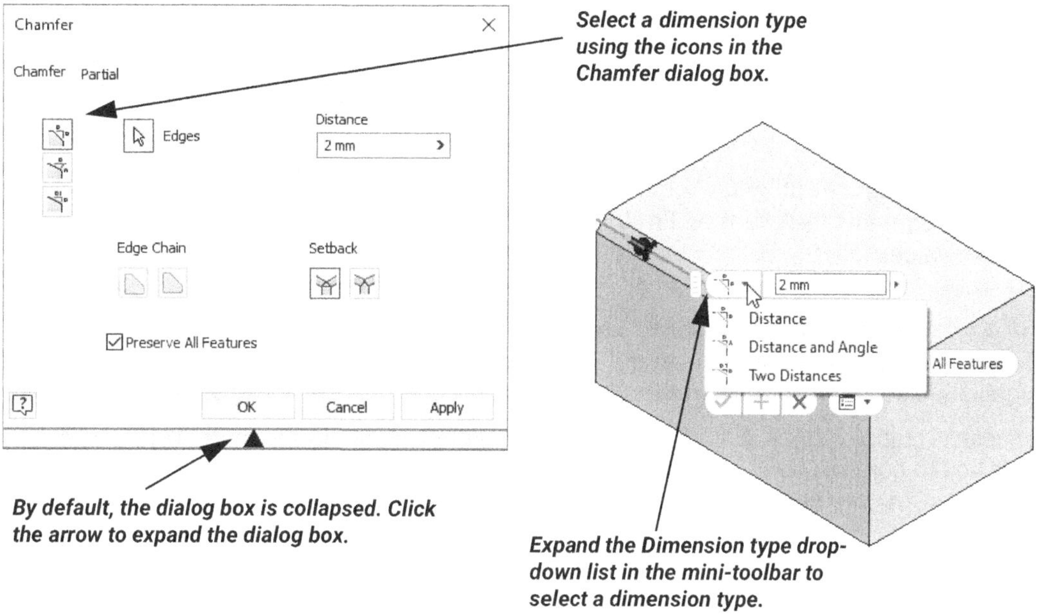

Figure 4–2

The dimension types are described as follows:

(Distance)	The chamfer is created at the same distance from the edge on each face.	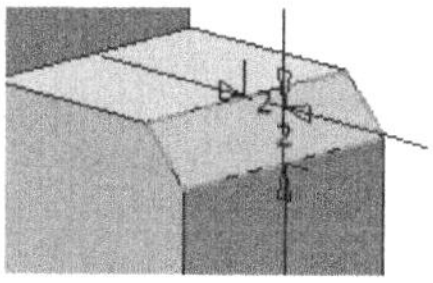
(Distance and Angle)	The chamfer is created at a distance from the edge on one face and at an angle to that face.	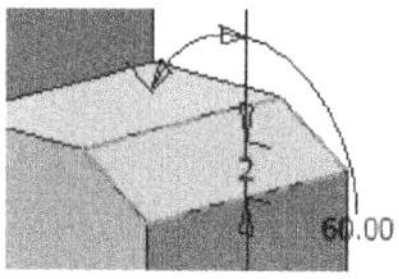
(Two Distances)	The chamfer is created at one distance from the edge of one face and a different distance from the edge of another.	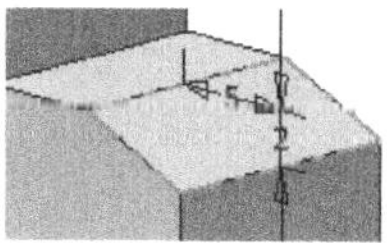

Step 3 - Select the placement references and enter distances.

The references and dimensions required to locate a chamfer depend on the dimension type that is used. Alternatively, you can select the reference before clicking (Chamfer).

- For a (Distance) chamfer, select the edge(s) to chamfer and enter a distance value from the edge to be removed.
- For a (Distance and Angle) chamfer, select the face and then select the edge(s) from the face that contains the chamfer. Enter a distance value from the edge to be removed and an angular value.
- For a (Two Distances) chamfer, select the edge and click or to toggle between the two surfaces that touch the edge. Enter a distance value to be removed from the highlighted surface. With this method, you can only chamfer one edge at a time.

If you select multiple edges, a single dimension is applied to all of the edges. This method enables you to control changes to all edges with a single value. To clear the selection of an edge, press <Ctrl> or <Shift> and reselect the edge.

Step 4 - Select additional options, as required.

Additional options (shown in Figure 4–3) enable you to further define the edges of the chamfer.

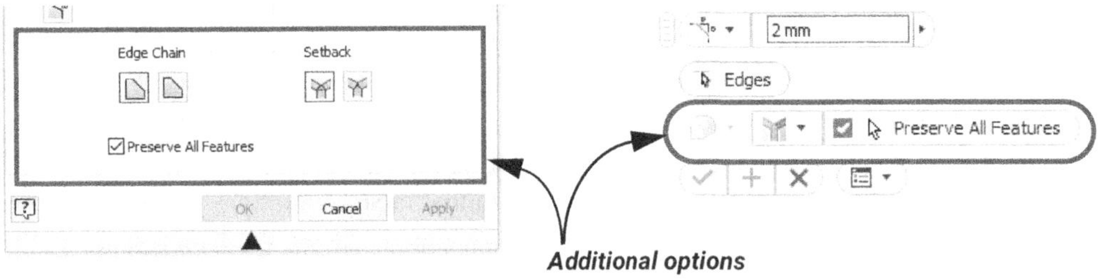

Figure 4–3

Note: *To toggle between the fields in the mini-toolbar, press <Tab> or select the field to activate it.*

The additional options are described as follows:

- The **Edge Chain** options determine how edges with curves are selected.
  - Click (All tangentially connected edges) to select all of the tangent edges.
  - Click (Single edge) to select each edge individually.
  - In the mini-toolbar, the options are available as shown in Figure 4–4.

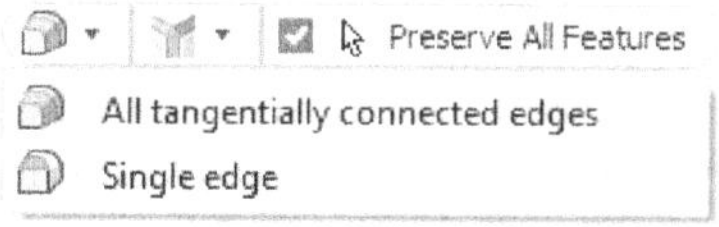

Figure 4–4

- Setback options control how chamfers meet at corners and are only available when using (Distance) chamfer type. The setback options are shown in Figure 4–5.

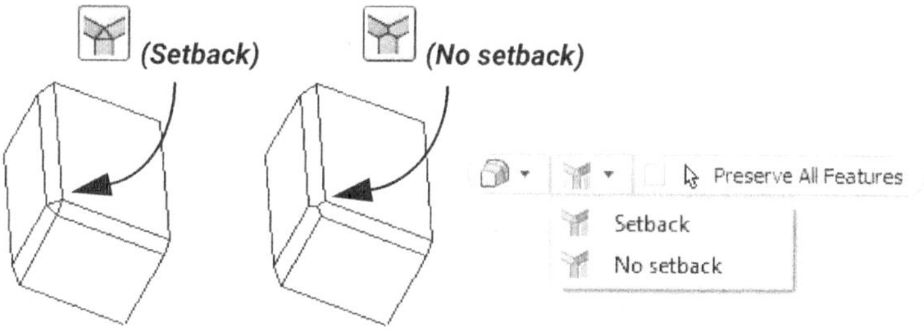

Figure 4–5

- The **Preserve All Features** option retains the existing features affected by the chamfer (e.g., a hole near the chamfered edge).

Step 5 - Select references to create a partial chamfer, as required.

To create a chamfer that does not fully extend the length of a selected reference edge, you can use the options on the *Partial* tab of the Chamfer dialog box. A partial chamfer cannot be defined using the mini-toolbar options. To define a partial chamfer on a selected reference, complete the following:

1. Select the *Partial* tab.
2. Select a point on the edge to define the end vertex. The start point is automatically set on the edge and is identified with a black dot. Once selected, the partial chamfer previews in the model and values populate in the dialog box.
3. The *Set Driven Dimension* option is set to **To End** by default. This sets the *To End* field as driven and prevents you from editing it. All changes to the size of the chamfer are made using the *To Start* and *Chamfer* fields. To adjust which fields are modifiable, you can change the option in the *Set Driven Dimension* option to **To Start** or **Chamfer**.
   - The **Chamfer** option enables you to enter distances from the start and end of the line to define the extent of the partial chamfer.
   - The **To Start** option enables you to enter a distance to the end and the chamfer length to define the extent of the partial chamfer on the edge.
4. Modify the values in the columns to define the extent of the partial chamfer. As changes are made, a preview displays in the graphics window, as shown in Figure 4–6.

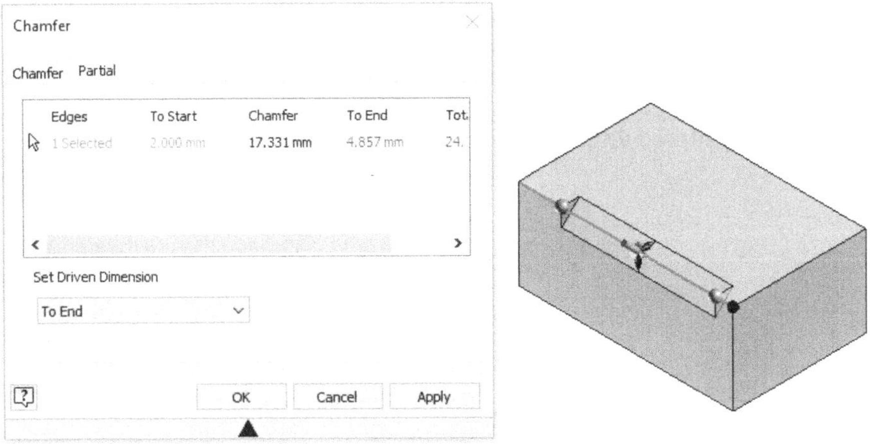

Figure 4–6

Step 6 - Complete the feature.

Once the edge chamfer is defined, you can complete the feature using any of the following options:

- Click in the mini-toolbar.
- Right-click in the graphics window and select **OK (Enter)**.
- Click **OK** in the Chamfer dialog box.
- Press <Enter>.
- Click **Apply** to add the chamfer and remain in the dialog box to continue adding additional chamfers.

The Chamfer feature is identified with the icon in the Model browser once created. If the icon displays in the mini-toolbar, it indicates that the chamfer cannot be created.

4.2 Constant Fillets

Fillets can add or remove material, as shown in Figure 4–7. A constant edge fillet has a constant radius along its entire reference edge.

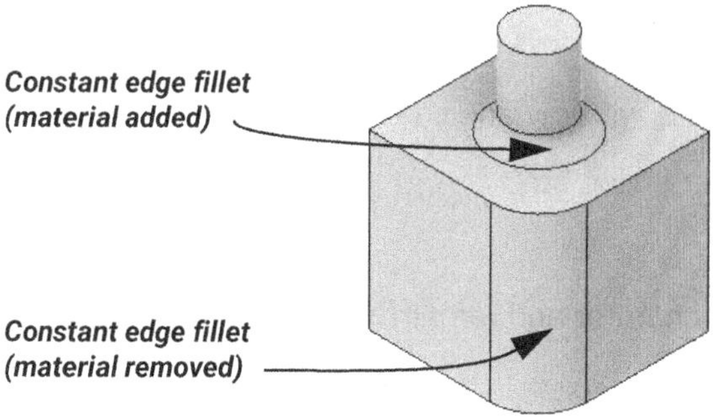

Figure 4–7

Use the following general steps to create a constant fillet:

1. Start the creation of the feature.
2. Select placement references.
3. Define the fillet size and shape.
4. Define the setbacks, as required.
5. Complete the feature.

Step 1 - Start the creation of the feature.

Use one of the following methods to create a fillet:

- Select the edge(s) to be filleted and click in the heads-up display on the model.
- In the *3D Model* tab>Modify panel, click (Fillet).
- Right-click anywhere in the graphics window and select **Fillet**.

Once the **Fillet** command is selected, the Properties panel and the Tool palette open, as shown in Figure 4–8. The Properties panel enables you to define the properties and values for the fillet and the Tool palette enables you to define the type of fillet and the reference selection priority.

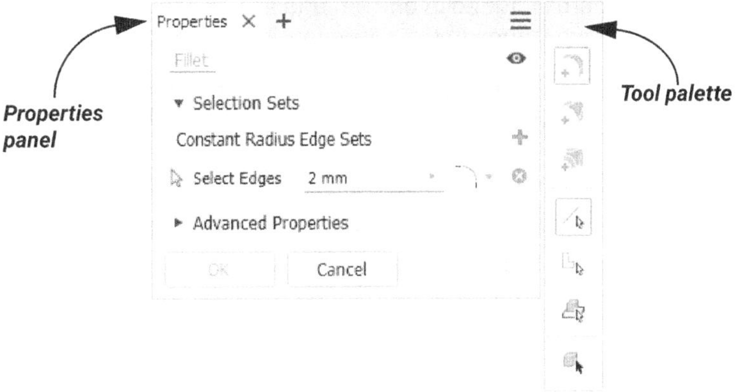

Figure 4–8

Step 2 - Select placement references.

On the Tool palette, enable the required reference selection priority. This determines the type of entity that is to be selected as the placement reference for the fillet. The options are described as follows:

	Selects one edge at a time. To select multiple edges to fillet, select each one independently.
	Selects all of the edges on a selected face.
	Selects all of the edges on a selected feature.
	Selects all of the edges on a selected solid body.

Based on the selection priority that is set, select edges, faces, or features to fillet them. If the  option is selected and there is only one solid body in the model, all edges are automatically selected.

Note: *To clear the selection of an edge, hold <Ctrl> or <Shift> and reselect the edge.*

By default, all selected edges are included in one set and are controlled by a single radius value. To add edges with unique radius values in the same feature, you must add additional sets. To add a set, select (Add constant radius edge set) in the Properties panel, as shown in Figure 4–9. Once the set is active, select new edges. To delete a selection set, click on the right-hand side of the edge set.

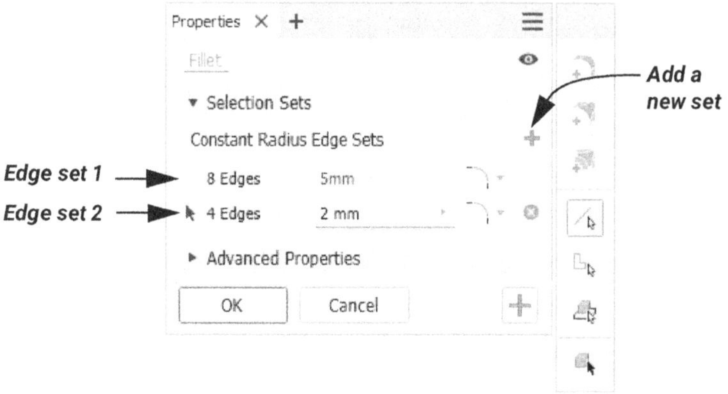

Figure 4–9

Step 3 - Define the fillet size and shape.

By default, the radius value that was last set during fillet creation is used as the default value. To modify the radius of the fillet, enter the new value in the on-screen entry field or in the Properties panel, as shown in Figure 4–10. As an alternative, you can also select and drag the radius handle that displays on the model to resize the fillet.

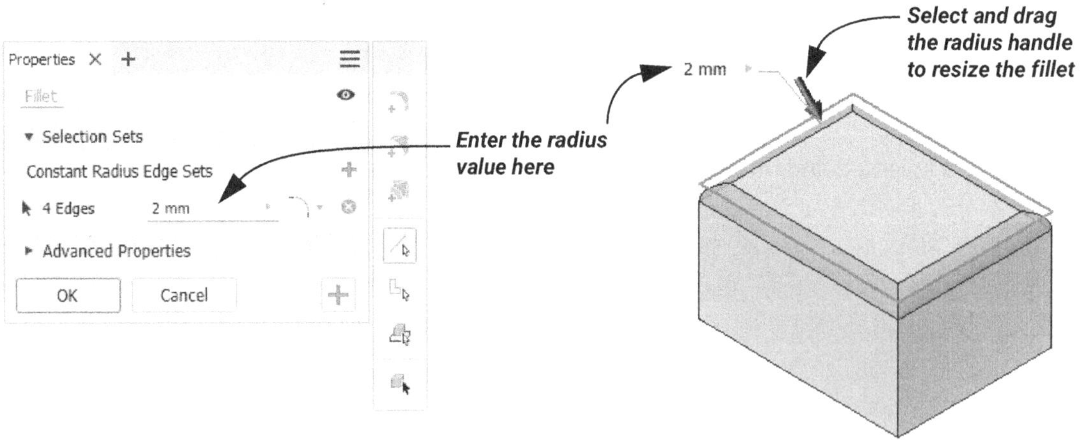

Figure 4–10

Continuity

Edge fillets can use one of three continuity options to further define the shape of the fillet geometry. The available options are shown in Figure 4–11.

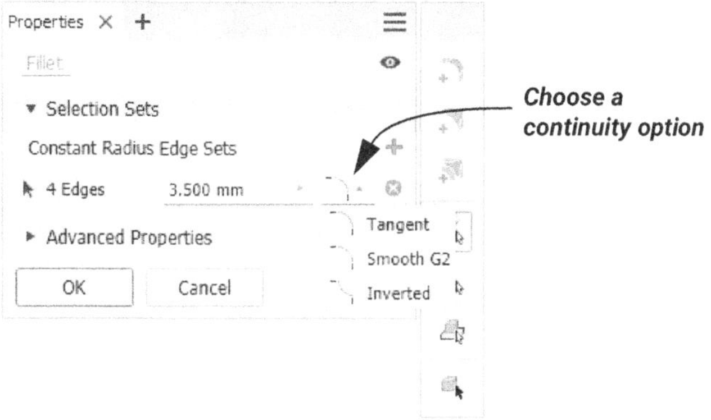

Figure 4–11

The continuity options are described as follows and are shown in Figure 4–12. Once the reference geometry is selected, you can assign a continuity option for each selection set.

- The **Tangent** setting ensures that the transition between the fillet and adjacent surfaces is tangent.
- The **Smooth G2** setting ensures the transition between the fillet and the adjacent surfaces is tangent and has a common curvature.
- The **Inverted** setting ensures that the transition between the fillet and the adjacent surfaces is perpendicular. This produces both concave and convex edges.

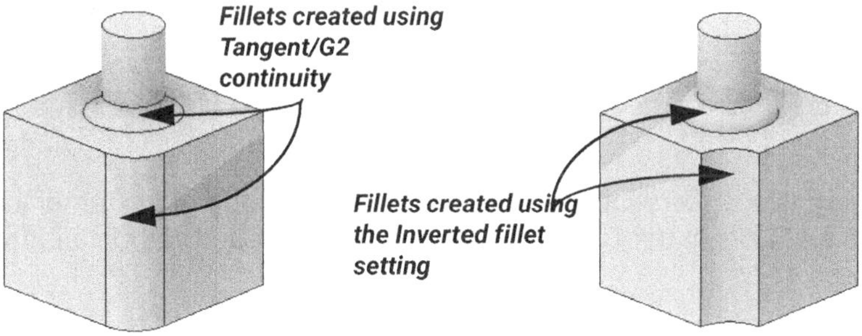

Figure 4–12

Additional Fillet Options

To display additional fillet options, expand the *Advanced Properties* area in the Properties panel, as shown in Figure 4–13.

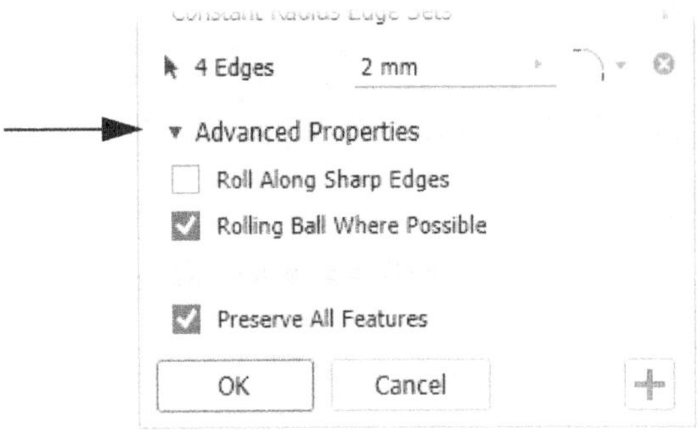

Figure 4–13

The options in the expanded area are described as follows:

Roll Along Sharp Edges	Varies the radius of the fillet, if required, to preserve the edges of the adjacent faces.
Rolling Ball Where Possible	Sets the corner style for fillets. If selected, the shape of surfaces that contain adjacent edges to which fillets are applied is maintained. The corner is not rounded.
Automatic Edge Chain	Determines how edges that contain curves are selected. When selecting an edge, any edge that is tangent to it is also selected.
Preserve All Features	All edges that intersect a fillet are calculated when a fillet is applied. When this option is cleared, only edges that are part of the fillet are calculated.

Step 4 - Define the setbacks, as required.

When three or more fillets intersect, you can define tangent continuous transitions between them by enabling setbacks in the Tool palette. Examples with and without setback distances are shown in Figure 4–14.

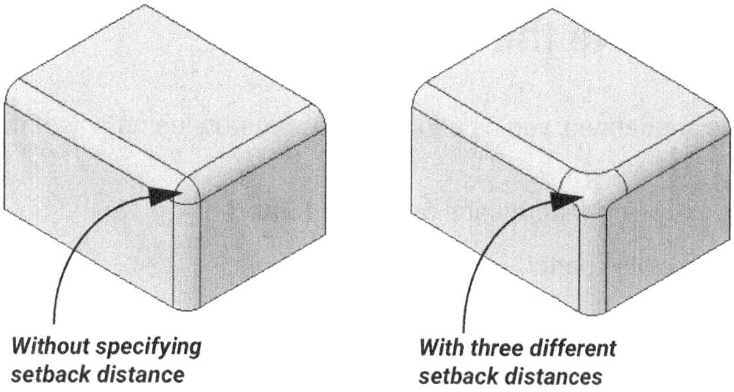

Figure 4–14

How To: Add a Setback

1. In the Tool palette, click (Add corner setback).
2. Select a vertex where the fillets intersect. Once selected, the intersecting edges are listed in the Properties panel, as shown in Figure 4–15.
3. In the Properties panel, enter setback values for each edge. The **Minimal** option enables you to define the setback values as the minimum allowable for that vertex.

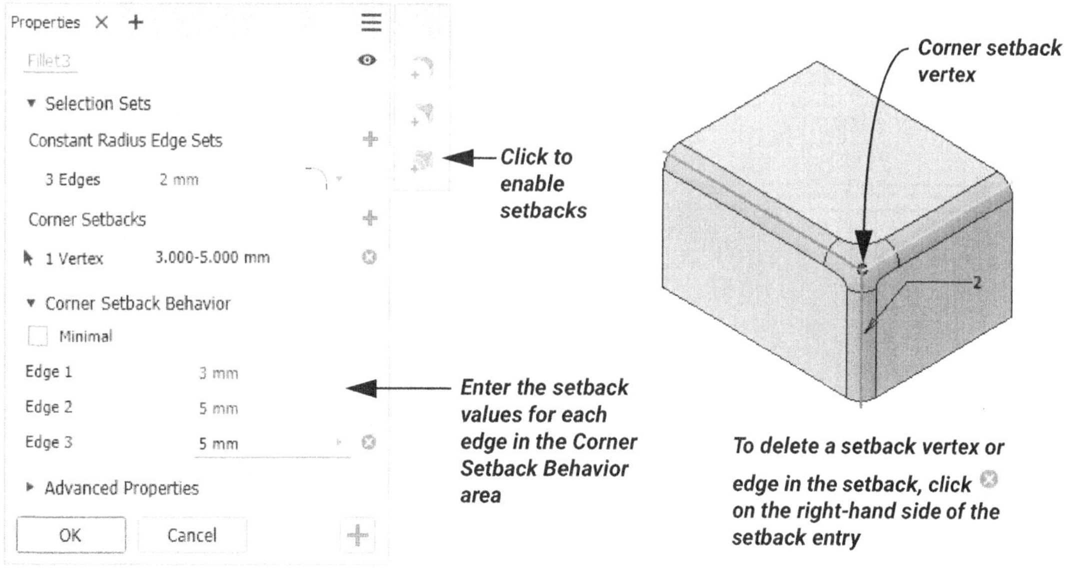

Figure 4–15

Step 5 - Complete the feature.

Once the references are defined, you can complete the feature using any of the following options:

- Right-click in the graphics window and select **OK (Enter)**.
- Click **OK** in the Properties panel.
- Press <Enter>.
- Click (Apply) to create the fillet and remain in the Properties panel to create another.

Once the fillet is created, the Model browser's fillet icon reveals whether the fillet was created as tangent ( ), smooth G2 ( ), or inverted ( ).

Hint: Constant Fillet Failures

The icon displays at the top of the Properties panel when the feature cannot be created. Click to open a window that attempts to describe why the fillet has failed. Click **Close** to return to the Properties panel to edit the fillet and resolve the failure.

4.3 Variable Fillets

A variable fillet's radius changes along the length of the edge. Radii values are applied to the ends of the edge and at intermediate points, if required. Each value can be independent. Two examples of variable fillets are shown in Figure 4–16.

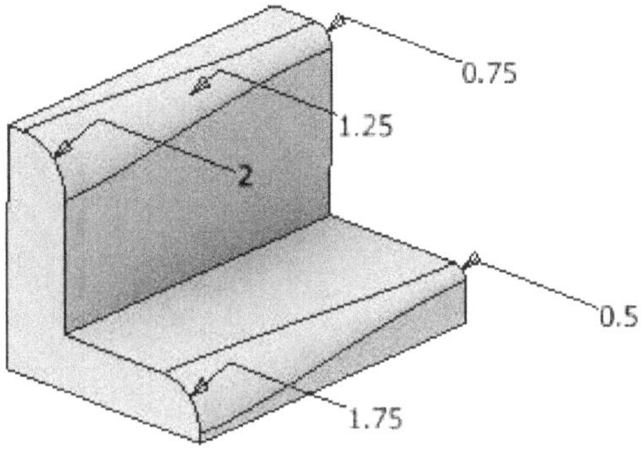

Figure 4–16

Use the following general steps to create a variable fillet:

1. Start the creation of the feature.
2. Select placement references.
3. Define the fillet size.
4. Define additional options, as required.
5. Complete the feature.

Step 1 - Start the creation of the feature.

Use one of the following methods to create a fillet:

- Select the edge(s) to be filleted and click  in the heads-up display on the model.
- In the *3D Model* tab>Modify panel, click  (Fillet).
- Right-click anywhere in the graphics window and select **Fillet**.

Once the **Fillet** command is selected, the Properties panel and the Tool palette open. By default, constant fillet is the default option. In the Tool palette, click (Add variable radius fillet) to define a variable fillet. The Properties panel and Tool palette update as shown in Figure 4–17. The Properties panel enables you to define the properties and values for the variable fillet.

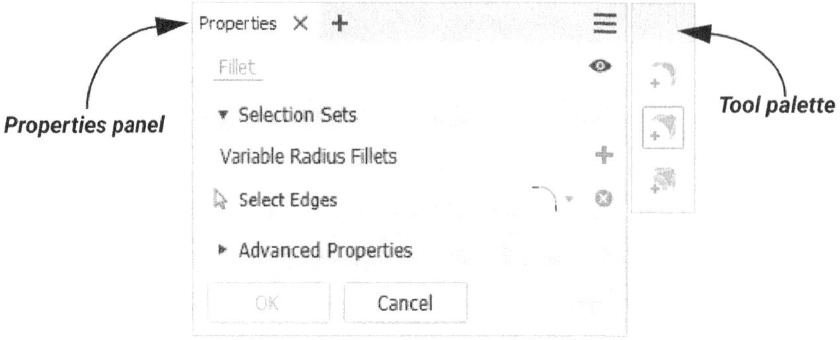

Figure 4–17

Step 2 - Select placement references.

Select an edge on the model to assign the variable fillet to. Only a linear or tangent edge can be selected for an individual fillet set. To clear the selection of an edge, hold <Ctrl> or <Shift> and reselect the edge.

To add other reference edges with unique radius values in the same feature, you must add additional sets. To add a set, select (Add variable radius fillet) adjacent to the *Variable Radius Fillets* area in the Properties panel, as shown in Figure 4–18. Once the set is active, select new edges. To delete a selection set, click on the right-hand side of the edge set.

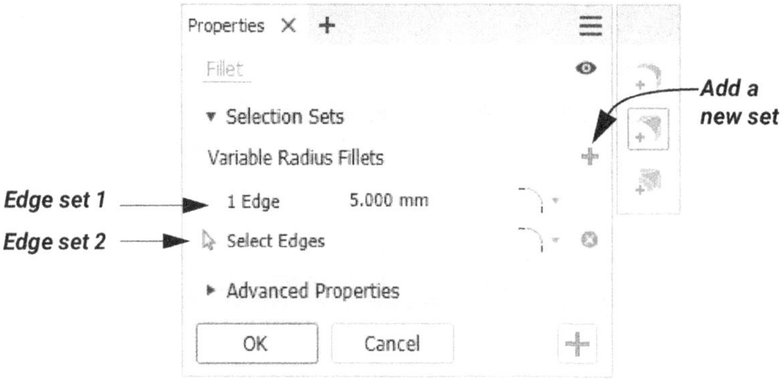

Figure 4–18

Step 3 - Define the fillet size.

By default, the radius value that was last set during fillet creation is used as the default value at both ends of the reference entity. To modify the radius values of the variable fillet, activate the required field (i.e., either end) and enter the new value in the on-screen entry field or in the Properties panel, as shown in Figure 4–19. As an alternative, you can also select and drag the radius handle that displays on the model to resize the fillet.

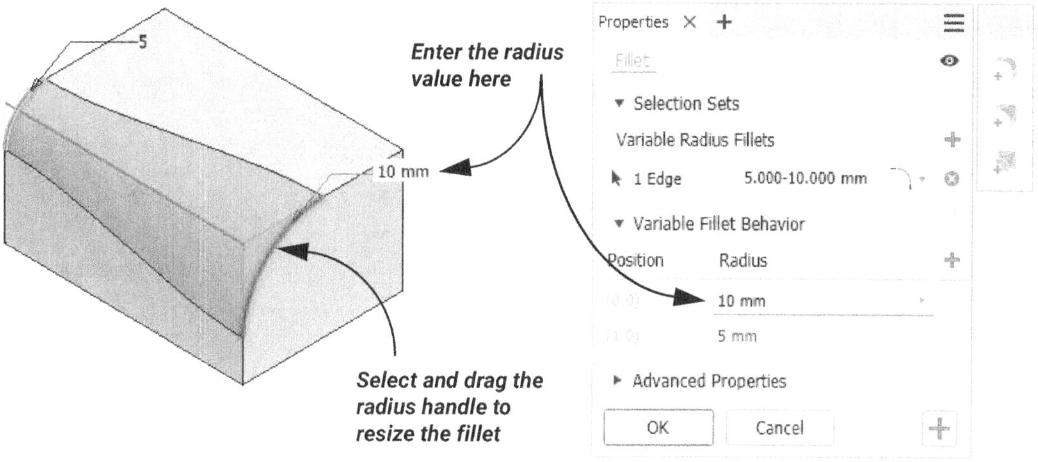

Figure 4–19

To vary the radius between the endpoints, you can add an intermediate point(s) using either of the following methods:

- In the Properties panel>*Variable Fillet Behavior* area, click +.
- In the graphics window, use your mouse and select a location on the edge that is being filleted.

If the intermediate point is added using the Properties panel, the point is automatically added at the midpoint of the edge (0.5 position). If you selected on the filleted edge, the point location is based on the selection location. Once the point is added, you can select the *Position* cell in the Properties panel or drag the point on the edge to modify its placement location. To modify the intermediate point's radius value, activate the radius handle or the *Radius* field in the Properties panel and modify it as needed. Figure 4–20 shows how an intermediate point was added, and where its position and radius can be modified.

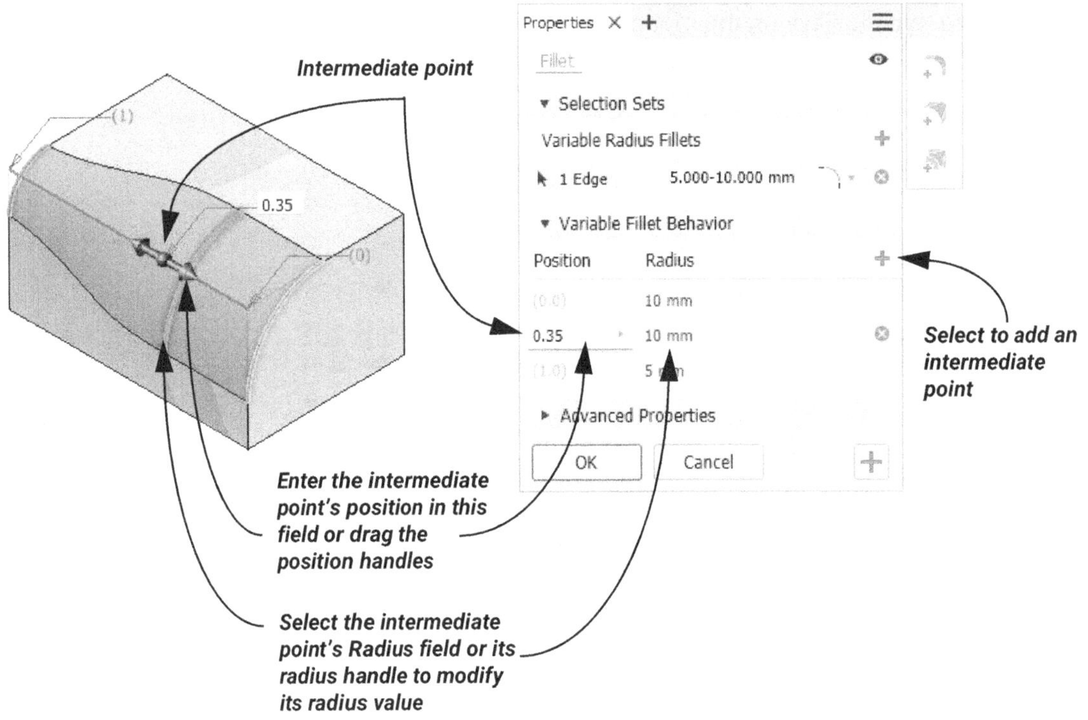

Figure 4–20

Step 4 - Define additional options, as required.

Consider using the following options to further control the variable fillet:

- Variable edge fillets are created with Tangent continuity by default. The continuity of a variable edge fillet can be changed to **Smooth G2**; however, unlike with constant edge fillets, you cannot invert a variable edge fillet. Defining continuity for a variable edge fillet is the same process as for a constant fillet, as shown in Figure 4–21.

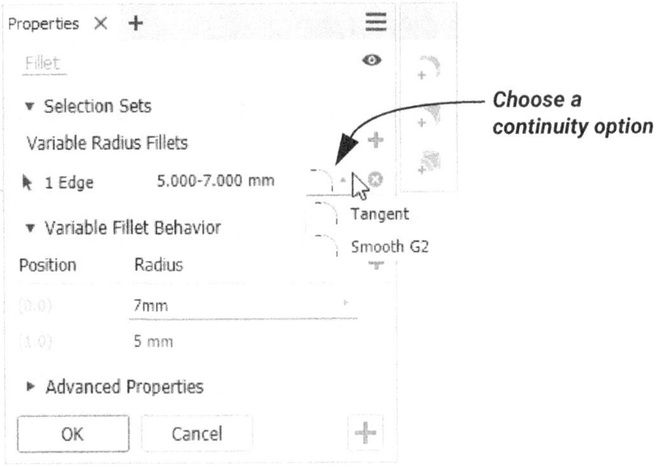

Figure 4–21

- Depending on how variable fillets and/or other fillets intersect, you may be able to define the setback for the intersecting vertex to customize the shape of the geometry. To add a corner setback, click  (Add corner setback) in the Tool palette. Once active, you will be prompted to select the intersecting vertex. If a vertex is unavailable, it will be identified in the Properties panel.
- Similarly to creating a constant fillet, you can access the same additional options to control the fillet's shape by expanding the *Advanced Properties* area, as shown in Figure 4–22. For variable fillets, the **Smooth Radius Transition** option can also be set to define how the fillet transitions between points. When enabled, the transition between adjacent points is a complex curve. This produces a fillet surface that is tangent to its adjacent surfaces. When disabled, the transition between the points is a straight line and is not necessarily tangent to its adjacent surfaces.

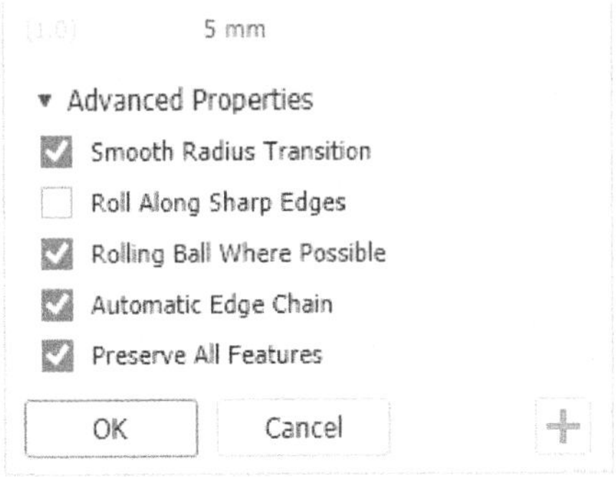

Figure 4–22

Step 5 - Complete the feature.

Once the references are defined, you can complete the feature using any of the following options:

- Right-click in the graphics window and select **OK (Enter)**.
- Click **OK** in the Properties panel.
- Press <Enter>.
- Click (Apply) to create the fillet and remain in the Properties panel to create another.

Once the fillet is created, the Model browser's fillet icon reveals whether the fillet was created as a tangent ( ) or smooth G2 ( ) variable fillet.

Hint: Variable Fillet Failures

The icon displays at the top of the Properties panel when the feature cannot be created. Click to open a window that attempts to describe why the fillet has failed. Click **Close** to return to the Properties panel to edit the fillet and resolve the failure.

4.4 Holes

Holes remove material from the model. Using the hole creation options that are available in the Properties panel, you can define multiple types of holes (as shown in Figure 4–23) that start and terminate in different configurations.

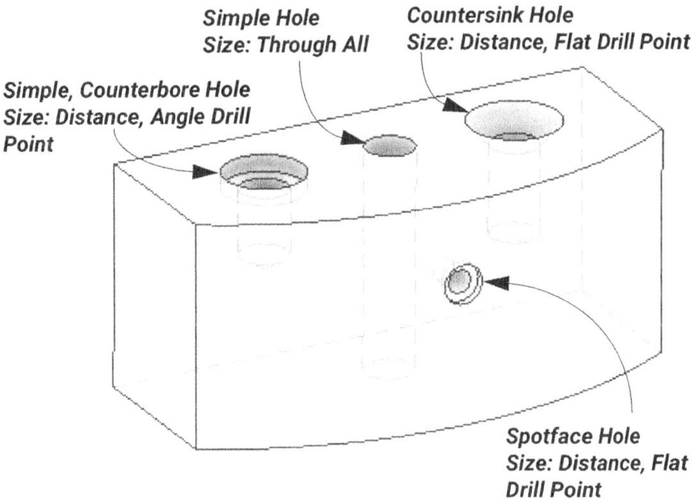

Figure 4–23

Use the following general steps to create a simple hole:

1. Start the creation of the feature.
2. Define the placement location for the hole.
3. Fully locate the hole on the placement plane.
4. Define the type of hole.
5. Define the size of the hole.
6. Complete the feature.

Step 1 - Start the creation of the feature.

The following methods can be used to create a new hole in a model:

- In the *3D Model* tab>Modify panel, click (Hole).
- Right-click anywhere in the graphics window and select **Hole**.
- Preselect a sketched point and click in the heads-up display on the model.

The Properties panel opens, similar to that shown in Figure 4–24.

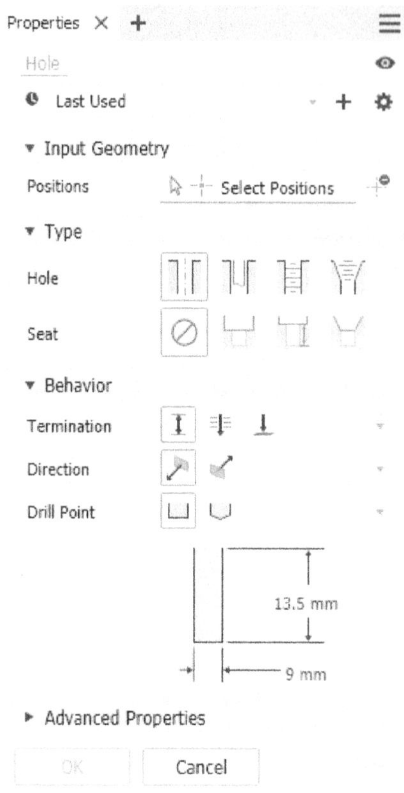

Figure 4–24

__Note:__ By default, __Last used__ is set as the hole preset at the top of the Properties panel. This presets all of the hole options to those that were used in the last hole operation. Creating unique hole presets are discussed later in the topic.

Step 2 - Define the placement location for the hole.

To locate the hole you must select a placement reference on which to locate the hole. Placement references can include the following:

- Sketch Points
- Faces
- Work Points

When selecting a placement location, you can use the **Allow Center Point Creation** option that is adjacent to the *Positions* field to control the type of reference that can be selected to locate a hole. Consider the following:

- When the **Allow Center Point Creation** option is OFF, its icon appears as in the Properties panel and only sketch geometry (i.e., points) or workpoints can be selected.
- When the **Allow Center Point Creation** option is ON, its icon appears as in the Properties panel and sketch geometry (i.e., points) or workpoints and faces can be selected.

Hole Placement on Sketched Points

If a single sketch is visible (and not consumed) and contains any sketched points, all of its points are automatically preselected as hole placement references. If two sketches are visible, no preselections are made by Inventor. Holes located based on the selection of a sketch point are extended perpendicularly from the face/sketch plane. References are listed in the *Input Geometry* area of the Properties panel, as shown on the left in Figure 4–25.

Hole Placement on a Face

To place a hole on a planar face, the (Allow Center Point Creation option ON) must be enabled in the Properties panel. Once on, select a hole placement location on a face using the left mouse button. A center point is added to the face and a preview of the hole displays. Holes located based on the selection of a face are extended perpendicular to the face. References are listed in the *Input Geometry* area of the Properties panel, as shown on the left in Figure 4–25.

Hole Placement on a Work Point

To place a hole on a work point, select it directly in the graphics window. Holes located using a work point require that an orientation reference also be selected. References are listed in the *Input Geometry* area of the Properties panel, as shown on the right in Figure 4–25.

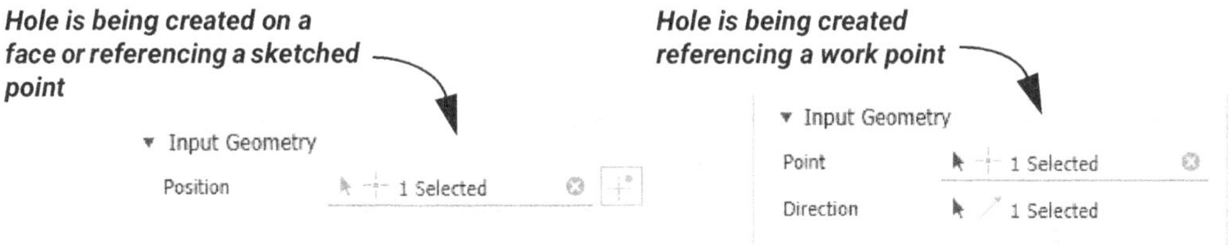

Figure 4–25

Note: *To clear a hole placement selection, you can either click adjacent to the field or press and hold <Ctrl> and select the point on the model to clear its selection.*

Hint: Sketch Creation

- When you select a planar face for hole placement, a sketch is immediately created and listed at the top of the Properties panel, as shown in Figure 4–26. In Step 3, you will learn how to access the sketch to fully locate the hole.

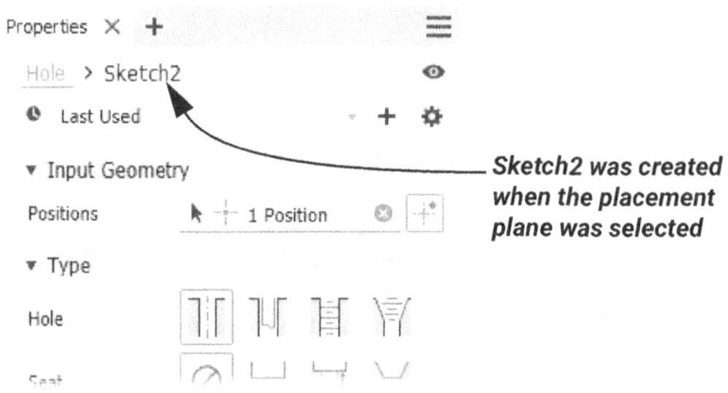

Figure 4–26

- If a sketch point is selected for hole placement, its sketch is listed at the top of the Properties panel. If a hole is added and subsequently removed, the center point remains in the sketch unless deleted in the Sketch environment.
- If a work point is selected for hole placement, no sketch is created because the work point alone fully defines its location in the model.

Step 3 - Fully locate the hole on the placement plane.

A hole placed on a face is not fully parametrically located with the selection of the placement plane alone. Although the hole is previewed once the placement plane is selected, its location on that plane must be defined. Holes that are created referencing a sketch point or work point are located based on the location of the points so no further location references are required. For linear or concentric holes, additional placements references are required.

Linear Placement

To fully locate a hole, you must constrain the center of the hole in two directions on its placement face. This can be done using different methods:

- In the graphics window, select the first linear edge and then select the second. Dimensions are created between each selected reference and the hole's center point, as shown in Figure 4–27. You can select on each entry field to activate it and modify the dimension value.

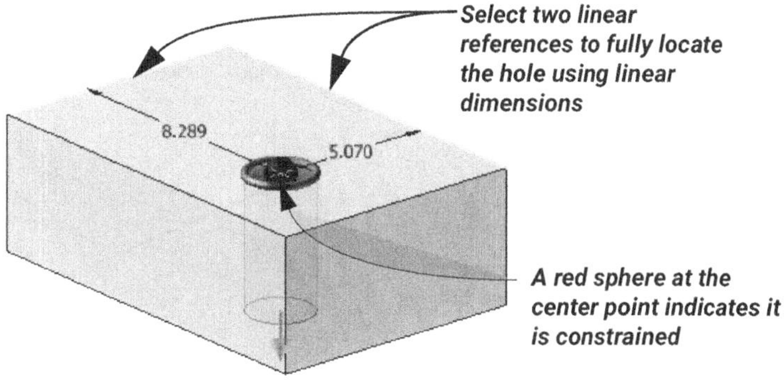

Figure 4–27

- In the graphics window, select and drag the center point of the hole so that it is coincident with the projected (fully constrained) origin point. A green circle displays when it snaps to the origin. Once you release the mouse button, a red sphere displays indicating the point is fully constrained. Figure 4–28 shows examples of how the center point can be constrained to the projected origin.

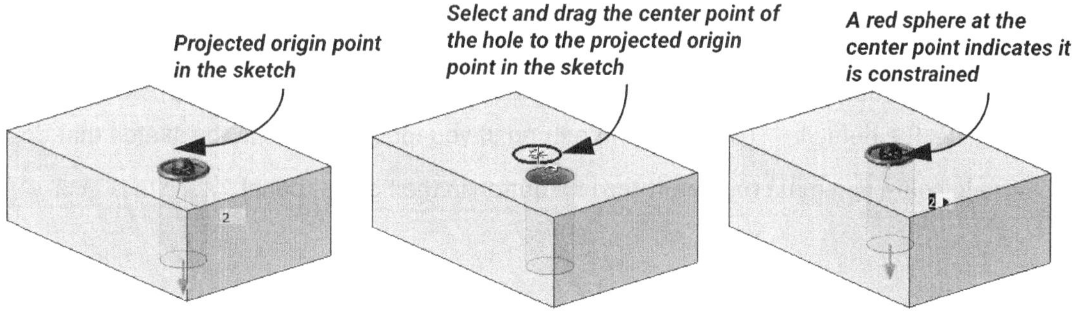

Figure 4–28

- In the header of the Properties panel, click **Sketch#** to open the hole's sketch, which provides access to the familiar Sketch ribbon, as shown in Figure 4–29. You can use all of the standard sketch tools to fully dimension and constrain the center point of the hole.

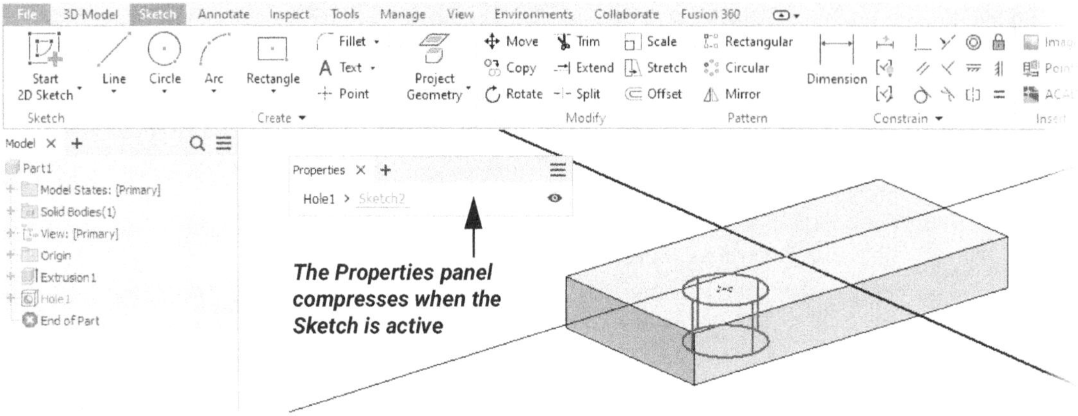

Figure 4–29

Once the center point has been constrained, click **Hole#** at the top of the Properties panel or click (Return to Hole) in the Sketch ribbon to reactivate the hole. If you select **Finish Sketch**, the hole is completed and placed based on the settings that were previously set in the Properties panel.

Hint: Point Creation in a Hole's Sketch

During hole creation (with the sketch active), additional holes are added if you place new points using the default (Center Point) setting. If you require points in the sketch that do not create holes, you must toggle off the button in the Format panel.

Concentric Placement

To locate a hole concentrically once it is placed on a plane, hover the cursor over the outside cylindrical face. Once the ◎ symbol displays adjacent to the cursor (as shown in Figure 4–30), select the face. This assigns the hole as a concentric hole to the selected face. Once the hole is constrained concentrically, a red sphere displays on the center point of the hole indicating it is fully constrained.

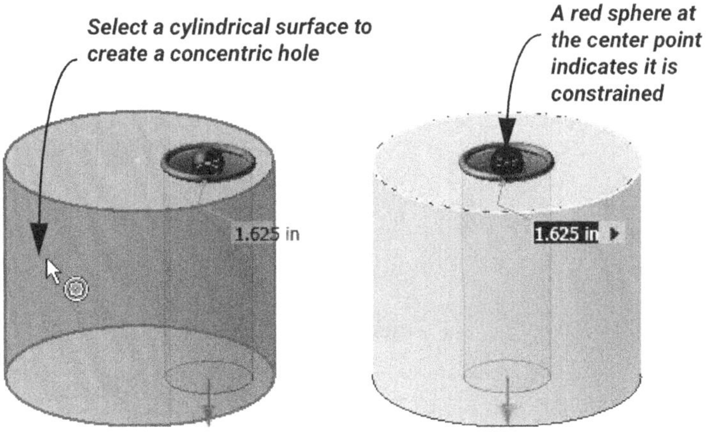

Figure 4–30

A sketch is created whenever a hole is placed on a plane. For a concentric hole, this sketch is still created; however, you are not required to access it unless you wanted to break the concentric alignment.

Hint: Fully Locating a Hole

A hole can be completed without its center point being parametrically constrained. This is not recommended! You should ensure that the center point is parametrically placed in such a way that it defines the hole's intent. To ensure it is fully located on its placement plane, confirm that a red sphere displays on the center point prior to completing the hole. Alternatively, hover the cursor over the center point and review the cursor symbol that displays. If the ✥ symbol displays adjacent to the cursor, it indicates the center point can be dragged and is therefore not constrained.

Step 4 - Define the type of hole.

The options available in the **Type** node enable you to define the hole. Its options are divided into how the hole is created and the type of seating that is to be assigned, as shown in Figure 4–31.

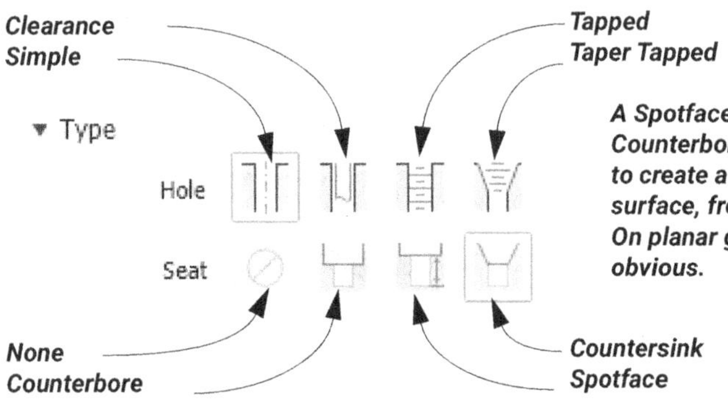

A Spotface hole is similar in geometry to a Counterbore hole, However, its purpose is to create a shallow flat area on an irregular surface, from which you can create a hole. On planar geometry, the difference is not obvious.

Figure 4–31

Step 5 - Define the size of the hole.

The options available in the **Behavior** node define how the hole is terminated, its direction, and the drill point type at the bottom of the hole, as shown in Figure 4–32.

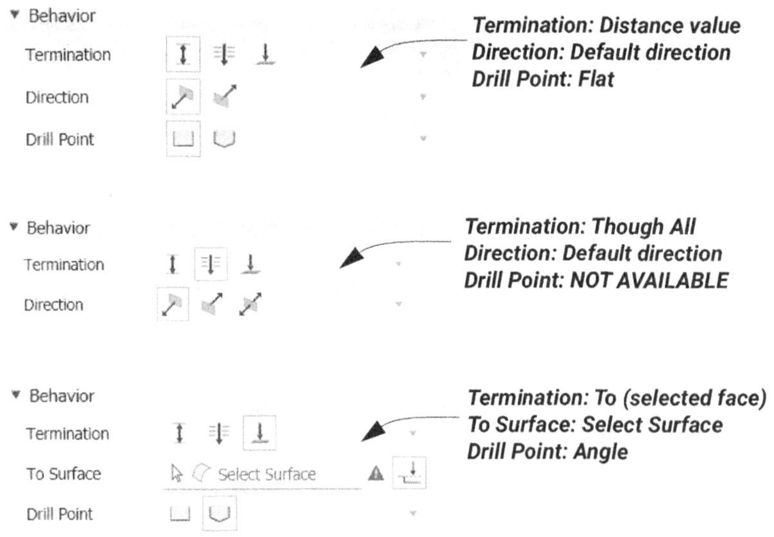

Figure 4–32

The termination options are described as follows:

Distance ( )	Creates a blind hole of a specified depth. Using the direction buttons you can define the direction of the hole.
Through All ( )	Creates a hole through the entire model. Using the direction buttons you can define the direction of the hole. For drilled simple holes, the direction can also be defined as symmetric.
To ( )	Creates a blind hole that terminates at a selected plane or at the extension of the selected plane. Toggle the (Terminate feature by extending the face ON) option when the selected termination plane does not completely intersect the hole.

Hint: Extend Start

You can enable the **Extend Start** option in the *Advanced Properties* area to extend the start plane to remove fragments, similar to the example shown in Figure 4–33. In this example, a hole and a fillet are intersecting and you can remove the material on the fillet using the **Extend Start** option. This option is only available to extend the start face in a single body.

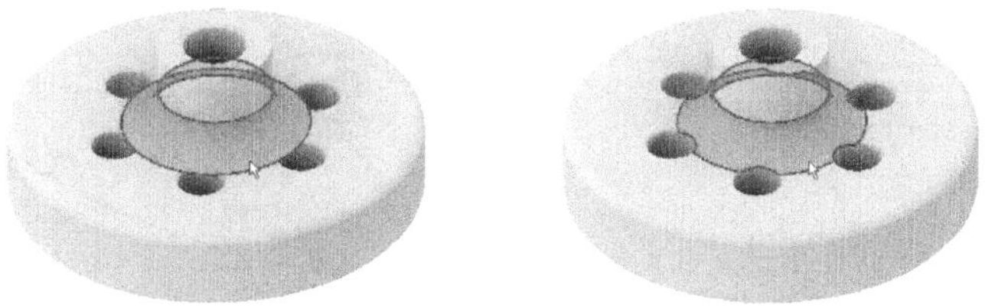

Extend Start disabled ***Extend Start enabled***

Figure 4–33

The hole size values can also be edited in the *Behavior* area by selecting and activating each dimension field and entering a value. The values can also be modified directly in the graphics window. Figure 4–34 shows two examples of holes and their active fields. To switch between fields, you can select the dimension fields in the Properties panel or the graphics window, or select the gold rings and arrows that display on the model.

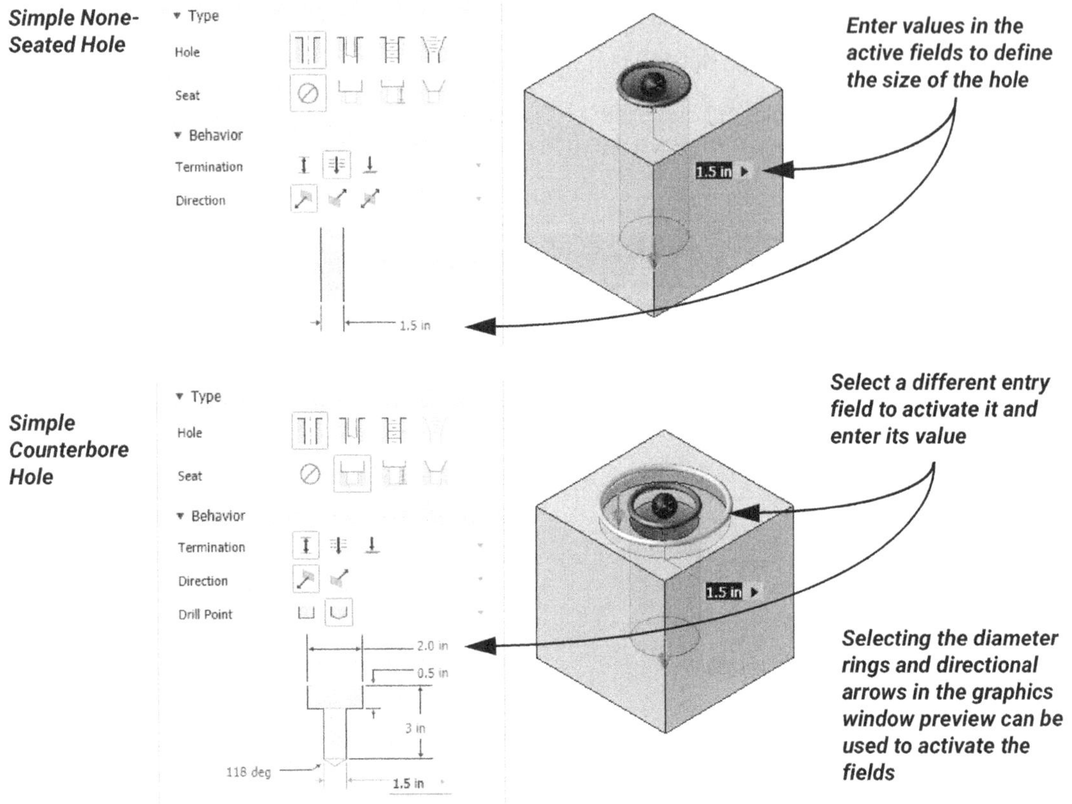

Figure 4–34

Step 6 - Complete the feature.

Once the hole is defined, you can complete the feature using any of the following options:

- Right-click in the graphics window and select **OK (Enter)**.
- Click **OK** in the Properties panel.
- Press <Enter>.
- Click (Apply) to create the hole and remain in the Properties panel to create another.

The **Hole** feature is identified with the icon in the Model browser once created.

Placing Multiple Holes

When the Properties panel is active, you can continue to place new center points to define multiple holes in the one Hole feature. All holes created in this way have the same settings and sizes. For unique settings, you must create a new hole feature.

Hole Presets

The **Hole** feature enables you to create and save unique and commonly used hole presets. By default, the preset list at the top of the Properties panel indicates that the **Last used** preset is active. This means that all of the settings that were used to create the last hole will be used for the creation of the new hole.

To create a custom preset, set the hole options in the *Type* and *Behavior* areas and click

+ (Create new preset) adjacent to the preset list, as shown in Figure 4–35. The preset is created with a system-defined name and you can immediately enter a new descriptive name.

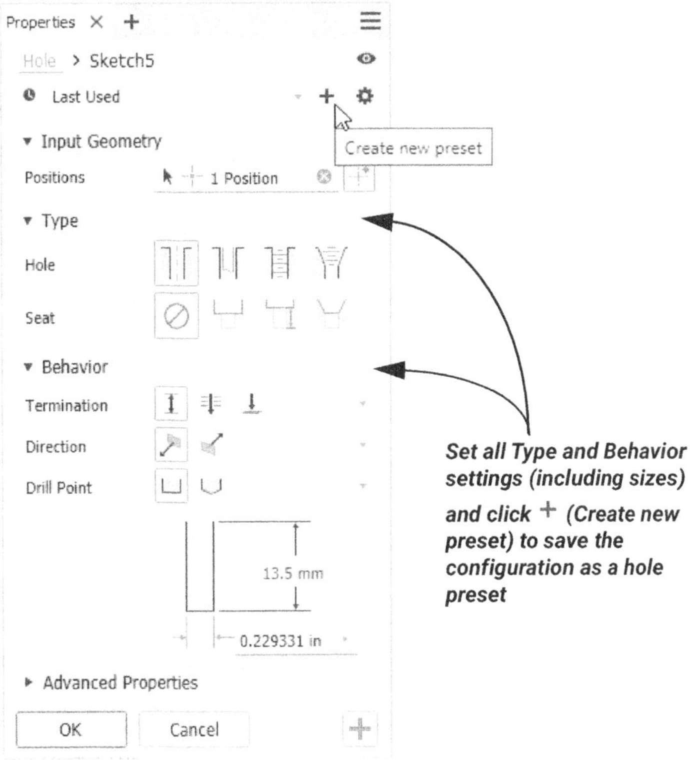

Figure 4–35

To use a saved preset, simply select it once the Hole feature has been activated, as shown in Figure 4–36. The hole is created using all the options that were saved when the preset was created.

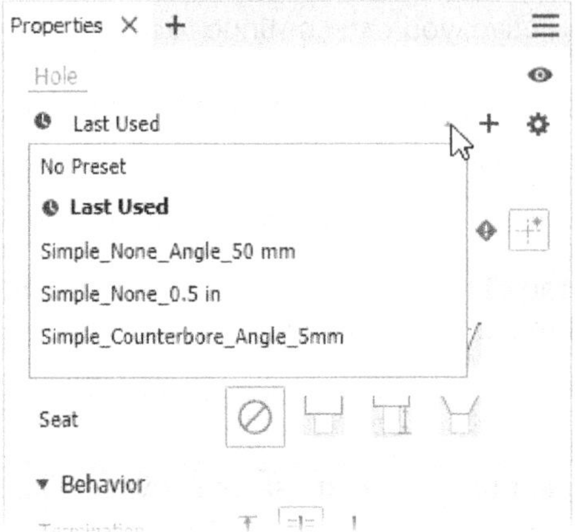

Figure 4–36

The preset settings are available by selecting (Preset Settings) adjacent to the preset list, as shown in Figure 4–37. These options enable you to save changes to a preset, rename a preset, and delete a preset. Additionally, you can customize the sort order for the preset list and define whether a new hole uses the **Last Used** or the current preset to create new holes.

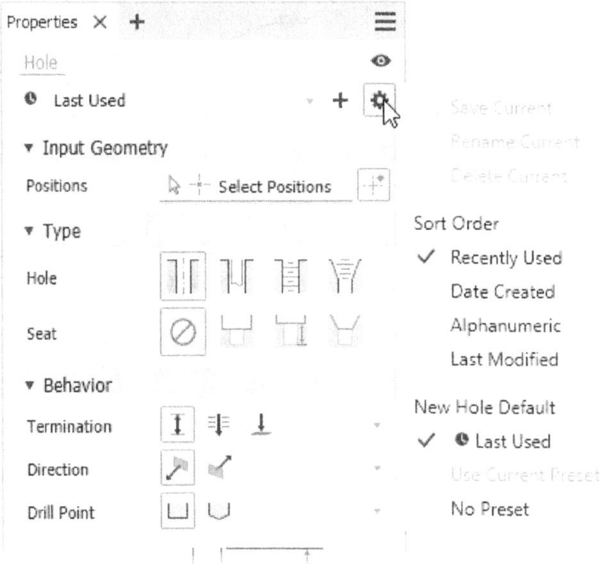

Figure 4–37

-

4.5 Editing Pick and Place Features

Once you have created a pick and place feature, you might need to modify it by changing dimension values, editing the properties of the feature, or in the case of a hole modify its location by editing the sketch that was generated when it was created. The following options enable you to make these changes.

- **Show Dimensions** - Displays the dimensions associated with the feature. You can double-click on the values once displayed to make dimensional changes.

- **Edit Sketch** ( ) - Accesses the feature's sketch to redefine any of the elements used to define the sketch. For pick and place features, this only applies to Hole features that generate a sketch during creation.

- **Edit Feature** ( ) - Opens the Properties panel or feature dialog box to redefine the settings used to define the feature.You can also double-click on the feature in the Model browser as an equivalent method to using the **Edit Feature** command.

The options can be accessed in the Model browser by right-clicking on the feature, as shown on the left in Figure 4–38, in the graphics window by selecting any face that is generated by the feature to bring up the toolbar options (shown in the center image), or by right-clicking on a feature geometry, as shown on the right.

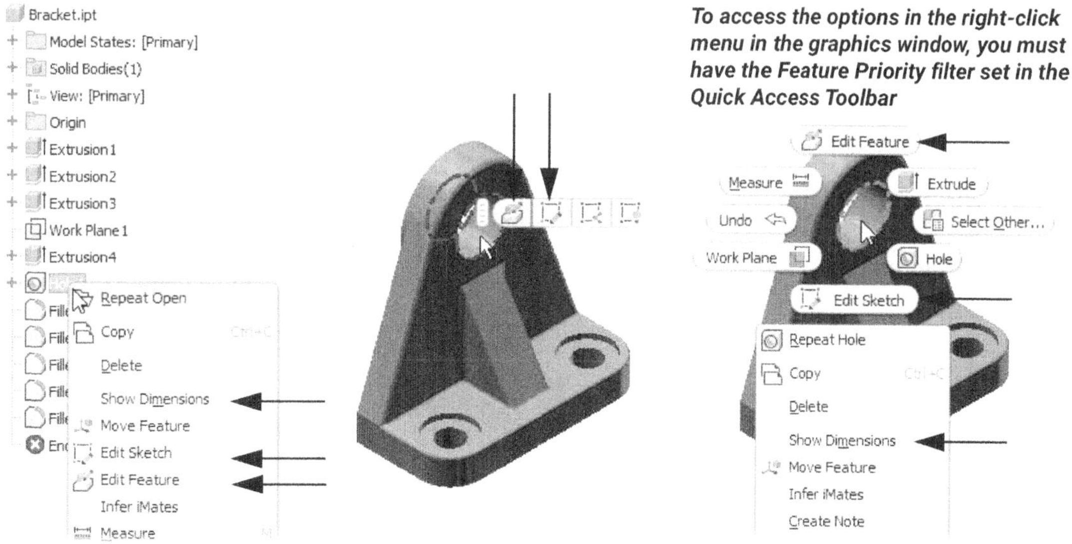

Figure 4–38

Practice 4a
Add Pick and Place Features

Practice Objectives

- Create constant and variable edge fillets along specific edges in the model.
- Create a From Sketch and Linear hole based on specific criteria.
- Create an edge chamfer along a specific edge in the model.

In this practice, you will add pick and place features to a model. The resulting model displays as shown in Figure 4–39.

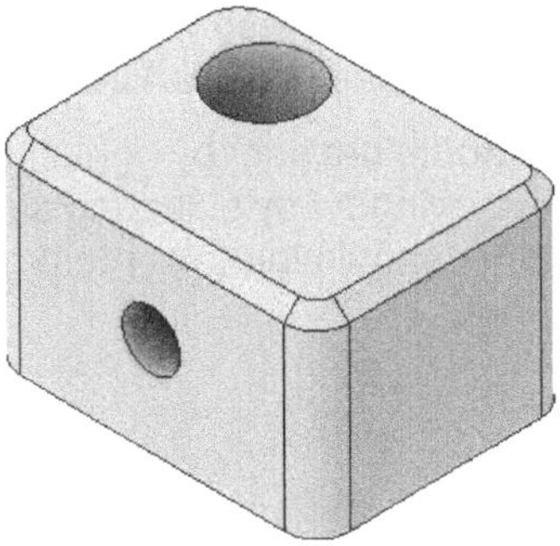

Figure 4–39

Task 1: Open a part file and create fillets.

1. Open **rectangle_1.ipt**.

2. In the *3D Model* tab>Modify panel, click  (Fillet). The Properties panel and Tool palette open, similar to that shown in Figure 4–40.

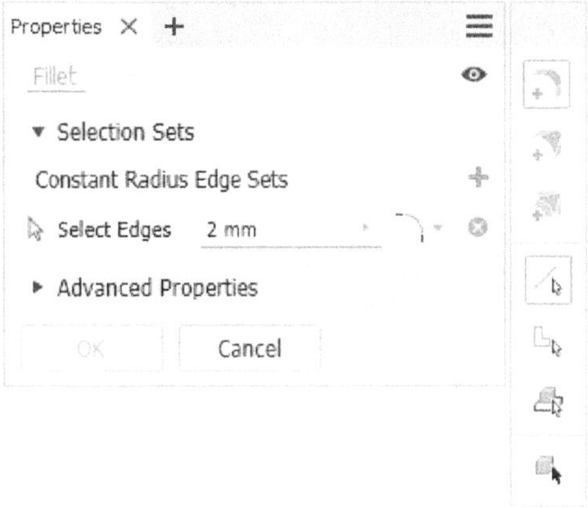

Figure 4–40

3. In the Tool palette, click  (Add constant radius edge set) to create a constant fillet, if not already active.

4. In the Tool palette, select  (Sets selection priority to edges), if not already active. Select the edges of the model shown in Figure 4–41. Selecting multiple edges ensures that the fillets are all the same radius and are driven by one dimension value. A default fillet automatically displays on the model.

   Note: *To clear the edges selected for fillets, press and hold <Ctrl> or <Shift> and select the referenced edge a second time.*

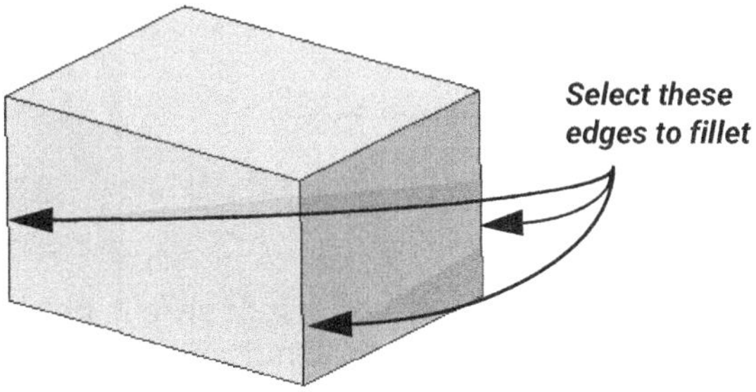

Figure 4–41

5. In the radius on-screen entry field or in the Properties panel, enter **2.54** as the radial dimension for the fillets, as shown in Figure 4–42. All three fillets act as one and update dynamically.

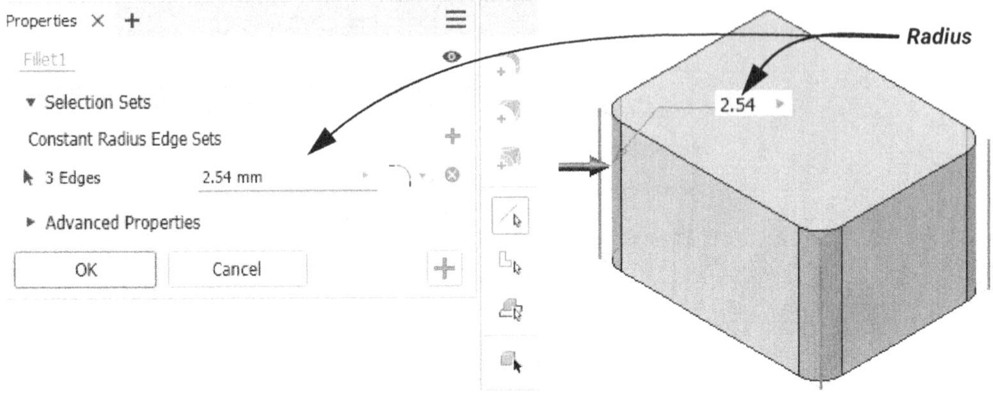

Figure 4–42

6. Click **OK** to complete the simple fillet. The model is shown in Figure 4–43. Note how the Model browser updates to display the single fillet feature.

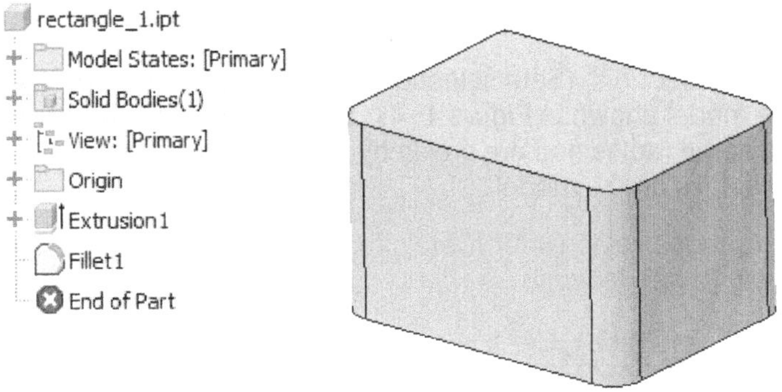

Figure 4–43

Task 2: Create the variable fillet.

1. Switch the model to Wireframe. The Wireframe visual style is being used for clarity in the upcoming images. You do not need to work in Wireframe to create a variable fillet.
2. In the graphics window, right-click and select **Fillet**.
3. In the Tool palette, select  (Add variable radius fillet). Note that the selection filters are cleared from the Tool palette for a variable fillet because only linear edges can be selected as references for variable fillets.

4. Select the vertical edge shown in Figure 4–44 on which to create the variable fillet.

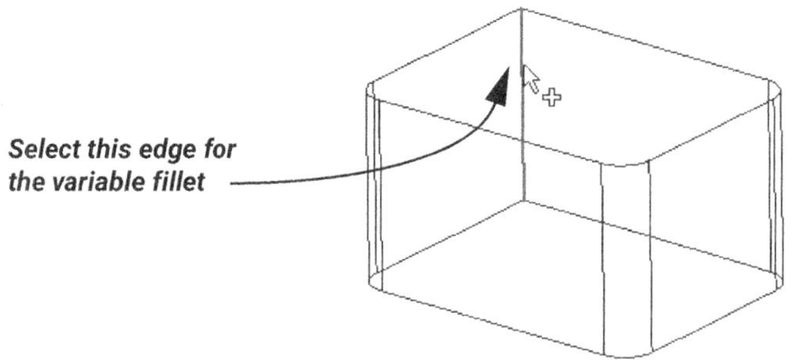

Figure 4–44

5. A variable fillet with the same radius at both ends is created by default. Modify the radius of both the start point (position 0,0) and end point (position 1,0) to **3.81** in the radius on-screen entry field or in the Properties panel, as shown in Figure 4–45.

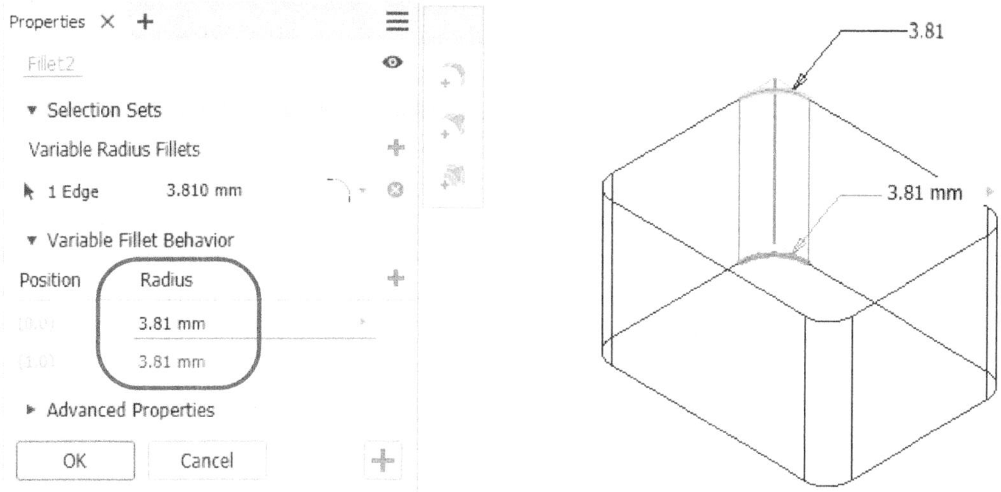

Figure 4–45

6. In the *Variable Fillet Behavior* area, click + (Add variable fillet point) to add an intermediate point on the same edge. The point is added at the midpoint of the line by default.

7. In the Properties panel, hover your cursor over the **0.5** *Position* field and note that you can edit this value if necessary. For this fillet, maintain the 0.5 position value to keep it at the midpoint of the selected edge.

8. Modify the radius of the intermediate point (position 0.5) to **7.62** in the radius on-screen entry field or in the Properties panel, as shown in Figure 4–46.

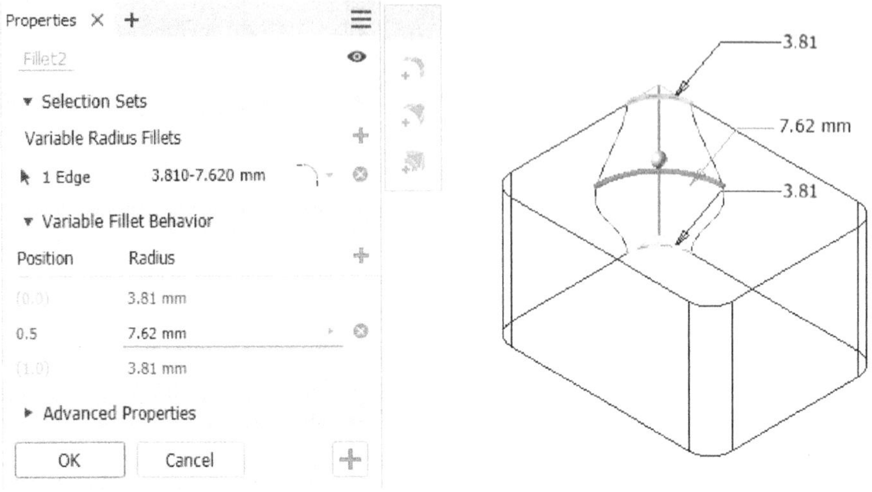

Figure 4–46

9. Click **OK** to complete the variable fillet. The model displays as shown in Figure 4–47. Note how the Model browser updates with a second fillet feature added.

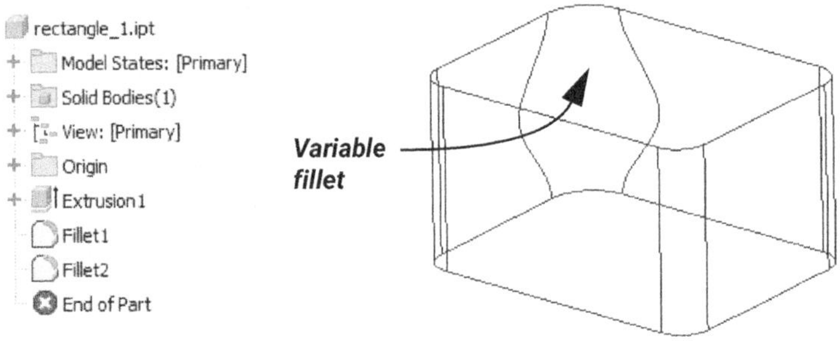

Figure 4–47

Task 3: Create a hole.

1. In the Modify panel, click  (Hole).

2. Complete the following in the Properties panel or graphics window (as shown in Figure 4–48). A preview of the hole displays in the graphics window as you make selections.

   - Select the location shown in Figure 4–48 to place the hole.
   - In the **Type** node, ensure that *Hole* is set to (Simple) and that *Seat* is set to (None).
   - In the **Behavior** node, ensure that *Termination* is set to (Through All) and that *Direction* is set to (Default).
   - Enter **7.5 mm** as the diameter of the hole in the Properties panel or in the on-screen entry field.

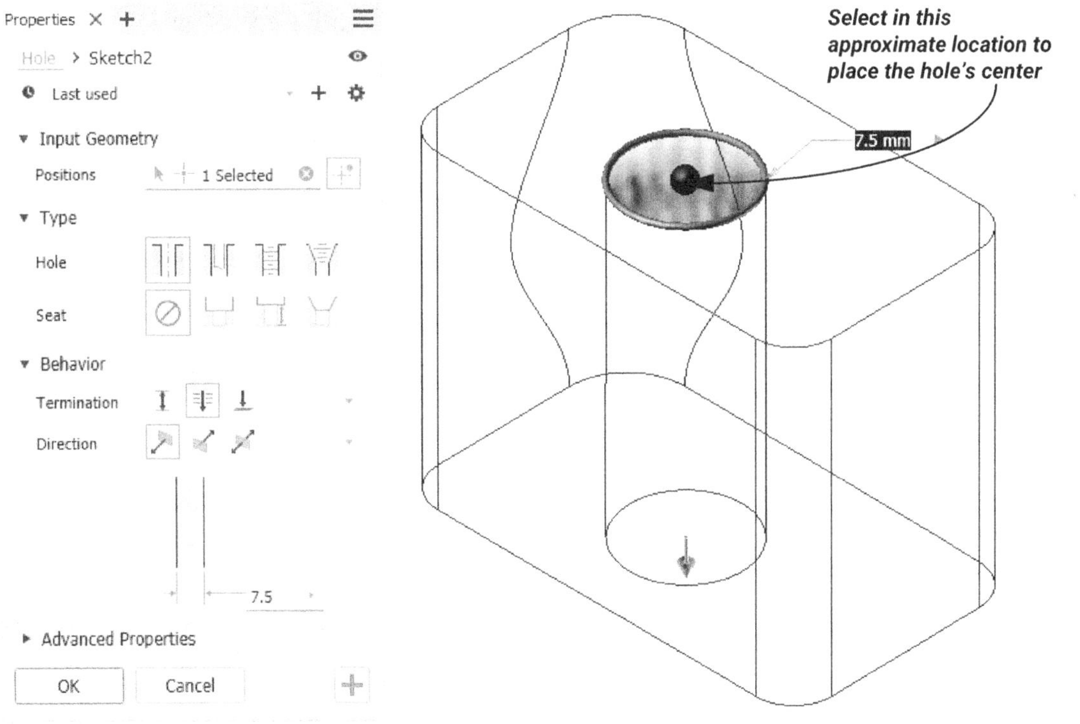

Figure 4–48

3. To fully locate the hole, additional positional references are required. Select the two edges shown in Figure 4–49 to create two linear dimensions that fully locate the hole.

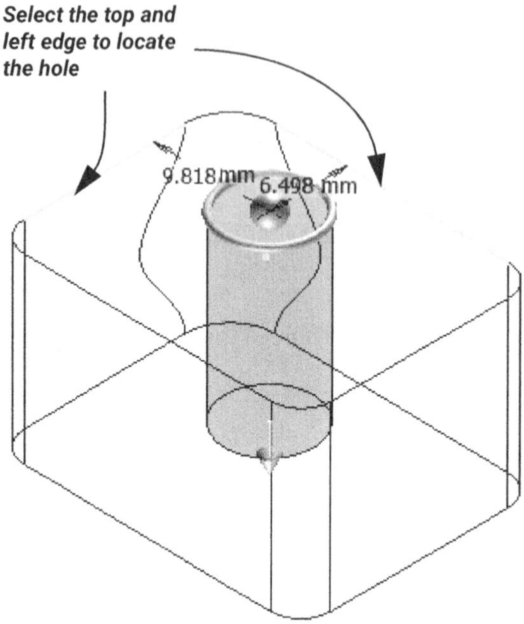

Figure 4–49

4. Reorient the model to the **TOP** view using the ViewCube.
5. The current values for the hole's center point dimensions display based on where you located the hole, similar to that shown in Figure 4–50. In the header of the Properties panel, click **Sketch2**. This accesses the sketch that was automatically created to define the hole's placement.

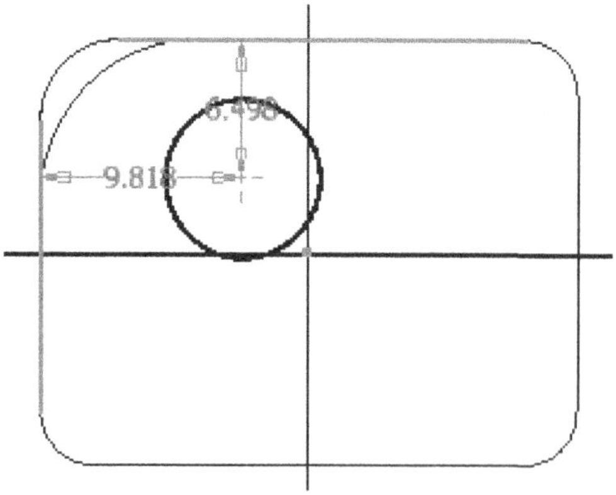

Figure 4–50

6. Note that the same Sketch ribbon and options are available. Modify the two values for the linear dimensions as shown in Figure 4–51.

   Note: You could have also edited the dimensions while still in the Properties panel, without accessing the sketch. This step is simply shown to explain that all sketching tools and constraints are still available to you to further define the hole's placement.

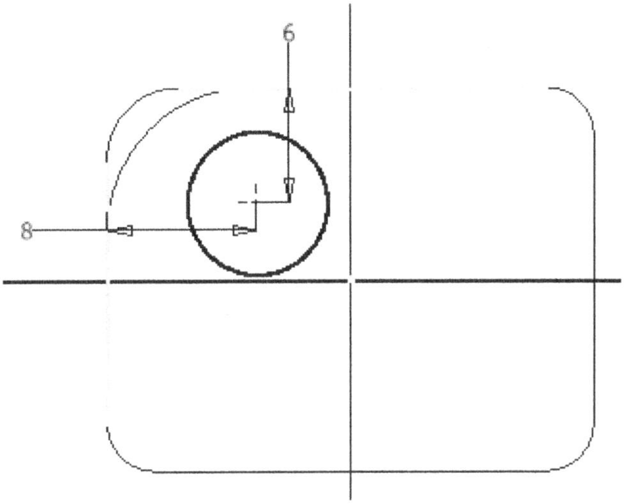

Figure 4–51

7. In the header of the Properties panel, click **Hole** to return to hole creation. Alternatively, in the *Sketch* tab, click (Return to Hole).
8. Click **OK** to complete the hole.

Task 4: Create a second hole.

1. In the Modify panel, click (Hole).

2. Complete the following in the Properties panel or graphics window (as shown in Figure 4–52). A preview of the hole displays in the graphics window as you make selections.Note that the default settings in the Properties panel are consistent with settings that were used in creating the previous hole because Last used is selected at the top of the panel.

    - Select the point shown in Figure 4–52 to place the hole.
    - In the **Type** node, ensure that *Hole* is set to (Simple) and that *Seat* is set to (None).
    - In the **Behavior** node, ensure that *Termination* is set to (Through All) and that *Direction* is set to (Default).
    - Enter **4.5** as the diameter of the hole in the Properties panel on in the on-screen entry field.

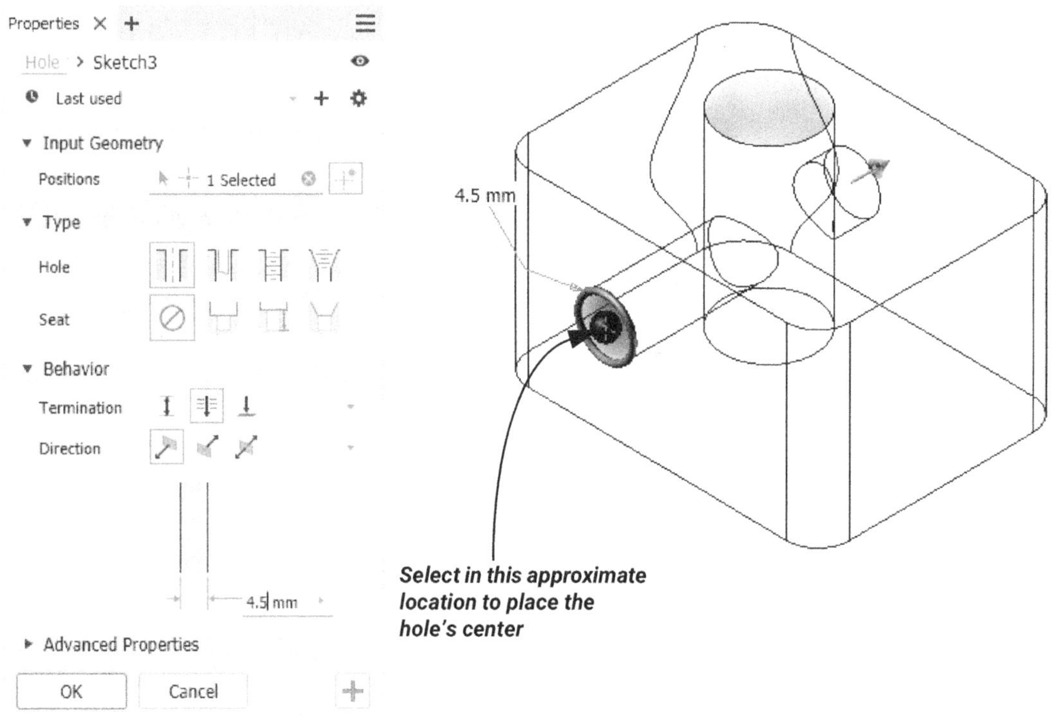

Figure 4–52

3. To fully locate the hole, additional positional references are required. The design intent requires that the hole is centered on the face. To accomplish this with constraints, you must go directly to the sketch. In the header of the Properties panel, click **Sketch3**.

4. The projected origin point exists in the middle of the face. Use the **Coincident** constraint type to constrain the hole center and the projected origin point, as shown in Figure 4–53. Alternatively, you can drag the center point to the projected origin point without accessing the sketch.

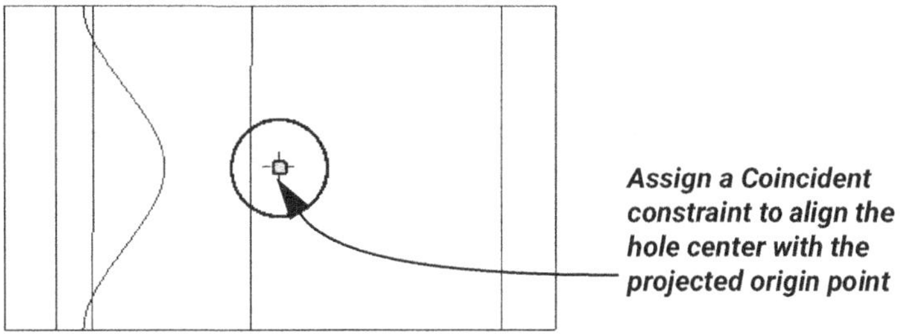

Figure 4–53

5. In the header of the Properties panel, click **Hole** to return to hole creation, or in the *Sketch* tab, click (Return to Hole).
6. Click **OK** to complete the hole.
7. Return the view display to **Shaded with Edges**.

Task 5: Create an edge chamfer.

1. Select the edge shown in Figure 4–54, and click in the heads-up display on the model. The edge chamfer automatically displays encompassing all four edges. This is because the fillets made the edges tangent to one another and all tangent edges are included.

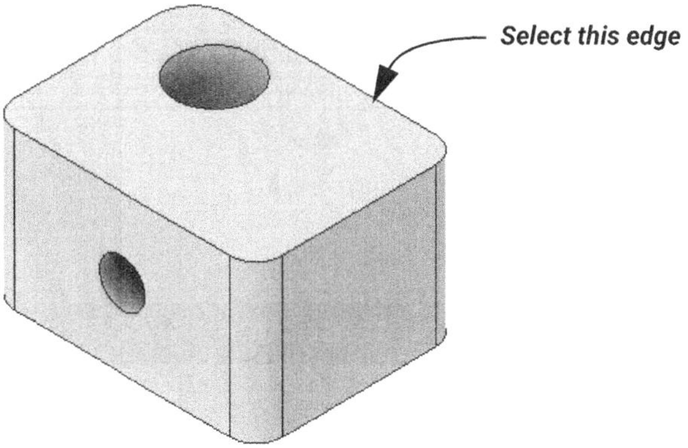

Figure 4–54

2. In the mini-toolbar, enter **1.20** in the *Distance* field, as shown in Figure 4–55.

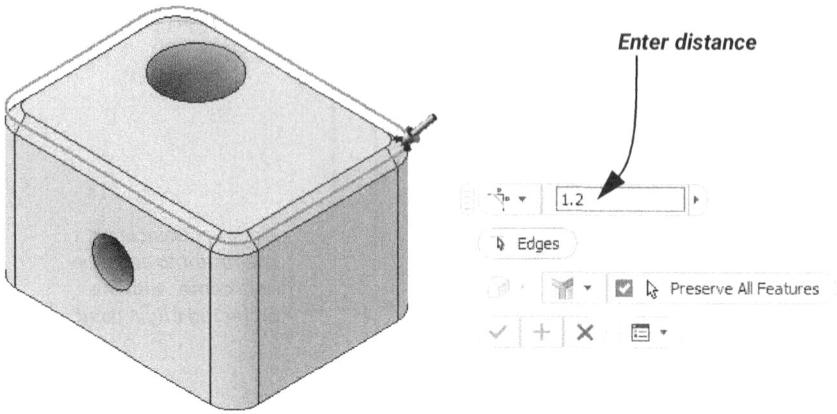

Figure 4–55

3. Click to complete the chamfer. The model displays as shown in Figure 4–56.

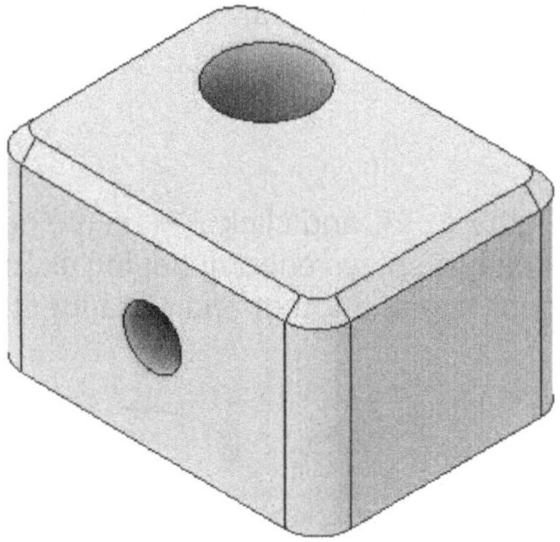

Figure 4–56

4. Save the model and close the window.

End of practice

Practice 4b
Create a Coaxial Hole

Practice Objectives

- Create a coaxial hole based on specific criteria.
- Make modifications and redefine the type of hole to achieve a required result.

In this practice, you will add a coaxial hole to the cylinder. The resulting model displays as shown in Figure 4–57.

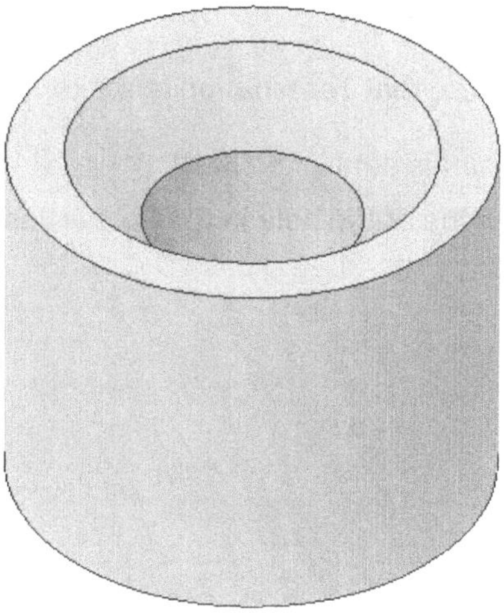

Figure 4–57

Task 1: Open a part file and create a concentric hole.

1. Open **cylinder_1.ipt**.
2. Right-click in the graphics window, and select **Hole**.

3. Complete the following in the Properties panel or graphics window (as shown in Figure 4–58). A preview of the hole displays in the graphics window as you make selections.
   - Select a location on the top face of the cylinder to place the hole.
   - Hover the cursor over the outside cylindrical face. Once the symbol displays adjacent to the cursor, select the face. This assigns the hole as a concentric hole and centers it on the top face.
   - In the **Type** node, ensure that *Hole* is set to (Simple) and that *Seat* is set to (None).
   - Enter **7.5** as the diameter of the hole in the Properties panel or in the on-screen entry field.
   - In the **Behavior** node, ensure that *Termination* is set to (Distance), *Direction* is set to (Default), and *Drill Point* is set to (Flat).
   - Enter **13.5** as the depth value of the hole in the Properties panel or in the on-screen entry field.

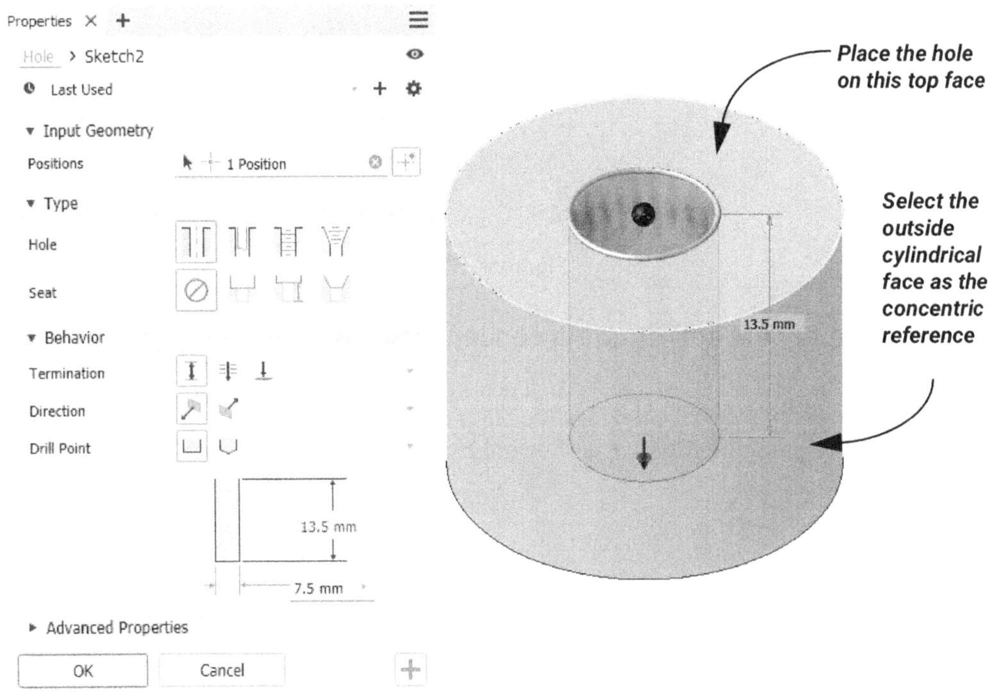

Figure 4–58

4. For Concentric holes, as described above, no additional references are required to define the hole's placement. Although a sketch is created, it does not need to be accessed unless its placement location is to be changed (i.e., linear dimensions are required). Click **OK** to complete the hole.

Task 2: Change the diameter of the coaxial hole.

1. Right-click on the hole in the Model browser and select **Show Dimensions**.
2. Double-click on the diameter dimension in the graphics window.
3. Enter **9.00** in the *Hole Diameter* field in the Hole Dimensions dialog box.
4. Click **OK** to close the dialog box.
5. In the Quick Access Toolbar, click (Local Update). Alternatively, you can double-click on the hole in the Model browser and simply edit the value in the Properties panel. Using this technique you do not have to update the model because it is automatically regenerated when you click **OK**.The updated model displays as shown in Figure 4–59.

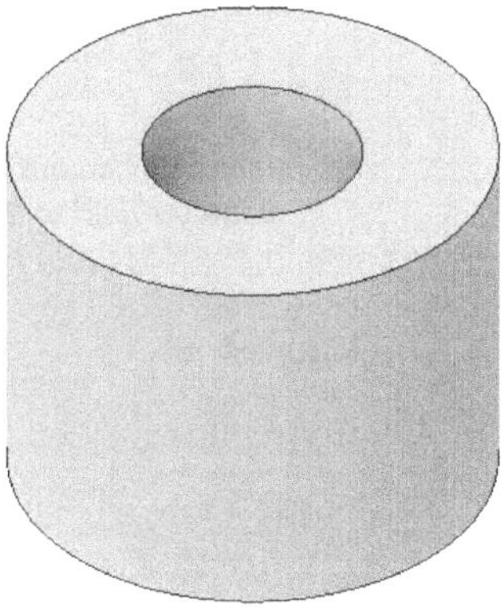

Figure 4–59

Task 3: Redefine the type of hole.

1. Right-click on the hole in the Model browser and select **Edit Feature**, or select any surface on the hole and click . The Properties panel opens.
2. In the **Type** node, set (Countersink) as the *Seat* type.

3. Activate the countersink diameter field (as shown in Figure 4–60) and enter **15.25** as the diameter of the hole.

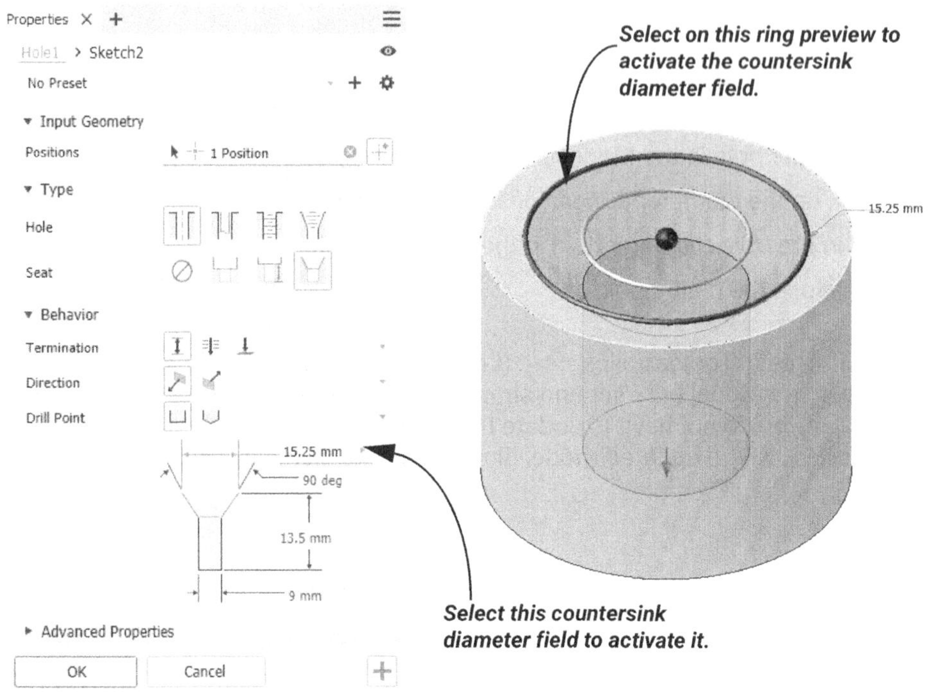

Figure 4–60

4. Click **OK** to complete the feature. The model displays as shown in Figure 4–61.

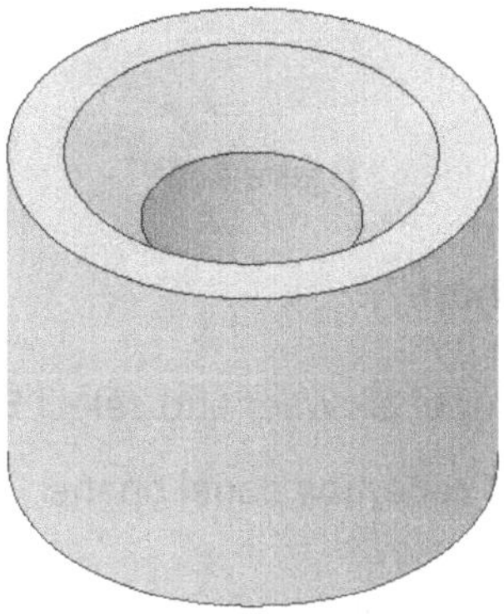

Figure 4–61

5. Save the model and close the window.

End of practice

Practice 4c
(Optional) Add Pick and Place Features

Practice Objective

- Create appropriate hole, chamfer, and fillet features to create the required geometry.

In this practice, you will continue to practice placing pick and place features on the model. The completed model displays as shown in Figure 4–62. Minimal instruction is provided for this practice.

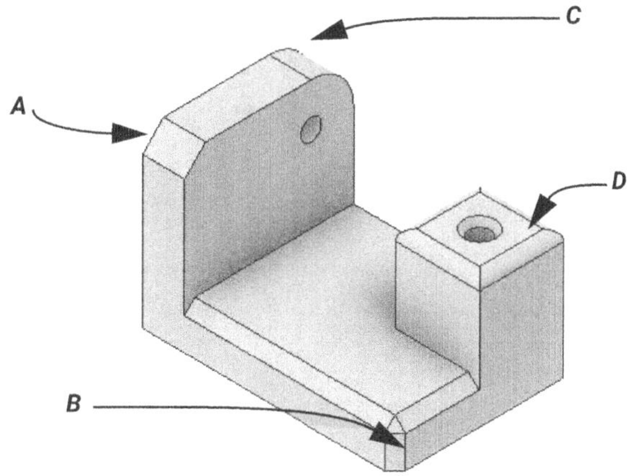

Figure 4–62

Task 1: Open a part and add features.

1. Open **placed_features.ipt**.
2. Add a **.5** chamfer to edge **A** and a **.25** chamfer to the three edges meeting at corner **B**.
3. Add a **1.0** constant radius fillet at edge **C**.
4. Create a **.5 dia.** hole through the part, concentric to fillet **C**.
5. Add a through all hole with a **.5** diameter and a **.75** countersink in the center of the surface **D** that is 2in by 2in.
6. Fillet the loop on surface **D**. Use a radius of **0.25**.
7. Save the model and close the window.

End of practice

Chapter Review Questions

1. Which chamfer type requires you to select a reference surface?
   a. Distance
   b. Distance and Angle
   c. Two Distances

2. In the fillet Tool palette, shown in Figure 4–63, which option enables you to fillet all of the edges of a feature?

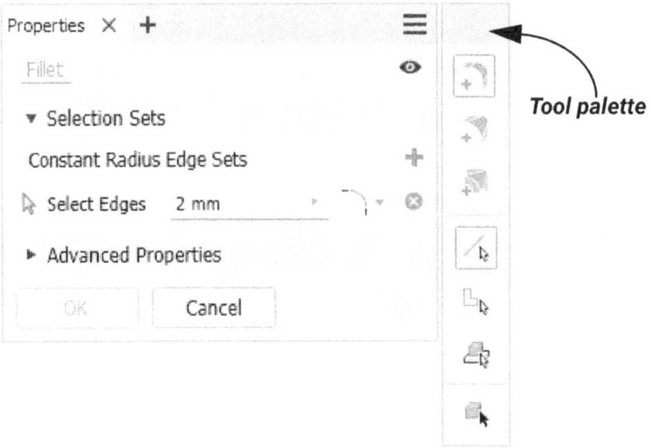

Figure 4–63

a. 

b. 

c. 

3. Chamfer features always remove material.
   a. True
   b. False

4. Fillet features can add or remove material.

a. True

b. False

5. Which keys on the keyboard can be used to clear the edges selected for a fillet or chamfer feature? (Select all that apply.)

a. <Tab>

b. <Ctrl>

c. <Shift>

d. <Alt>

6. Fillets on multiple edges can be controlled by one dimension.

a. True

b. False

7. How many separate Fillet features are listed in the Model browser if you click **OK** to create Fillet2, shown in the Properties panel in Figure 4–64?

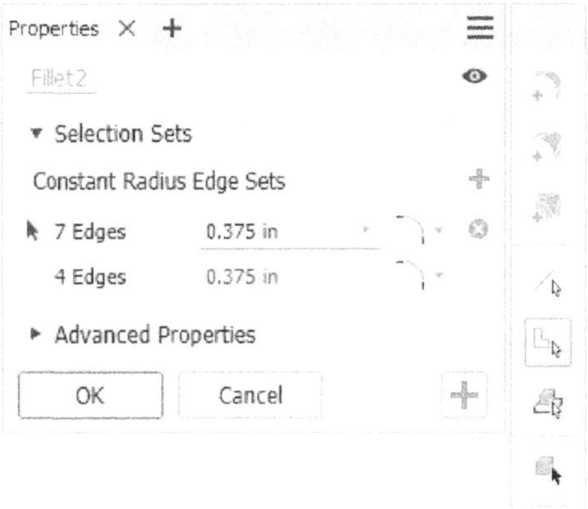

Figure 4–64

a. 1

b. 2

c. 4

d. 11

8. When defining the location reference for a concentric hole, which of the following can be selected?
    a. Planar Face
    b. Cylindrical Face

9. How can you modify an existing placed feature, such as a fillet or chamfer?
    a. Return to the sketch mode and change the sketch profile.
    b. Double-click on the feature in the model or in the Model browser.
    c. Select the same tool used to create the feature to edit it.

10. Which option do you select to change the reference edges for a chamfer?
    a. Show Dimensions
    b. Edit Feature
    c. Edit Sketch
    d. Suppress Features

Command Summary

Button	Command	Location
	**Chamfer (feature)**	• **Ribbon:** *3D Model* tab>Modify panel • **Heads-up Display:** In the graphics window with an entity selected
	**Face Fillet**	• **Ribbon:** *3D Model* tab>Modify panel>expanded Fillet command
	**Fillet**	• **Ribbon:** *3D Model* tab>Modify panel • **Context Menu:** In the graphics window • **Heads-up Display:** In the graphics window with an entity selected
	**Full Round Fillet**	• **Ribbon:** *3D Model* tab>Modify panel>expanded Fillet command
	**Hole**	• **Ribbon:** *3D Model* tab>Modify panel • **Context Menu:** In the graphics window

Chapter 5

Feature Duplication Tools

Incorporating the use of duplication techniques when creating similar geometry enables you to efficiently create models.

Learning Objectives

- Create a rectangular pattern of features that translate along a first and second direction.
- Create a circular pattern of features that rotate about a selected axis.
- Edit Pattern features to make changes to the original geometry.
- Delete Pattern features from a model.

5.1 Rectangular Feature Patterns

You can create multiple copies of parts or features on a part by creating a pattern. An example of a rectangular feature pattern is shown in Figure 5–1.

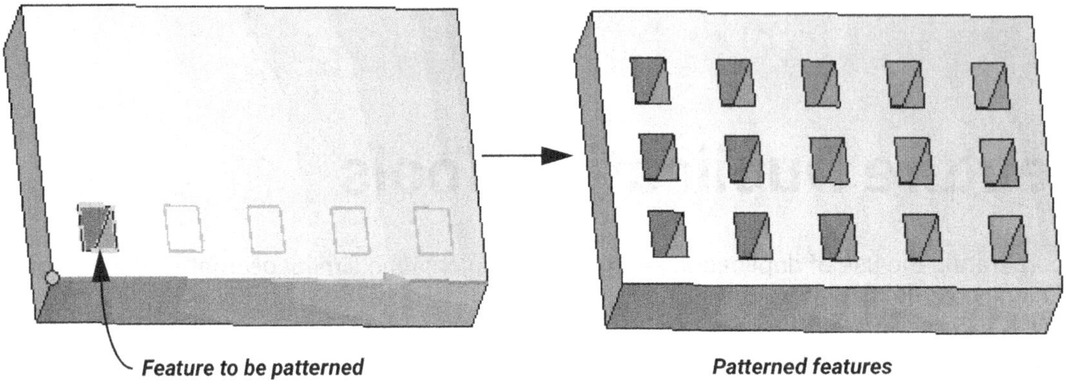

Figure 5–1

Use the following general steps to create a rectangular pattern of features on a part:

1. Start the creation of the pattern.
2. Define the object(s) to pattern.
3. Define the pattern in the first direction.
4. Define the pattern in the second direction, as required.
5. Define additional pattern options, as required.
6. Complete the pattern.

Step 1 - Start the creation of the pattern.

In the *3D Model* tab>Pattern panel, click (Rectangular Pattern). The Rectangular Pattern dialog box opens as shown in Figure 5–2.

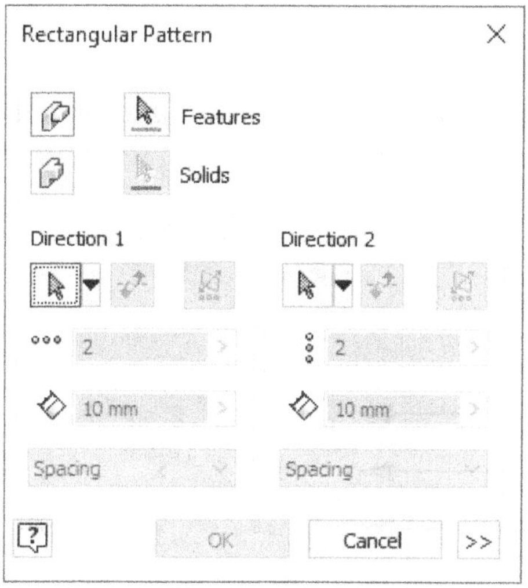

Figure 5–2

Step 2 - Define the object(s) to pattern.

To select the object(s) to pattern, use the options at the top of the dialog box to determine the object type to be patterned:

- Click (Pattern individual features) to create a pattern of individually selected features. This is the default option.
- Click (Pattern a solid) to pattern the entire solid model.

Once the object type is active, select the appropriate feature(s) or the solid model to pattern. Consider the following:

- Work and surface features can also be included in a pattern.
- Dependent features are not automatically patterned if their parent is selected.
- Dependent features cannot be patterned themselves unless the parent feature is selected.

Step 3 - Define the pattern in the first direction.

To define the first pattern path direction, click [icon] in the *Direction 1* area (as shown in Figure 5–3) and select a sketch entity, a part edge, or work a work plane or axis to define the direction. You can also conveniently select an axis using the [icon] drop-down list as an alternative to selecting from the Model browser. The path does not have to be linear and it can be open or closed. Define the remaining options in the Direction 1 area to define the pattern:

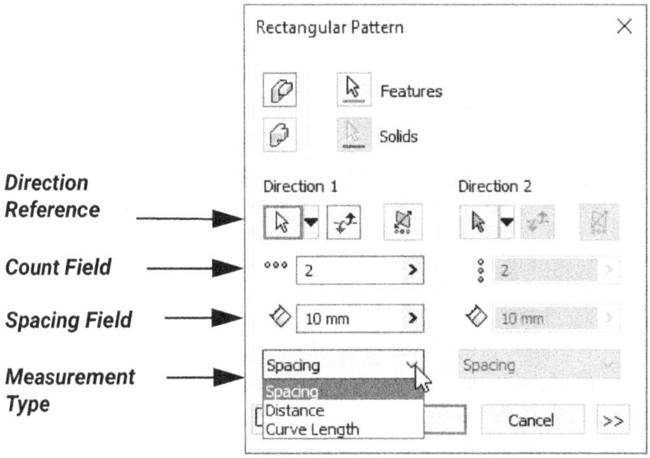

Figure 5–3

Enter the number of occurrences (including the selected geometry) in the ◦◦◦ *(Count)* field, as shown in Figure 5–3.

The distance between each occurrence is defined in the [icon] *(Spacing)* field. How the value is applied to the model depends on the measurement type that is used in the drop-down list shown in Figure 5–3.

- Use **Spacing** to set the entered spacing value as the distance between individual occurrences, as shown in Figure 5–4.

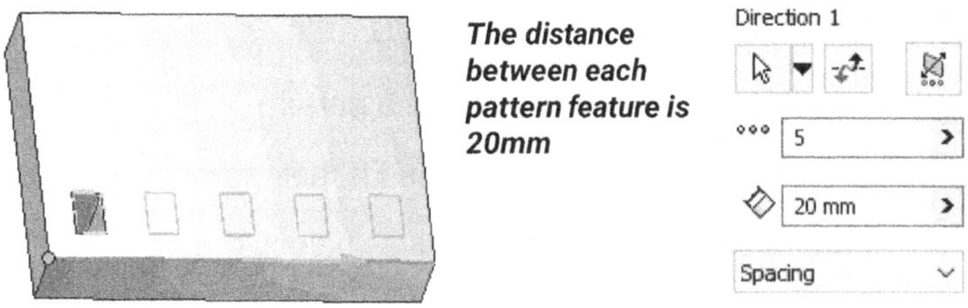

Figure 5–4

- Use **Distance** to set the entered spacing value as the total distance between the first and last occurrence, as shown in Figure 5–5.

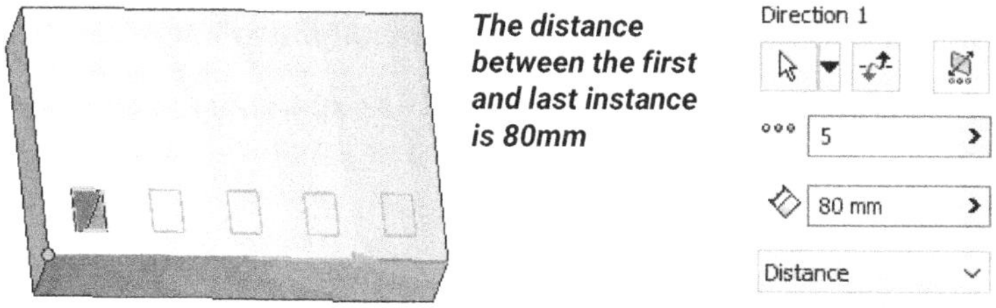

Figure 5–5

- Use **Curve Length** to set the length of the pattern equal to that of a selected curve (e.g. line), as shown in Figure 5–6. If this option is used the *Spacing* field is not available. The number of occurrences is equally spaced along the curve.

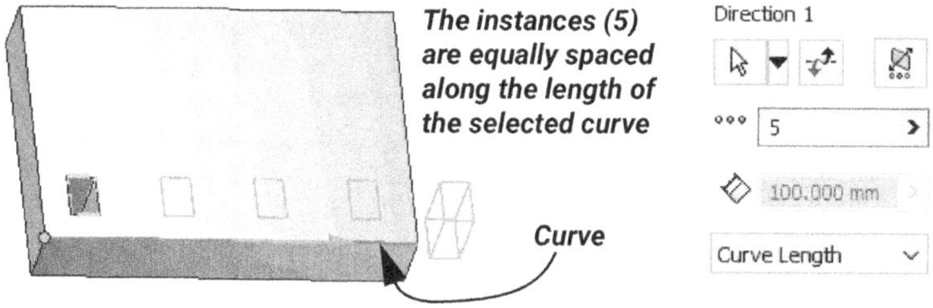

Figure 5–6

Step 4 - Define the pattern in the second direction, as required.

To define the second pattern path, click  in the *Direction 2* area and select a different direction reference, as shown in Figure 5–7. The second direction does not need to be perpendicular to the first. Similar to the *Direction 1* area, set the number of occurrences, spacing, and measurement type to define how the pattern is be created in the second direction.

Figure 5–7

Step 5 - Define additional pattern options, as required.

Consider the use of the *Direction*, *Compute*, and *Orientation* areas in the expanded dialog box (>>) to refine how the feature pattern is generated. The expanded dialog box is shown in Figure 5–8.

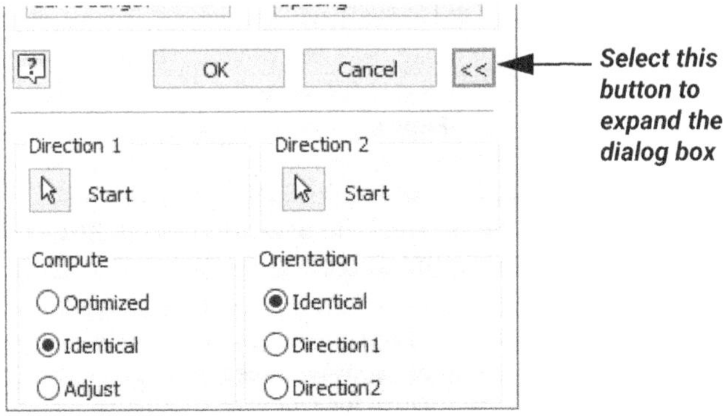

Figure 5–8

- The Start references in the *Direction 1* and *Direction 2* areas enable you to assign a specific point on the model as the start point for the first occurrence. This can be established independently in both directions, if required. For best patterning results, it is recommended to place the first occurrence on or relative to the start point of the path.
- The *Compute* area contains options to control how the pattered geometry is calculated. The three options are described as follows:

Optimized	Optimized patterns are the fastest and also the most restrictive. Optimized patterns have the following restrictions: • Features cannot lie on different surfaces. • Features cannot break edges of the part. • Features cannot intersect with each other.
Identical	Identical patterns create identically patterned features. This is the default pattern option. Identical patterns generate the following types of occurrences: • Features that can lie on different surfaces. • Features that can break the edge of the part. • Features that can intersect with each other. • Feature depth of all occurrences is the same value as the pattern leader (regardless of its depth option).
Adjust	Adjusted patterns create occurrences similar to the Identical pattern type while also using feature depth settings. Each occurrence is patterned individually, which increases the computation time for the pattern.

The patterned features in Figure 5–9 show the differences between the **Identical** and **Adjust** compute options. An **Optimized** pattern is explicitly recommended when the pattern results in a large number of occurrences and is used to optimize performance.

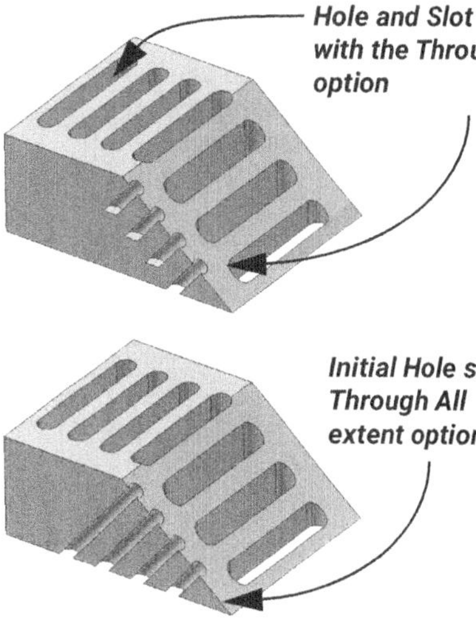

Figure 5–9

- The *Orientation* area contains options to define how the patterned features are oriented relative to the first selected feature being patterned. The options are as follows:

Identical	Enables you to orient the patterned occurrences such that they are oriented in the same way as the first feature selected for patterning.
Direction1/ Direction2	Enables you to orient the patterned occurrences such that they are the oriented based on either the Direction1 or Direction2 reference paths. Orientation of the occurrences is such that the first feature that was selected for patterning maintains its orientation to the 2D tangent vector of the Direction1 or Direction2 reference path throughout the pattern.

The pattern shown in Figure 5–10 was created by assigning 23 occurrences in *Direction 1* and uses the **Curve Length** measurement type. The **Identical** orientation option was used, which maintains the orientation in the same way as the first occurrence relative as it travels along the curve. The resulting pattern does not produce the required results.

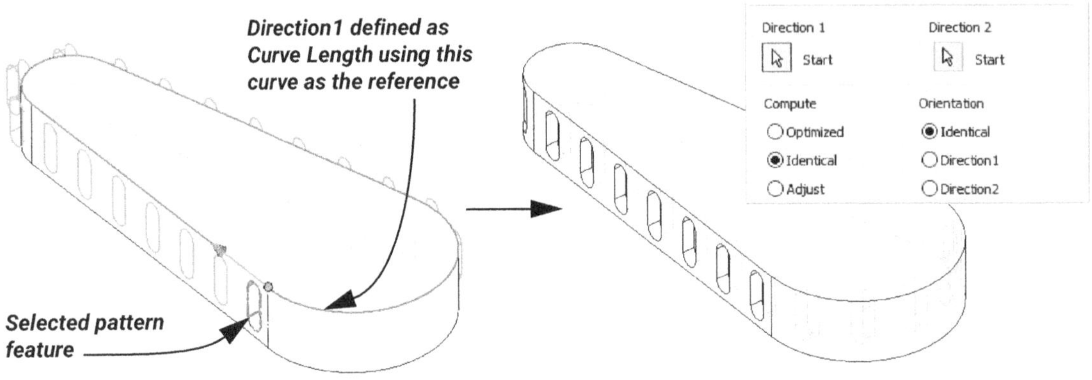

Figure 5–10

The previous pattern was edited. A start reference for *Direction 1* was defined (as shown in Figure 5–11) and the **Direction1** Orientation option was set. These edits produced the required results.

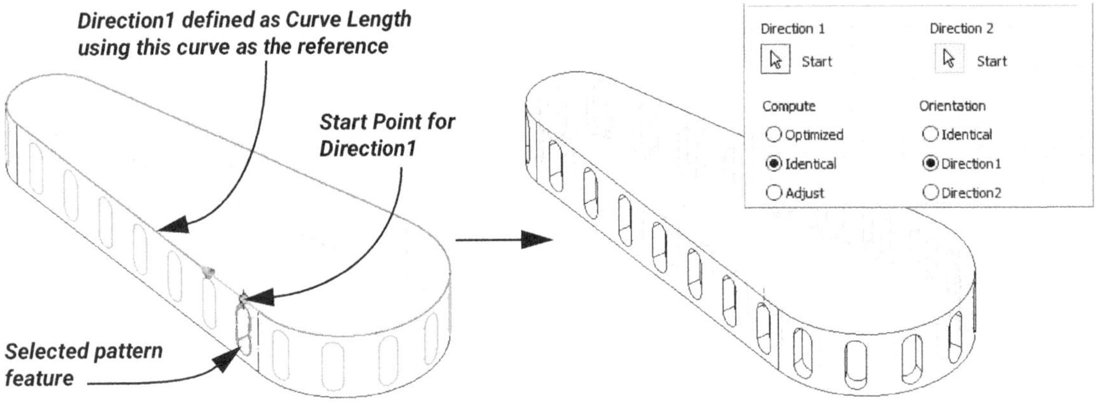

Figure 5–11

Step 6 - Complete the pattern.

Click **OK** to complete the pattern. Alternatively, you can right-click and select **OK (Enter)**.

5.2 Circular Feature Patterns

You can create multiple copies of parts or features on a part by creating a pattern. An example of a circular pattern of holes is shown in Figure 5–12.

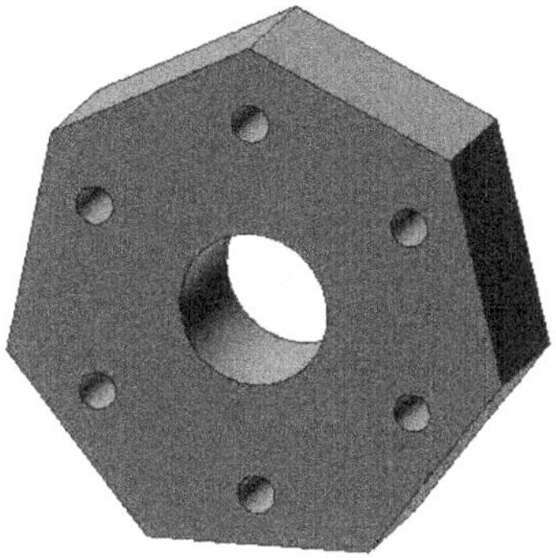

Figure 5–12

Use the following general steps to create a circular pattern:

1. Start the creation of the pattern.
2. Define the object(s) to pattern.
3. Define the rotation axis.
4. Define the pattern placement.
5. Define the pattern orientation.
6. Define additional pattern options, as required.
7. Complete the pattern.

Step 1 - Start the creation of the pattern.

In the *3D Model* tab>Pattern panel, click (Circular Pattern). The Circular Pattern dialog box opens as shown in Figure 5–13.

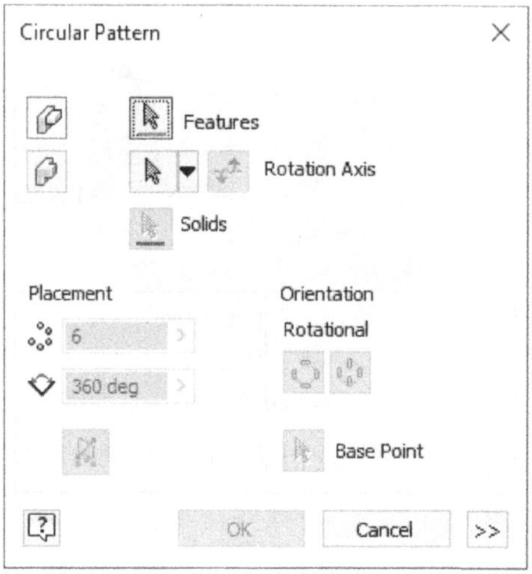

Figure 5–13

Step 2 - Define the object(s) to pattern.

Similar to a Rectangular pattern, select one of the object types to be patterned ((Pattern individual features) or (Pattern a solid)) and select the object(s) in the Model browser or in the graphics window. Refer to the Rectangular Pattern topic for more information on selecting features for patterning.

Step 3 - Define the rotation axis.

To define the axis about which to create the pattern, click (Rotation Axis) in the Circular Pattern dialog box and select the reference. You can select a cylindrical or conical face, a work axis, or an edge for the pattern axis. You can also conveniently select an axis using the drop-down list as an alternative to selecting from the Model browser. If required, click to reverse the direction of the pattern around the assigned axis of rotation.

Step 4 - Define the pattern placement.

Once objects are selected for patterning and the axis is defined, you can enter values in the *Placement* area to define the pattern.

- Enter the number of occurrences (including the selected geometry) in the (*Count*) field, as shown in Figure 5–14.
- Enter the angle between the first and last occurrence in the (*Angle*) field, as shown in Figure 5–14.

In the example shown in Figure 5–14, a hole is being patterned radially about the larger hole's axis. The values being used are shown in the Circular Pattern dialog box.

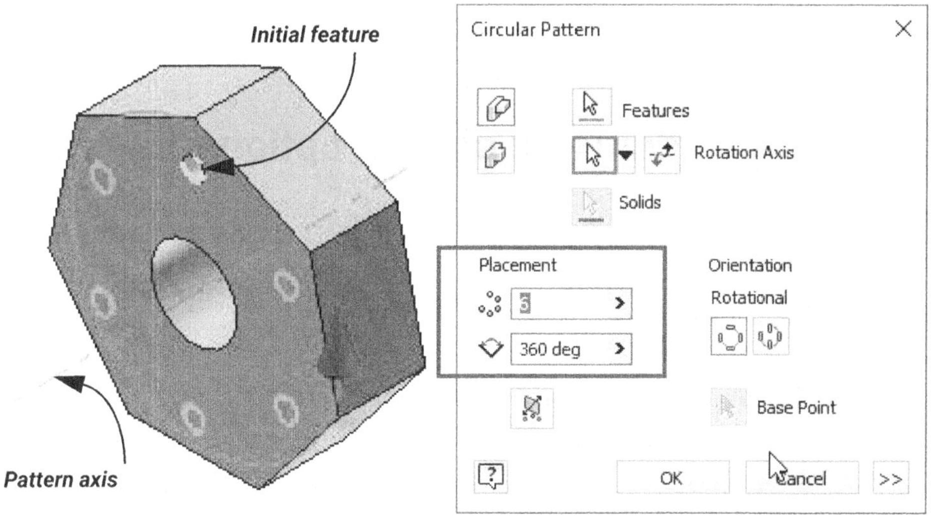

Figure 5–14

Step 5 - Define the pattern orientation.

In the *Orientation* area of the Circular Pattern dialog box, select the required pattern orientation.

- Select (Rotational) to ensure that the patterned feature's orientation is rotated, as it extends through the pattern angle.
- Select (Fixed) to ensure that the patterned feature's orientation remains the same as the original feature, as it extends through the pattern angle. When defining a **Fixed** orientation you can change the default Base Point, if required.

Figure 5–15 shows examples of both orientation options that are available.

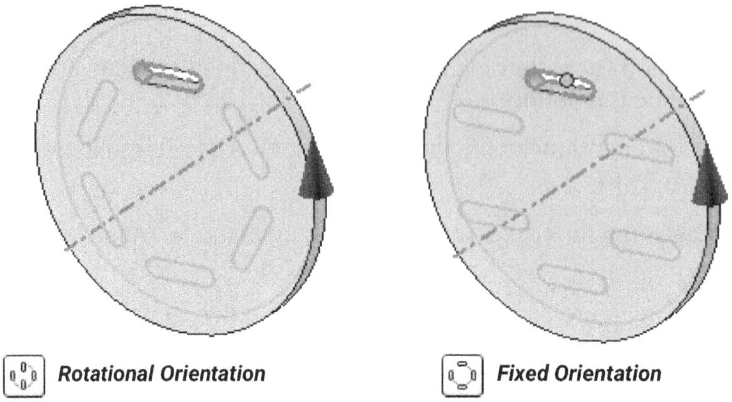

Figure 5–15

Step 6 - Define additional pattern options, as required.

Consider the use of the *Creation Method* and *Positioning Method* areas in the expanded dialog box (>>) to refine how the feature pattern is generated. The expanded dialog box is shown in Figure 5–16.

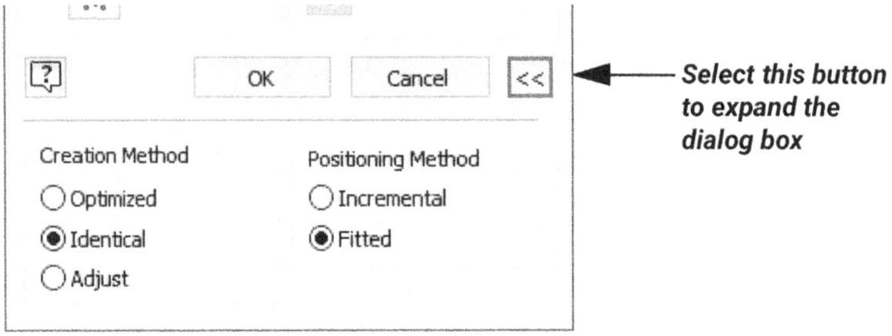

Figure 5–16

- The *Creation Method* area contains options to control how the pattered geometry is calculated. The three options are the same as those in the *Compute* area for rectangular patterns. Refer to their description in the Rectangular pattern topic for more information. Figure 5–17 illustrates the differences between the **Identical** and **Adjust** creation methods for a circular pattern.

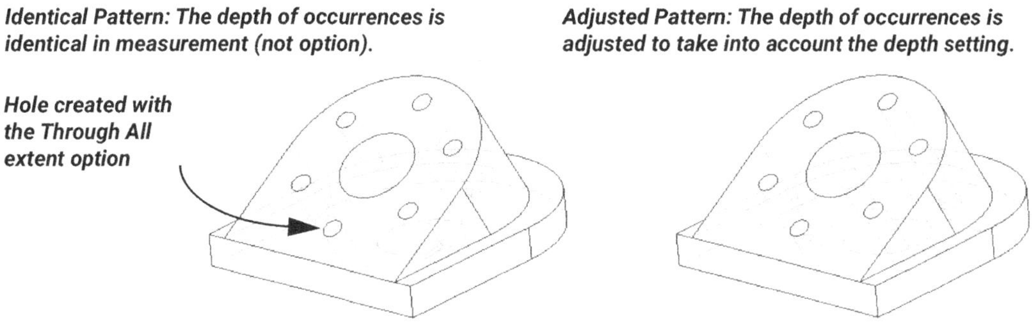

Figure 5–17

- The *Positioning Method* area enables you to position the pattered feature in the model. The options are as follows:

Incremental	Enables you to use the Angle value to incrementally define the spacing between the patterned features. For example, an incremental pattern of 3 occurrences at 90 degrees. 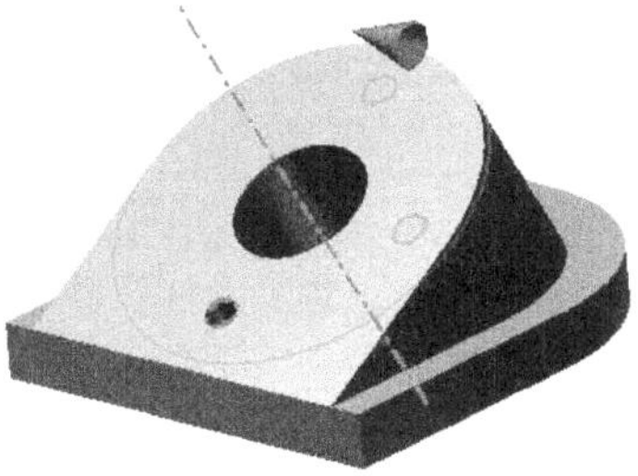
Fitted	Enables you to use the Angle value to define the angular range of pattern. The number of occurrences are fit into this value. For example, a fitted pattern of 3 occurrences at 90 degrees. 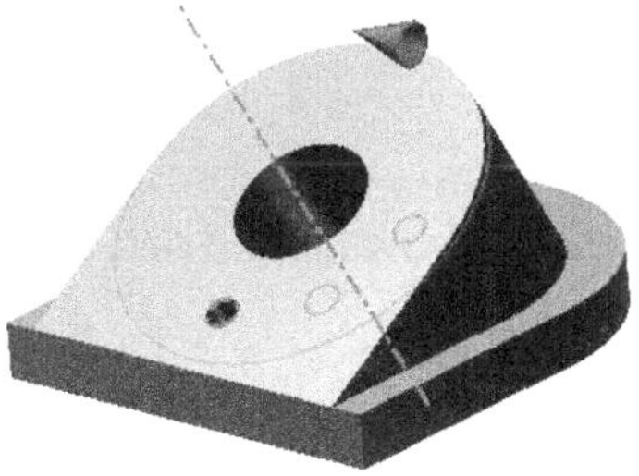

Step 7 - Complete the pattern.

Click **OK** to complete the pattern. Alternatively, you can right-click and select **OK (Enter)**.

5.3 Manipulating Patterns

Suppress Patterns

To suppress a pattern, right-click on the pattern in the Model browser and select **Suppress Features**. To suppress individual pattern features, expand the pattern feature in the Model browser, right-click on the occurrence you want to suppress, and select **Suppress**, as shown in Figure 5–18.

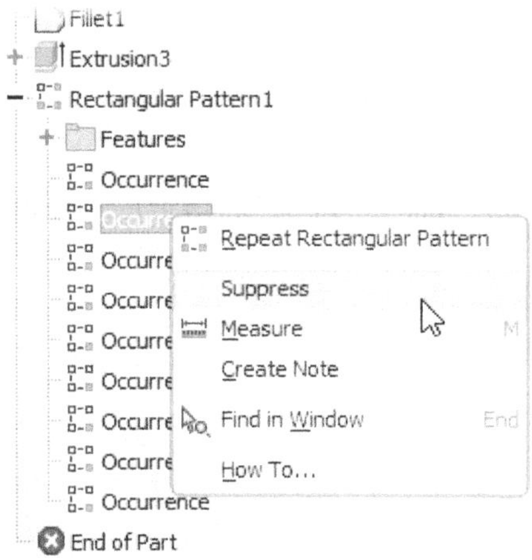

Figure 5–18

- The suppressed occurrence displays in the Model browser with a line across it. To display this occurrence again, right-click on it and select **Suppress** again.
- You cannot suppress the first occurrence (original feature) of the pattern.

Edit Pattern

You can edit patterns and mirrored features at any time by right-clicking on the pattern or mirrored feature in the Model browser and selecting **Edit Feature**.

Delete Patterns

You can delete patterns and mirrored features at any time by right-clicking on the pattern or mirrored feature in the Model browser and selecting **Delete**. All occurrences of the pattern or mirrored feature are deleted except for the original occurrence.

Practice 5a
Pattern Features

Practice Objectives

- Create a rectangular pattern of features that translate along a single direction.
- Create a circular pattern of features that rotate about a selected axis.
- Create a rectangular pattern driven by a curve.

In this practice, you will pattern ribs and holes using the pattern tools to create model geometry, as shown in Figure 5–19.

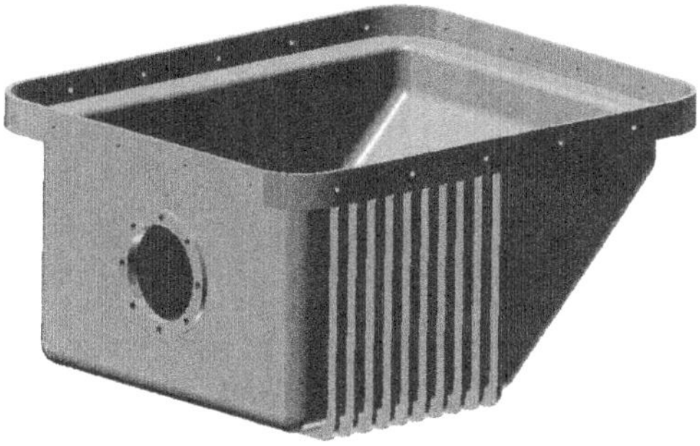

Figure 5–19

Task 1: Open a part file.

1. Open **Air-Box.ipt**. The model displays as shown in Figure 5–20.

Figure 5–20

Task 2: Create a rectangular pattern.

1. In the Pattern panel, click (Rectangular Pattern). The Rectangular Pattern dialog box opens, as shown in Figure 5–21.

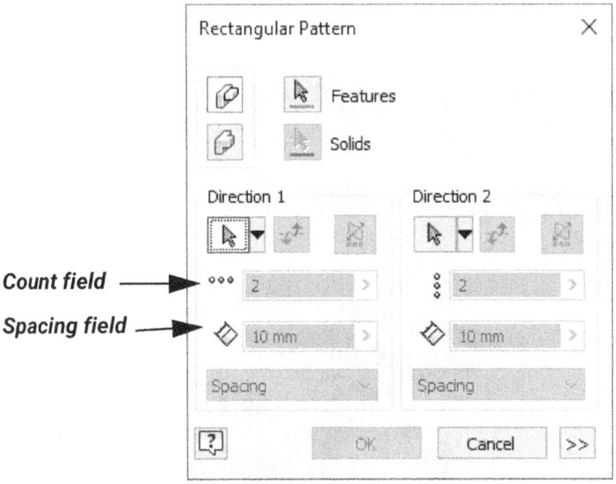

Figure 5–21

2. Verify that (Features) is toggled on. Select **Rib1** and **Fillet4** in the Model browser.

3. Click (Direction 1) and select the **YZ Plane** in the Model browser. The pattern previews as shown in Figure 5–22. If required, change the pattern direction by clicking .

   Note: *Alternatively, you could define the direction for the pattern by selecting* ***X Axis*** *in the drop-down list.*

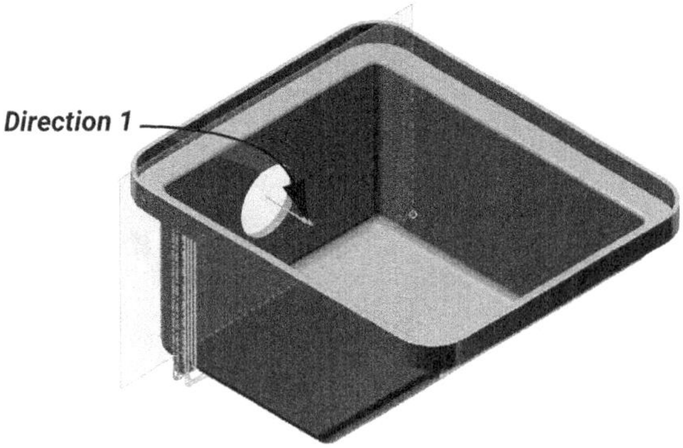

Figure 5–22

4. In the *Direction 1* area, set the (*Count*) field to **10** and the (*Spacing*) field to **110**.
5. Expand the drop-down list below the *Spacing* field and select **Distance**. This equally spaces the 10 occurrences over the 110 length.
6. A second direction is not required to create this pattern. Click **OK** to apply the pattern. The model displays as shown in Figure 5–23.

Figure 5–23

Task 3: Create a circular pattern.

1. In the Pattern panel, click (Circular Pattern). The Circular Pattern dialog box opens, as shown in Figure 5–24.

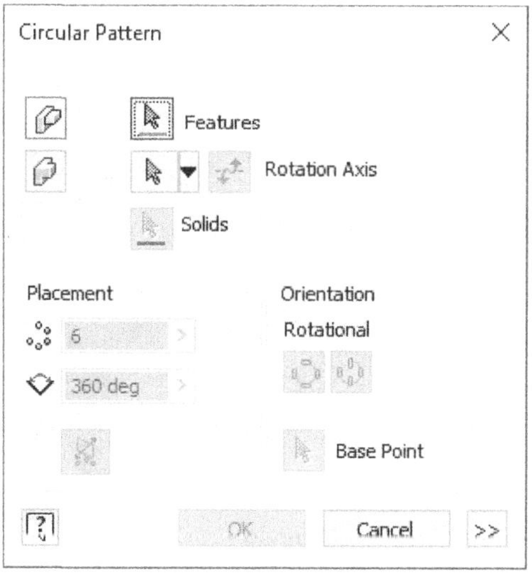

Figure 5–24

2. Verify that (Features) is toggled on. Select the hole shown in Figure 5–25.

3. Click (Rotation Axis) and select the central hole face for the axis, as shown in Figure 5–25.

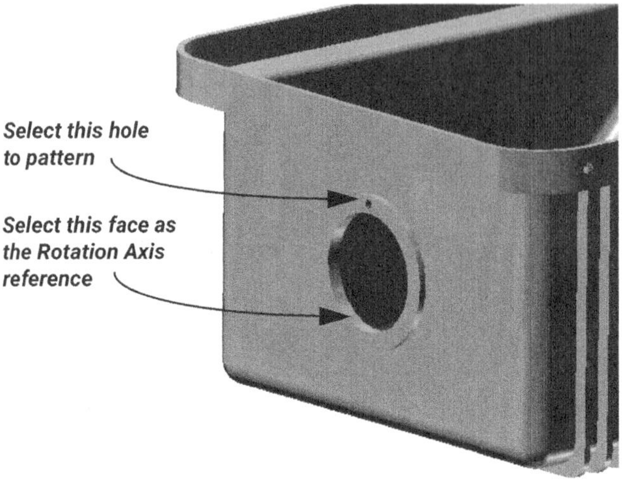

Figure 5–25

4. Enter **8** in the *(Count)* field and accept the default (360deg) in the *(Angle)* field.
5. Click **OK**. The model displays as shown in Figure 5–26.

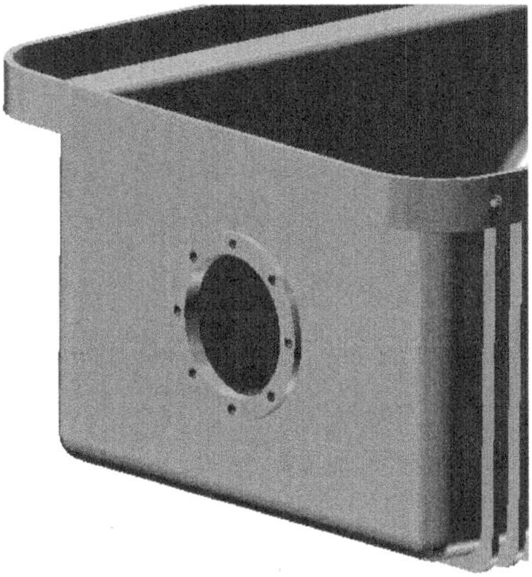

Figure 5–26

Task 4: Create a second rectangular pattern driven by a curve.

In this task, you will create a rectangular pattern along the outside lip of the model, as shown in Figure 5–27. To accomplish this pattern a point and hole have been created for you, but you will create a curve that will be used to drive the path of the patterned hole.

Figure 5–27

1. Create a sketch and select the top edge of the model as the sketch plane, as shown in Figure 5–28. Project the outside edges that intersect this plane onto the sketch plane. Finish the sketch.

Figure 5–28

2. In the Pattern panel, click (Rectangular Pattern). The Rectangular Pattern dialog box opens.

3. Verify that (Features) is toggled on. Select the hole shown in Figure 5–29.

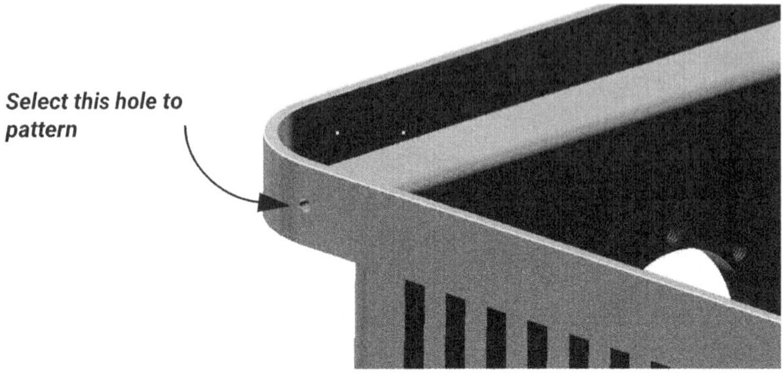

Figure 5–29

4. Click (Direction 1) and select the outer curve that was created in the sketch. Ensure that the entire curve around the model is selected, not just a single entity.
5. In the *Direction 1* area, set the ∘∘∘ *(Count)* field to **20**. The preview of the holes reveal an incorrect pattern.
6. For *Direction 1,* expand the Spacing drop-down list and select **Curve Length**. The preview of the holes still reveals an incorrect pattern. Customization of the additional options is required.
7. Click >> at the bottom of the dialog box to expand it.
8. In the *Direction 1* area, click (Start).

   Note: *It is recommended that you place the first occurrence on the start point of the path, as was done.*

9. Select the vertex on the sketched curve, as shown in Figure 5–30, as the reference for the Start Direction. This sets the start point for the first patterned occurrence.

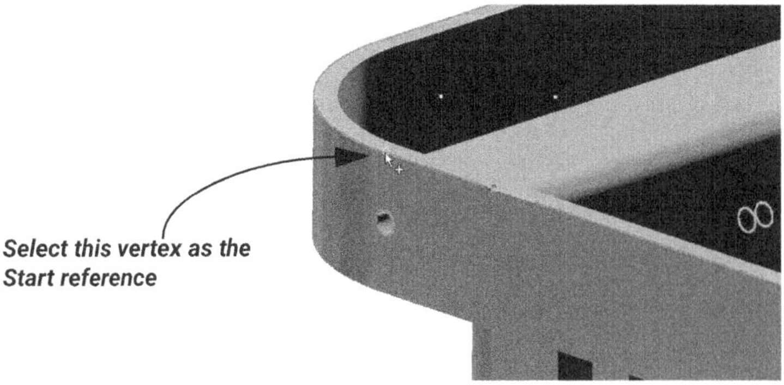

Figure 5–30

10. In the *Orientation* area, select **Direction1** to ensure that the orientation of the patterned holes follows the tangent vector of the curve that was selected as the Direction1 reference.
11. Click **OK** to complete the pattern. The model displays as shown in Figure 5–31.

Figure 5–31

12. Save the model and close the window.

End of practice

Chapter Review Questions

1. The direction references selected to create a rectangular feature pattern must be linear.

a. True

b. False

2. The model shown in Figure 5–32 has a pattern of extruded cuts created in one direction. What is the number of pattern occurrences that are defined in the dialog box?

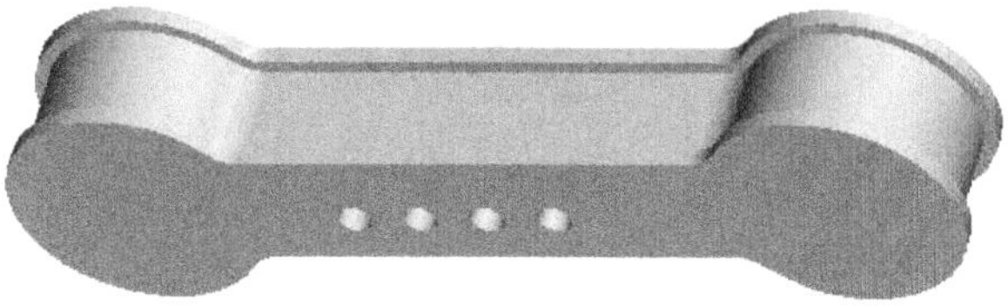

Figure 5–32

a. 1

b. 2

c. 3

d. 4

3. Which entities can be used as the rotation axis for a circular pattern? (Select all that apply.)

a. Work plane

b. Edge

c. Work axis

d. Cylindrical face

4. What should you do if the preview of your rectangular pattern is in the wrong direction along a selected path? (Select all that apply.)

a. Select a new direction reference that is in the correct direction.

b. Click the **Flip** direction icon in the Rectangular Pattern dialog box to change the direction.

c. Enter a negative value as the *Spacing* value.

d. Expand the additional options at the bottom of the dialog box and change the Compute method.

5. Which of the following statements is true for removing specific occurrences from within a pattern?

   a. You can suppress the first occurrence of the pattern (original).

   b. You can suppress all but the first occurrence of the pattern.

   c. You can select individual occurrences in the pattern for deletion.

   d. You can use the **Delete** command to delete the first occurrence in the model.

6. Which of the following are valid characteristics of patterned features when using an Identical Compute method, as shown in Figure 5–33? (Select all that apply.)

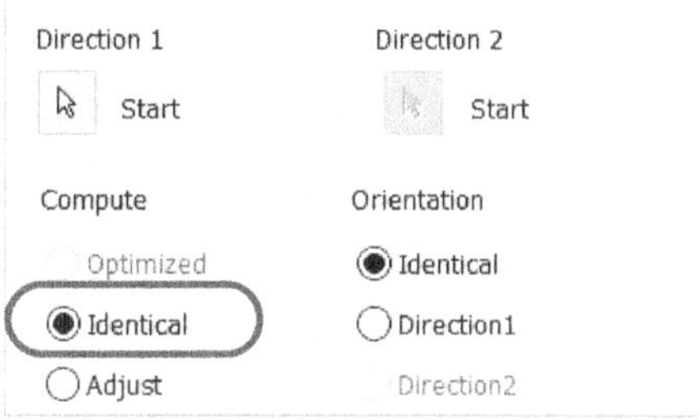

Figure 5–33

   a. The created features cannot lie on different surfaces.

   b. The created features can break edges of the part.

   c. The created features cannot intersect with each other.

   d. Feature depth of all occurrences is the same value as the pattern leader (regardless of the depth option set for the feature).

Command Summary

Button	Command	Location
	**Circular Pattern (feature)**	• **Ribbon:** *3D Model* tab>Pattern panel
N/A	**Delete (entire pattern)**	• **Context Menu**: In Model browser
	**Rectangular Pattern (feature)**	• **Ribbon:** *3D Model* tab>Pattern panel
N/A	**Suppress Feature (pattern)**	• **Context Menu:** In Model browser

Chapter 6

Model and Display Manipulation

Learning how to manipulate and control existing and new features in your model provides flexibility in designing and making changes to your models. Tools such as section and design views provide additional viewing tools to review the model.

Learning Objectives

- Change the order of features in the Model browser.
- Use the End of Part marker to change the location in which new features are added to a model.
- Remove a feature temporarily from being included in the model geometry.
- Create quarter, half, and three-quarter section views in a model to help visualize the interior of a 3D model.
- Create and activate custom design views that store display settings for a model.

6.1 Reordering Features

A model is generated in the order in which the features display in the Model browser. In certain situations, the resulting geometry varies, depending on the feature creation order. To achieve the required geometry, you can reorder the features to change the way the part is constructed. To reorder a feature, select it in the Model browser and drag it below or above its current position. You cannot drag a feature above a feature that it references or below a feature that references it.

Consider the following example shown in Figure 6–1. Shell and fillet features are to be added to the model. Due to the order in which the existing features were initially added, the resulting geometry after the addition of the shell is not wanted. Reordering the hole after the shell and adding the fillet before the shell results in the completed part shown in Figure 6–1.

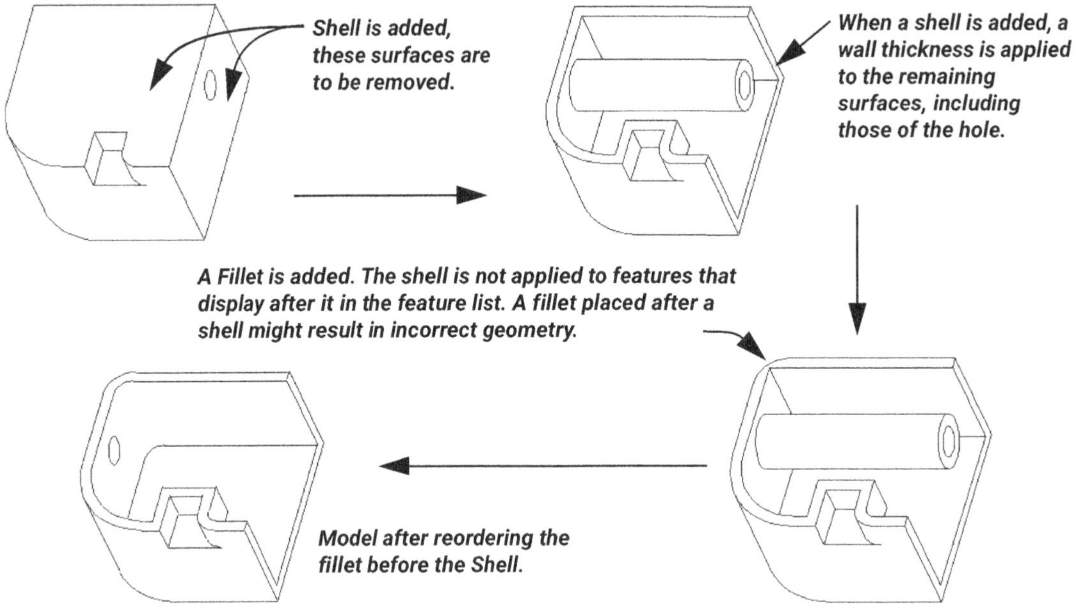

Figure 6–1

6.2 Inserting Features

By default, when features are added to the model, they are added to the end of the feature list.

To insert features at any earlier point, you must move the End of Part marker from the bottom of the Model browser to the location at which you want to insert a feature. You can use this technique when you need to create a feature earlier in the design process. Use any of the following techniques to move the End of Part marker:

- Right-click a feature in the Model browser and select **Move EOP Marker**. The End of Part is placed after the feature.
- Select and drag the End of Part marker in the Model browser to the location at which you want to insert a feature.

Figure 6–2 shows an example of a model and its Model browser before (left-hand side) and after (right-hand side) moving the End of Part marker. Once moved, all of the features below it are temporarily removed from the model and a new feature can be added.

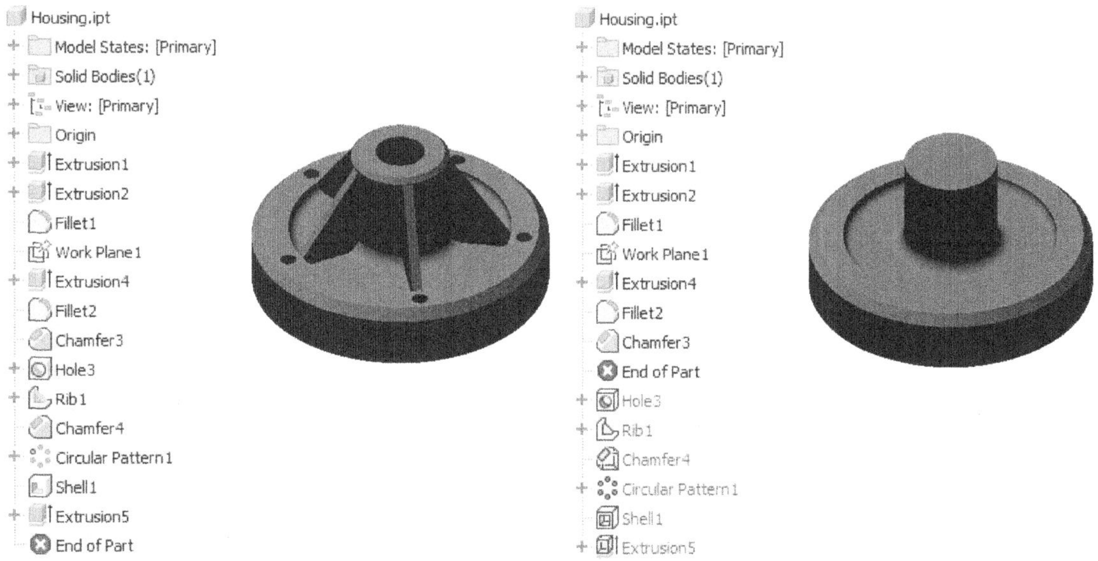

Figure 6–2

To return the End of Part marker to the bottom of the Model browser use one of the following techniques:

- Right-click End of Part and select **Move EOP to End**.
- Drag the End of Part to the bottom of the Model browser.

6.3 Suppressing Features

As you work on a complex part, you might find it difficult to identify or select features in the graphics window. You can simplify the appearance of a model by suppressing a feature to make it temporarily invisible. To suppress a feature, right-click on it in the Model browser and select **Suppress Features**, as shown on the left in Figure 6–3. If you suppress a feature, all of its dependent features are also suppressed. Suppressed features and any of its dependent features are displayed in gray and are crossed out in the Model browser, as shown on the right in Figure 6–3.

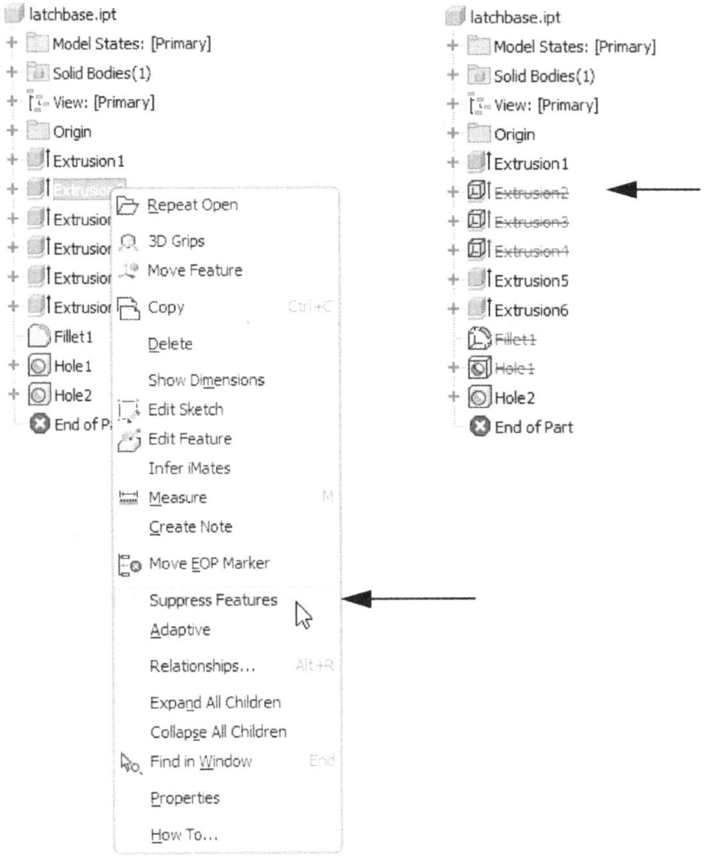

Figure 6–3

> ***Note:*** *You can select features for suppression directly in the graphics window if the* ***Select Features*** *feature priority setting is set.*

To unsuppress a feature, right-click on the feature in the Model browser and select **Unsuppress Features**. The dependent features that were suppressed are also unsuppressed.

Hint: Rule-Based Suppression

Using the Feature Properties dialog box, you can establish rule-based suppression. To access the dialog box, right-click the feature and select **Properties**. In the *Suppress* area of the dialog box, you can set the appropriate situation for suppressing the feature. The suppression options are shown in Figure 6–4.

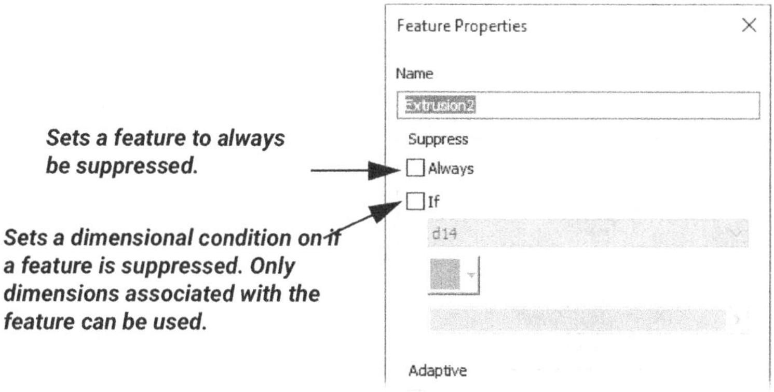

Figure 6–4

If a suppression condition is set, you must unsuppress it to return it to the model. Just unsuppressing the parent geometry does not resume it.

6.4 Sectioning Part Models

Section views help visualize a 3D model by providing a section view of it. There are three types of section views that can be created. Figure 6–5 shows these views and the selected planes required to create them.

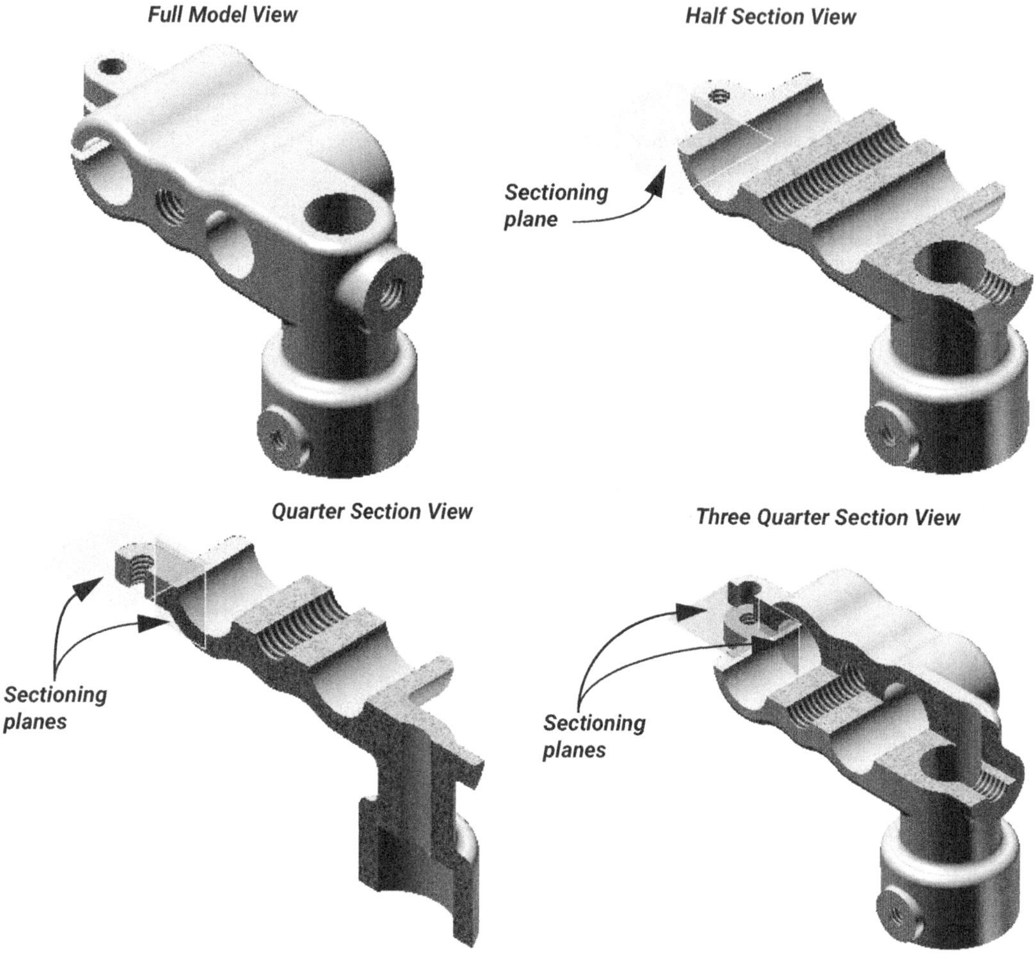

Figure 6–5

How To: Section a Part

1. In the *View* tab>Visibility panel, select the type of section view in the drop-down list, as shown in Figure 6–6.

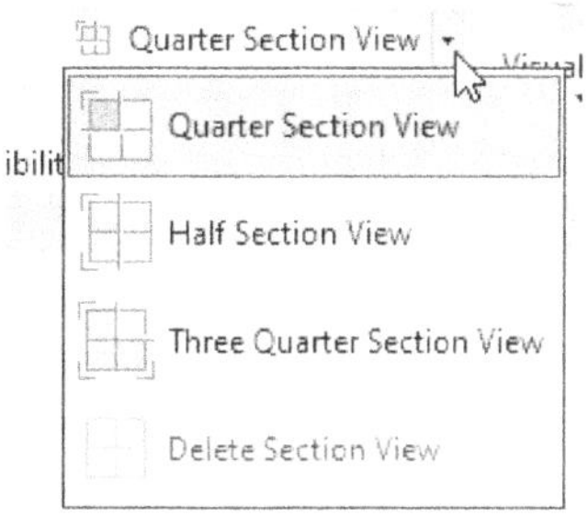

Figure 6–6

2. Select the plane to section about. The mini-toolbar appears in the graphics window as shown in Figure 6–7.

Figure 6–7

3. If required, move the selected plane using one of the following techniques with the  option selected.
   - In the mini-toolbar, enter a value in the offset field.
   - In the graphics window, drag the arrow that appears on the section plane.
   - In the mini-toolbar, use the scroll wheel in the Offset field to offset incrementally. To change the scroll increments when modifying section plane placement, right-click in the graphics window and select **Scroll Step Size**, enter an increment value, and click .

Note: *To rotate the plane, select* 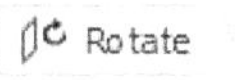 *and enter or drag the rotation handle as needed.*

4. If required, flip the section about the plane by selecting .

5. If creating a quarter or three quarter section view, click to continue or click to combine the section.
6. Select an additional plane to section about. If required, enter an offset value or flip the direction of the new plane using the same techniques as mentioned above. The mini-toolbar appears as shown in Figure 6–8 when a quarter or three quarter section view is being created.

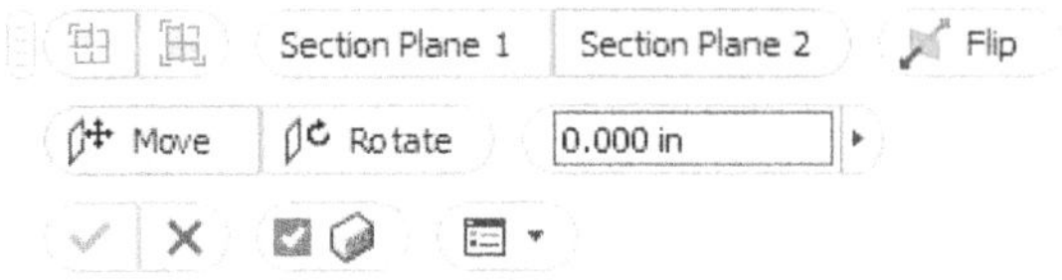

Figure 6–8

7. To further modify the offset from a selected plane, the correct plane must be active. In the mini-toolbar select Section Plane 1 or Section Plane 2, as needed, to switch the active plane and then modify as required.

   Note: *If creating a Quarter Section or a Three Quarter Section View you can toggle between the two. This can be done in the mini-toolbar by selecting (Three Quarter Section View) or (Quarter Section View), as needed.*

8. Right-click and select **OK (Enter)** or click to complete the view.
9. To return to a view of the entire part, select **Delete Section View** in the Section View drop-down list.

Section views are temporary unless used in conjunction with design views. Once you select **Delete Section View**, the created section view is lost and must be recreated if required again. If created in a design view, do not select **Delete Section View** to maintain the section view in the design view. Unless a section view is saved as a Design View, it cannot be redefined and you would need to recreate it to make changes. If stored in a Design View, you can modify the section, by right-clicking its name and selecting **Section View** > **Edit** to make changes to the section or **Section View** >**Suppress** to suppress the section view in the Design View.

6.5 Part Design Views

A representation of the part's display can be saved using a design view. Model configuration settings that you might want to save include: part color, work feature (not origin features) and sketch visibility, camera position, section views, orientation, and zoom level. Any of these settings can be saved using a design view. Additionally, design views can be used when creating drawing views.

How To: Save a Design View

1. Right-click on the **View** node and select **New**, as shown in Figure 6–9. Additional views are created to capture alternate configurations. When a new view is created it is automatically set to be active.

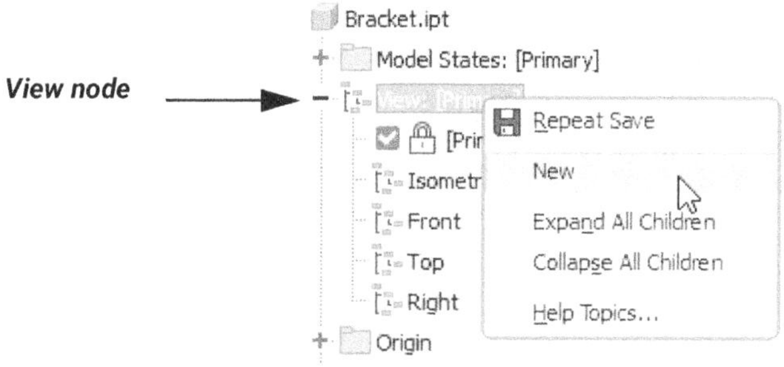

Figure 6–9

Note: As of Autodesk Inventor 2017, models created with a default template contain four additional default design views. For models created prior to 2017, only a single Primary Design View is provided in the default template.

2. Configure the view display (e.g., change the part orientation, set a section view, set the part color, toggle off the visibility of work features or sketches, or change the camera position).
3. Rename the design view. Select the new view, click again (do not double-click) and enter a descriptive name for the view.
4. (Optional) To lock the design view, right-click on the view name in the Model browser and select **Lock**. Locking restricts you or others from making changes to the design view representation.

To display an alternate design view, right-click on its name in the Model browser and select **Activate**. Alternatively, you can double-click on its name.

Practice 6a
Section and Design Views

Practice Objectives

- Create section views using a work plane as the cutting reference.
- Create a design view to capture a model's view display.

In this practice, you will work with a part model and create both section and design views in the model. The model that will be used is shown in Figure 6–10.

Figure 6–10

Task 1: Create design views in a model.

1. Open **Bracket_Display.ipt**.
2. In the Model browser, right-click on the **View** node and select **New**.
3. Expand the **View** node of the Model browser, if it does not automatically expand. A new **View1** design view is created and is set to be active (indicated by the checkmark).

4. Select **View1**, and then select it again to rename it. Enter **Quarter Section View** as its name, as shown in Figure 6–11.

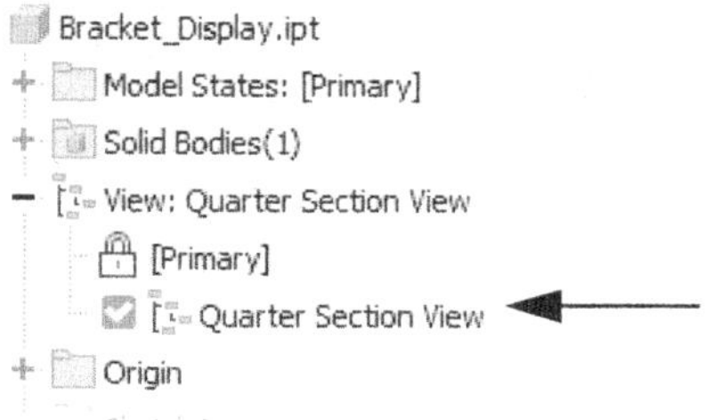

Figure 6–11

5. Select the *View* tab>Visibility panel and expand the drop-down list associated with (Quarter Section View). The command displayed might vary depending on which command was last selected.

6. Click (Half Section View), as shown in Figure 6–12.

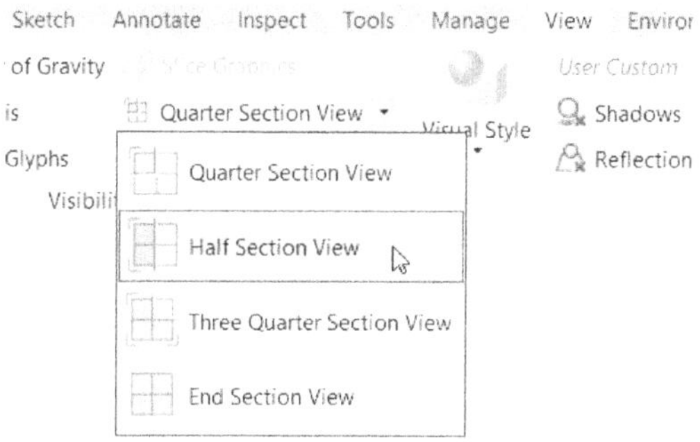

Figure 6–12

7. Select **XY Plane** in the Model browser. In the offset prompt that displays you can enter an offset value to reposition the section plane. For this section, leave the value at 0.00 in. The model displays as shown in Figure 6–13.

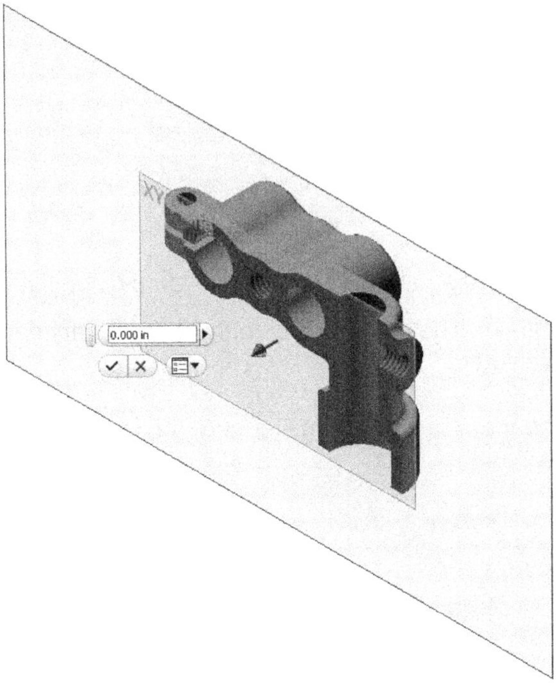

Figure 6–13

8. Right-click anywhere in the graphics window and select **Scroll Step Size**. Accept the default value of .25 in and click .
9. Place the cursor in the *Offset* entry field and scroll the middle mouse button. Note that the sectioning plane moves in .25 in increments to progress you through multiple section views.
10. Alternatively, you can hover the cursor over the offset direction arrow and drag it. The drag uses a smaller increment to produce a more gradual sectioning movement.
11. Click to complete the section view at its current offset value.
12. In the Visibility panel, expand the view types and click (Delete Section View) to delete the section view.
13. In the Visibility panel, click (Quarter Section View).
14. Select **XY Plane** in the Model browser. In the offset prompt that displays, accept the 0.00 in offset and click to continue to the selection of the second plane.

15. Select **XZ Plane** in the Model browser. In the offset prompt that displays, accept the 0.00 in offset. The model displays as shown in Figure 6–14.

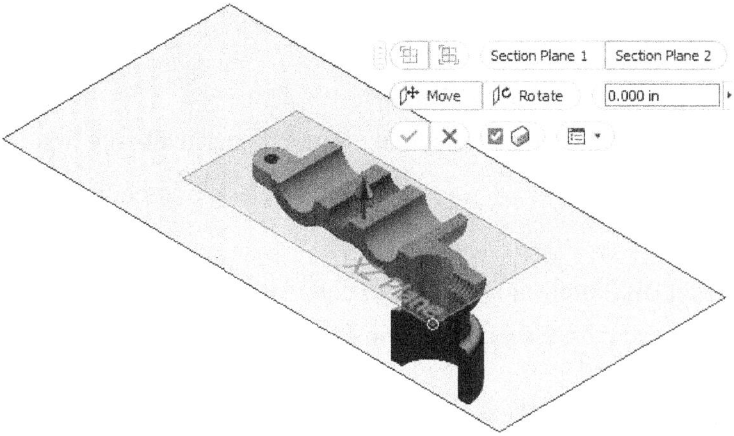

Figure 6–14

16. Select  **.** This flips the direction of section based on the currently active **Section Plane 2**, as shown in Figure 6–15.

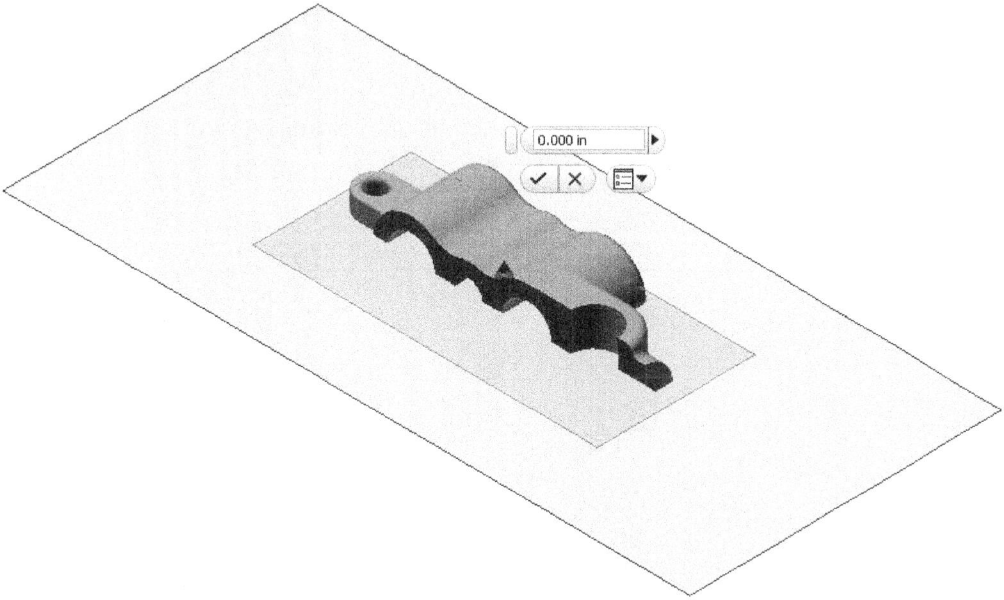

Figure 6–15

17. In the mini-toolbar, select (Three Quarter Section View). Because two planes would also be required to create a three quarter view you can quickly switch between these two views using this option and the (Quarter Section View) options.
18. Return to the (Three Quarter Section View).
19. The last plane to be selected is active (Section Plane 2). To activate the first cutting plane for modification, select Section Plane 1. Drag the section plane or modify the offset value in the mini-toolbar to change the plane placement.
20. Right-click and select **OK (Enter)** or click to complete the definition of the section view.
21. Double-click on **Primary** in the **View** node in the Model browser. The model display returns to the original, non-sectioned view.
22. Double-click on **Quarter Section View** in the **View** node in the Model browser. The model displays as sectioned again. The section that was previously created was saved in this view.
23. Save the part and close the window.

End of practice

Chapter Review Questions

1. In the example shown in Figure 6–16, **Hole1** is a **Through All** hole and **Extrusion2** is the solid cylindrical feature. What can you do to include **Extrusion2** in the **Hole1** feature (i.e., have the hole pass through the cylinder)?

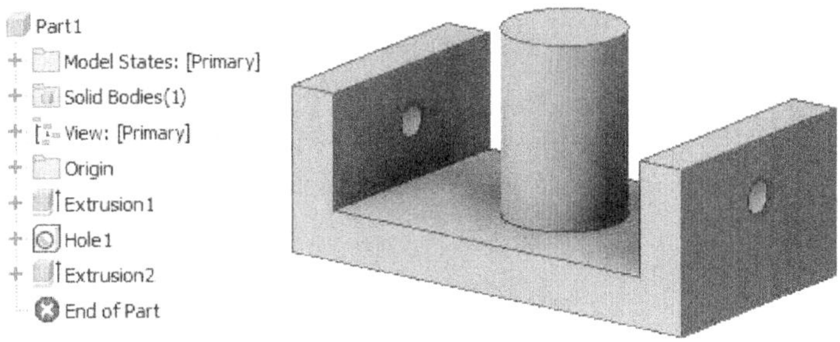

Figure 6–16

   a. Suppress Hole1 and then recreate Extrusion2.
   b. In the Model browser, drag the End of Part marker above Hole1.
   c. Make Extrusion2 Adaptive.
   d. In the Model browser, drag Extrusion2 above Hole1.

2. Which of the following statements are true for reordering features in a model? (Select all that apply.)
   a. Reordering enables you to drag and drop features so that you can rearrange the feature creation order.
   b. When reordering, features can be moved anywhere.
   c. Base features can be moved anywhere in the model.
   d. You can insert new features between existing features.

3. Any features below the End of Part marker in the Model browser are still displayed, but you cannot select them as references when creating new features.
   a. True
   b. False

4. If you suppress a feature, all dependent features are also suppressed.

a. True

b. False

5. Which items in the Model browser shown in Figure 6–17 are *Suppressed* in the model? (Select all that apply.)

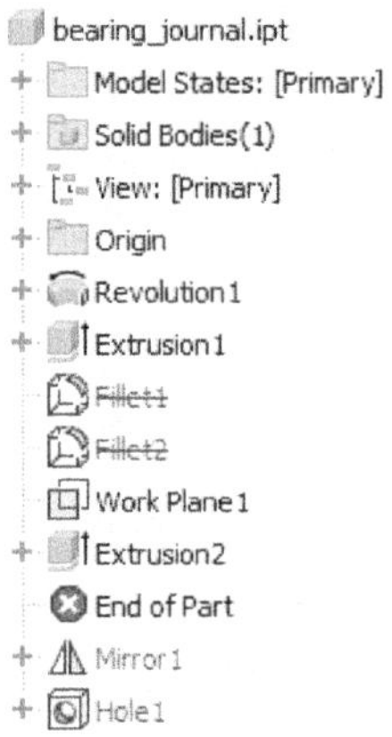

Figure 6–17

a. Solid1

b. Sketch3

c. Fillet1

d. Fillet2

e. Work Plane1

f. Mirror1

g. Hole1

6. How can a section view be saved with the model?

a. A section view is saved with the model and can be retrieved in the Navigation Bar.

b. A section view is saved with the model and can be retrieved in the Appearance panel in the *View* tab.

c. A section view is saved with the model in a design view and can be retrieved in the Model browser.

d. A section view cannot be saved with the model.

7. Once completed, a section view can be modified.

a. True

b. False

Command Summary

Button	Command	Location
	**End Section View**	• **Ribbon:** *View* tab>Visibility panel
	**Half Section View**	• **Ribbon:** *View* tab>Visibility panel
N/A	**Move EOP Marker**	• **Context Menu:** In Model browser with a feature selected
N/A	**Move EOP to End**	• **Context Menu:** In Model browser with the End of Part node selected
N/A	**New (Design View)**	• **Context Menu:** In Model browser with the View node selected
	**Quarter Section View**	• **Ribbon:** *View* tab>Visibility panel
N/A	**Suppress Features**	• **Context Menu:** In Model browser with a feature selected • **Context Menu:** In graphics window with a feature selected
	**Three Quarter Section View**	• **Ribbon:** *View* tab>Visibility panel
N/A	**UnSuppress Features**	• **Context Menu:** In Model browser with a suppressed feature selected

Chapter 7

Work Features

During the design process, the features that currently exist in the model might not provide the references required to place a new feature. In these situations, you can use work features to create the required references.

Learning Objectives

- Use the work plane creation types to create new work planes in a model.
- Use the work axes creation types to create new work axes in a model.
- Use the work point creation types to create new work points in a model.
- Describe how using work planes, work axes, and work points in a model can assist you in creating geometry that cannot otherwise be created using existing planes or geometry.

7.1 Work Planes

Work planes are non-solid features. They do not have thickness or mass and are used as references when creating other features in a model. When creating a part, three origin work planes are automatically created in the default templates.

Additional work planes can be created if a feature's sketching plane is not satisfied by any of the three origin work planes or existing geometry. Multiple work planes might be required to create a required work plane.To create the extrusions shown in Figure 7–1, additional work planes were required.

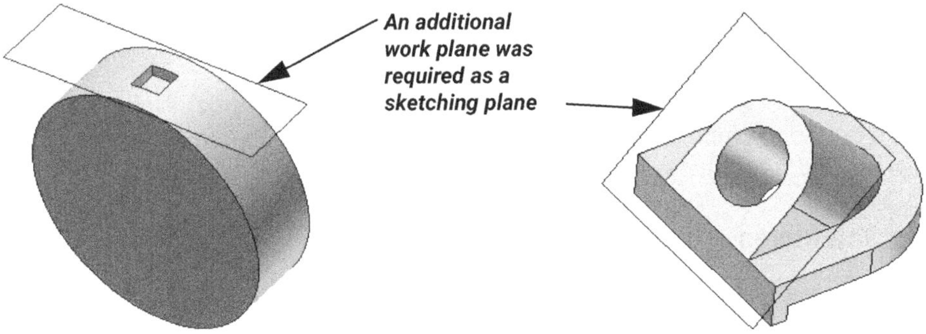

Figure 7–1

How To: Create a Work Plane

1. Start the creation of a work plane using one of the following techniques. The end result of any of these methods is the same. However, by selecting a plane placement type you are guided as to which references to select.
    - In the *3D Model* tab>Work Features panel, click (Plane).
    - In the *3D Model* tab>Work Features panel, expand (Plane) and select a plane placement type. Note that some of the methods are not available in Assembly mode.
    - In the graphics window, right-click and select **Work Plane**.
2. Once you have started the creation of a work plane, you must select references to locate it. References can include Origin features, Work features (plane, axis, point), edges, construction lines, vertices, or faces (planar or cylindrical). The reference type required depends on the work plane being created. Once the selected references fully define the work plane's placement, it displays. Alternatively, you can select the reference before clicking (Plane).

The different work plane placement types are described as follows:

Type	Example
Offset from Plane: Creates a work plane parallel to an existing plane. Place the cursor over a reference plane or face, hold the left mouse button, and drag away from the face. Enter the required offset distance.	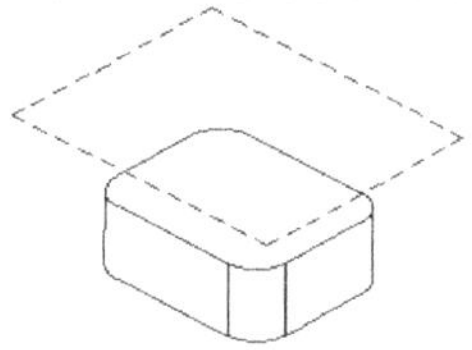
Parallel to Plane through Point: Creates a work plane that is parallel to another plane or face and passes through an edge, axis, or point. Select the reference plane and then select a point.	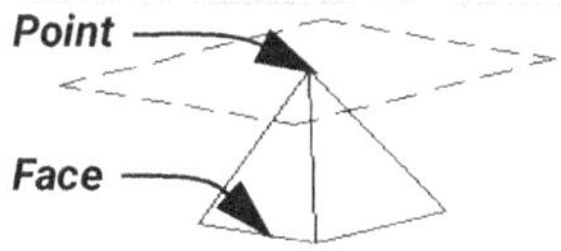
Midplane between Two Planes: Creates a work plane in the middle of two planes (parallel or non-parallel). Select two planes to create a work plane evenly spaced between them.	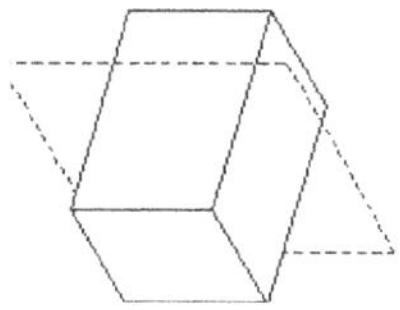
Midplane of Torus: Creates a work plane through the center or mid-plane of a torus. Select the torus to place the plane at its mid-plane.	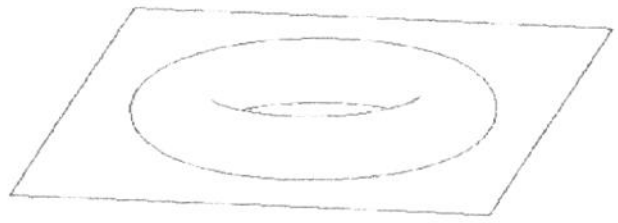
Angle to Plane around Edge: Creates a work plane at an angle to an existing plane or face. Select the plane to which the work plane is referenced. Select the edge or axis through which the work plane passes. Enter the required angle in the mini-toolbar to create a plane perpendicular to another plane.	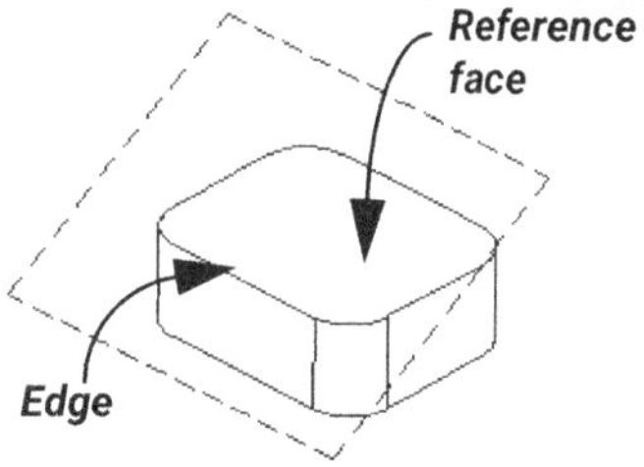
Three Points: Creates a work plane through three selected points (midpoints, end points, and/or work points). Select three point references to place the plane.	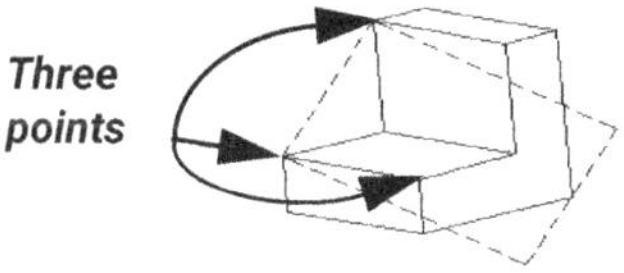
Two Coplanar Edges: Creates a work plane by selecting two coplanar straight edges or work axes. Select the two linear references to place the plane.	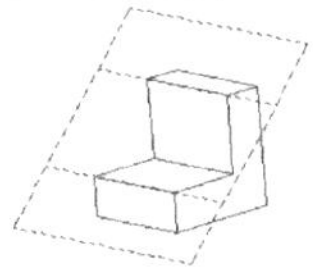

Tangent to Surface through Edge: Creates a work plane that lies on the curved surface or its projection and passes through an edge or axis. To create the work plane, select the edge and the curved face.

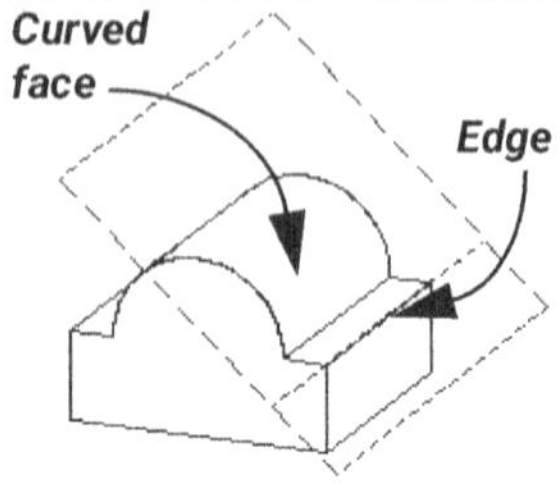

Tangent to Surface through Point: Creates a work plane that is tangent to a cylindrical face at a point defined by a construction line. The construction line should be drawn on a plane perpendicular to the cylindrical surface and from the center line of the cylinder to a point on the cylinder

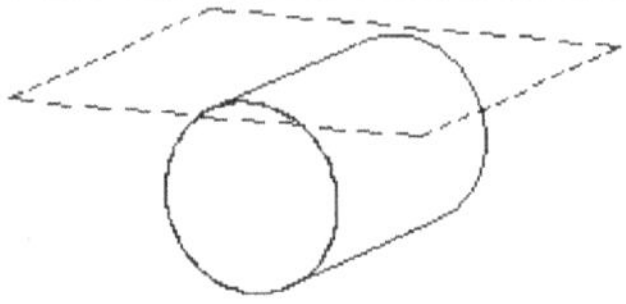

Tangent to Surface and Parallel to Plane: Creates a work plane that is tangent to a cylindrical face and parallel to a planar surface. To create the work plane, select the cylindrical face and the planar surface.

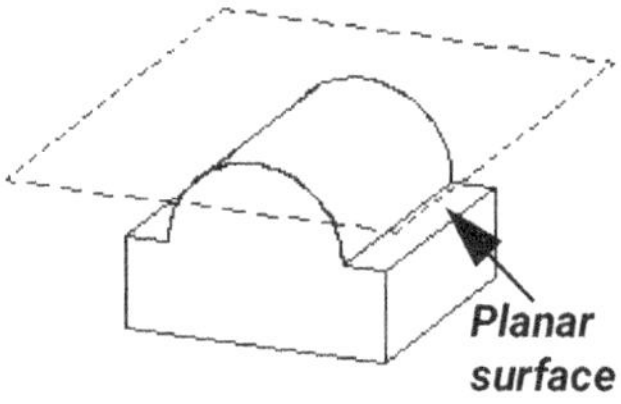

Normal to Axis through Point: Creates a work plane that is perpendicular to an axis and passes through a selected point. To create the work plane, select the axis or edge to which it is perpendicular and select the point (i.e., end point, midpoint, or work point).

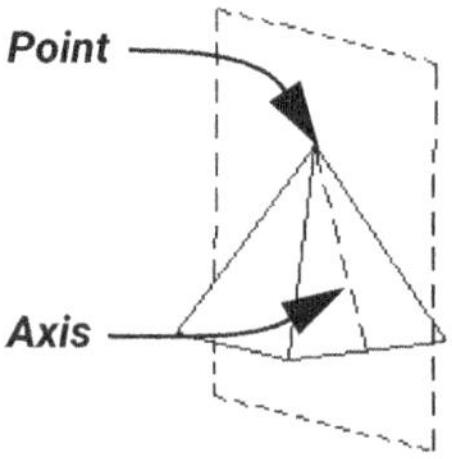

Normal to Curve at Point: Creates a work plane that is perpendicular to a non-linear sketch curve at a work point, sketch point, vertex, or the midpoint of an edge. To create the work plane, select the edge or sketch curve and select the point.

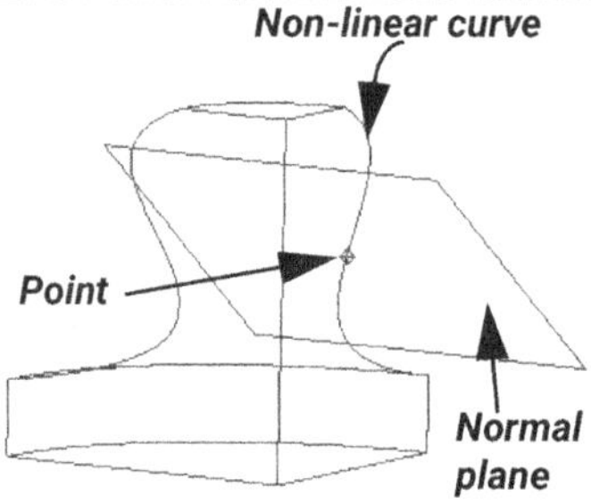

Consider the following when working with work planes:

- In situations where you have started to define a sketch and realize that a required plane does not exist, you can create an offset work plane on-the-fly. To create an offset work plane while (Start 2D Sketch) is active, select and drag the plane from a reference plane, and enter an offset value.

- Work axes and work points can be created during work plane creation and used as references. To do so, start the creation of the work plane (using either the **Plane** option or a specific work plane placement type), right-click, and select **Create Point** or **Create Axis**, as shown in Figure 7–2. Once the references have been selected, the work plane is created.

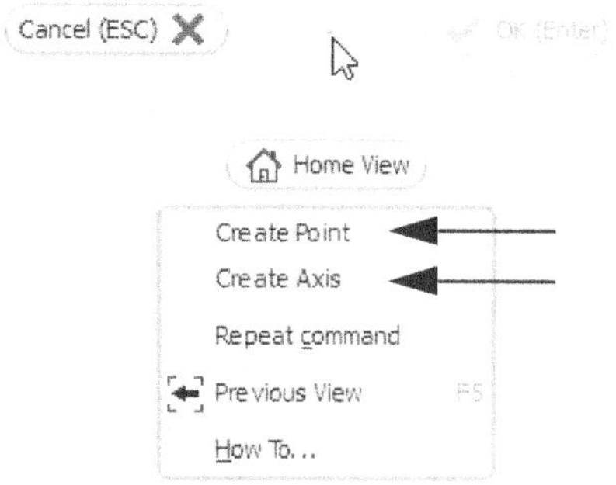

Figure 7–2

- To change the name of the work plane, select it in the Model browser and select it again (do not double-click) and enter a new name.
- To redefine the references of a work plane, right-click on the work plane, select **Redefine Feature**, and select new references.
- To modify the dimension values associated with work planes, double-click on the work plane in the graphics window or Model browser or right-click and select **Edit Dimension**. Once the dimension value displays, enter a new value.
- Work planes are infinite in size, but are sized to fit the geometry. To change its size, select its corner, wait until  displays, and drag. To automatically resize to fit the model, right-click on the work plane and select **Auto-Resize**. To manually change size, **Auto-Resize** must be toggled off.
- The two sides of a work plane are different colors. The normal side is a lighter color than the non-normal side. The normal side of the work plane can be reversed by right-clicking on the work plane and selecting **Flip Normal**. When entering offset values, the positive direction is always taken from the normal side of the plane.
- To toggle a work plane's visibility, right-click on the work plane and select **Visibility**. Alternatively, you can select the work plane in the Model browser and press <Alt> + V.
- To globally control work plane display, use the  (Object Visibility) options (*View* tab>Visibility panel).

7.2 Work Axes

A work axis is a type of feature that can be used to help create work planes, revolved features, or any other feature in the model. For example, a construction line can be sketched to serve as the axis of rotation for rotational features. However, creating a permanent work axis in the model is more efficient if the axial location is referenced by subsequent features (e.g., work plane). The plane shown in Figure 7–3 passes through the center of the rotational feature (work axis) and at an angle to the vertical face.

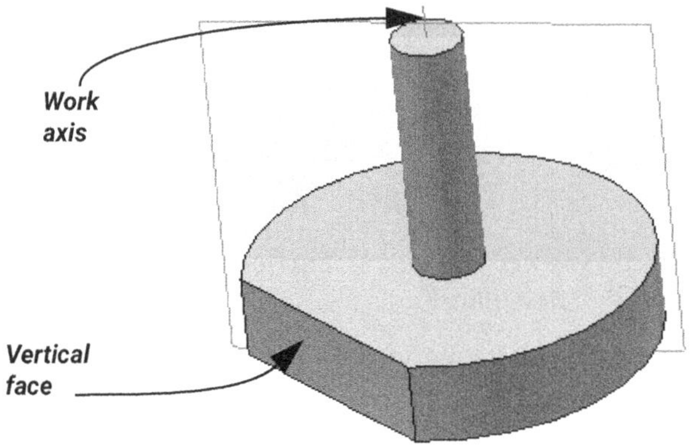

Figure 7–3

How To: Create a Work Axis

1. Start the creation of a work axis using one of the following methods. The end result of either method is the same. However, by selecting an axis placement type option, you are guided as to which references to select.
   - In the *3D Model* tab>Work Features panel, click (Axis).
   - In the *3D Model* tab>Work Features panel, expand (Axis) and select an axis placement type.
2. Once you have started the creation of a work axis, you must select references to locate it. References can include edges/curves, planar faces, work planes, cylindrical surfaces, work points, vertices, or sketched lines. The reference type required depends on the work axis being created. Once the selected references fully define the work axis' placement, the work axis displays. Alternatively, you can select the reference before clicking (Axis).

The different work axis placement types are described as follows:

Type | **Example**

On Line or Edge: Select a line or linear edge. The resulting axis is along that line or edge.

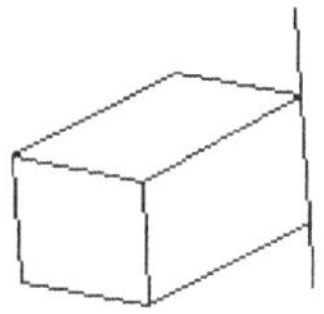

Parallel to Line through Point: Select a point and then an edge, work axis, or sketched line. The resulting axis is parallel to the edge, work axis, or sketched line and goes through the point.

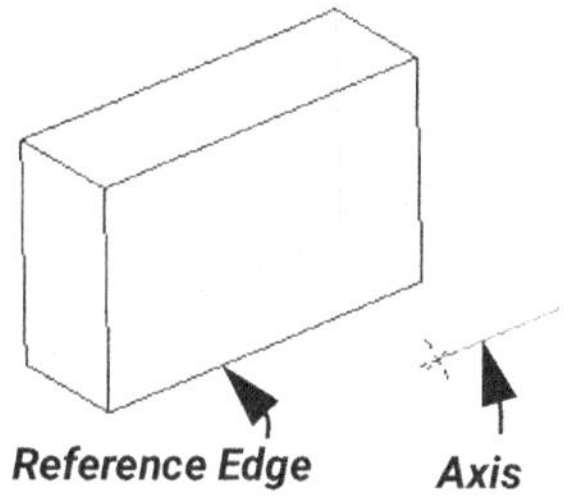

Through Two Points: Select two end points, center points, or work points. The resulting axis passes through those points.

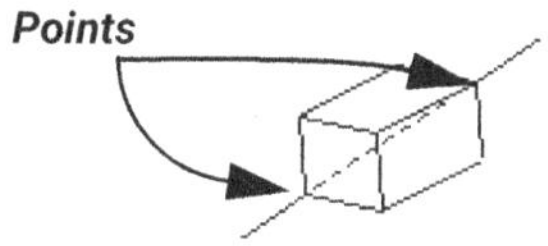

Intersection of Two Planes: Select two work planes or planar faces. The resulting axis is located along the intersection of the two planes.

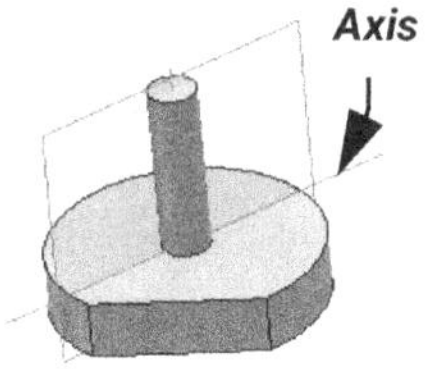

Normal to Plane through Point: Select a point and a surface. The resulting axis is normal to the surface and goes through the point.

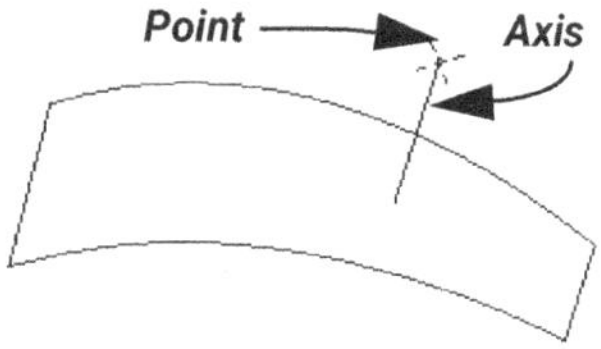

Through Center of Circular or Elliptical Edge: Select an edge of a circular or elliptical feature. The resulting axis passes through the center line of the edge.

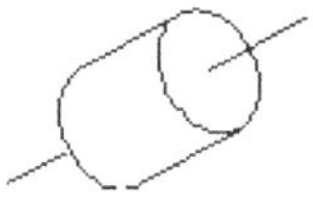

Through Revolved Face or Feature: Select a face or feature of a revolved feature to create an axis that passes through the feature's center line.

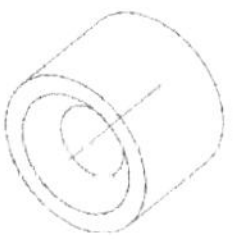

Consider the following when working with work axis:

- Work planes and work points can be created during work axis creation and used as references. To do so, start the creation of the work axis (using either the **Axis** option or a specific work axis placement type), right-click, and select **Create Plane** or **Create Point**, as shown in Figure 7–4.

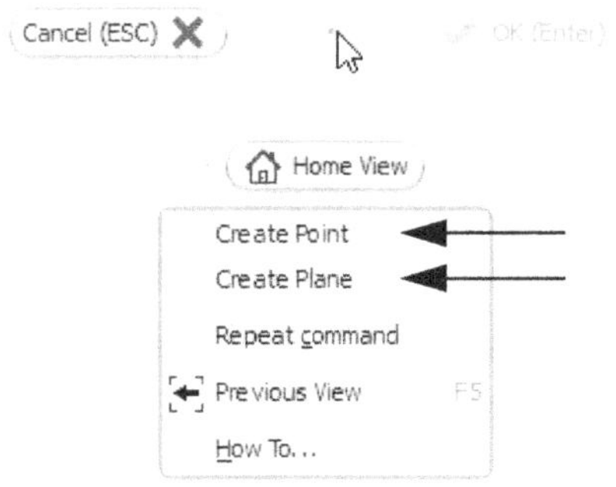

Figure 7–4

- To change the name of the work axis, select it in the Model browser and select it again (do not double-click). Enter a name.
- To redefine the references of a work axis, right-click on the work axis, select **Redefine Feature**, and select new references.
- Work axes are infinite in length, but on screen they are sized to fit the overall geometry. To change the display size, select one of its ends and drag it. To automatically resize the work axis to fit the model, right-click on it and select **Auto-Resize**. Once toggled on, the work axis automatically resizes. To manually change the size, **Auto-Resize** needs to be toggled off.
- To change a work axis' visibility, right-click on the work axis and select **Visibility**. Alternatively, you can select the work axis in the Model browser and press <Alt> + V.
- To globally control work axis display, use the (Object Visibility) options (*View* tab> Visibility panel).

7.3 Work Points

Work points can be used as references when creating work planes, work axes, or other features in the model. In the example shown in Figure 7–5, various methods are used to create work points.

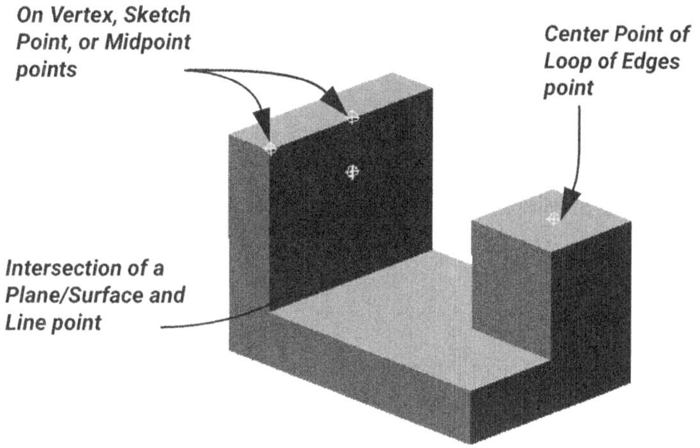

Figure 7–5

How To: Create a Work Point

1. Start the creation of a work point using one of the following methods. The end result of either method is the same. However, by selecting a point placement type, you are guided as to which references to select.

   - In the *3D Model* tab>Work Features panel, click (Point).
   - In the *3D Model* tab>Work Features panel, expand (Point) and select a point placement type.

2. Once you have started the creation of a work point, you must select references to locate it. Reference can include work points, vertices, sketched points, midpoints, work planes, edges, work axes, or solid geometry. The reference type required depends on the work point being created. Once the selected references fully define the work point's placement, it displays. Alternatively, you can select the reference before clicking (Point).

The different work point placement types are described as follows:

Type	Example
Grounded Point: Select an existing point and convert it to a grounded point. Grounded work points have all degrees of freedom removed and are fixed in space.	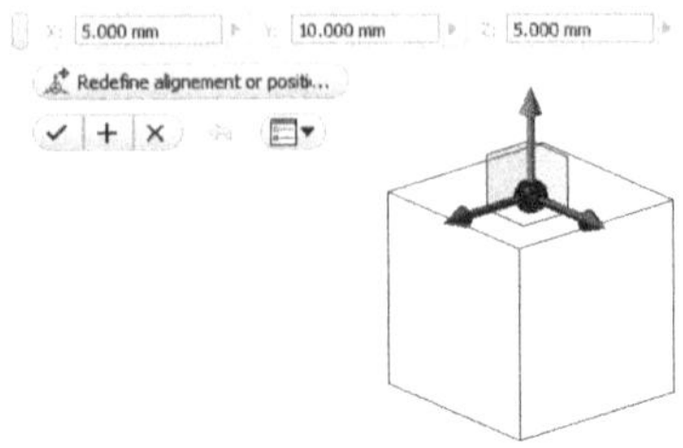
On Vertex, Sketch point, or Midpoint: Select the end point or midpoint.	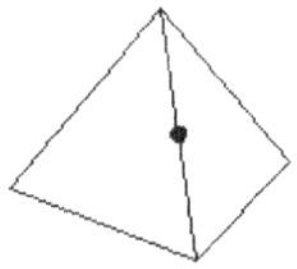
Intersection of Three Planes: Select three work planes or planar faces. The work point is located at their intersection.	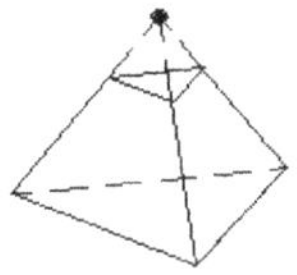
Intersection of Two Lines: Select the two edges, work axes, or lines. The work point is located at their intersection.	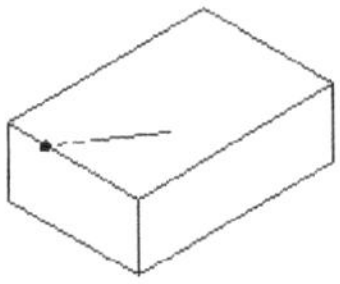
Intersection of a Plane / Surface and Line: Select a plane and sketch line, curve, edge, or axis. The work point is located at their intersection.	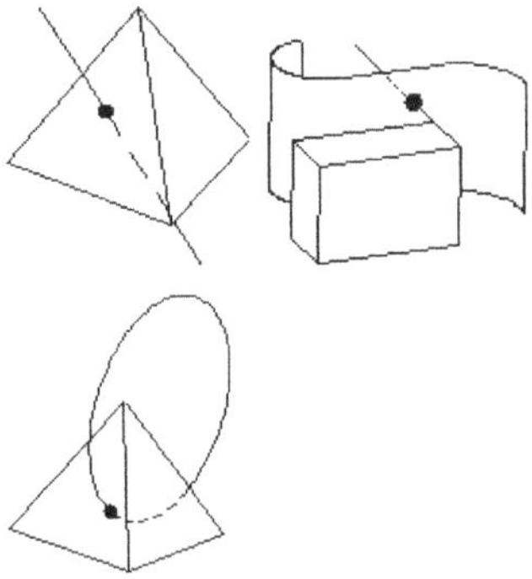
Center Point of Loop of Edges: Toggle on Loop Select Mode in the shortcut menu and select a circle, arc, or edge. A point is created at the center of the loop whether it is circular or not.	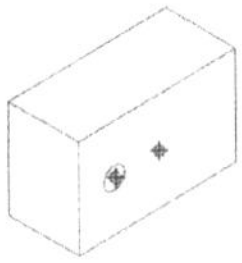

Center of Torus: Select the torus surface. A point is created at the center of the selected surface.

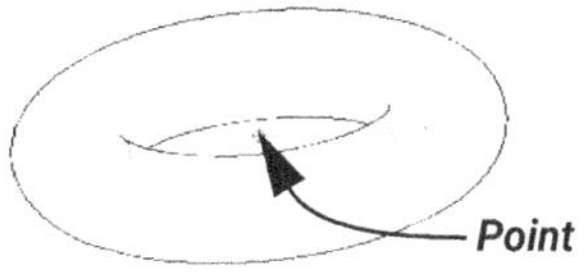

Center of Sphere: Select the sphere surface. A point is created at the center of the selected surface.

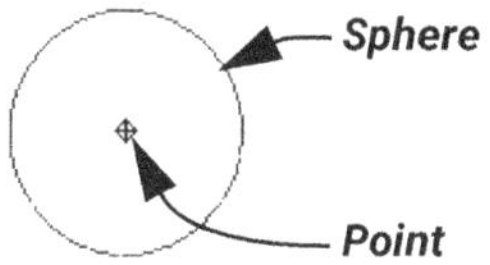

Consider the following when working with work points:

- Work planes and work axes can be created during work point creation and used as references. To do so, start the creation of the work point (using either the **Point** option or a specific work point placement type), right-click and select **Create Axis** or **Create Plane**, as shown in Figure 7–6.

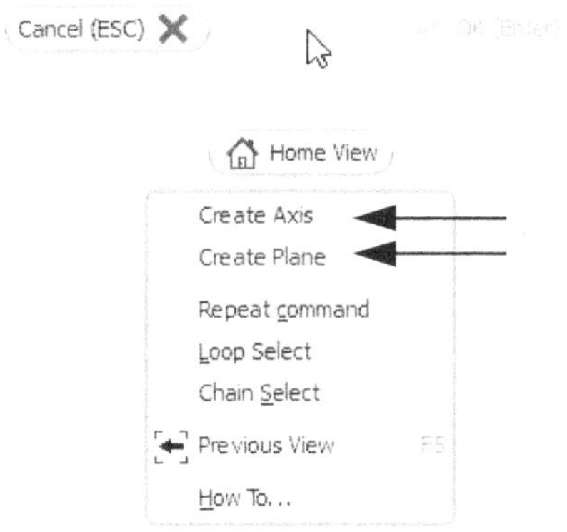

Figure 7–6

- To change the name of the work point (feature) select it in the Model browser and select it again (do not double-click). Enter a new name.
- To redefine the references of a work point, right-click on the work axis, select **Redefine Feature**, and select new references.
- To change a work point's visibility, right-click on the work point and select **Visibility**. Alternatively, you can select the work point in the Model browser and press <Alt> + V.
- To globally control work point display, use the (Object Visibility) options (*View* tab>Visibility panel)

Practice 7a
Work Features for Inventor CAM

Practice Objective

- Create work features that can be used as references in the creation of solid geometry and be used in future Inventor CAM toolpaths.

In this practice, you will create the model shown on the left in Figure 7–7. To machine this model with an Inventor CAM toolpath, a custom tool orientation and boundary could be used to machine the contoured face (as shown on the right). To do this, you would need to create additional sketch geometry in the model that can be referenced in the toolpath. In this exercise, along with creating the solid geometry, you will also create this sketch geometry to provide further practice using the sketch environment and creating work features.

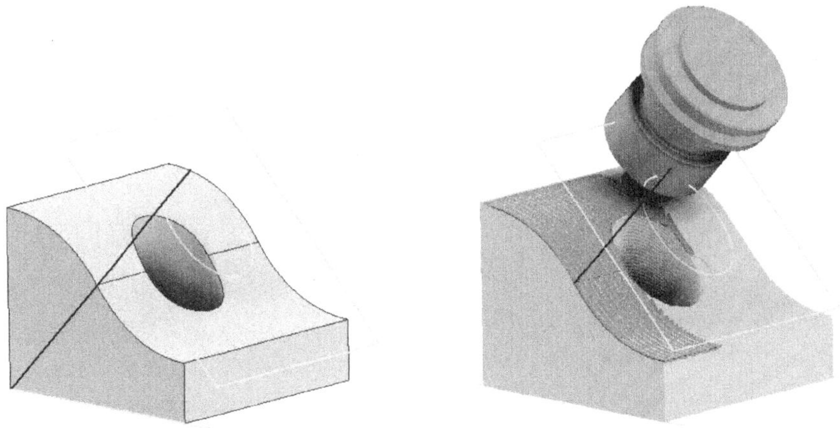

Final geometry that will be created in this exercise.

Sample toolpath shown using the exercise's sketched geometry.

Figure 7–7

Task 1: Create a new part and create a sketch.

1. Create a new part using the standard imperial (in) template.
2. Save the file as **Machining Boundary.ipt**.
3. In the Model browser, expand the *Origin* node.
4. In the Model browser, select the XY plane. In the *3D Model* tab>Sketch panel, click (Start 2D Sketch) to start a new sketch.

5. Sketch, dimension, and constrain the three lines and two arcs shown in Figure 7–8. To fully constrain the sketch with only the three dimensions shown, consider the following:
   - Ensure that the center points for the centers of the arcs are aligned with the vertical sketched lines.
   - Constrain the two arcs as equal.

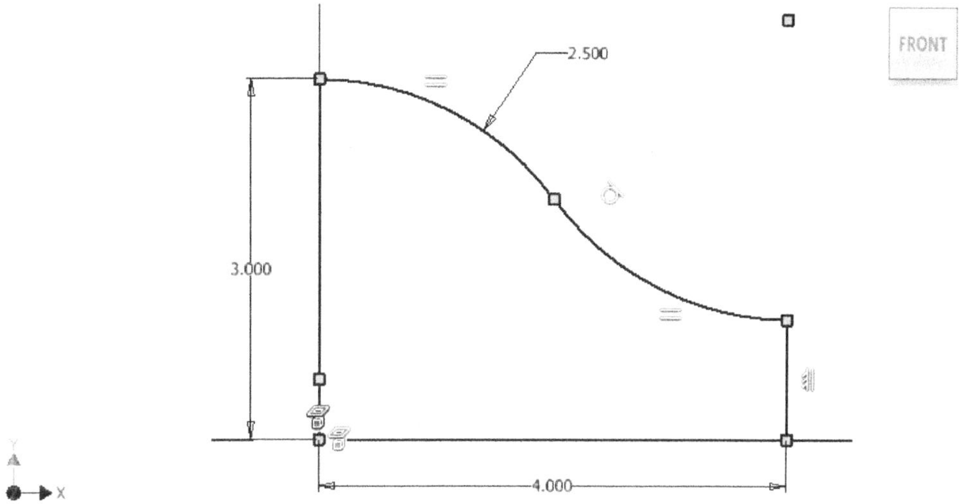

Figure 7–8

6. In the Exit panel, click (Finish Sketch) to complete the sketch.

7. In the *3D Model* tab>Create panel, click (Extrude). Extrude the section **4 in** in the -Z direction and complete the feature. The model should appear as shown in Figure 7–9.

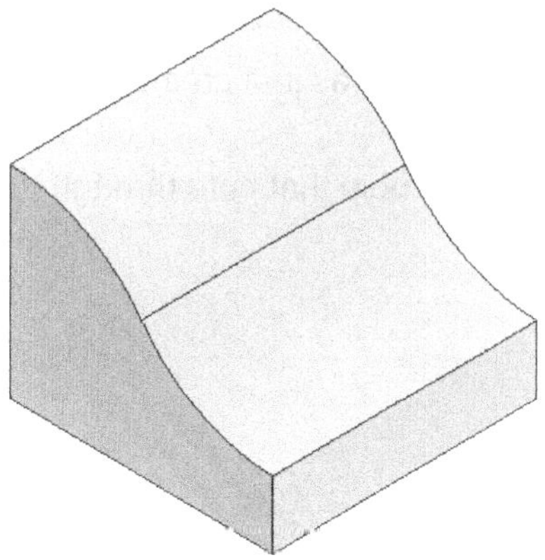

Figure 7–9

Task 2: Create a hole centered on a face.

In this task, you will create a hole that will remain centered on a selected face, regardless of changes to the model that would change the size of the face. To accomplish this, you will create a work point and create the hole based on that point. In a later task, you will make changes to the model to ensure that the hole placement updates correctly.

1. In the Work Features panel, expand  (Point) and select **Center Point of Loop of Edges** to create a work point.
2. Rotate the model and select the loop of edges, as shown in Figure 7–10.

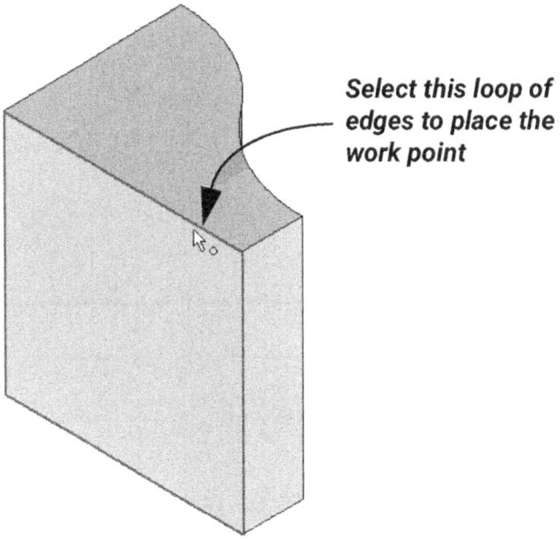

Figure 7–10

3. A point displays, centered on the face that is bounded by the selected loop.
4. Right-click in the graphics window and select **Hole**.
5. Place the hole on the work point that was just created. Define the hole's direction by selecting the **Y Axis** in the *Origin* node.
6. Further define the hole as a simple hole that cuts through the entire model and has a diameter of **1.5 in**.

7. Complete the feature. The model displays as shown in Figure 7–11.

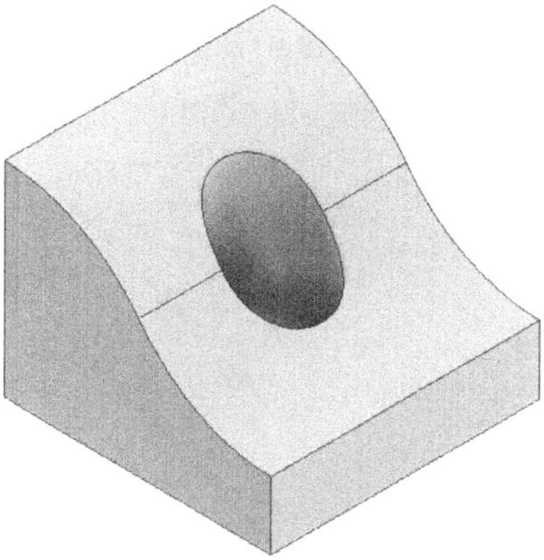

Figure 7–11

Task 3: Create a sketched line to define tool orientation.

When working in the CAM environment, you may have situations where the pre-defined orientation of the stock does not meet the needs for a specific toolpath's tool orientation. In these cases, you can use linear entities (edges, axis, sketched lines) to define the tool orientation for that specific toolpath. In this task, you will create a sketch that could be used to define a tool's orientation.

1. In the *3D Model* tab>Sketch panel, click (Start 2D Sketch).
2. Select the face shown in Figure 7–12 as the sketch plane.

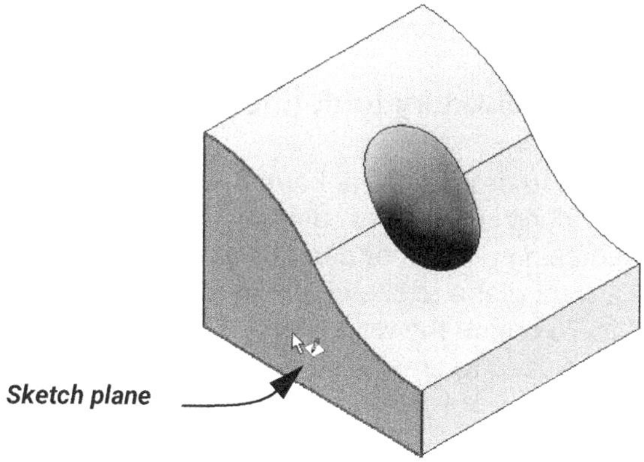

Figure 7–12

3. Sketch, dimension, and constrain the line as shown in Figure 7–13. To fully constrain the sketch with only the two dimensions shown, consider the following:
   - Ensure that the line starts on the projected origin center point.
   - Dimension the line at **45°** to the projected XZ plane.

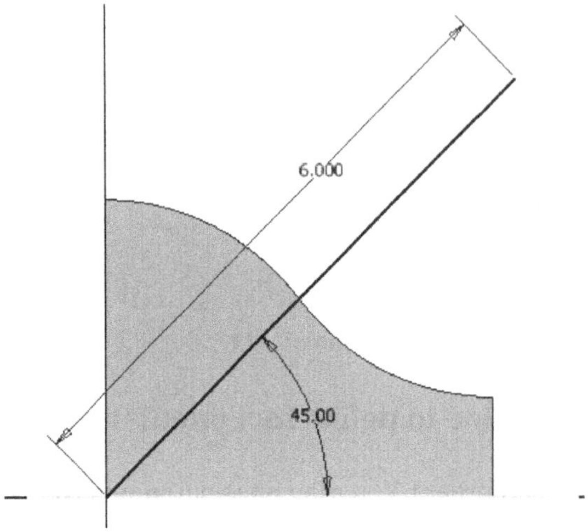

Figure 7–13

4. In the Exit panel, click (Finish Sketch).
5. In the Model browser, slowly double-click on the new sketch and rename it **Tool Orientation**.
6. By default, the sketch is shown in the graphics window with its dimensions. Right-click on the newly named sketch and clear the **Dimension Visibility** option. The sketch remains displayed but the dimensions have been removed.

Task 4: Create a sketched boundary to define the cutting boundary.

In addition to creating a sketch to define the tool orientation, you may also need to define your machining boundary when working in the CAM environment. To create the machining boundary, you often will not have a sketching plane that can be easily selected from the model geometry, so you will need to create a work plane to sketch on. In this task, you will create the work plane and sketch a boundary on it. To create the work plane, you will use the **Normal to Axis through Point** option because it can be used to create the required plane normal to the sketched line that defines the tool orientation.

1. Reorient the model similar to that shown in Figure 7–14.
2. In the Work Features panel, expand (Plane) and select **Normal to Axis through Point** to create a work plane.
3. Select the linear sketched line created in the previous task and then select the point shown in Figure 7–14. As soon as you hover your mouse over the point, the work plane preview will display to help you identify if it is being created correctly.

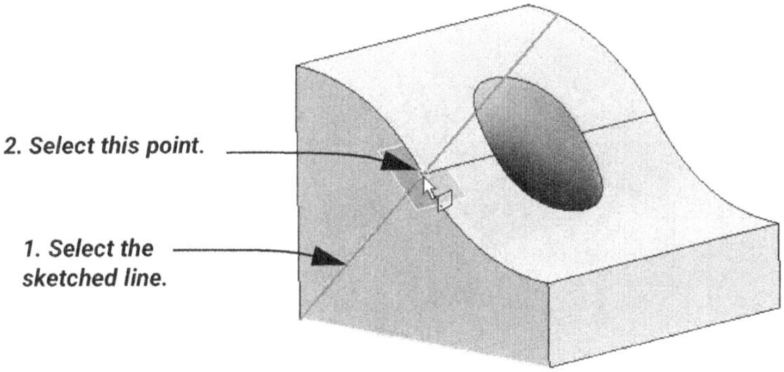

Figure 7–14

4. Right-click on **Work Plane1** in the Model browser and select **Auto-Resize**. The work plane should resize, as shown in Figure 7–15, to encompass the entire model geometry. This is not required, but can be easier for visualization purposes.

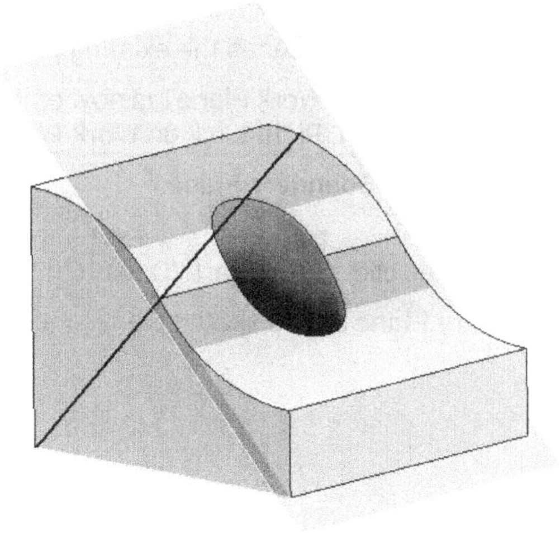

Figure 7–15

5. This work plane alone cannot be used as the sketch plane for the machining boundary because it intersects the model geometry. In the Work Features panel, expand (Plane) and select **Offset from Plane.**
6. Select **Work Plane1** in the graphics window. Drag the offset arrow or enter **1 in** in the offset field, as shown in Figure 7–16.

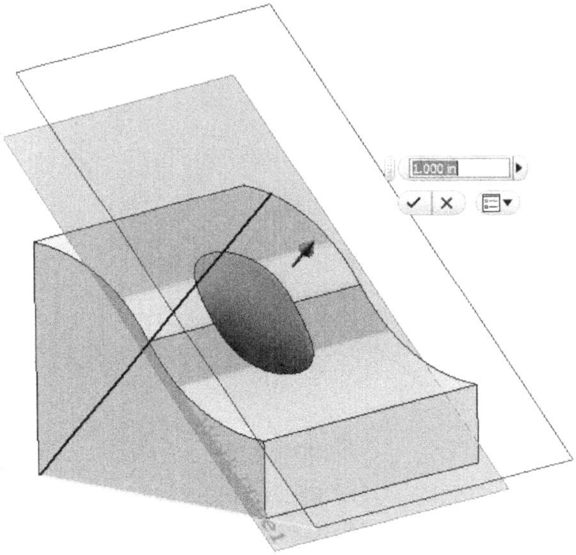

Figure 7–16

7. Click .to create a work plane that references the existing plane.
8. Review the Model browser and note that Work Plane1 is now embedded within Work Plane2 because it referenced it during creation. Right-click on **Work Plane1** and clear its visibility.
9. Rename Work Plane2 as **Machining Boundary Plane**.
10. In the *3D Model* tab>Sketch panel, click (Start 2D Sketch).
11. Select the **Machining Boundary Plane** as the sketch plane.

12. Once oriented into the 2D sketch orientation, select  (Project Geometry) and select the edges as described in Figure 7–17. The projected edges will all appear yellow, indicating they are referenced geometry.

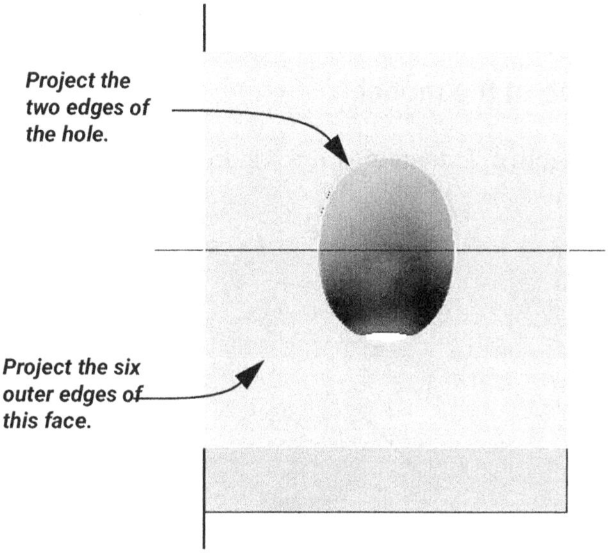

Figure 7–17

13. Note that the sketch is fully constrained. In the Exit panel, click  (Finish Sketch) to complete the sketch as shown in Figure 7–18.

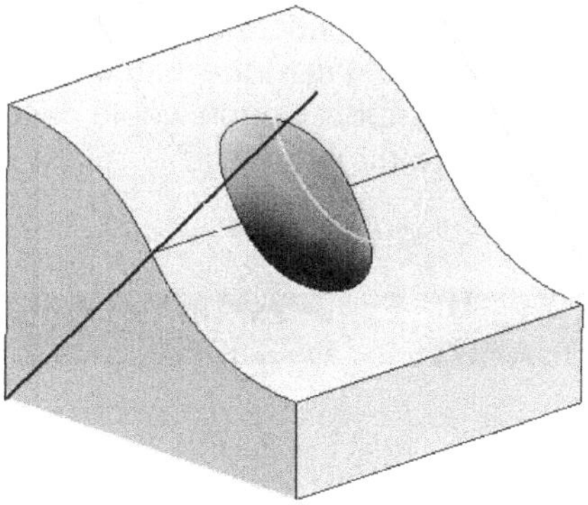

Figure 7–18

In this sketch, you did not create any additional sketched entities as the projected geometry will be sufficient to define a selected machining boundary. As an alternative, you could have sketched entities on the **Machining Boundary Plane**, as required, if the projected edges did not properly define the required boundary. The important steps are that the work plane is created normal to the tool orientation reference and that the work plane does not intersect any geometry as it will be the cutting plane for the model once in Inventor CAM.

Task 5: Modify the size of the model.

1. Modify the extruded depth of Extrusion1 from 4 in to **6 in**, as shown in Figure 7–19. Update the model.

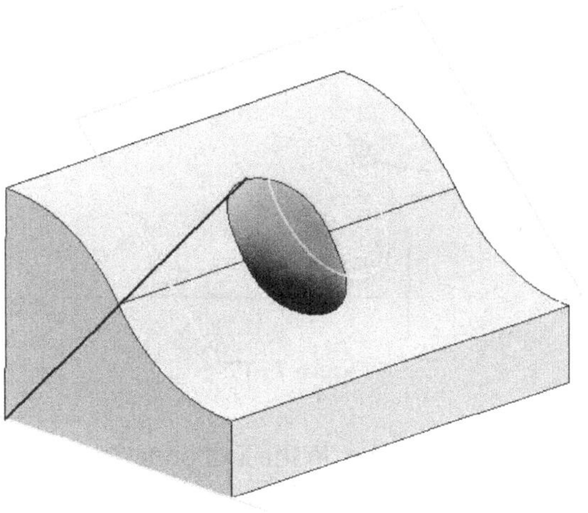

Figure 7–19

The model should update such that the hole remains centered on its face (because the work point updated) and the sketched boundary updates to reflect the size change (because projected edges were used). If the model had been used in Inventor CAM and had toolpaths been assigned, only the **Generate** option would need to be selected to update the toolpath to incorporate the change to the model.

2. Save the model.

End of practice

Chapter Review Questions

1. Origin planes are the only work planes that can exist in a model.
   a. True
   b. False

2. Which of the following are possible uses for work planes similar to those shown in Figure 7–20? (Select all that apply.)

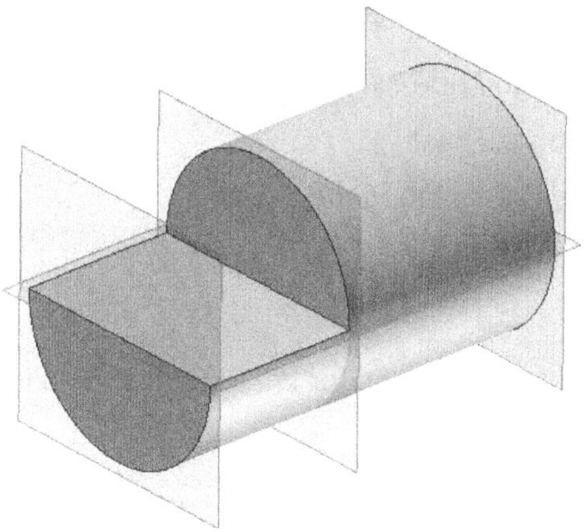

Figure 7–20

   a. To create another work plane.
   b. To define a sketch plane.
   c. To serve as the boundary for the depth of an extrusion.
   d. To set up a drawing sheet.

3. Which of the following are valid options to create a work plane? (Select all that apply.)
   a. Through a Plane and Parallel to an Axis
   b. Offset from Plane
   c. Tangent to Surface and Parallel to Plane
   d. Three Points

4. Which option enables you to create the work plane shown in Figure 7–21?

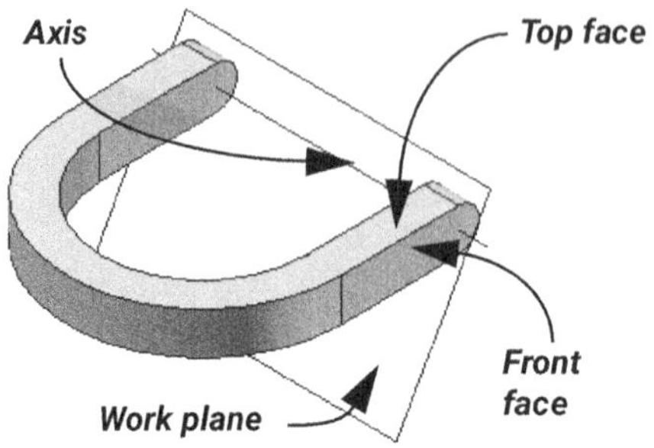

Figure 7–21

a. Tangent to Surface through Edge
b. Tangent to Surface through Point
c. Tangent to Surface and Parallel to Plane
d. Angle to Plane around Edge

5. Which of the following are valid options for creating a work axis? (Select all that apply.)
   a. Intersection of Two Planes
   b. Through Two Points
   c. Parallel to a Line
   d. On Line or Edge

6. A work axis can be used as a reference when creating a work plane.
   a. True
   b. False

7. Which option creates a work point centered on a face and remains centered even after the size of the face changes?
   a. On Vertex, Sketch Point, or Midpoint
   b. Center Point of Loop of Edges
   c. Center of Torus
   d. Through Center of Circular or Elliptical Edge

8. You can create work planes during work point creation to reference and constrain the work point.

a. True

b. False

Command Summary

Button	Command	Location
	**Angle to Plane around Edge**	• **Ribbon:** *3D Model* tab>Work Features panel>expand **Plane**
	**Axis**	• **Ribbon:** *3D Model* tab>Work Features panel
	**Center Point of Loop of Edges**	• **Ribbon:** *3D Model* tab>Work Features panel>expand **Plane**
	**Center Point of Sphere**	• **Ribbon:** *3D Model* tab>Work Features panel>expand **Plane**
	**Center Point of Torus**	• **Ribbon:** *3D Model* tab>Work Features panel>expand **Plane**
	**Grounded Point**	• **Ribbon:** *3D Model* tab>Work Features panel>expand **Plane**
	**Intersection of a Plane/ Surface and Line**	• **Ribbon:** *3D Model* tab>Work Features panel>expand **Plane**
	**Intersection of Three Planes**	• **Ribbon:** *3D Model* tab>Work Features panel>expand **Plane**
	**Intersection of Two Lines**	• **Ribbon:** *3D Model* tab>Work Features panel>expand **Plane**
	**Intersection of Two Planes**	• **Ribbon:** *3D Model* tab>Work Features panel>expand **Axis**
	**Midplane between Two Planes**	• **Ribbon:** *3D Model* tab>Work Features panel>expand **Plane**
	**Midplane of a Torus**	• **Ribbon:** *3D Model* tab>Work Features panel>expand **Plane**
	**Normal to a Curve at Point**	• **Ribbon:** *3D Model* tab>Work Features panel>expand **Plane**
	**Normal to Axis through Point**	• **Ribbon:** *3D Model* tab>Work Features panel>expand **Plane**
	**Normal to Plane through Point**	• **Ribbon:** *3D Model* tab>Work Features panel>expand **Axis**
	**Offset from Plane**	• **Ribbon:** *3D Model* tab>Work Features panel>expand **Plane**
	**On Line or Edge**	• **Ribbon:** *3D Model* tab>Work Features panel>expand **Axis**

Button	Command	Location
	**On Vertex, Sketch point, or Midpoint**	• **Ribbon:** *3D Model* tab>Work Features panel>expand **Plane**
	**Parallel to Line through Point**	• **Ribbon:** *3D Model* tab>Work Features panel>expand **Axis**
	**Parallel to Plane through Point**	• **Ribbon:** *3D Model* tab>Work Features panel>expand **Plane**
	**Plane**	• **Ribbon:** *3D Model* tab>Work Features panel • **Context Menu:** In the graphics window
	**Point**	• **Ribbon:** *3D Model* tab>Work Features panel
	**Tangent to Surface and Parallel to Plane**	• **Ribbon:** *3D Model* tab>Work Features panel>expand **Plane**
	**Tangent to Surface through Edge**	• **Ribbon:** *3D Model* tab>Work Features panel>expand **Plane**
	**Tangent to Surface through Point**	• **Ribbon:** *3D Model* tab>Work Features panel>expand **Plane**
	**Three Points**	• **Ribbon:** *3D Model* tab>Work Features panel>expand **Plane**
	**Through Center of Circular or Elliptical Edge**	• **Ribbon:** *3D Model* tab>Work Features panel>expand **Axis**
	**Through Revolved Face or Feature**	• **Ribbon:** *3D Model* tab>Work Features panel>expand **Axis**
	**Through Two Points**	• **Ribbon:** *3D Model* tab>Work Features panel>expand **Axis**
	**Two Coplanar Edges**	• **Ribbon:** *3D Model* tab>Work Features panel>expand **Plane**

Chapter 8

Assembly Environment

An assembly file in Autodesk® Inventor® enables you to combine the components that have been modeled to create a top-level assembly that communicates how all the components are combined. Both parts and other assemblies, referred to as subassemblies, can be referenced in an assembly.

Learning Objectives

- Create a new assembly file using a standard template.
- Place, constrain, and edit components in an assembly file.
- Use the Model browser to find items, filter information, and switch between the Modeling and Assembly views for an assembly.
- Save new and existing assembly files.

8.1 Assembling Components Using Constraints

You place and constrain components to create an assembly. Constraints are specified to locate components parametrically with respect to other components. Similar to the dependencies between features in a part, relationships also exist in an assembly when components are assembled relative to one another.

Use the following general steps to create an assembly and place components:

1. Create an assembly file.
2. Place components in the assembly file.
3. Drag parts and display degrees of freedom.
4. Select a constraint type.
5. Select references on the components.
6. Assign an offset value, as required.
7. Repeat Step 4 to Step 6 until the components are fully constrained.
8. Complete the component placement.
9. Edit the component placement, as required.

Step 1 - Create an assembly file.

The first step in creating an assembly is to start a new file based on an assembly template. This can be done using the default template that is assigned in the software or you can start the assembly by selecting a template. These methods are described:

- To create an assembly using the default template, expand **New** on the Home page and select Assembly. Alternatively, on the Quick Access Toolbar, expand (New) and click Assembly, or in the File menu, expand **New** and click Assembly.
- To access the Create New File dialog box to select a specific assembly template, click **New** on the Home page. Alternatively, on the Quick Access Toolbar, click (New) or in the File menu, click **New**.

Step 2 - Place components in the assembly file.

To add a component to the assembly, in the *Assemble* tab>Component panel, click (Place). In the Place Component dialog box, select the component to add and click **Open**. It is possible to select multiple components by holding <Ctrl> or <Shift> while selecting.

> ***Note:*** *Components that can be added to an assembly include parts (.IPT), library components, and other assembly models called subassemblies (.IAM). Subassemblies act as single components.*

To locate the first component, you can freely place it in the assembly or ground it to the assembly coordinate system (0,0,0).

- To freely locate the component in the assembly, click in the graphics window with the left mouse button to place it. However, before locating a component in the assembly, you can use **Rotate X 90**, **Rotate Y 90**, or **Rotate Z 90** to reorient the model before placement.
- To ground the component, right-click and select **Place Grounded at Origin** in the marking menu as shown in Figure 8–1.

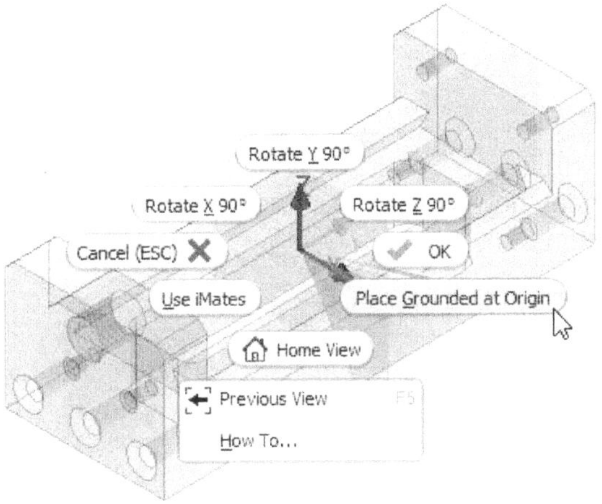

Figure 8–1

Once placed freely or grounded, a second instance of the component is immediately available for further placement. To complete the operation without assembling any additional instances of the same component, right-click and select **Cancel [Esc]** or **OK**. Alternatively, you can press <Esc>.

- Grounded components are indicated by the  pushpin symbol in the Model browser, as shown in Figure 8–2.
- The [•] icon indicates that the component is fully constrained.
- The cursor changes from  to  when you hover over a grounded component in the model.

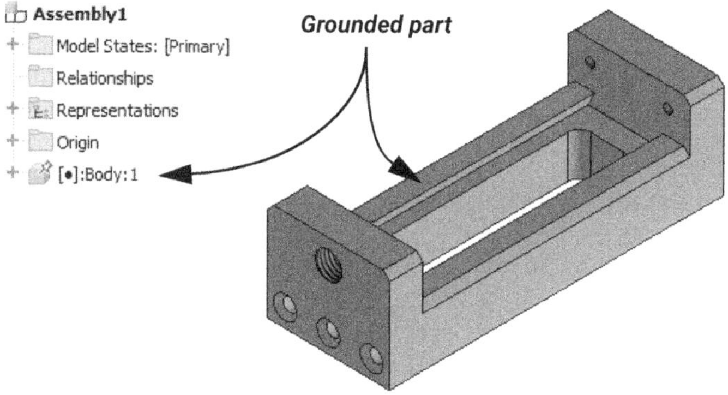

Figure 8–2

- To unground a component, right-click on it in the assembly window or Model browser and clear the **Grounded** option.

Note: It is good practice to ground at least one component. This component serves as the base on which the rest of the assembly is built. To automatically ground the first assembled component, set the ***Place and ground first component at origin*** *option in the Assembly tab in the Application Options dialog box.*

In the *Assemble* tab>Component panel, click (Place) to add a second component to the assembly. To freely locate the component in the assembly, click in the graphics window with the left mouse button to place it. The [▫] icon in the Model browser indicates that the component is not fully constrained, as shown in Figure 8–3.

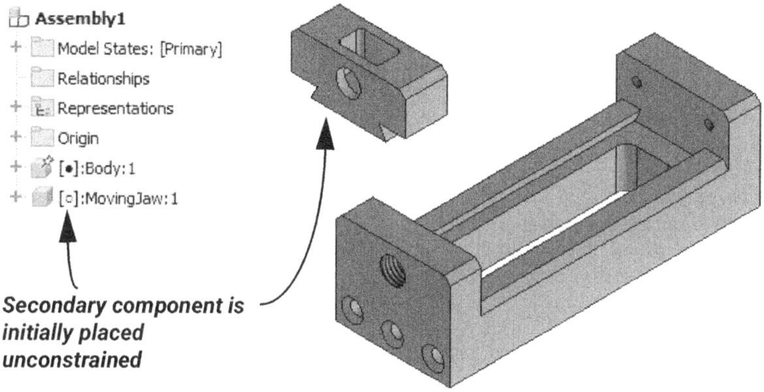

Figure 8–3

Note: Any secondary component can also be grounded, if required, by right-clicking and selecting ***Place Grounded at Origin*** *in the marking menu.*

Step 3 - Drag parts and display degrees of freedom.

Once components are placed in the assembly, you can begin constraining any non-grounded components. To prepare for constraining you might want to move them. This can be done using any of the following methods:

- To drag a part, select it and drag it to a new location in the assembly window (hold the left mouse button while dragging). Alternatively, you can use (Free Move) in the *Assemble* tab>Position panel.
- To rotate a single component in the assembly, in the *Assemble* tab>Position panel, click (Free Rotate) and select the component. Similar to globally rotating the assembly, hold the left mouse button while dragging to rotate only the selected component.

To display the degrees of freedom for components, in the *View* tab>Visibility panel, click (Degrees of Freedom). By default, they are not displayed. A completely unconstrained component (as shown in Figure 8–4) has six degrees of freedom, as indicated by green arrows on the component. It can translate in three directions (X, Y, and Z) and rotate about three axes (X, Y, and Z), as shown in Figure 8–4. Note that degrees of freedom symbols do not display on a grounded part because the part does not have any degrees of freedom.

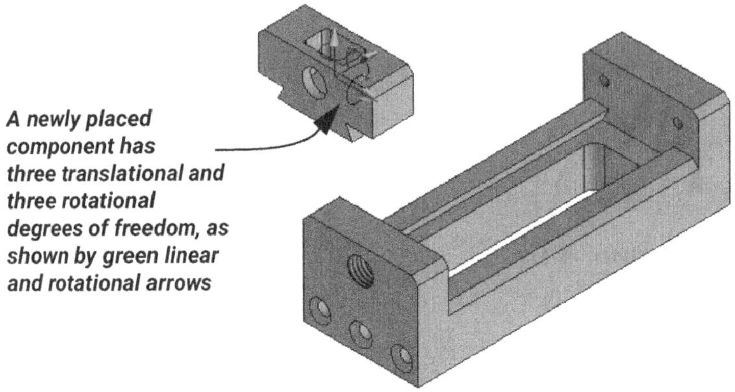

Figure 8–4

Hint: Degree of Freedom Analysis

The **Degree of Freedom Analysis** command provides a summary of the degrees of freedom remaining in all of the components in the assembly. To open the Degree of Freedom Analysis dialog box, in the *Assemble* tab>Productivity panel, click (Degree of Freedom Analysis). This dialog box lists all assembly components and lists the translational and rotational degrees of freedom remaining for each component.

- To graphically display the remaining degrees of freedom in the graphics window, select a component name in the dialog box.
- To visually animate the degrees of freedom remaining, select **Animate Freedom** in the dialog box and select a component name.

Step 4 - Select a constraint type.

In the *Assemble* tab>Relationships panel, click (Constrain) to open the Place Constraint dialog box. In this dialog box, you select the constraint type in the *Type* area and define how the components are oriented relative to one another in the *Solution* area. Depending on the type of constraint being created, the dialog box updates appropriately to provide the required options. The available constraint types are described as follows:

Mate

The Mate constraint ( ) positions two components adjacent to each other. It can be assigned between two planes, edges, center points, or work points. The Plane-Plane Mate constraint removes one translational and two rotational degrees of freedom. When planes or the center point of a circular edge are selected, the Mate orientation solutions are shown in Figure 8–5.

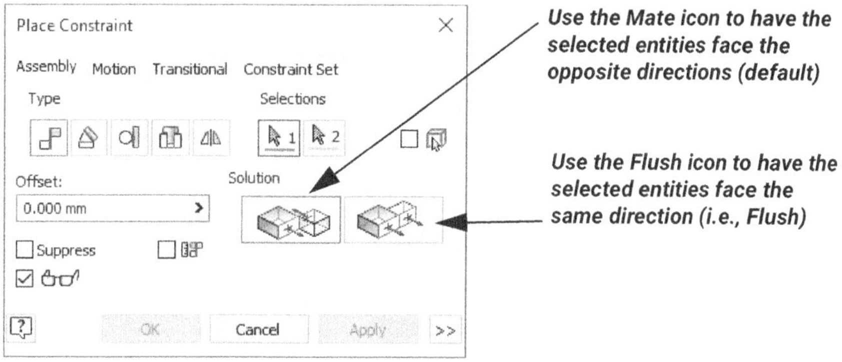

Figure 8–5

When linear edges or axes selected, the Mate orientation solutions are shown in Figure 8–6.

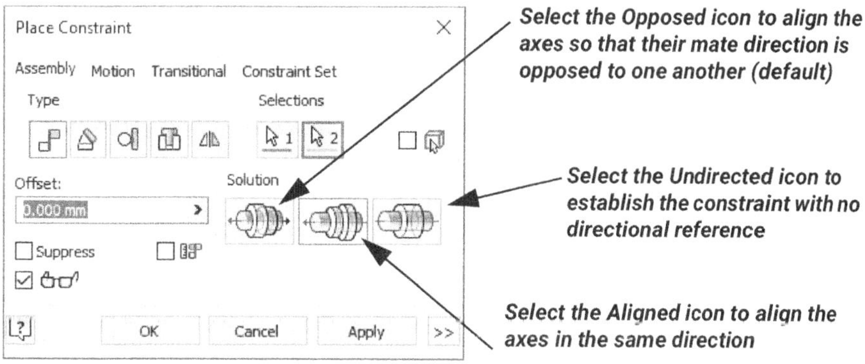

Figure 8–6

Angle

The Angle constraint ( ) specifies the angle between two edges, two planes, or an edge and a plane of the components. This constraint removes only two rotational degrees of freedom. The available Angle orientation solutions are shown in Figure 8–7.

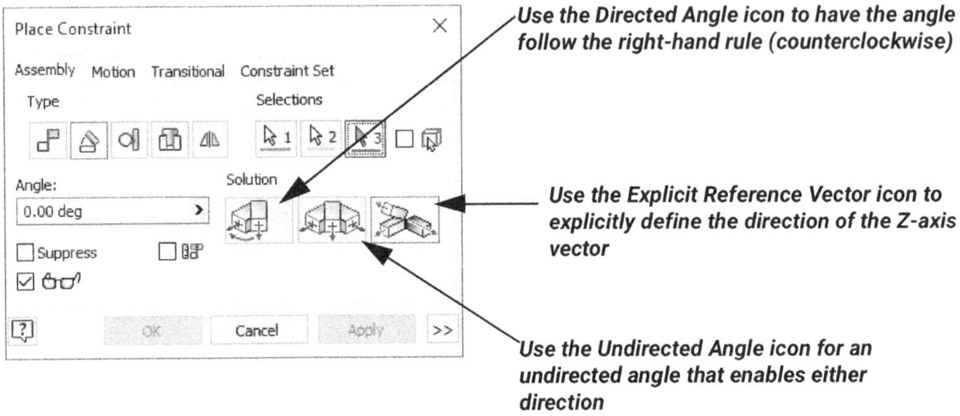

Figure 8–7

Tangent

The Tangent constraint ( ) positions two components tangent to each other. This constraint only removes one translational degree of freedom. The available Tangent orientation solutions are shown in Figure 8–8.

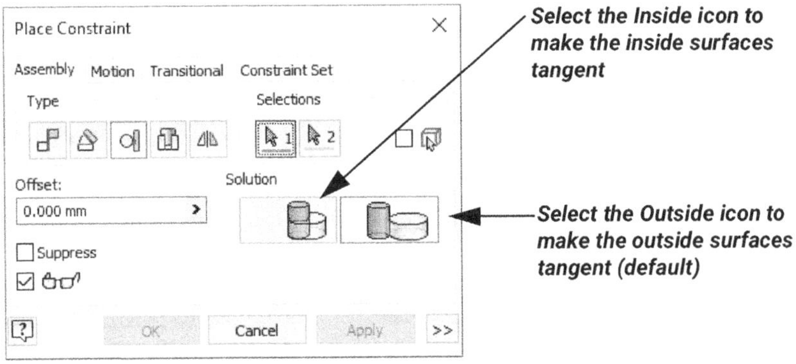

Figure 8–8

Insert

The Insert constraint ( ) enables you to position two components to fit into each other. This constraint removes three translational and two rotational degrees of freedom by mating the axis of two components, as well as applying a Mate constraint between two planar faces. To remove the final rotation degree of freedom, enable (Lock Rotation). The available Insert orientation solutions are shown in Figure 8–9.

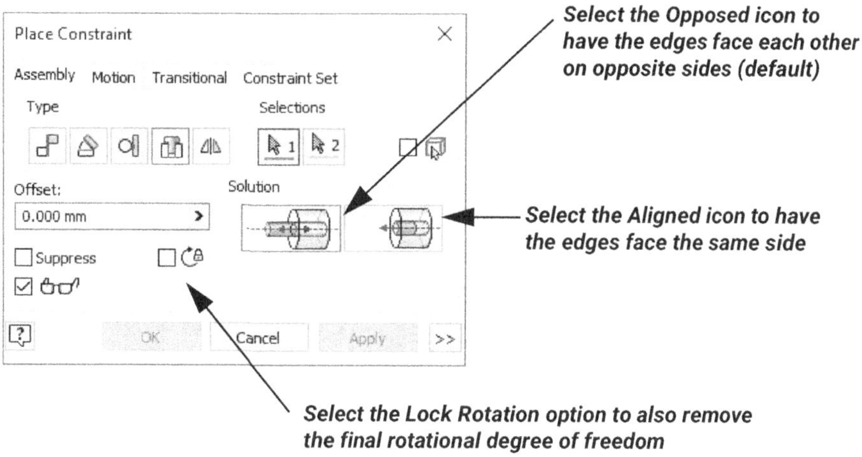

Figure 8–9

Note: *The Model browser icon used to identify an Insert constraint varies depending on whether* ***Lock Rotation*** *has been set. The icon indicates constaints where a rotational degree of freedom is still available and the icon indicates constraints where it has been locked.*

Symmetry

The Symmetry constraint ( ) enables you to position two components symmetrically about a plane or planar face. This constraint removes one translational and two rotational degrees of freedom by creating symmetry between reference planes or edges. When you place a Symmetry constraint, the dialog box opens as shown in Figure 8–10.

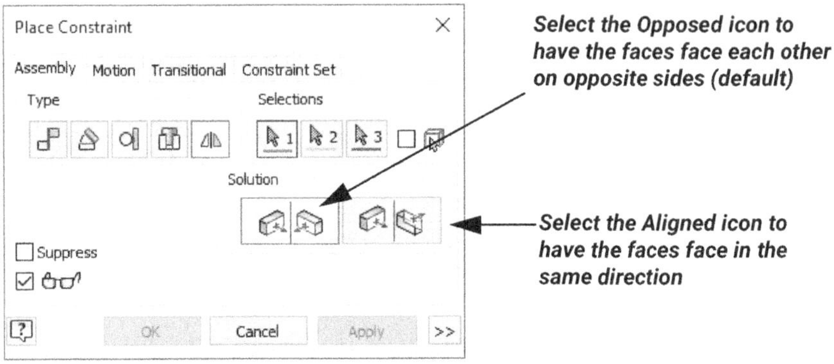

Figure 8–10

UCS

A UCS constraint enables you to position two components so that the UCS in each component is selected to be constrained to the other. This constraint removes three translational and three rotational degrees of freedom. It can be assigned on the *Constraint Set* tab in the Place Constraint dialog box, or using the **UCS to UCS** assemble option, as shown in Figure 8–11.

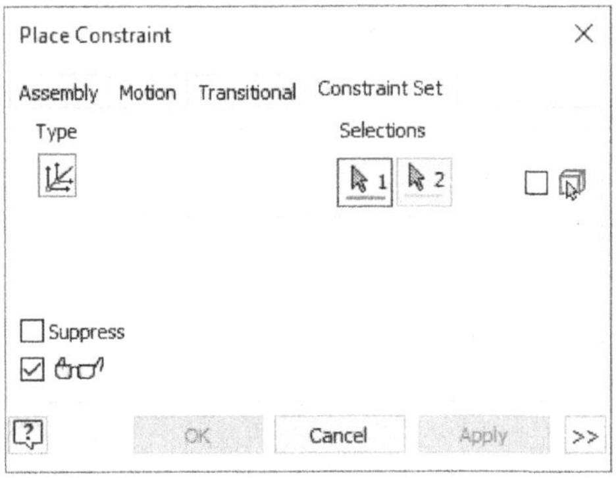

Figure 8–11

Step 5 - Select references on the components.

Reference selection on both components is required to fully define each constraint. Depending on the type of constraint being defined, you can select any of the following geometry types to define the reference:

- Faces
- Planes
- Lines (edges, curves, or axes)
- Points (work points, center points, or vertices)

> ***Note:*** *When selecting references, you can select faces through parts by hovering the cursor over the face and selecting it in the Select Other drop-down list.*

How To: Assign References

1. Ensure the (First Selection) field is active.
2. Select the geometry reference on the first component that is appropriate for the constraint type.
3. Ensure the (Second Selection) field is active.
4. Select the geometry reference on the second component that is appropriate for the constraint type.

To preview the effect of the added constraint in the assembly, click (Show Preview).

Hint: Isolating Components During Reference Selection

To isolate a component so that you can only select specific reference geometry on that component, click (Pick part first) in the Place Constraint dialog box and then select the component to isolate. This option is valuable during reference selection when components are close to each other or when one component obscures another.

Step 6 - Assign an offset value, as required.

You can assign an offset value between selected references in the Place Constraint dialog box.

- If the (Predict Offset and Orientation) option is enabled when you select two component references, the current distance (offset value or angle) between them automatically displays in the *Offset* field in the dialog box. The option is only available for the Mate and Angle constraints.

Step 7 - Repeat Step 4 to Step 6 until the components are fully constrained.

Once references and any offset value has been selected, click **Apply** to complete the constraint definition. Continue adding constraints between components until all required degrees of freedom are removed and the [•] icon appears in the Model browser for the component, indicating that the component is fully constrained.

Step 8 - Complete the component placement.

Once the components have been fully constrained, click **Cancel** to close the Place Constraint dialog box. Alternatively, right-click in the graphics window and select **Cancel (ESC)**.

- The default naming convention for a constraint includes the constraint type and a sequential numerical number. To rename a constraint, double-click on the constraint name in the Model browser and enter a new name.
- The assembly file stores links to and constraint information for the components used in the assembly. The geometry of the components is still defined in the individual .IPT (part) files.

Hint: Showing Constraints in the Graphics Window

To show glyphs in the model that indicate an assigned constraint, click (Show) in the Relationships panel and select a component. Preselecting all of the components and selecting this option displays all of the glyphs. Use (Hide All) to clear them from the display.

Step 9 - Edit the component placement, as required.

Constraints are listed in the Model browser under the component(s) to which they are applied. Expand the component in the Model browser to display all of its constraints. Additionally, all of the constraints are listed in the **Relationships** node at the top of the Model browser. Consider the following:

- To modify an offset value, select the constraint in the Model browser and enter a new offset value in the field that displays at the bottom of the Model browser.
- To edit a constraint, right-click on the constraint in the Model browser and select **Edit**. The original Edit Constraint dialog box opens and you can change any of the elements.
- To review failed (sick) constraints, click (Show Sick) in the Relationships panel. Edit the references as required to resolve the issues.
- To delete a constraint or a sick constraint, right-click on its glyph and select **Delete** or delete it in the Model browser.

  Note: *When components are copied and pasted, their constraints are only copied with them if both of the components used in defining the constraint are copied.*

Assembly Examples

The following examples use different combinations of Mate constraint references to create fully constrained assemblies. The components to be placed are shown in Figure 8–12.

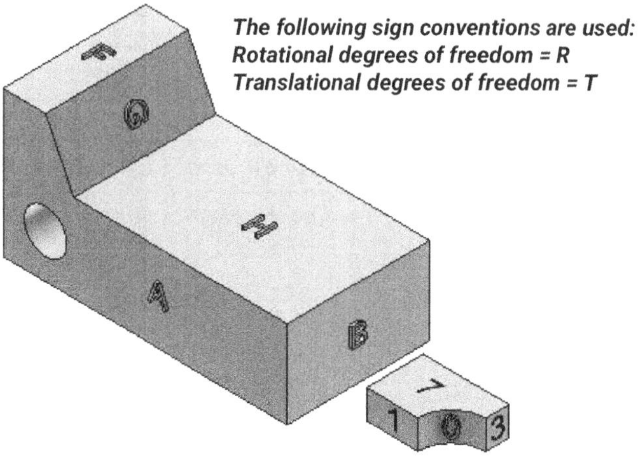

Figure 8–12

Example 1: Mate (Plane-Plane)

The combination of constraints and references shown in Figure 8–13 is used to create the fully constrained assembly.

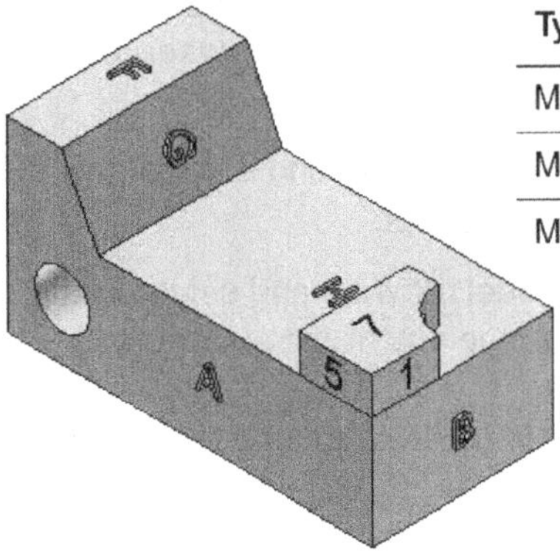

Type	References	Offset	DOF removed
Mate	Faces 6 and H	0.00mm	Two **R** and one **T**
Mate (Flush)	Faces 5 and A	0.00mm	One **R** and one **T**
Mate (Flush)	Faces 1 and B	0.00mm	One **T**

Figure 8–13

Hint: Mate constraints orient components so that surface normals are facing one another. This can sometimes make reference selection difficult, as it can hide references. Alternatively, consider using the Mate - Flush constraint until all of the references have been selected and then switch back to the Mate constraint.

Example 2: Mate (Line - Plane)

The combination of constraints and references shown in Figure 8–14 is used to create the fully constrained assembly.

Type	References	Offset	DOF removed
Mate	Faces 6 and H	0.00mm	Two **R** and one **T**
Mate	Face 1 and Face A edge	0.00mm	One **R** and one **T**
Mate	Face 3 and Face B edge	0.00mm	One **T**

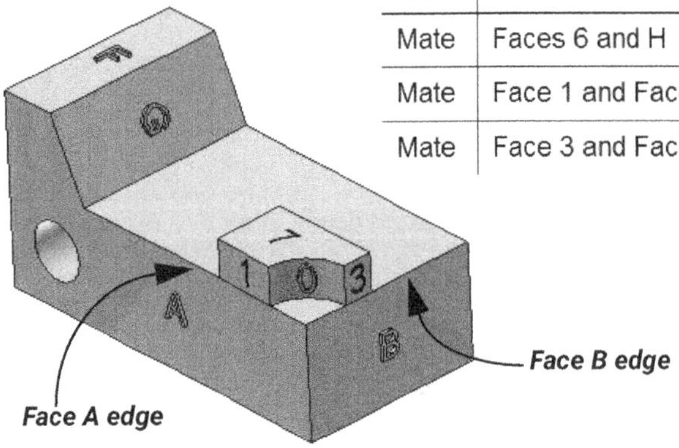

The Line-Plane Mate constraint type removes one translational and one rotational degree of freedom

Figure 8–14

Example 3: Mate (Line - Line)

The combination of constraints and references shown in Figure 8–15 is used to create the fully constrained assembly.

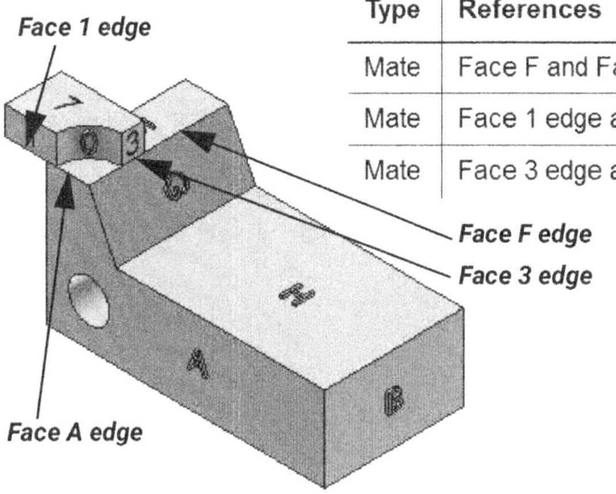

Type	References	Offset	DOF removed
Mate	Face F and Face 6	0.00mm	One **T**
Mate	Face 1 edge and face A edge	0.00mm	Two **R** and two **T**
Mate	Face 3 edge and face F edge	0.00mm	One **R** and one **T**

The Line-Line Mate constraint type removes two translational and two rotational degrees of freedom

Figure 8–15

Example 4: Mate (Work Point - Work Point)

The combination of constraints and references shown in Figure 8–16 is used to create the fully constrained assembly.

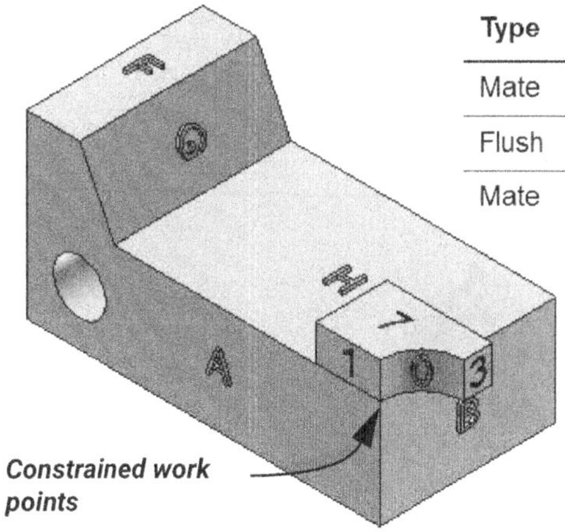

Type	References	Offset	DOF removed
Mate	Point from each part	0.00mm	Three **T**
Flush	Faces 1 and A	0.00mm	Two **R**
Mate	Faces 6 and H	0.00mm	One **R**

The Mate constraint type between work points removes three translational degrees of freedom

Figure 8–16

Example 5: Tangent and Angle

The combination of constraints and references shown in Figure 8–17 is used to create the fully constrained assembly.

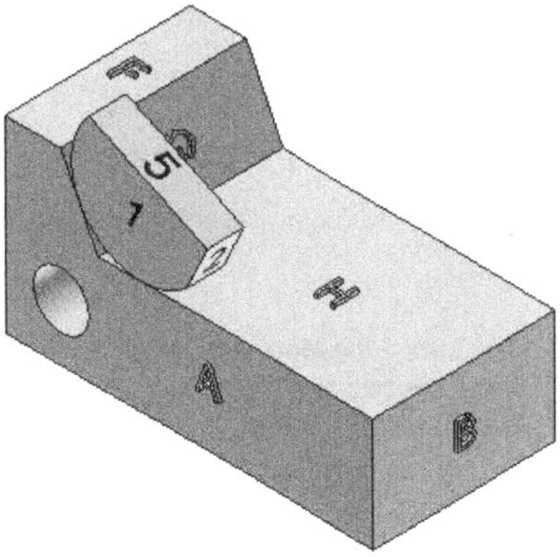

Type	References	Offset	DOF removed
Tangent	Faces H and 4	0.00mm	One **R** and one **T**
Flush	Faces 1 and A	0.00mm	One **R** and one **T**
Tangent	Faces G and 4	0.00mm	One **T**
Angle	Faces F and 5	25deg	One **R**

Figure 8–17

Example 6: Insert and Mate

This example uses different combinations of constraints to create the fully constrained assembly. You can create this assembly with only one constraint (Insert). However, if you want to orient the bolt in a certain direction, add an additional Mate constraint (Flush) or an Angle constraint. The components to be placed are shown in Figure 8–18.

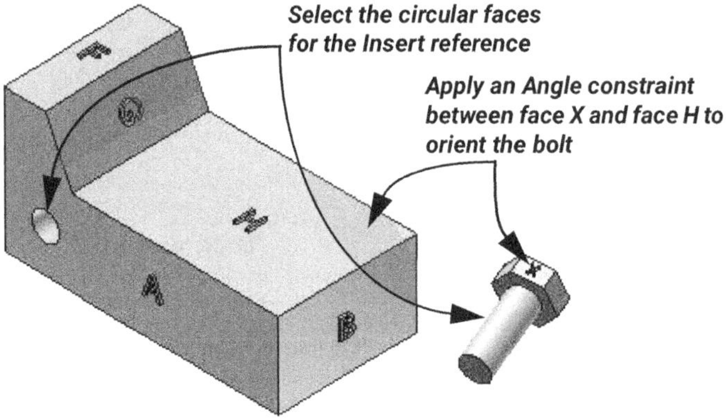

Figure 8–18

The combination of constraints and references shown in Figure 8–19 are used to create the fully constrained assembly.

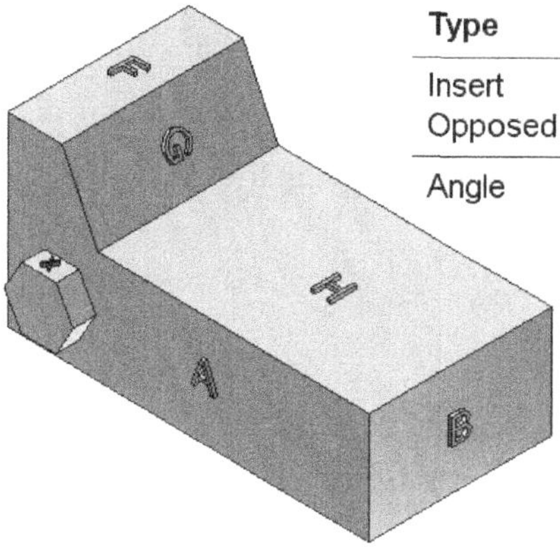

Type	References	Offset	DOF removed
Insert Opposed	The circular faces	0.00mm	Two **R** and Three **T**
Angle	Face H and X	0.00deg	One **R**

The Insert constraint removes three translational and two rotational degrees of freedom

Figure 8–19

8.2 Assembly Browser

The Model browser lists all of the parts, subassemblies, and representations and model states that make up an assembly. The following can be done using the Model browser.

- You can change the Model browser's display style. Select **Modeling** at the top of the Model browser to display component features and select **Assembly** to display the constraints, as shown in Figure 8–20.

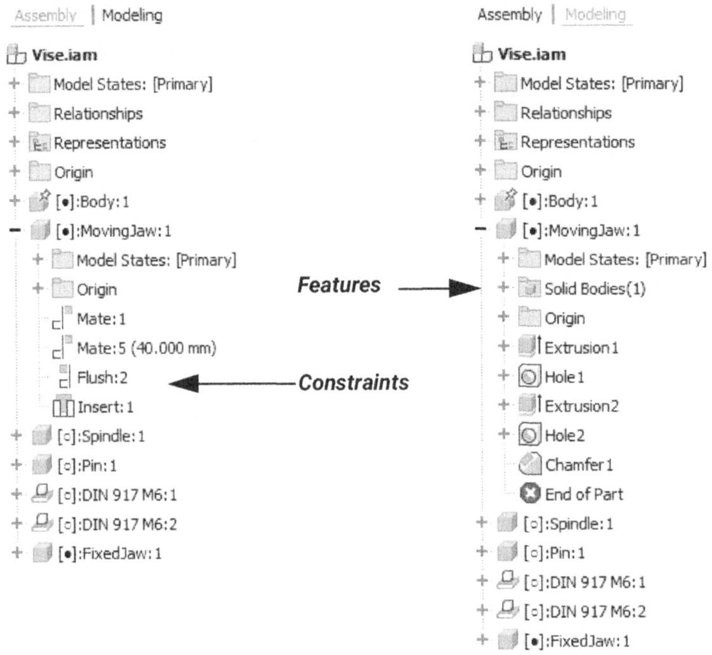

Figure 8–20

- You can find objects using the Model browser options:
  - Use (Find) in the Model browser header to search for objects, such as components, features, constraints, and sketches. If an item is located, the browser display updates to only show the located item(s).
  - Expand (Advanced Settings Menu) and click **Find**. The Find Assembly Components dialog box opens, providing advanced search options. This icon opens the same dialog box and options as when you click (Find Component) in the *Tools* tab>Find panel.
- You can identify the types of components in the assembly by the component icons adjacent to the names (e.g., parts ( ), subassemblies ( ), or content center items ( )).

- You can identify if components are fully constrained in the Model browser by reviewing the constraint states of components.
  - The (Pushpin) icon adjacent to a component name indicates that it is grounded (fully constrained).
  - The [•] icon adjacent to a component name indicates that the component is fully constrained.
  - The [◦] icon adjacent to a component name indicates that the component is not fully constrained. To review which degrees of freedom remain, you must review the existing constraints.
  - The [-] icon adjacent to a component name indicates that the component constraint status is unknown. To attempt to resolve it, in the *Manage* tab>Update panel, click **Rebuild All** or review constraints and assign as needed.

Hint: Enabling the Display of Constraint States

Constraint states were introduced in Inventor 2022, and the current default templates have them set to display by default. If they are not displayed, the assembly may have been created in an older version. To turn on constraint states, expand (Advanced Settings Menu) and select **Display Preferences>Show Constraint State**. Alternatively, you can set the **Show Constraint State in Browser** option from the *Tools* tab>**Document Settings**>*Modeling* tab.

- To open a component from the Model browser, right-click on the component in the Model browser and select **Open**. The part or subassembly opens in a separate window.
- You can open a drawing directly from the Model browser by right-clicking the assembly name and selecting **Component>Open Drawing**. If a drawing with the same name as the assembly exists, it automatically opens. If not, the Open dialog box opens for you to select the filename.
- You can create a drawing file directly from the Model browser by right-clicking on the assembly name and selecting **Create Drawing View**. You are immediately prompted to select a template. You can then begin the placement of the base view and any of its dependent projected views. Similarly, you can create a presentation file by right-clicking and selecting **Create Presentation**.

- You can manipulate the display of the Model browser using the **Display Preferences** options shown in Figure 8–21.
  - There are options that enable you to hide work planes, notes, documents, and warnings.
  - Using the **Show Children Only** option, you can list only first-level components in the Model browser (components in subassemblies are not listed).
  - Use **Hide Fully Constrained** to quickly turn off the display of components that are fully constrained in the assembly.
  - Enable **Show Constraint State** to display the icons ([-], [▫], [•]) to help you identify the constraint status of a component. You can disable this option to turn off the display of the icons.

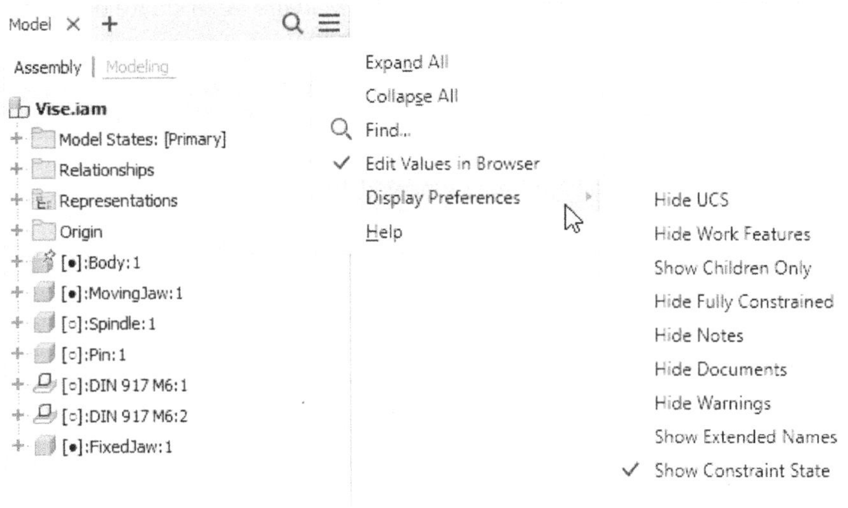

Figure 8–21

8.3 Saving Assembly Files

To save an assembly file, click (Save) in the Quick Access Toolbar or click **Save** in the **File** menu. If the assembly has not been saved before, the Save As dialog box opens. Enter a name for the assembly and click **Save**. If the assembly has been saved before, the Save dialog box opens as shown in Figure 8–22.

The Save dialog box lists the components that require saving and their checkout status (if a Vault project is active), and it enables you to set whether or not to save each file. The *Save State* column provides some information on why the file needs saving. If a row appears in red, it indicates the file is outside the active project folder.

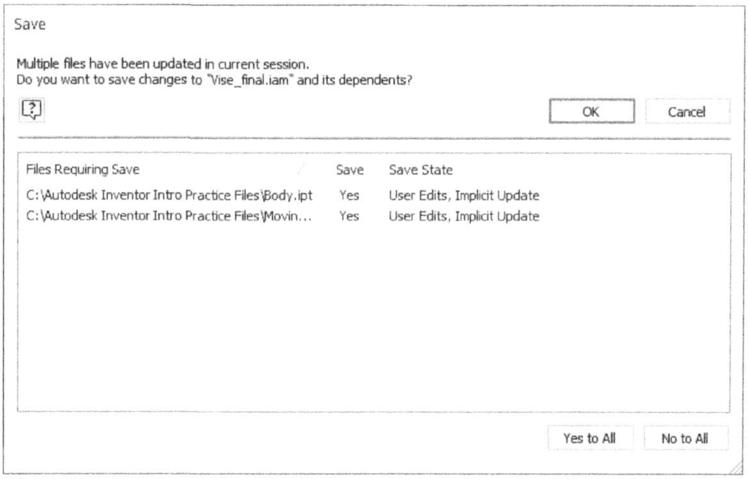

Figure 8–22

Note: *By default, all of the modified files are marked to be saved. Clicking **Yes to All** saves all files regardless if changes were made. Additionally, if you are working with the Autodesk Vault software, all of the saved files receive new versions based on the save date, not based on whether the physical model was actually changed.*

- If you do not want to save a particular file, change the **Yes** to **No** by clicking on it in the *Save* column.
- Files available for checkout (which you have edited without checking out) are marked **Yes** for saving and the file is saved and available for check out. If you click **Yes** to change it to **No**, the file is not saved.

Once you have decided which files to save, click **OK** to save the selected files.

Practice 8a
Assembly Basics I (Constraints)

Practice Objectives

- Place and constrain components in an assembly.
- Place a Content Center component in an assembly.
- Modify assembly dimensions to change the position of components relative to one another.
- Edit existing component placement references.

In this practice, you will create a new assembly and assemble the components, as shown in Figure 8–23. In addition, you will redefine the original constraints and references, and make modifications.

Figure 8–23

Task 1: Create an assembly and assemble the first component.

1. Create a new assembly file using the **Standard(mm).iam** template.
2. In the *Assemble* tab>Component panel, click  (Place). You might need to expand the Placement drop-down list to access this option.
3. Select **Body.ipt** in the Place Component dialog box and click **Open**. The component is added to the assembly.
4. If the component displays in a 2D orientation, return the model to its default Home view using the ViewCube. If the default orientation isn't as shown in Figure 8–24, right-click and select the **Rotate X 90**, **Rotate Y 90**, or **Rotate Z 90** to reorient it as shown. Once reoriented, right-click on the model and select **Place Grounded at Origin** to ground the component.
5. Right-click and select **OK** to assemble a single instance of the component into the assembly. If you select again an additional **Body** component is added.

6. Review the Model browser. Note that the base part has been added to the browser with (Pushpin) next to it, as shown in Figure 8–24. This indicates that the component is grounded. A grounded part is fixed to a location in the assembly and is not dependent on other parts. The [•] icon indicates that the component is fully constrained. Hover the cursor over the **Body.ipt** component in the graphics window and note that the cursor symbol has changed to , indicating that it is grounded.

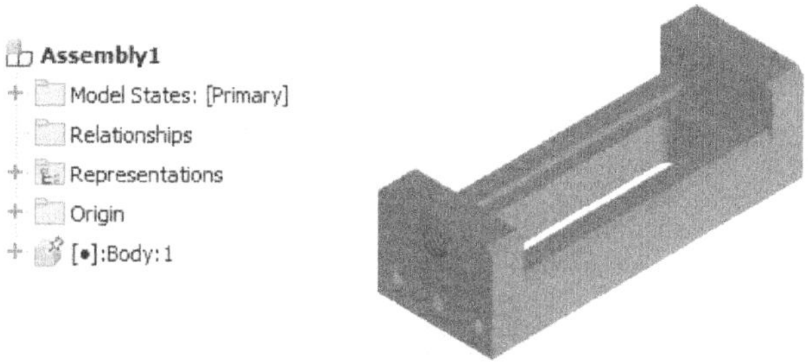

Figure 8–24

Task 2: Add another part and apply the first constraint.

In this task, you will add and apply the first constraint to place the **MovingJaw** component in the assembly. The final placement of the component in the assembly is shown in Figure 8–25.

Figure 8–25

1. In the Component panel, click (Place).
2. Select **MovingJaw.ipt** in the Place Component dialog box and click **Open**.

3. Right-click on the model and select **Rotate X 90**. Continue to right-click and select **Rotate X 90** to rotate the component into a more convenient orientation for constraining, as shown in Figure 8–26.
4. Position **MovingJaw.ipt** as shown in Figure 8–26, and click the left mouse button to place it.
5. Right-click and select **OK** to place a single instance of the component in the assembly.
6. Select the *View* tab. In the Visibility panel, click (Degrees of Freedom). Note that there are six degrees of freedom for **MovingJaw.ipt** as indicated by the symbol that displays on the model.

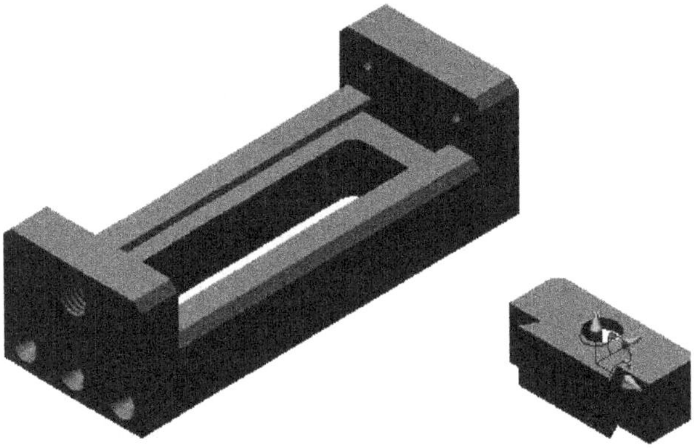

Figure 8–26

7. Note in the Model browser that the icon appears adjacent to the MovingJaw component. This indicates that the component is not fully constrained.
8. Select the *Assemble* tab and in the Relationships panel, click (Constrain). The Place Constraint dialog box opens.

9. Leave (Mate) selected. Select the face of the **MovingJaw** and the face of the base, as shown in Figure 8–27. Note how the references remain highlighted once selected.

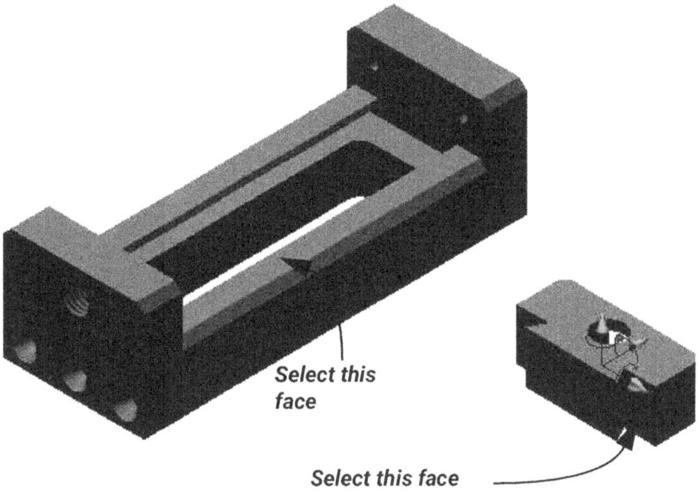

Figure 8–27

Note: When selecting references, you can select faces through parts by hovering the cursor over the face and selecting it in the Select Other drop-down list.

10. Click **Apply** to apply the constraint. The assembly displays similar to that shown in Figure 8–28. Once applied, the references are no longer highlighted. Note that the component can still rotate and translate.

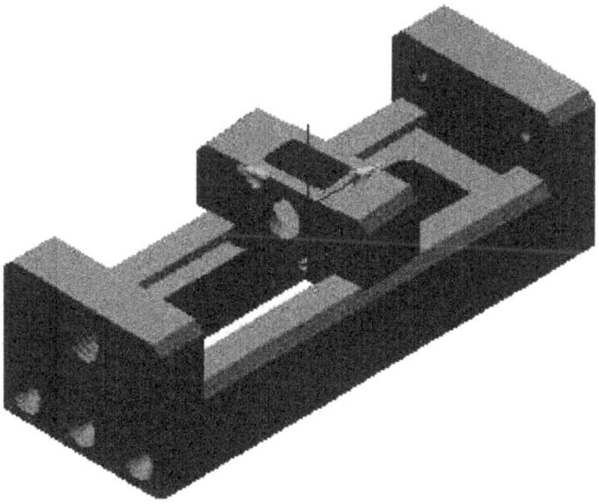

Figure 8–28

Task 3: Apply a second constraint.

The second constraint flushes the XZ origin planes of the two components with a zero offset. Where possible, assembling to origin features is preferable as these features are never deleted or modified.

1. The  (Mate) constraint type remains selected by default in the Place Constraint dialog box.
2. Click 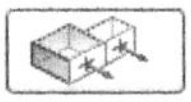 (Flush) in the *Solution* area in the dialog box.
3. Select the XZ origin planes in each of the components. The planes can be selected in the model (if displayed) or in the Model browser.
4. Enter **0.00** in the *Offset* field.
5. Apply the constraint. The assembly displays as shown in Figure 8–29. Note that one degree of freedom still exists in the model.

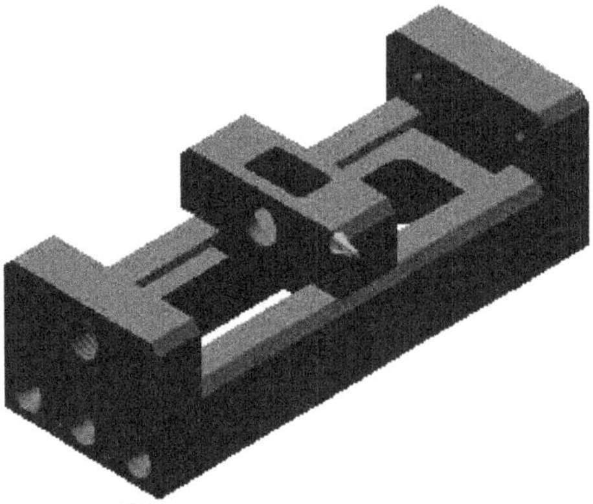

Figure 8–29

Task 4: Apply a third constraint.

The third constraint flushes the YZ origin planes of the two components with a zero offset.

1. Select the YZ origin plane from the **Body** and **MovingJaw** parts ( (Mate) and 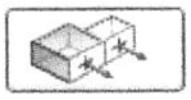 (Flush) are still active) to constrain the final degree of freedom.
2. Enter **0.00** in the *Offset* field.
3. Apply the constraint. The assembly displays as shown in Figure 8–30. Note that the degrees of freedom are completely removed and the [•] icon displays adjacent to the component name in the Model browser, which means that **MovingJaw.ipt** is fully constrained.

Figure 8–30

4. Click **Cancel** to close the Place Constraint dialog box.
5. Expand the two component's nodes in the Model browser and note that the constraints are listed. Expand the **Relationships** node at the top of the Model browser and note that the constraints are also listed in this node.

   Note: *Constraints are only listed in the component nodes if the Assembly View of the Model browser is active. The* ***Relationships*** *node is available in either the Assembly or Modeling View.*

Task 5: Add and constrain the spindle part.

In this task, you will add and constrain **Spindle.ipt** into the assembly. The final placement of the **Spindle** part in the assembly is shown in Figure 8–31.

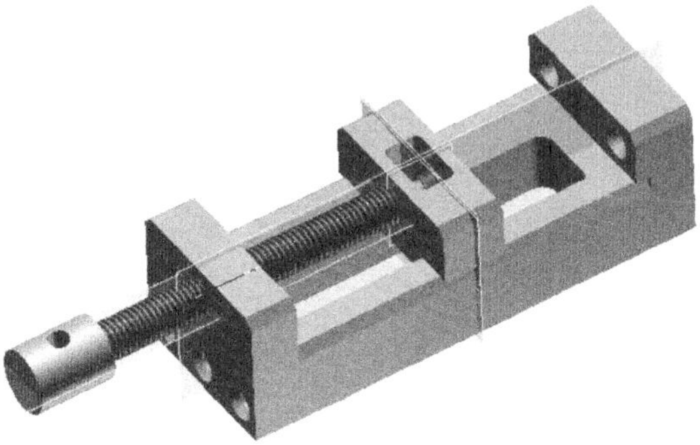

Figure 8–31

1. Toggle on the display of the origin planes in the models, if they have been toggled off.
2. In the Component panel, click  (Place).

3. Select **Spindle.ipt** in the Place Component dialog box and click **Open**.
4. Position **Spindle.ipt** as shown in Figure 8–32 and click the left mouse button to place it.
5. Right-click and select **OK** to assemble a single instance of the component in the assembly.

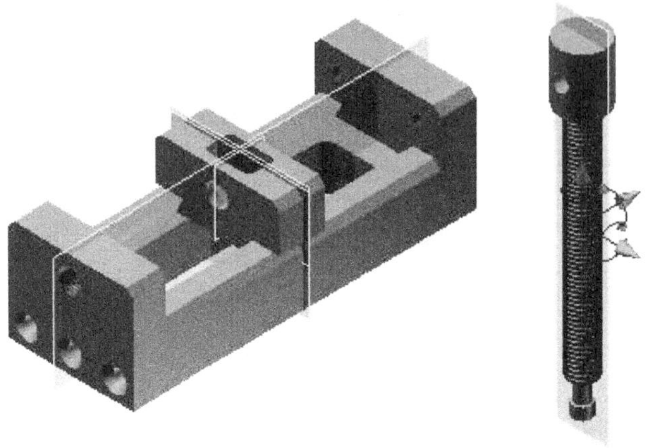

Figure 8–32

6. In the Relationships panel, click (Constrain). The Place Constraint dialog box opens.
7. Click (Insert) in the Place Constraint dialog box.
8. Ensure that (Opposed) is selected in the *Solution* area in the dialog box.
9. Hover the cursor over the hole in the **MovingJaw**, as shown in Figure 8–33. When the edge of the hole and the axis highlight, click to select them.

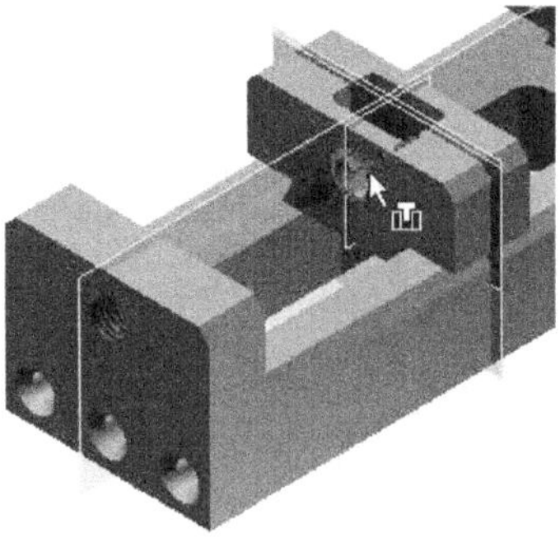

Figure 8–33

10. Hover the cursor over the area shown in Figure 8–34. When the edge and axis highlight, click to select them. An Insert constraint is applied between the two highlighted axes.

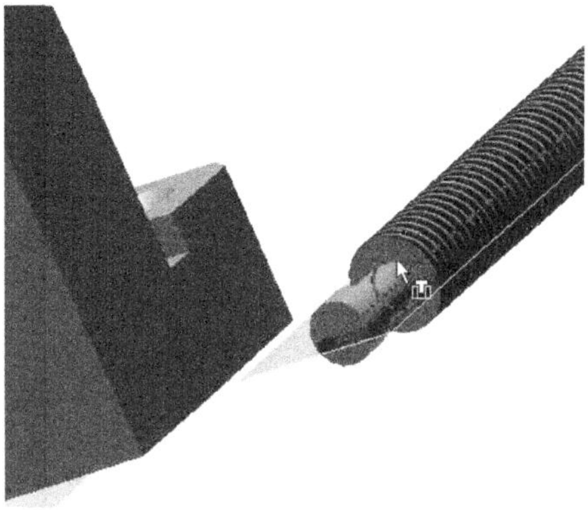

Figure 8–34

Note: *Activating the **Free Rotate** command to rotate a component independent of another in the assembly cancels the current command. To spin during component placement, use the global **Orbit** command to rotate the entire assembly.*

11. Click **OK** to apply the constraint and close the dialog box. The assembly displays similar to that shown in Figure 8–35.

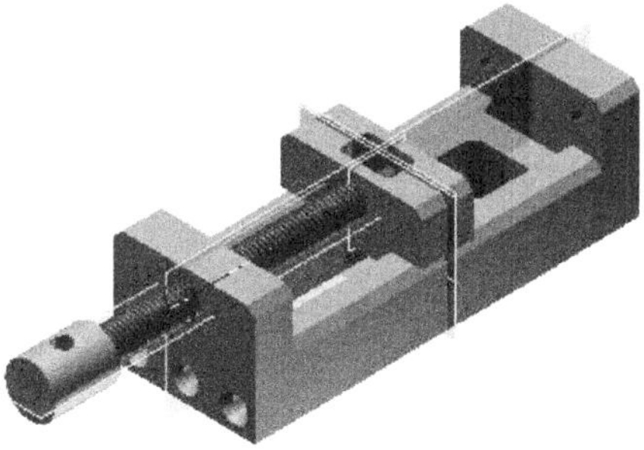

Figure 8–35

A rotational degree of freedom remains. This degree of freedom will not be removed, and the spindle will be allowed to rotate about its axis. The [◦] icon displays for this component in the Model browser, indicating it is unconstrained.

Task 6: Add and constrain the pin part.

In this task, you will add and constrain **Pin.ipt** into the assembly. Its final placement is shown in Figure 8–36.

Figure 8–36

1. Place one instance of **Pin.ipt** into the assembly, as shown in Figure 8–37.

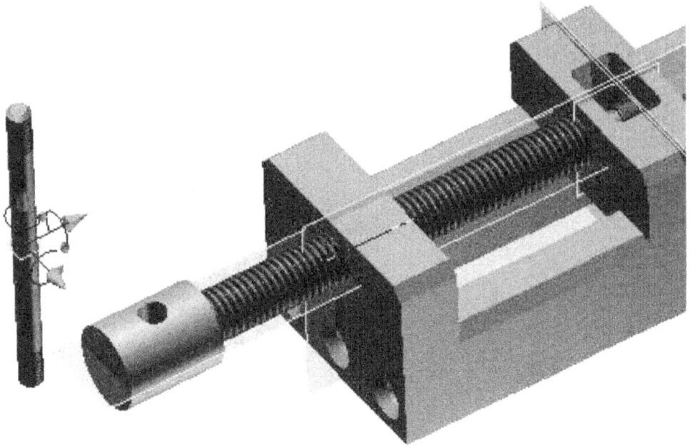

Figure 8–37

2. In the Relationships panel, click (Constrain).

3. In the Place Constraint dialog box, ensure that (Mate) is selected.

4. Select the axis of the pin and spindle, as shown in Figure 8–38. In the *Solution* area, also ensure that 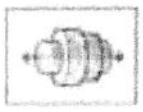 (Opposed) is selected.

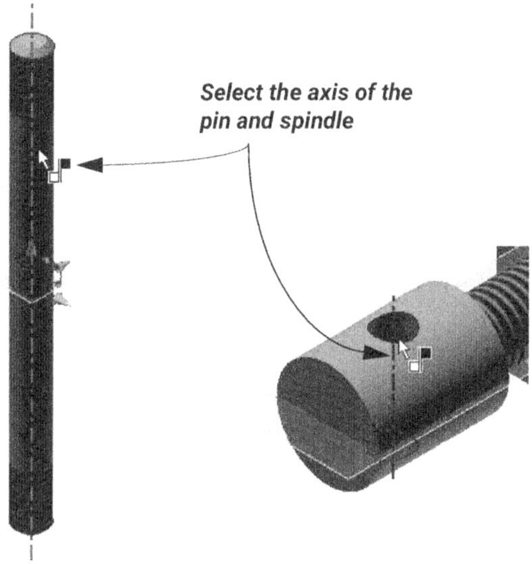

Figure 8–38

5. Click **Apply** to apply the constraint.

6. Select  (Mate) and 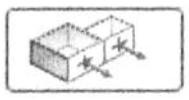 (Flush) in the Place Constraint dialog box and select the XZ origin plane of the spindle and the XY origin plane of the pin, as shown in Figure 8–39.

Figure 8–39

7. Click **Apply** to apply the constraint.

8. A rotational degree of freedom remains. This degree of freedom will not be removed, and the pin will be allowed to rotate about its axis. Click **Cancel** to close the Place Constraint dialog box.

Task 7: Assemble cap nuts.

In this task, you will add and apply constraints to place two cap nut components in the assembly.

1. Place one instance of **DIN 917 - M6 x 1 10 copy.ipt** into the assembly. This is a part file that has been provided for you that was originally from the Autodesk Content Center. Your company may or may not use the Content Center for standard fasteners. Note how the icon is different than that of a part file that you have modeled.
2. In the Relationships panel, click  (Constrain).
3. In the Place Constraint dialog box that opens, click  (Insert).
4. Ensure that 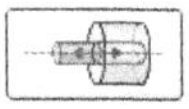 (Opposed) is selected in the *Solution* area in the dialog box.
5. Hover the cursor over the hole in the nut, as shown in Figure 8–40. When the edge of the hole and the axis highlights, click to select it.

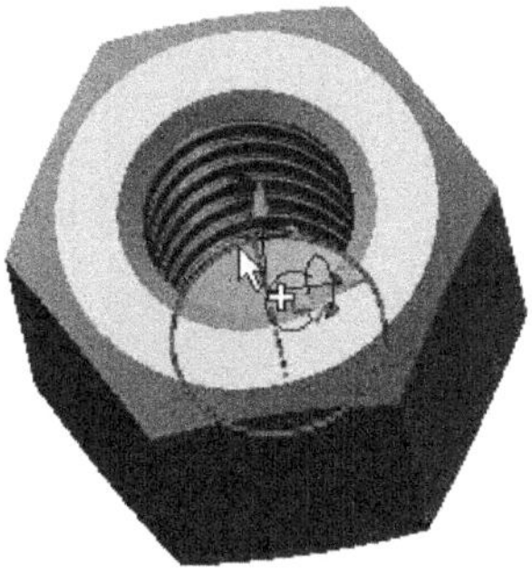

Figure 8–40

6. Hover the cursor over the area shown in Figure 8–41. When the edge and axis highlight, click to select them. An Insert constraint is applied between the two highlighted edges.

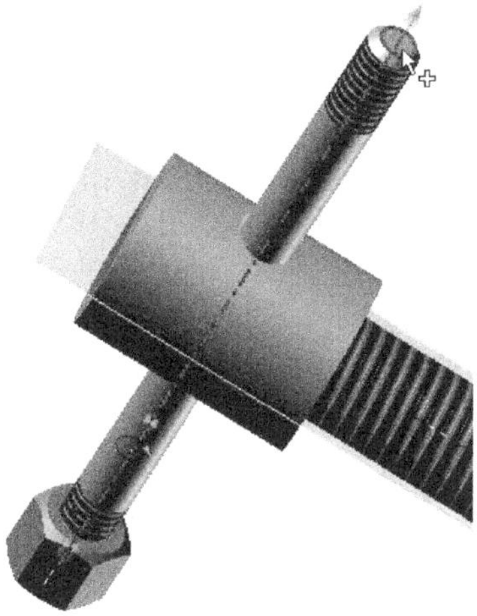

Figure 8–41

7. Apply the constraint and close the Place Constraint dialog box.
8. Create a copy of the cap nut component. Select **DIN 917 M6:1** in the Model browser, right-click, and select **Copy**.
9. Place the cursor anywhere in the graphics window, right-click, and select **Paste** to create a copy of the nut. Alternatively, you could have dragged **DIN 917 M6:1** in the Model browser into the model to include a second instance in the assembly.
10. Assign the same insert constraint to constrain the second cap nut component. The assembly displays as shown in Figure 8–42.

Figure 8–42

Task 8: Assemble and constrain the fixed jaw.

The Assemble mini-toolbar provides an alternative to using the Place Constraint dialog box to constrain components. It enables you to quickly select references in components without activating any constraint tool. On placement, you begin selecting references and a constraint is assigned based on the references that are selected. If the assumed constraint is incorrect, you can select the appropriate option in the drop-down list. Depending on the user preference, you can use the Assemble mini-toolbar or **Constrain** option. However, once you become more familiar with assembling components, the Assemble mini-toolbar can be more efficient.

1. Place one instance of **FixedJaw.ipt** in the assembly. Rotate the model as shown in Figure 8–43. A second component remains attached to the cursor. Do Not right-click and select **OK**.
2. Only the newly placed component is active for reference selection. Hover the cursor over the first circular edge reference, shown on **FixedJaw.ipt** in Figure 8–43 and select it.
3. The Assemble mini-toolbar opens immediately. Select the second circular edge reference on the **Body.ipt** component. as shown in Figure 8–43. The (Insert) constraint is assumed and displays in the Assemble mini-toolbar.

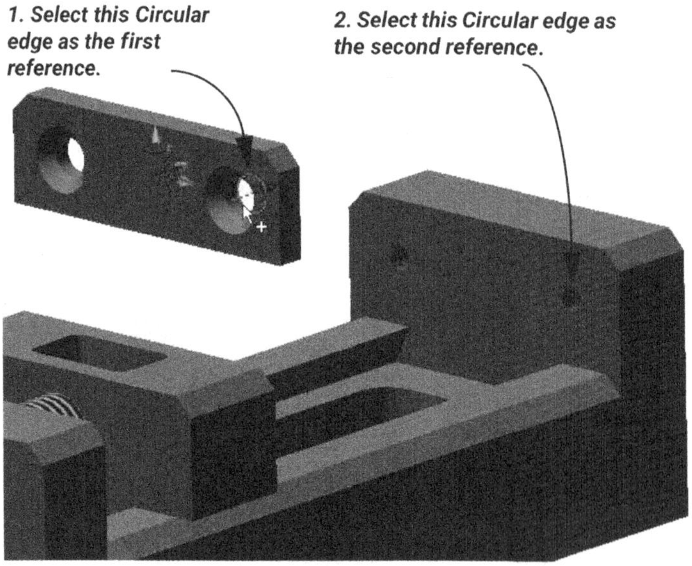

Figure 8–43

4. Click to apply the constraint.
5. Select the equivalent edges on the **FixedJaw** and **Body** parts for the left-hand hole.
6. Click to apply the constraint.

7. Click to apply the constraint and close the Assemble mini-toolbar.
8. The component is now fully located in the assembly. Because the constraints were assigned immediately on component placement, you can continue to place a second instance of **FixedJaw.ipt**. Right-click and select **OK** to end component placement. Activating and using the Assemble mini-toolbar in this way is excellent if repeating the assembly of the same component multiple times or to quickly constrain components without having to interact with the assembly commands in the ribbon.

Task 9: Modify the constraint references.

In this task, you will modify the constraint references between the **MovingJaw** and the **Body** components. The **MovingJaw** will be able to move along the **Body** in the Y-direction. In this task, you will modify the references so that a zero offset will place the **MovingJaw** against the front wall of the **Body** component. Entering positive offset values will simulate its motion in the Y-direction.

1. For clarity, hide all of the visible work planes and the *Degrees of Freedom*. Select the *View* tab. In the Visibility panel, expand (Object Visibility) and clear the **Origin Planes** option. Click (Degrees of Freedom) to remove the degrees of freedom from display.
2. Expand the **MovingJaw** branch in the Model browser and select **Flush:1** to verify that this is the constraint that is to be edited. (Your constraint might be labeled differently. Locate the constraint that flushed the XZ origin planes of the **Body** and the **MovingJaw**.)
3. In the Model browser, double-click on **Flush:1** to open the *Edit Dimension* field. To display the components (as shown in Figure 8–44), set the *offset* value to **20** and press <Enter>. Depending on the order of reference selection you might need to enter **-20**.

4. Right-click on **Flush:1** in the Model browser and select **Edit**. The Edit Constraint dialog box opens with the constraint references highlighted on the model, as shown in Figure 8–44. The constraint selections are color-coded to indicate the selection numbers that correspond in the model.

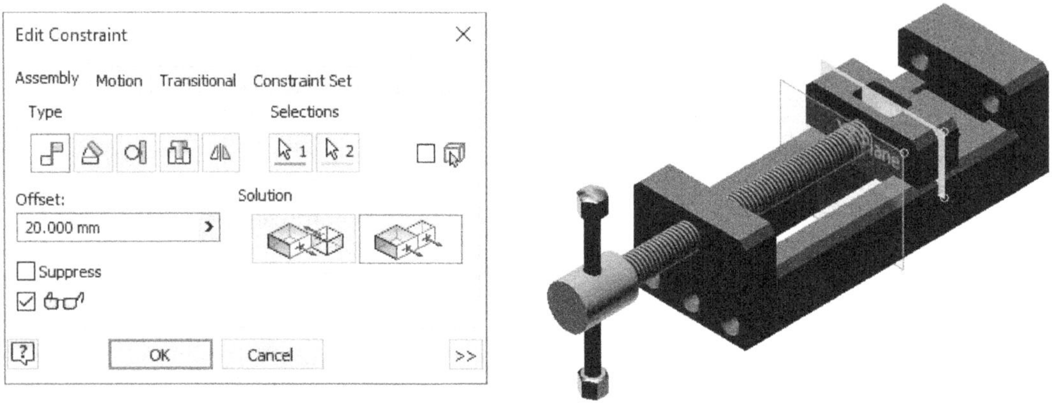

Figure 8–44

5. In the *Solution* area, click 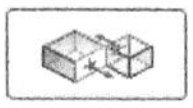 (Mate).
6. In the *Selections* area, click the icon associated to the XZ origin plane on the **MovingJaw**. Select the face on the **MovingJaw**, as shown in Figure 8–45.
7. In the *Selection* area, click the icon associated with the XZ origin plane on the base. Select the face on the base as shown in Figure 8–45.

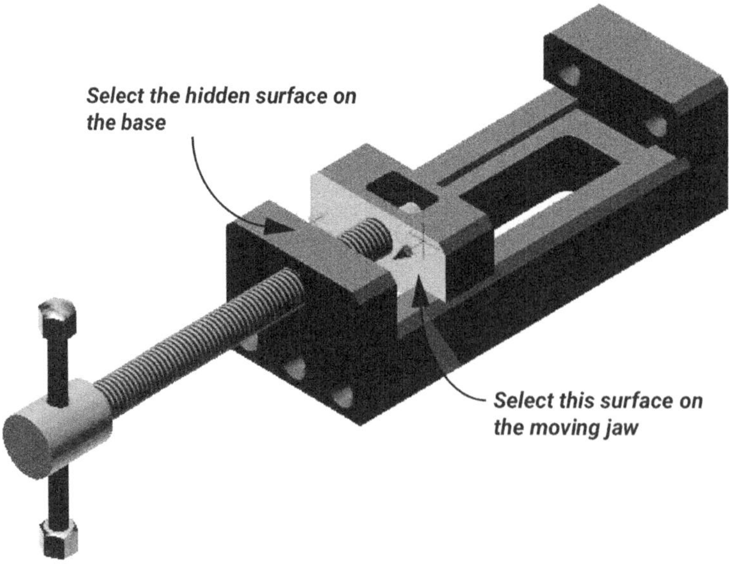

Figure 8–45

8. Click **OK**.
9. Modify the offset value of the new Mate constraint to view the motion of the **MovingJaw** along the **Body**.
10. Save the assembly. Enter **Vise** as the filename.
11. Close the window.

End of practice

Chapter Review Questions

1. You cannot assemble components so that two parts occupy the same space at the same time.
   a. True
   b. False

2. In the Assembly browser, shown in Figure 8–46, what does the Pushpin icon next to the **Base_vise** part indicate?

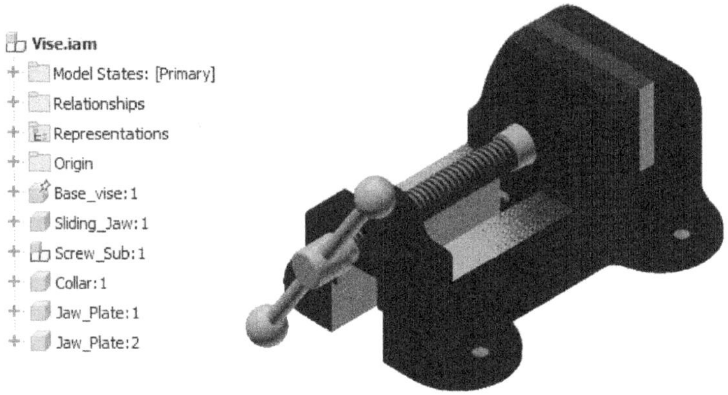

Figure 8–46

   a. The component requires additional constraints.
   b. The component is adaptive (size adjusts to fit constraints).
   c. The component was imported in SAT format (not parametric).
   d. The component is grounded (does not move).

3. How many rotational degrees of freedom (R) and translational degrees of freedom (T) does an unconstrained part or subassembly have?
   a. 1 R and 3 T
   b. 3 R and 3 T
   c. 2 R and 2 T
   d. 3 R and 1 T

4. In the Place Constraint dialog box, four areas are circled, as shown in Figure 8–47. Which area enables you to assign a constraint between two parallel surfaces as **Flush**?

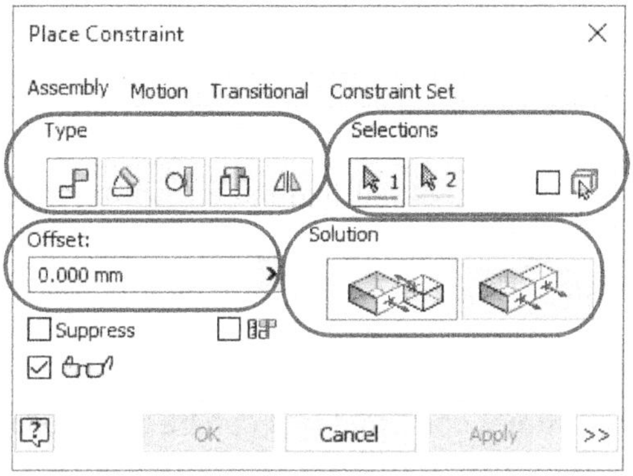

Figure 8–47

a. Type
b. Solution
c. Offset
d. Selections

5. Which of the following constraint types is highlighted in the Place Constraint dialog box, as shown in Figure 8–48?

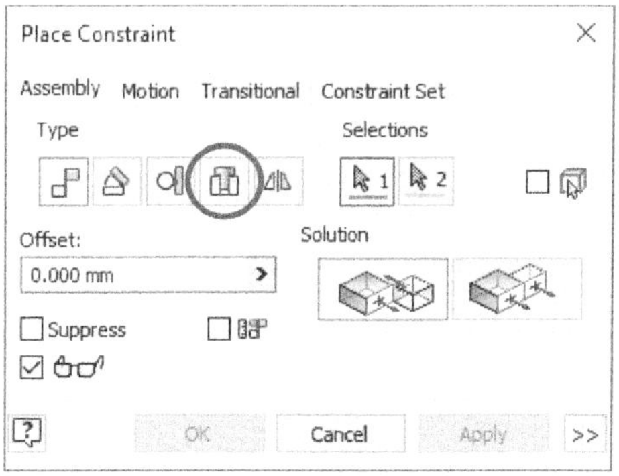

Figure 8–48

a. Pin
b. Flush
c. Insert
d. Mate

6. How would you determine how many degrees of freedom exist on a partially constrained part?

a. All degrees of freedom are automatically displayed in the model when the Place Constraint dialog box is open.

b. Right-click in the graphics window and select Degree of Freedom in the marking menu.

c. In the *Assemble* tab>Productivity panel, expand the commands and click  (Degree of Freedom Analysis).

d. Degrees of Freedom can only be reviewed in a sketch, not in an assembly.

7. Which of the following constraint combinations can be used to create the assembly shown on the right in Figure 8–49?

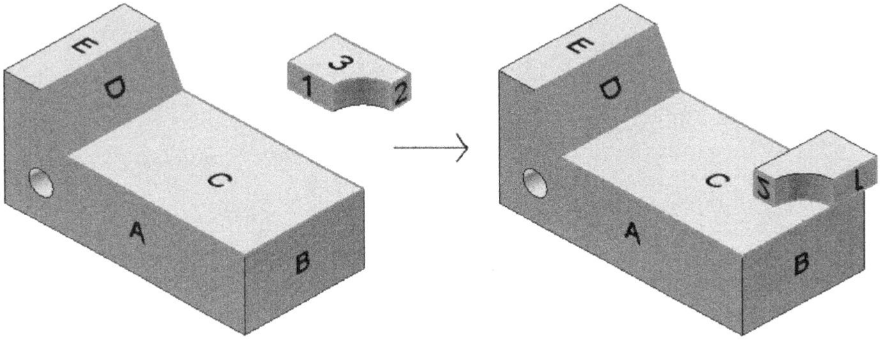

Figure 8–49

a. Flush 1 and B, Flush Offset A and 2, Flush C and 3

b. Mate 1 and B, Mate Offset A and 2, Flush C and 3

c. Flush 1 and B, Flush Offset A and 2, Mate C and 3

d. Flush 1 and B, Flush Offset A and 2, Insert C and 3

e. Mate 1 and B, Mate Offset A and 2, Insert C and 3

f. Mate 1 and B, Mate Offset A and 2, Mate C and 3

8. The pin is constrained in the holes on the part, as shown in Figure 8–50. How would you precisely control the distance between the pin heads and the sides of the part?

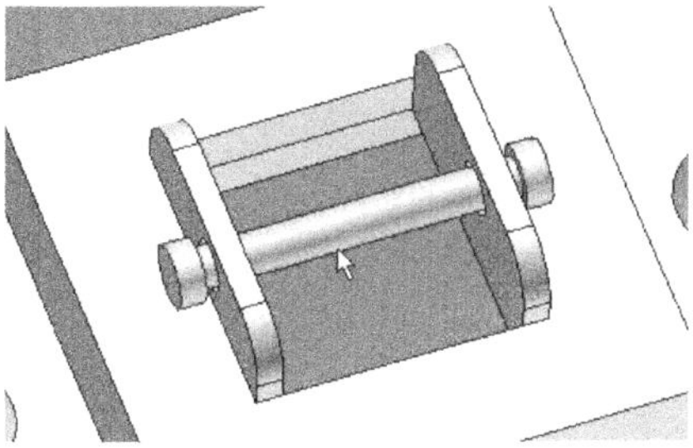

Figure 8–50

a. Set the offset value for the constraint.
b. Use Move Component.
c. Use Tweak Component.
d. Apply a model dimension in the assembly.

9. Which of the following statements are true of subassemblies? (Select all that apply.)

a. They are always grounded in the assembly.
b. They can contain other subassemblies.
c. They are always stored as .IAM files.
d. They act like a single component in the assembly.

10. What happens when you use the **Place** command to place an assembly file?

a. It becomes a subassembly in the assembly.
b. The parts of the assembly are placed as individual components at the top level of the assembly.
c. It becomes a grounded component in the assembly no matter how many components have been assembled before it.
d. The parts of the assembly are placed but are not enabled.

11. Which constraint type creates a Flush constraint, as shown in Figure 8–51?

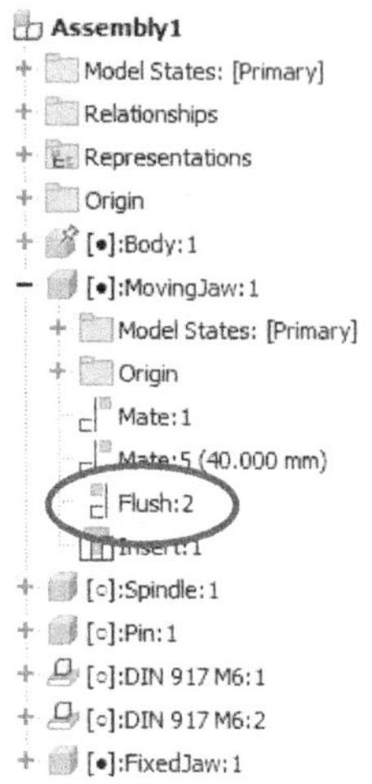

Figure 8–51

a. Insert
b. Tangent
c. Mate
d. Angle

12. What type of entities can be constrained with the Insert constraint?

a. Cylindrical entities
b. Linear entities
c. Flat entities
d. Points

13. When you set the Model browser to **Assembly View**, which of the following are listed in the Model browser display? (Select all that apply.)

a. Origin features
b. Assembly constraints
c. Assembly features
d. Part features

Command Summary

Button	Command	Location
	**Assemble**	• **Ribbon:** *Assemble* tab>Relationships panel
	**Constrain**	• **Ribbon:** *Assemble* tab>Relationships panel
	**Degrees of Freedom**	• **Ribbon:** *View* tab>Visibility panel
	**Degrees of Freedom Analysis**	• **Ribbon:** *Assemble* tab>Productivity panel
	**Free Move**	• **Ribbon:** *Assemble* tab>Position panel
	**Free Rotate**	• **Ribbon:** *Assemble* tab>Position panel
	**Hide All**	• **Ribbon:** *Assemble* tab>Relationships panel
	**Place**	• **Ribbon:** *Assemble* tab>Component panel
	**Show**	• **Ribbon:** *Assemble* tab>Relationships panel
	**Show Sick**	• **Ribbon:** *Assemble* tab>Relationships panel

Chapter 9

Joint Connections

The use of Joint connections to join components in an assembly is an alternative technique to assigning constraints. Depending on the Joint type selected, the assigned connections remove multiple degrees of freedom at once and enable you to test the movement between components based on the references you select.

Learning Objectives

- Use the **Joint** command to connect components in an assembly while maintaining the defined degree of freedom.
- Edit a joint connection so that the type, its references, or its values can be changed.

9.1 Assembling Components Using Joints

The **Joint** command offers an alternative to using the **Constrain** and **Assemble** commands. Joints enable you to define the allowable movement of a component by selecting a joint connection type. Based on the allowable movement for the selected type, all of the required degrees of freedom are removed at the same time.

Use the following general steps to join components:

1. Launch the **Joint** command.
2. Select a joint type.
3. Select references on the components.
4. Assign a gap value, as required.
5. Assign limits, as required.
6. Complete the joint.
7. Edit the joint, as required.

Step 1 - Launch the Joint command.

To join components using the **Joint** command, in the *Assemble* tab>Relationships panel, click (Joint) or select the <J> keyboard shortcut key. The Place Joint dialog box and the mini-toolbar interface open, as shown in Figure 9–1.

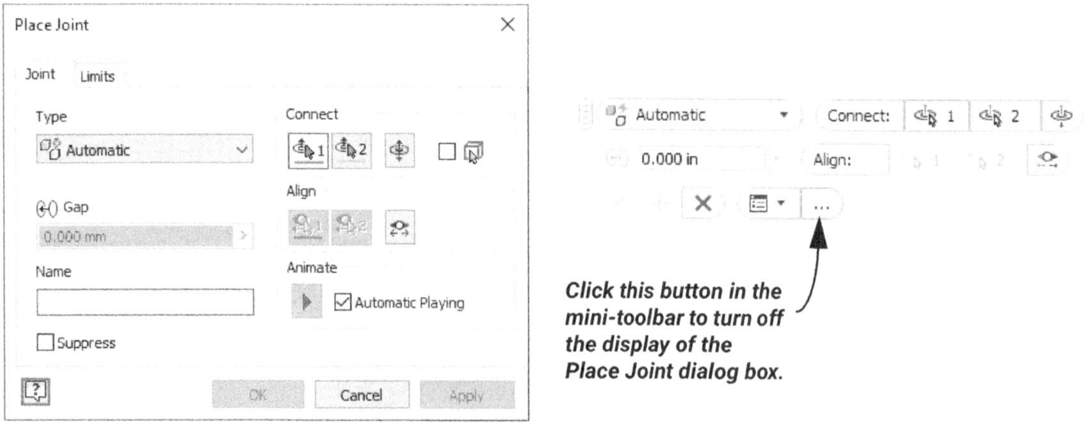

Figure 9–1

The Place Joint dialog box contains the same options as the mini-toolbar as well as the following options that can't be accomplished in the mini-toolbar:

- You can toggle the visual animation when components are joined (**Automatic Playing**).
- You can assign a name to a Joint.
- The *Limits* tab enables you to specify a limit on the range of motion for a specific connection.

Step 2 - Select a joint type.

The (Automatic) joint type is used by default. Alternatively, you can manually select a joint type in the drop-down lists, as shown in Figure 9–2.

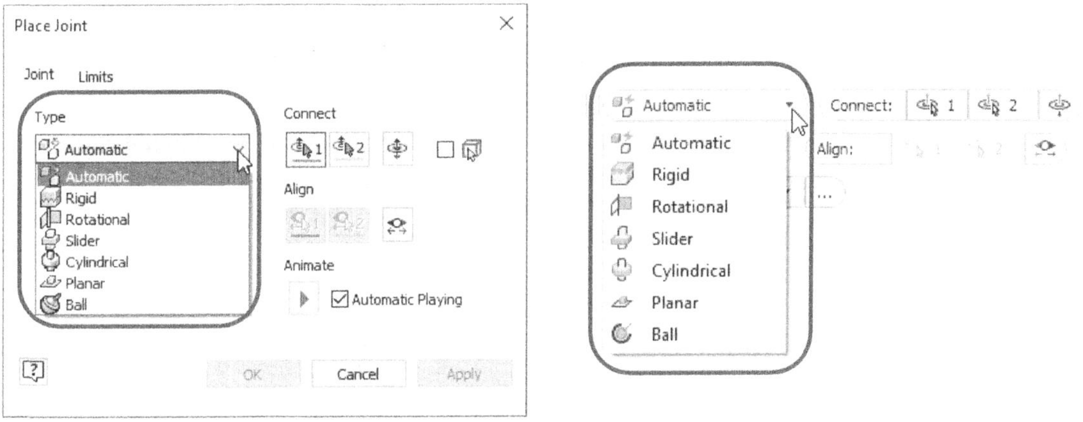

Figure 9–2

Each joint type connection removes various Degrees of Freedom (DOF). The degrees of freedom that remain permit the type of movement indicated by the joint type. The Automatic ( ) joint type enables the software to assume the joint type based on the selected references. Once assumed, the type can be changed if the software's assumption is incorrect.

The available joint types are listed as follows:

Joint Type	Icon	Remaining DOF
Rigid		0 Translational, 0 Rotational
Rotational		0 Translational, 1 Rotational
Slider		1 Translational, 0 Rotational
Cylindrical		1 Translational, 1 Rotational
Planar		2 Translational, 1 Rotational
Ball		0 Translational, 3 Rotational

Step 3 - Select references on the components.

References are required to fully define a joint type. Based on the selected references, the components are joined to one another and the selected joint type defines the allowable movement between the components. All of the references required for the joint types are assigned in the *Connect* and *Align* areas, as shown in Figure 9–3.

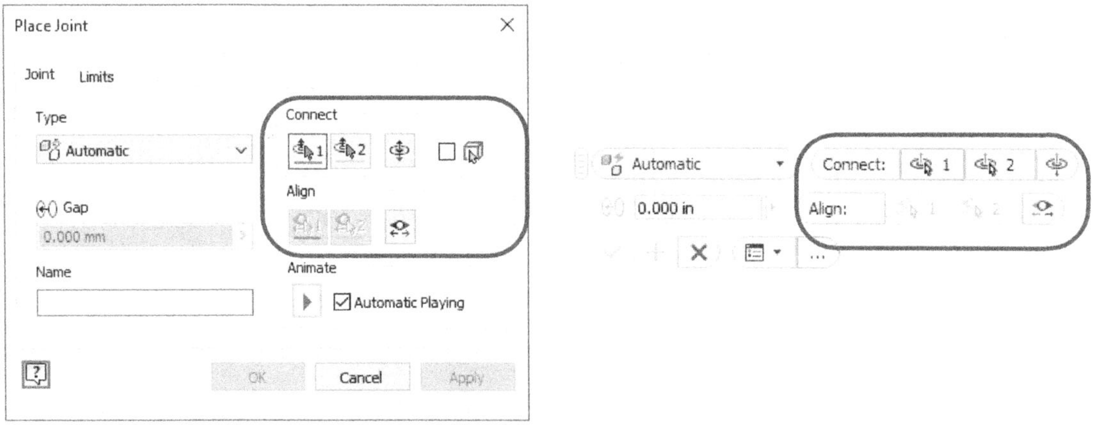

Figure 9–3

By default, once a joint type is selected, the reference selection fields are automatically active.

The first reference selected is assigned to the  *(First Origin)* field and the second to the  *(Second Origin)* field.

Before selecting a reference, it is important to note the active green dot on the highlighted entity. This point represents the Joint origin and is the point to which the joint is assigned. The location of the cursor on the entity controls which point is active. If the required point is not active, move the cursor closer to the required point to activate it. The entity on which it resides plays a secondary role in defining the orientation or alignment.

> ***Note:*** *When selecting references, you can select faces through parts by hovering the cursor over the face and selecting it in the Select Other drop-down list.*

The selectable entity types are described as follows:

Entity Type	Description
Face	For a rectangular face, the active point can be on: • A corner, • The midpoint of an edge (as shown on the right), or • At the center point of the face (as shown on the left). The location of the cursor when selecting defines which point is assigned. 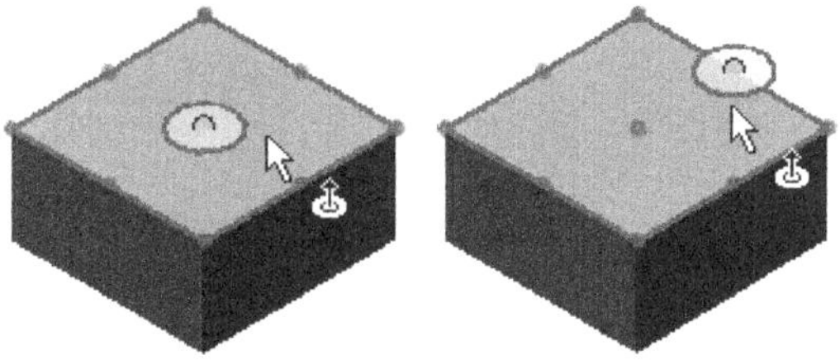
Edge (linear)	For a straight edge, the active point can be: • At either end (as shown on the right), or • At the center point of the edge (as shown on the left). The location of the cursor when selecting defines which point is assigned. 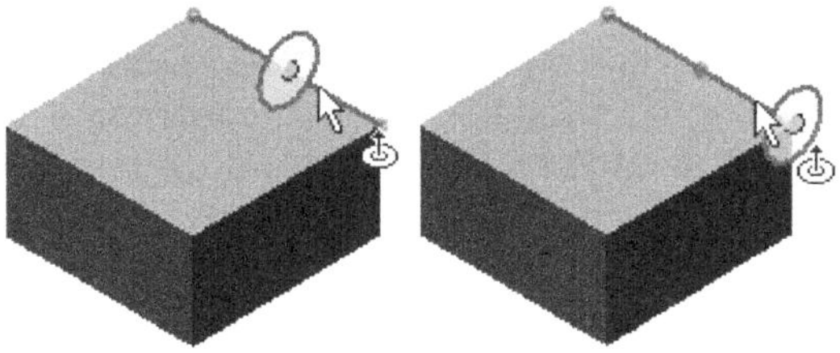

Entity Type	Description
Edge (circular)	For a circular edge or face, the active point is always at the center of the edge. 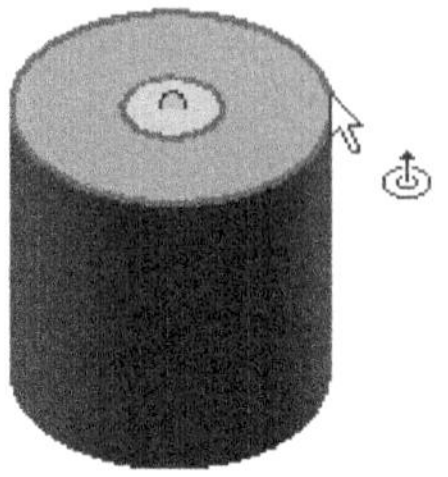
Spherical	For spherical geometry, the active point can be: • At the center of the geometry (as shown on the left), or • At points where geometry intersects with the surface of the sphere (as shown right). The location of the cursor when selecting defines which point is assigned. 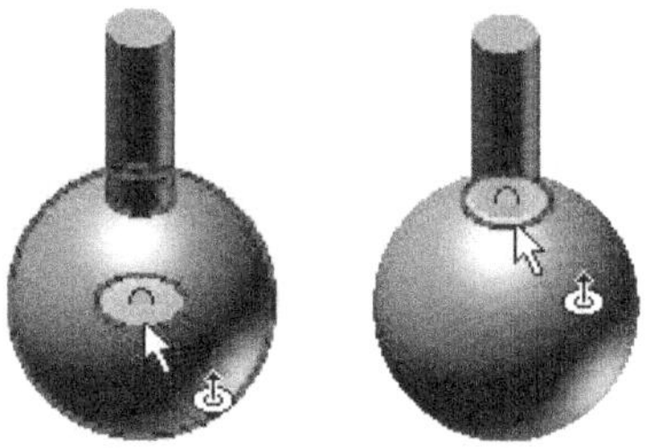

Hint: Working with Joint Origins

A new Joint Origin can be created by right-clicking and selecting **Between Two Faces**. Once active, select two faces to create the Joint Origin between them. Alternatively, you can right-click and select **Offset Origin** and then enter offset values to locate a Joint Origin. These two options are only available as you hover over the reference and right-click, as shown in Figure 9–4. By default, the **Infer Origin** option infers the origin based on the existing geometry.

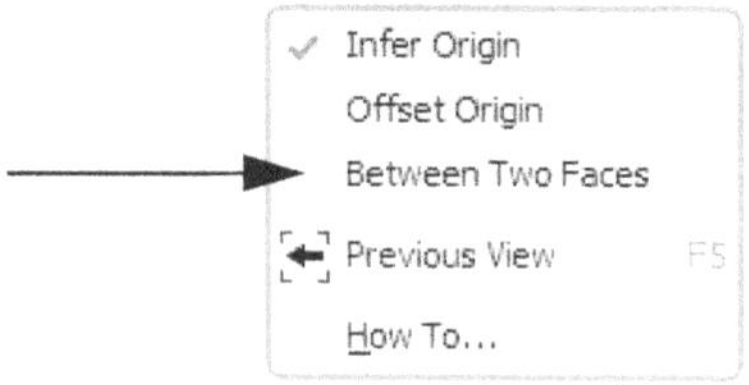

Figure 9–4

- Use (Pick part first) in the Place Joint dialog box to isolate a selected component so that you can ensure that the correct references on the isolated component are selected. Alternatively, you can use the **Isolate** option to isolate specific components for constraining. This is valuable when components are close to each other, or when one component obscures another.
- When selecting references, the first component you select is the component that is going to move. If it is a grounded component, you are prompted that a grounded component has been selected to be moved. You can accept this and the component remains grounded, but doing so changes the orientation of the grounded component.

Once the First and Second Origin references have been defined the alignment is automatically assumed based on the selected references, and the components automatically move into position. A short animation is played indicating the type of motion that remains between the components.

> ***Note:*** *To toggle off the animation preview when references are selected, clear the* ***Automatic Playing*** *option in the Animate area in the Place Joint dialog box. Click* *to play the animation at any time.*

If the component is assembled in the wrong direction, consider the following:

- Click (Flip Component) in the *Connect* area to flip the component's orientation.
- Click (Invert Alignment) in the *Align* area to try inverting the alignment.
- In the Align area, select (First Alignment) or (Second Alignment) and select new references (e.g., faces, edges, or work geometry), similar to that shown in Figure 9–5.

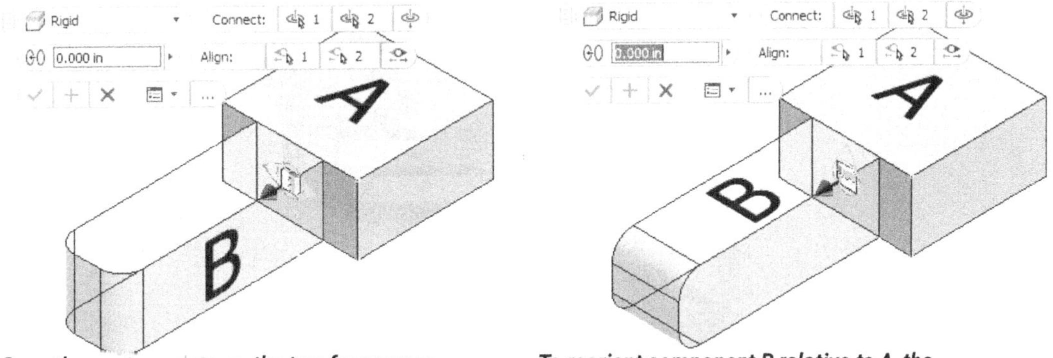

Once the center points on the two faces were selected as references, a Rigid joint was added and the components were automatically aligned.

To reorient component B relative to A, the alignment references were edited and both the A and B faces were selected.

Figure 9–5

The following examples explain how components were joined using the various joint types.

Rigid

The (Rigid) joint type removes all of the degrees of freedom, eliminating any relative motion between it and its referenced component. Welded or bolted connections are examples of the **Rigid** joint type, similar to that shown in Figure 9–6.

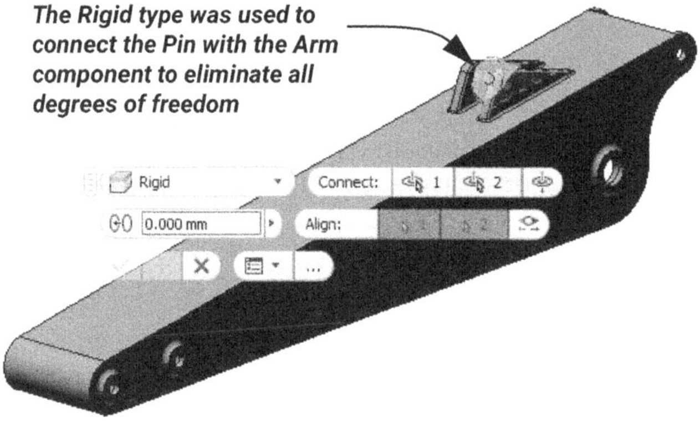

Figure 9–6

Rotational

The (Rotational) joint type allows for rotation about an axis, similar to that shown in Figure 9–7. This joint type removes five degrees of freedom.

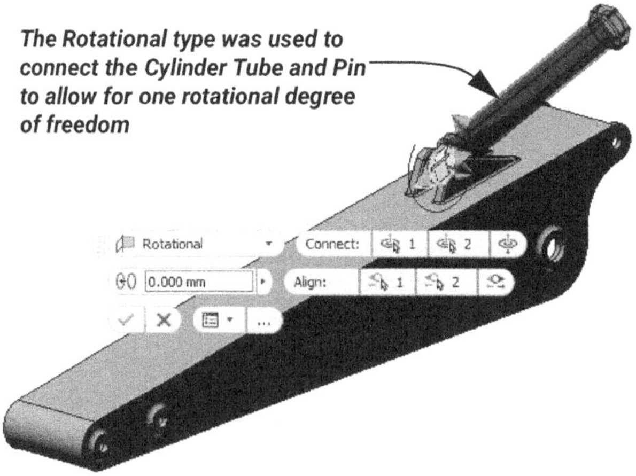

Figure 9–7

> ***Note:*** *Once a joint has been assigned, you can use (Degrees of Freedom) to graphically display the remaining degrees of freedom to help with visualization.*

Slider

The (Slider) joint type allows for translational movement along an axis, as shown in Figure 9–8. This joint type removes five degrees of freedom.

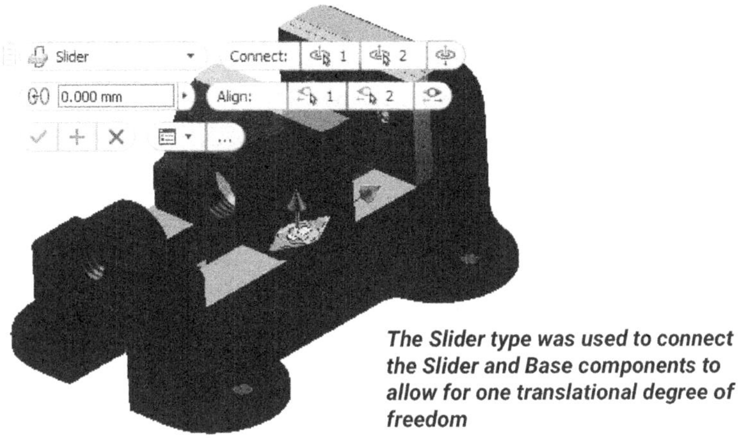

Figure 9–8

Cylindrical

The (Cylindrical) joint type enables a component to translate and rotate about a specific axis leaving two degrees of freedom available, as shown in Figure 9–9.

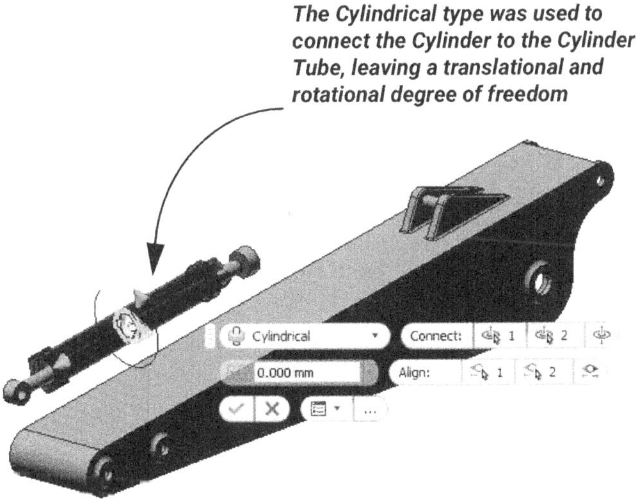

Figure 9–9

Note: *The preview for a new joint type does not maintain previous connections. Once assigned, the relationships between all of the joint connections display.*

Planar

The (Planar) joint type enables a component to move in a plane, as shown in Figure 9–10. Two translational and one rotational degree of freedom remain with the component.

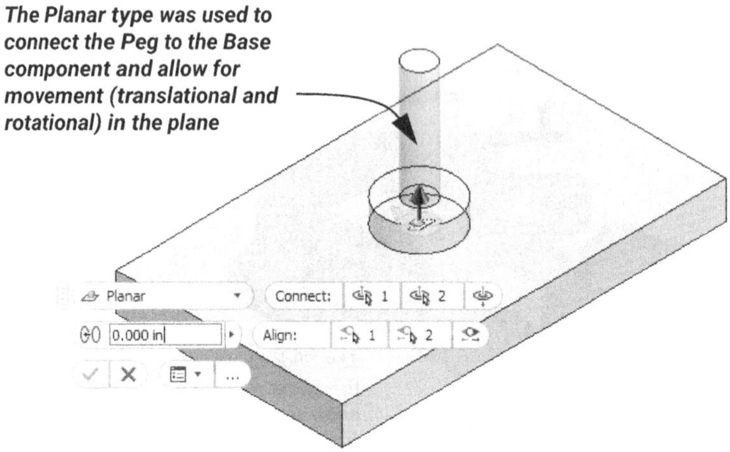

Figure 9–10

Ball

The (Ball) joint type enables a component to rotate in any direction about the origin joint, as shown in Figure 9–11. All translational degrees for freedom are removed.

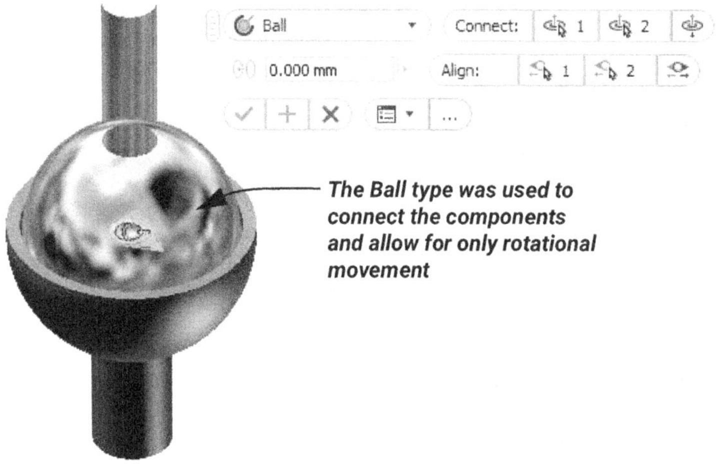

Figure 9–11

Step 4 - Assign a gap value, as required.

You can assign an gap value between selected references in the Place Joint dialog box or in the mini-toolbar. Entering a *Gap* value provides you with the flexibility of joining Origins that are at locations other than the end and center points.

Step 5 - Assign limits, as required.

To further control the motion that is permitted by a joint, you can define a specific range of motion. This is done by selecting the *Limits* tab in the Place Joint dialog box and entering values in the *Angular* and *Linear* areas, as shown in Figure 9–12. Limits can only be assigned in the Place Joint dialog box. You cannot set limits in the mini-toolbar.

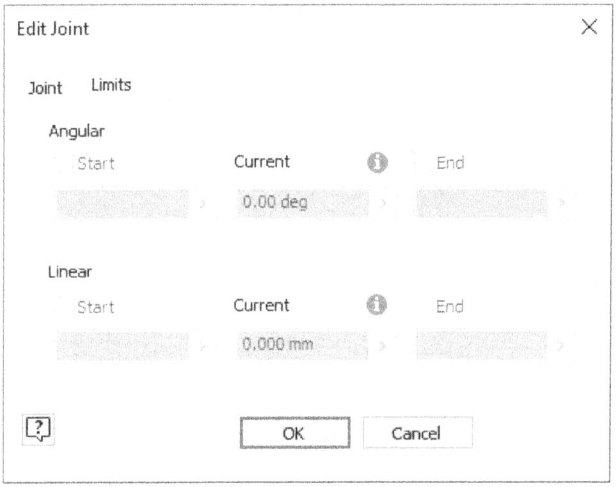

Figure 9–12

Note: *Limits cannot be specified for any option that is disabled, because the degree of freedom does not exist in the model.*

To specify a range, select **Start** or **End** and enter values to define a limit on the range of motion. For example, the angular range for a **Rotational** joint type can be controlled and a linear range can be specified for a **Slider** joint type. The *Current* value listed in each area defines the current position of the component in the assembly.

Step 6 - Complete the joint.

Click **OK** in the Place Joint dialog box or click ✓ in the mini-toolbar to complete the joint. Alternatively, you can right-click in the graphics window and select **OK (Enter)** or press <Enter> to complete the joint.

- The default name for a Joint is its type, followed by a number that indicates the number of joints of that type that have been assigned. Double-click on a joint's name in the Model browser to rename it. Alternatively, it can be renamed in the *Name* field of the dialog box.
- Use the **Lock** option (shown in Figure 9–13) to maintain the current position of the component without disabling the degrees of freedom that have been set in the component. A locked component cannot be selected to be moved. However, it updates if the connected components are moved, as opposed to grounding a component, which would lock the component in place regardless of any changes made.
- Use the **Protect** option (shown in Figure 9–13) to enable whether you should be prompted if relationships violate the degrees of freedom that have been assigned to the component with the use of a joint.

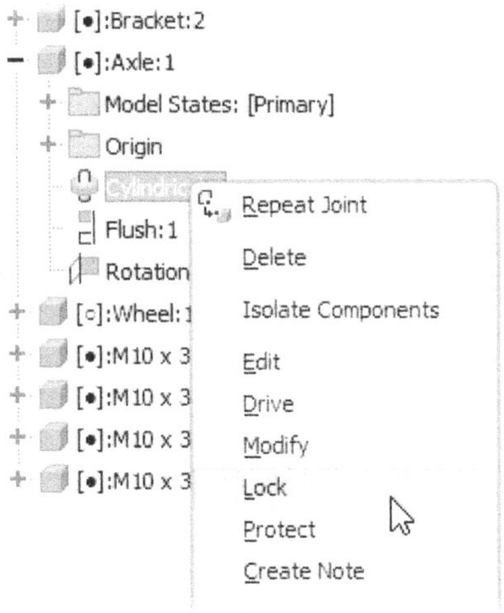

Figure 9–13

*Note: The **Lock** and **Protect** options are only available for joints, not for constraints.*

Hint: Combine Joints with Constraints

You can use the **Constrain** or **Assemble** commands to add additional constraints between components to further constrain any open degrees of freedom.

Step 7 - Edit the joint, as required.

Joints are listed in the Model browser under the component(s) to which they have been applied, as well as in the **Relationships** node at the top of the Model browser. Consider the following to edit a joint:

- To modify any value associated with a joint, double-click on the joint's name in the Model browser or right-click and select **Modify**. A mini-toolbar displays that enables you to enter the new values for linear or gap values.
- To change references used for a joint, right-click on the joint name in the Model browser and select **Edit**. The Edit Joint dialog box opens and you can change any of original references.
- To delete a joint, right-click the joint name in the Model browser and select **Delete**.
- To review the relationships between components, click (Free Move) and drag a component. The connections are indicated by connecting lines, and glyphs indicate the type of joints that were used, as shown in Figure 9–14.

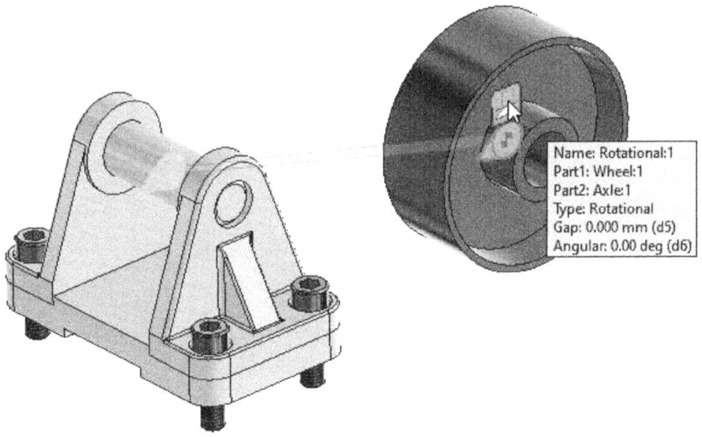

Figure 9–14

- Use (Show) in the Relationships panel to display the glyphs for any selected components. Preselecting all of the components and selecting this option displays all of the glyphs. Use (Hide All) to clear them from the display.
- You can right-click on the icons to suppress or delete a joint type. You can also select **Suppress** in the Joint dialog box to suppress a joint during creation or editing.
- If any of the joints are failing you can use (Show Sick) in the Relationships panel to review them. This command is only available if there are sick joints in the assembly. Edit the references as required to resolve the issues or delete the Joint.

Practice 9a
Assembly Basics II (Joints)

Practice Objectives

- Use the **Joint** command to fully connect components in an assembly.
- Drag components to verify the movement in the assembly.

In this practice, you will create a new assembly and assemble the components as shown in Figure 9–15. To assemble the components, you will use the **Joint** command, which will connect components relative to one another so that the assembly can easily be tested for movement.

Figure 9–15

Task 1: Create a new assembly and assemble the first component.

1. Create a new assembly file using the **Standard(mm).iam** template file.
2. In the Component panel, click  (Place).
3. Select **Plate.ipt** in the Place Component dialog box and click **Open**. The component is added to the assembly.
4. If the component displays in a 2D orientation, return the model to its default Home view using the ViewCube.

5. If the default orientation isn't as shown in Figure 9–16, right-click and select the **Rotate X 90**, **Rotate Y 90**, or **Rotate Z 90** to reorient it as shown. Once reoriented, right-click on the model and select **Place Grounded at Origin** to ground the component. The model displays as shown in Figure 9–16.

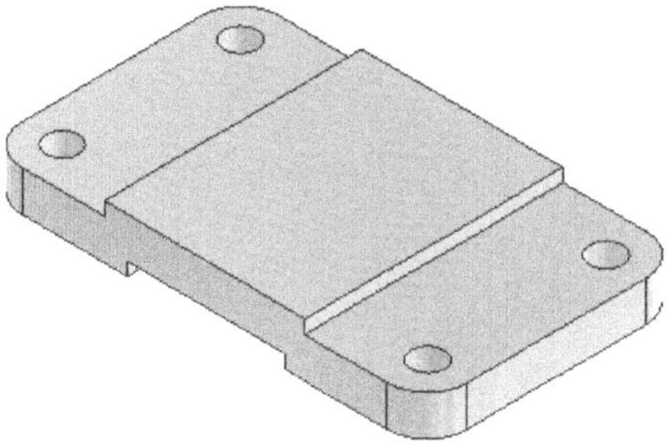

Figure 9–16

Note: *The assembly's visibility style has been set to* ***Shaded with Edges*** *for clarity in the images.*

6. Right-click and select **OK** to assemble a single instance of the component into the assembly.

7. Review the Model browser and note the pushpin ( ) symbol next to the **Plate**, as shown in Figure 9–17. This indicates that the component is grounded. The [•] icon indicates that the component is fully constrained. Hover the cursor over the **Plate.ipt** component in the graphics window. The cursor symbol also indicates that it is grounded.

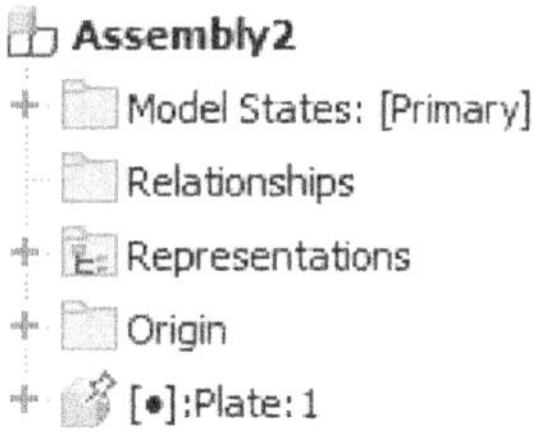

Figure 9–17

Task 2: Assemble the Bracket component.

1. Select the *Assemble* tab, and in the Component panel, click (Place).
2. Select **Bracket.ipt** in the Place Component dialog box and click **Open**. The component is added to the assembly.

3. Right-click on the model and select **Rotate Z 90** to rotate the component, right-click again and select **Rotate Y 90** to rotate is into a more convenient orientation for reference selection.

4. Use the left mouse button to locate the component next to the **Plate** component, as shown in Figure 9–18. Right-click and select **OK** to place a single instance.

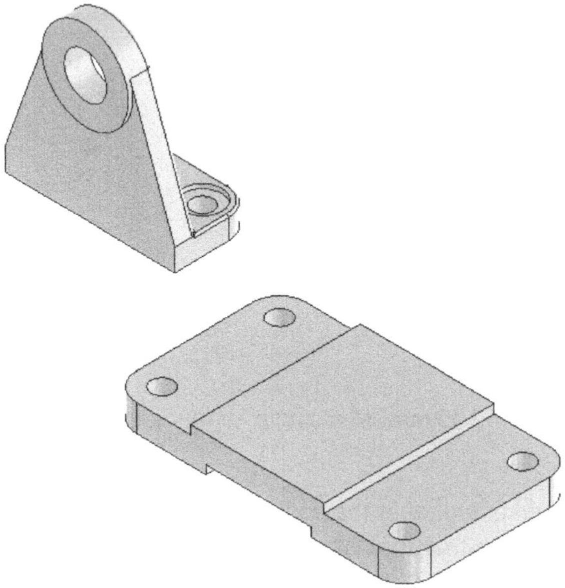

Figure 9–18

5. In the *Assemble* tab>Relationships panel, click  (Joint). Alternatively, you can press <J> on the keyboard. The Place Joint dialog box and mini-toolbar open. If the mini-toolbar is not displayed, enable it in the *View* tab>Windows panel in the User Interface list.

6. In the mini-toolbar, click to toggle off the display of the Place Joint dialog box. You will use the mini-toolbar to join components.

   Note: *Once the Place Joint dialog box is toggled off, it must be enabled again to open it.*

7. In the Type drop-down list in the mini-toolbar, select **Rigid**.

8. Rotate the assembly as shown in Figure 9–19.
9. On the **Bracket** component (first reference), hover the cursor over the edge shown in Figure 9–19. It will display in red with a green dot at the midpoint of the edge. Use the left mouse button to select the reference.
10. On the **Plate** component (second reference), hover the cursor over the edge shown in Figure 9–19. It will display in red with a green dot at the midpoint of the edge. Use the left mouse button to select the reference.

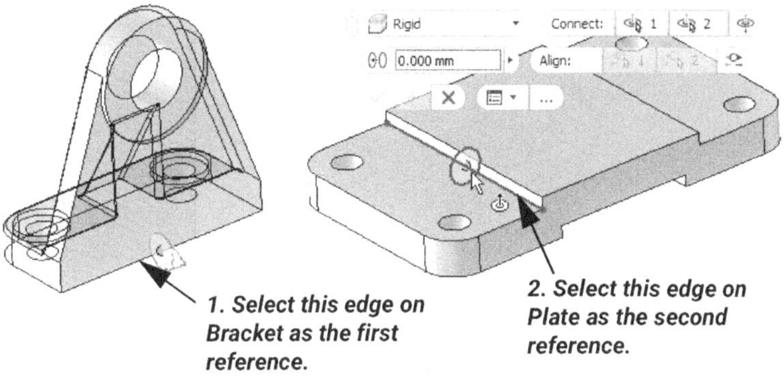

Figure 9–19

Note: Figure 9–19 shows the reference on ***Bracket*** *already selected and the reference on* ***Plate*** *highlighted. The images displaying the reference selection in this practice will be shown in this way for the remainder of the practice. The images may also be reoriented for clarity. You can spin the model, as required, to select the required references.*

The **Bracket** component (reference 1) moves into position and displays animated movement indicating its allowable degrees of freedom. In this case, it is a rigid joint, and because no movement is permitted, the animated movement is very small.

Note that you did not have to activate any of the fields in the mini-toolbar. The first reference field is immediately active and the second is activated once the first reference has been selected. Selecting the reference fields in the *Connect* field is only required when redefining a reference.

11. The components assemble in the wrong orientation. In the *Connect* area in the mini-toolbar, click (Flip Component) to flip the component.
12. Note that while the **Bracket** component has been flipped, the alignment must also be inverted to correct the orientation. In the *Align* area in the mini-toolbar, click (Invert Component) to invert the component.

13. Click (Flip Component) again to locate the component, if required.
14. Click in the mini-toolbar to complete the joint. The assembly displays as shown in Figure 9–20.

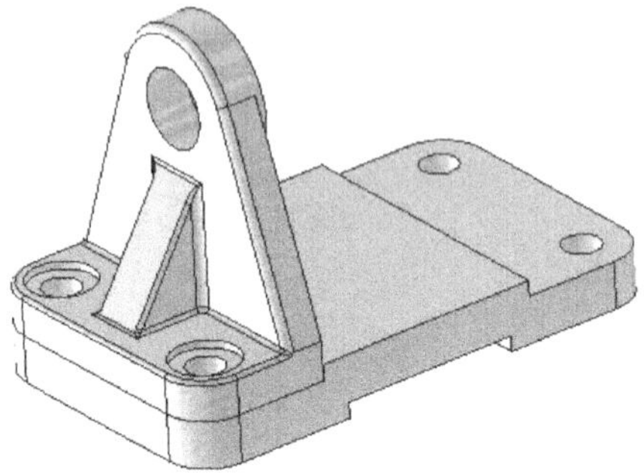

Figure 9–20

15. Expand the **Relationships** node and note that the **Rigid** joint has been added. A **Rigid** joint is also listed in the nodes for the two components. The [•] icon is added to the Model browser for the Bracket, indicating it is fully constrained.

Task 3: Assemble a second instance of the Bracket component.

1. In the Component panel, click (Place).
2. Select **Bracket.ipt** in the Place Component dialog box and click **Open**. The component is added to the assembly.
3. Right-click on the model and select **Rotate Z 90** and **Rotate Y 90** (twice) to rotate the component into a more convenient orientation, similar to that shown in Figure 9–21.
4. Use the left mouse button to locate the component next to the **Plate** component, as shown in Figure 9–21. Right-click and select **OK** to place a single instance.

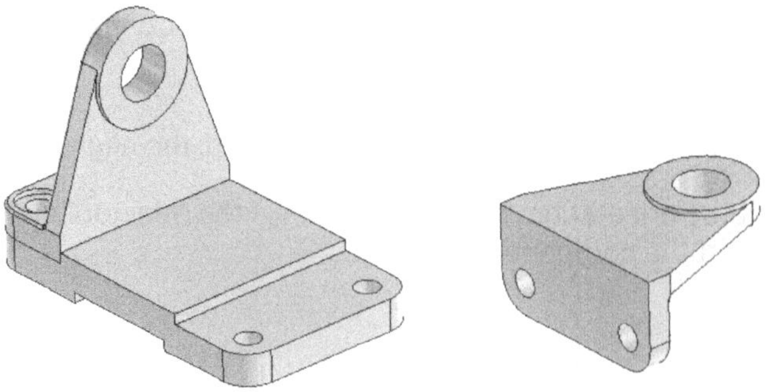

Figure 9–21

5. In the *Assemble* tab>Relationships panel, click (Joint) or select the <J> keyboard key.
6. In the Type drop-down list in the mini-toolbar, select **Rigid**.

   Previously, the two components were joined using reference edges, but for this component, faces will be used. Faces are generally the more stable selection reference.
7. On the **Bracket** component (first reference), hover the cursor over the surface shown in Figure 9–22. It will display in red. Continue to move the cursor so that the green dot displays at the midpoint of the top edge. Use the left mouse button to select the reference.
8. On the **Plate** component (second reference), hover over the face shown in Figure 9–22. It will display in red. Continue to move the cursor so that the green dot displays at the midpoint of the long edge. Use the left mouse button to select the reference.

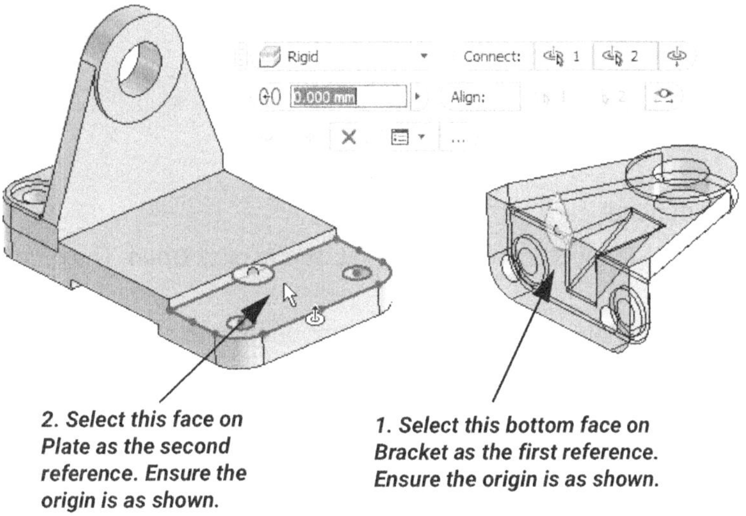

Figure 9–22

9. The **Bracket** component (reference 1) moves into position. If the components assemble in the wrong orientation, use the (Flip Component) and (Invert Component) options to reposition the component, as required.

10. Click in the mini-toolbar to complete the joint. The assembly displays as shown in Figure 9–23.

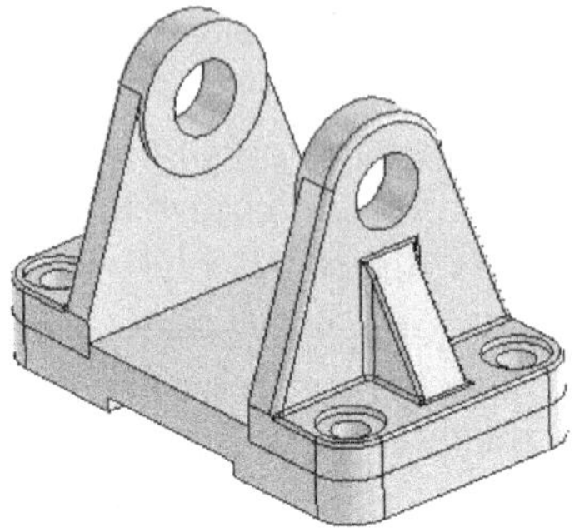

Figure 9–23

Task 4: Assemble the Axle component.

1. In the Component panel, click (Place).
2. Select **Axle.ipt** in the Place Component dialog box and click **Open**. The component is added to the assembly.
3. Use the shortcut menu options to rotate the component into a more convenient orientation.
4. Use the left mouse button to locate the component next to the assembly, as shown in Figure 9–24. Right-click and select **OK** to place a single instance.

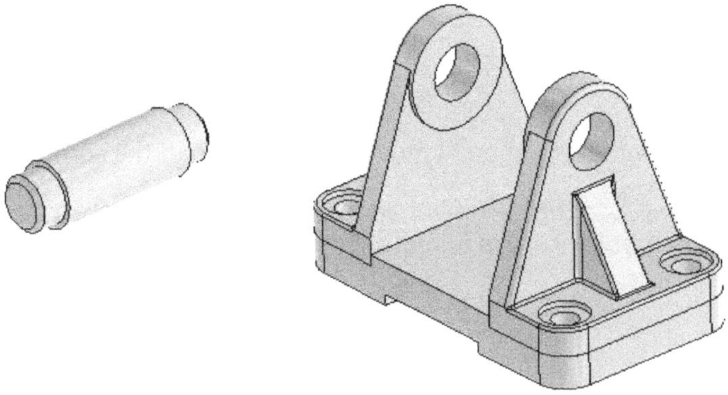

Figure 9–24

5. In the *Assemble* tab>Relationships panel, click (Joint).

   Ideally, the **Axle** component should join the midpoint of its central axis to a point midway between the two **Bracket** components. Joint references must be selected in a single component. To join the **Axle** you will be required to use both a **Joint** and **Constraint** option.

6. In the Type drop-down list in the mini-toolbar, select **Cylindrical**. This type allows for 1 translational and 1 rotational degree of freedom. The translational degree of freedom will be removed in a later step using a Mate constraint.
7. On the **Axle** component (first reference), hover the cursor over the midpoint of the cylindrical surface, shown in Figure 9–25. It will display in red with a green dot at the center point of the central axis. Use the left mouse button to select the reference.
8. On the **Bracket** component (second reference), hover over the edge shown in Figure 9–25. It will display in red with a green dot at the midpoint of the edge. Use the left mouse button to select the reference.

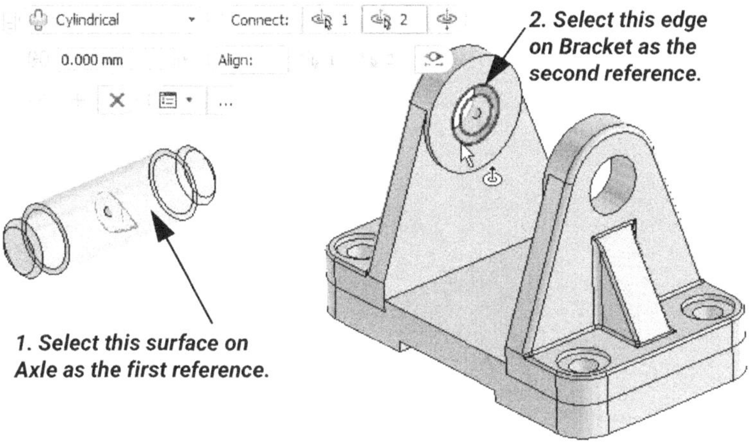

Figure 9–25

9. Click in the mini-toolbar to complete the joint. The assembly displays as shown in Figure 9–26.

Figure 9–26

10. Drag the **Axle** and note how it moves. It can rotate in the hole and translate along the axis of the hole.

11. In the *Assemble* tab>Relationships panel, click (Constrain). Constraints can be used to remove any unwanted degrees of freedom that result from a joint connection. In this case, you will remove the translational degree of freedom in the **Axle** component.
12. Assign a Mate (Flush) constraint that aligns the XY plane in the **Axle** with the YZ plane of the assembly.
13. Click **OK** to complete the constraint definition. Drag the **Axle** and note that only one rotational degree of freedom remains. To visually identify the remaining rotational degree of freedom, in the *View* tab>Visibility panel, click (Degrees of Freedom). The assembly displays as shown in Figure 9–27. Note that the [◦] icon appears adjacent to the component name, indicating it is not fully constrained. This is as expected as the rotational degree of freedom still remains.

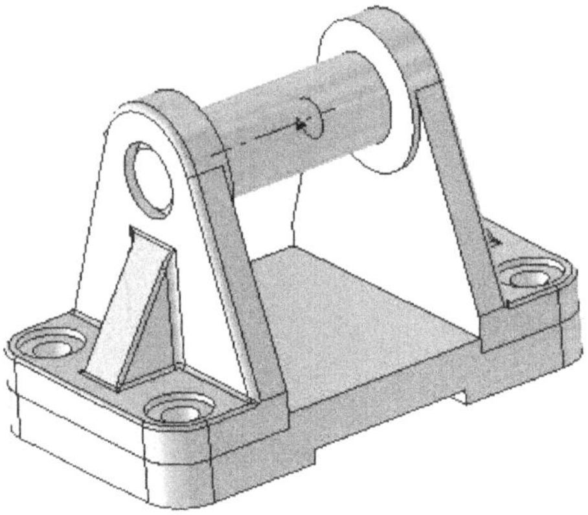

Figure 9–27

14. To further remove any degrees of freedom from the assembly, you can lock joint connections. Right-click on the Cylindrical joint connection and select **Lock**. This removes the remaining rotational degree of freedom and the [•] icon now displays.
15. Expand the **Relationships** node and note that the Cylindrical joint and Flush constraint have been added.

Alternatively, you can use a **Rigid** joint and set the correct offset value to locate the Axle.

Task 5: Assemble the Wheel component.

1. Place one instance of the **Wheel** component, similar to the orientation shown in Figure 9–28.

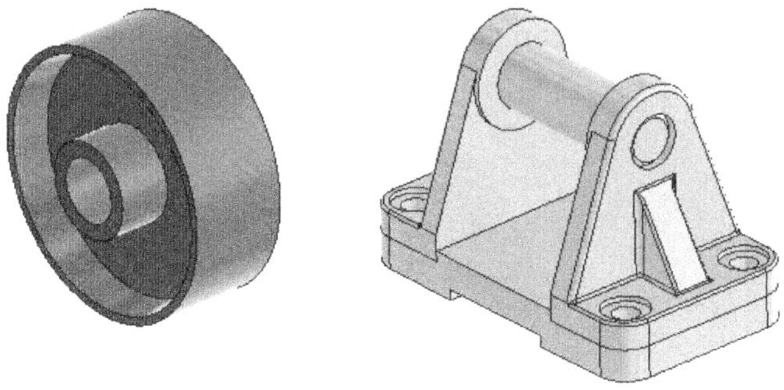

Figure 9–28

2. In the *Assemble* tab>Relationships panel, click (Joint).
3. In the Type drop-down list in the mini-toolbar, leave **Automatic** as the joint type.
4. On the **Wheel** component (first reference), select the midpoint of the inner cylindrical surface, shown in Figure 9–29, as the origin reference. To ensure that you are snapping to the proper reference, once you hover over the required surface (inner cylindrical face), press and hold <Ctrl> to maintain surface selection. You are now able to move between the origin references while remaining on the original surface.
5. On the **Axle** component (second reference), select the midpoint of the cylindrical surface shown in Figure 9–29, as the origin reference.

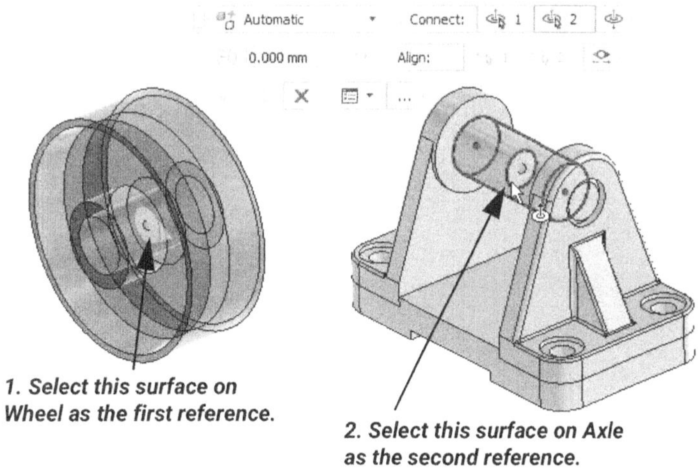

Figure 9–29

The **Wheel** component (reference 1) moves into position and displays animated movement indicating its allowable degrees of freedom. Note that the system assumed a Cylindrical joint type. A Rotational joint is required.

6. In the Type drop-down list in the mini-toolbar, select **Rotational**.

7. Click ✓ in the mini-toolbar to complete the joint. The assembly displays as shown in Figure 9–30.

Figure 9–30

Task 6: Assemble the Bolt components.

1. Place one instance of the **M10 x35** component.
2. Begin the creation of a new joint. In the Type drop-down list in the mini-toolbar, select **Rotational**.
3. On the **M10 x35** component (first reference), hover the cursor over the bottom face of the bolt head so that the origin reference is shown as in Figure 9–31. Select to assign the reference.
4. On the **Bracket** component (second reference), hover the cursor over the bottom face of the counterbore hole so that the origin reference is shown as in Figure 9–31. Select to assign the reference.

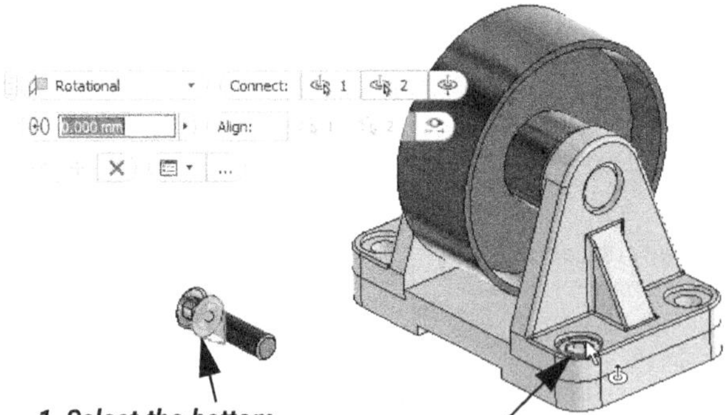

Figure 9–31

5. The component moves into position and displays its remaining rotational degree of freedom. Complete the joint. The assembly displays as shown in Figure 9–32.

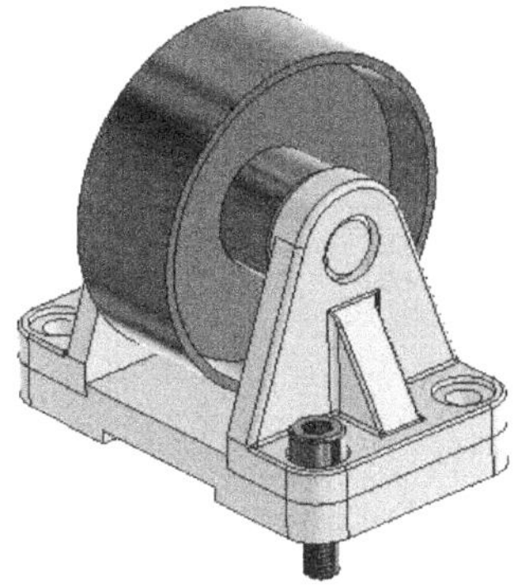

Figure 9–32

6. Right-click on the **Rotational** joint in the Model browser and select **Lock** to remove its rotational degree of freedom.

   Note: *In general, it is recommended to remove degrees of freedom to eliminate the possibility to unexpected changes and so that Inventor is not forced to calculate the open movement after each update.*

7. Place a second instance of the **M10 x35** component. Instead of using a **Rotational** joint, assign a **Rigid** joint connection to remove all degrees of freedom with a single constraint.

8. Add and join the remaining bolt components, as shown in Figure 9–33. Ensure all degrees of freedom are removed from the bolts using either of the two methods. Review the Model browser icons to verify that the Wheel is the only component that is not fully constrained.

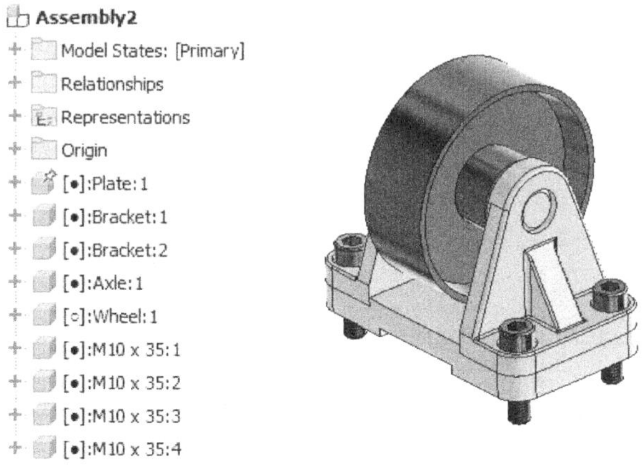

Figure 9–33

9. Save the assembly as **Assembly_Joints.iam.**

End of practice

Chapter Review Questions

1. Once a Joint connection type has been added between components in an assembly, additional constraints can be used to further eliminate any degrees of freedom.
   a. True
   b. False

2. Match the joint type in the column on the left with its icon.

Icon

a. Rigid
b. Rotational
c. Slider
d. Cylindrical
e. Planar
f. Ball

3. Which of the following cannot be accomplished using the mini-toolbar shown in Figure 9–34? (Select all that apply.)

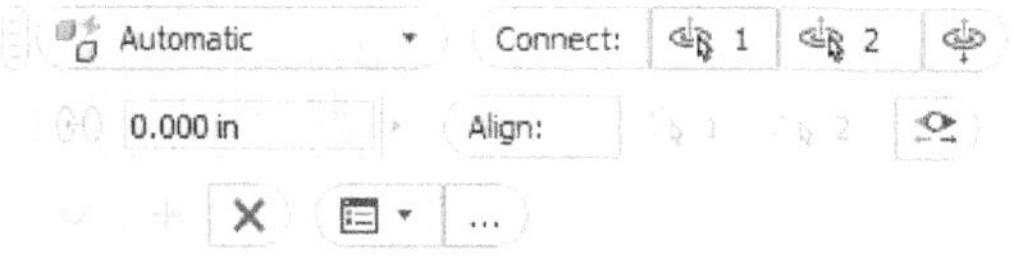

Figure 9–34

a. Define a gap value for offsetting references.
b. Define a limit value for range of motion.
c. Flip components.
d. Control whether an animation displays when components are joined.
e. Assign a name for the joint.

4. Match the joint type in the column on the left with the degrees of freedom that remain in the assembled component after it has been assigned.

	Degrees of Freedom
a. Rigid	1 Translational, 1 Rotational
b. Rotational	2 Translational, 1 Rotational
c. Slider	0 Translational, 0 Rotational
d. Cylindrical	0 Translational, 3 Rotational
e. Planar	1 Translational, 0 Rotational
f. Ball	0 Translational, 1 Rotational

5. The Automatic joint type assumes the joint type without requiring you to select references on the two components being joined.

a. True

b. False

6. The alignment references between two components are defined by default based on the selected references. Which of the following buttons in the Place Joint dialog box enables you to invert the default alignment?

a. 

b. 

c. 

d. 

7. Which of the following entity types can be selected as references for joint connections? (Select all that apply.)

a. Work Points

b. Work Planes

c. Work Axes

d. Faces

e. Edges

f. Spherical Geometry

8. The first component reference selected to define the placement of a joint connection represents the component that is going to remain stationary when joined.

a. True

b. False

9. Which of the following best describes the **Lock** option when used to lock a joint?

a. A locked component cannot be selected to be moved, but it updates if connected components are moved.

b. A locked component is similar to a grounded component. It is locked in place regardless of changes made to connected components.

10. Which of the following options enables you to redefine the alignment references that were assigned when a joint connection was assigned?

a. Modify

b. Edit

c. Free Move

d. Show Sick

Command Summary

Button	Command	Location
	**Degrees of Freedom**	• **Ribbon:** *View* tab>Visibility panel
	**Joint**	• **Ribbon:** *Assemble* tab>Relationships panel • Keyboard Shortcut: <J> keyboard key
	**Place**	• **Ribbon:** *Assemble* tab>Component panel • Keyboard Shortcut: <P> keyboard key

Chapter 10

Manipulating Assembly Display

You have learned that components are constrained to one another to form assemblies. The constraints that you use result in feature relationships between the components. You now learn how to use a number of other tools in Assembly mode to evaluate and review an entire assembly.

Learning Objectives

- Temporarily relocate a constrained component to a new location in an assembly by moving or rotating it.
- Suppress constraints in an assembly.
- Control component display in an assembly.
- Create section views in an assembly that display portions of an overall assembly based on selected planes.
- Create design view representations that store assembly display configurations.
- Use appropriate selection priority options to efficiently make selections in an assembly.

10.1 Moving and Rotating Components

Viewing or selecting references in components of a large assemblies can be challenging. Moving and rotating components is a simple way of temporarily relocating assembly components.

Moving Components

To move components in an assembly, click  (Free Move) in the *Assemble* tab>Position panel, and select the component to move in the graphics window. Alternatively, you can select the component in the graphics window, right-click and select **Free Move**. Hold the left mouse button, and drag the component to a new location. Once you have moved the component, release the mouse button to drop the component. When moving components, you can only select one component to move at a time and grounded components cannot be moved.

- If the component being moved is constrained, the **Free Move** command displays relationships as elastic bands between the constraint references. Icons indicate the original constraint type, as shown in Figure 10–1. Relationships are not displayed between unconstrained components.

Figure 10–1

- Select any of the constraint icons once a moved component has been placed and right-click to display the marking menu, as shown in Figure 10–2. The commands in the marking menu enable you to **Edit**, **Suppress**, **Delete**, or **Modify** (offset value) the selected constraint.

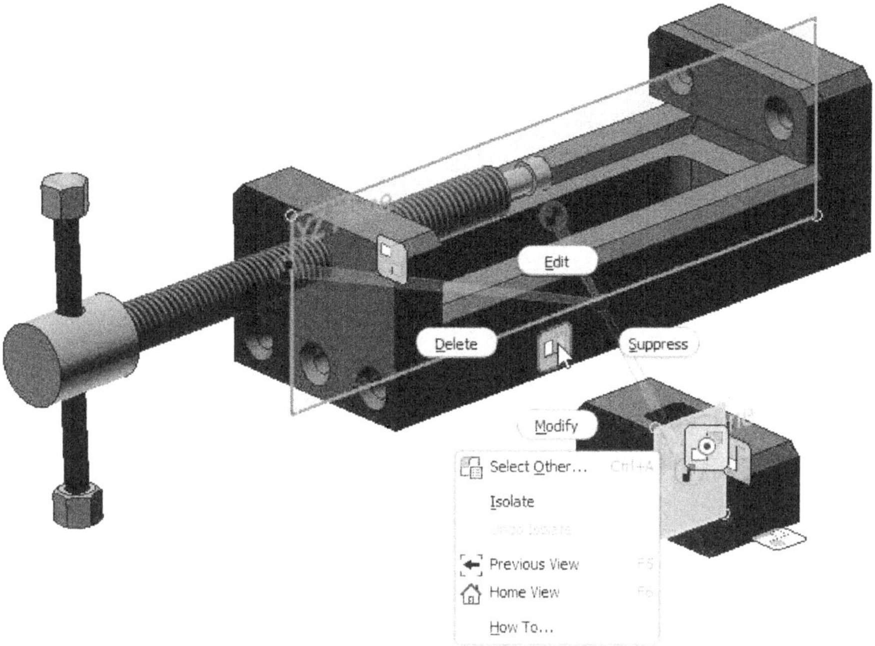

Figure 10–2

- To clear the relationship display from the model, press <Esc>, or right-click and select **OK**.

Rotating Components

Rotating components enables you to manipulate the orientation of selected assembly components independent of the overall assembly and can help with constraint selection. Unlike the **Free Move** command, the **Free Rotate** command does not function differently for constrained and unconstrained components. Grounded components cannot be rotated.

To rotate assembly components, click (Free Rotate) in the *Assemble* tab>Position panel and select the component to rotate in the graphics window. Alternatively, you can select the component in the graphics window, right-click and select **Free Rotate**. A rotation circle displays in the assembly window, as it does when using the **Orbit** command.

Use the following methods to rotate (hold the left mouse button while dragging the mouse):

- Click inside the circle to rotate freely.
- Use the left or right handles to rotate about the Y-axis.
- Use the top or bottom handles to rotate about the X-axis.
- Click outside the circle to rotate about the Z-axis.

When you have finished rotating the component(s), press <Esc> or right-click and select **OK**.

Updating the Assembly

To return the parts to their constrained positions after moving or rotating them, click (Local Update) in the Quick Access Toolbar. The update options for assemblies are shown in Figure 10–3.

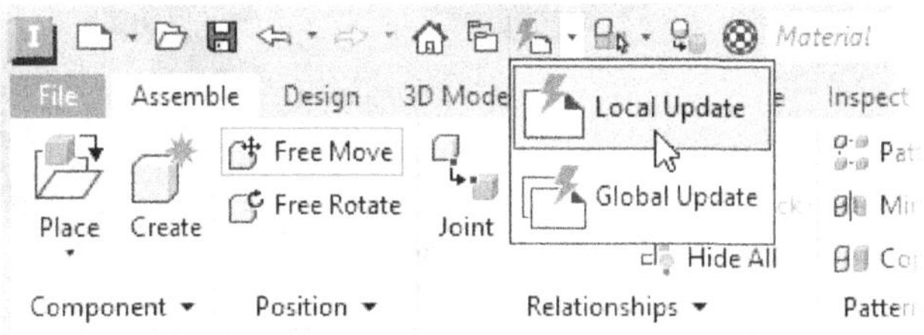

Figure 10–3

- Select (Local Update) to update an individual part or subassembly. This option is useful for large assemblies with long update times.
- Select (Global Update) to update the entire assembly. All subassemblies including the top-level assembly are updated.

10.2 Suppressing Constraints or Joints

In complex assemblies, suppressing constraints or joints is useful to help ease the assembly of other components. Once suppressed, a component can be easily moved to allow for selecting references or to test an alternate constraint. A suppressed constraint or joint displays in the Model browser as a grayed symbol. To suppress a constraint (shown in Figure 10–4):

- Right-click on the constraint (or joint) in the Model browser and select **Suppress**.
- With constraint (or joint) symbols shown in the model, right-click on the symbol and select **Suppress**.
- In the Edit Constraint (or Edit Joint) dialog box, select **Suppress**.

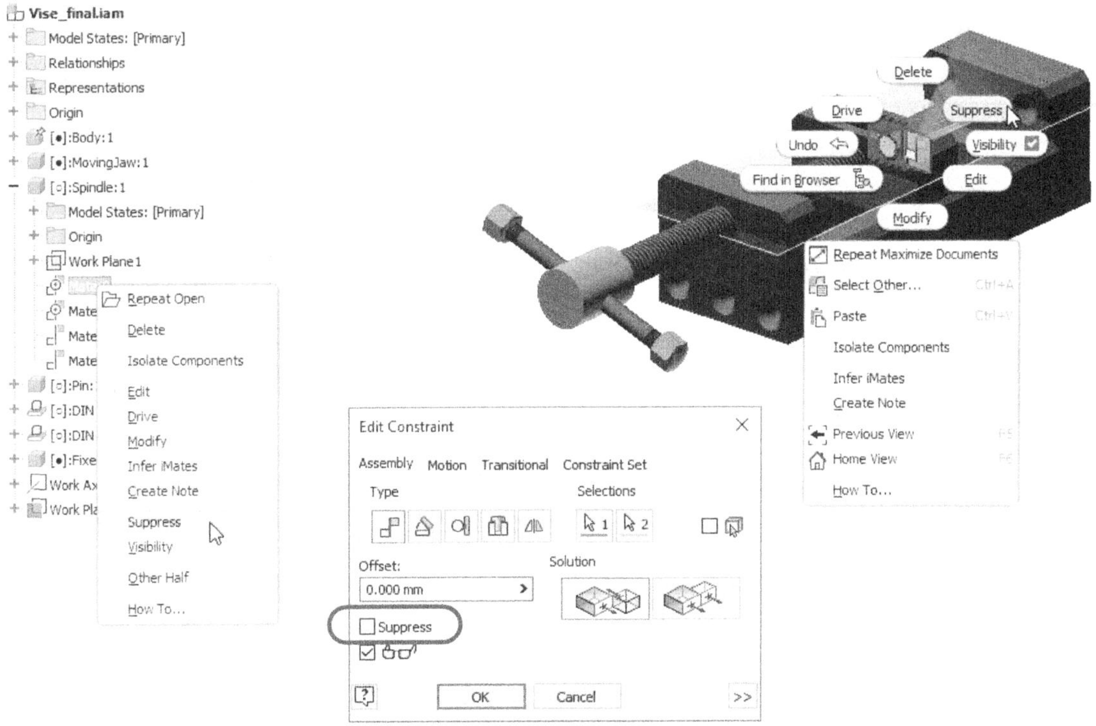

Figure 10–4

- If you have suppressed any constraints or joints, you must reactivate them if you want them to update. To resume them, right-click on the constraint or joint in the Model browser and clear the **Suppress** option or clear the **Suppress** option in the Edit Constraint or Edit Joint dialog boxes.

10.3 Controlling Component Display

When you add components to an assembly, they are visible and enabled by default. The following tools are available to simplify the display of assembly components:

Visible Components

You can toggle off the visibility of a component to more easily modify components, as shown in Figure 10–5. To toggle off the visibility of a component, right-click on a component in the Model browser and select **Visibility** so that it is toggled off. Alternatively, you can right-click on the component in the graphics window and select **Visibility**. The component symbol in the Model browser displays in gray and the model is no longer displayed in the graphics window, as shown in Figure 10–5. To display the component again, right-click on it in the Model browser and select **Visibility** so that it is toggled on.

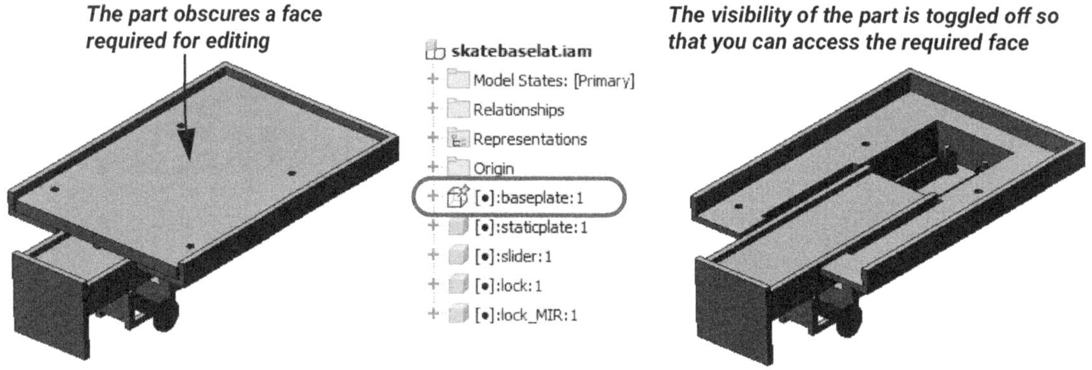

Figure 10–5

Enabling Components

You can restrict a component from being selected by disabling it, as shown in Figure 10–6. To disable a component, right-click on the component in the Model browser or in the graphics window and select **Enabled** so that it is toggled off. The component symbol in the Model browser displays in green and the model displays in a lighter shading, as shown in Figure 10–6. To re-enable the component, right-click on the component in the Model browser and select **Enabled** so that it is toggled on.

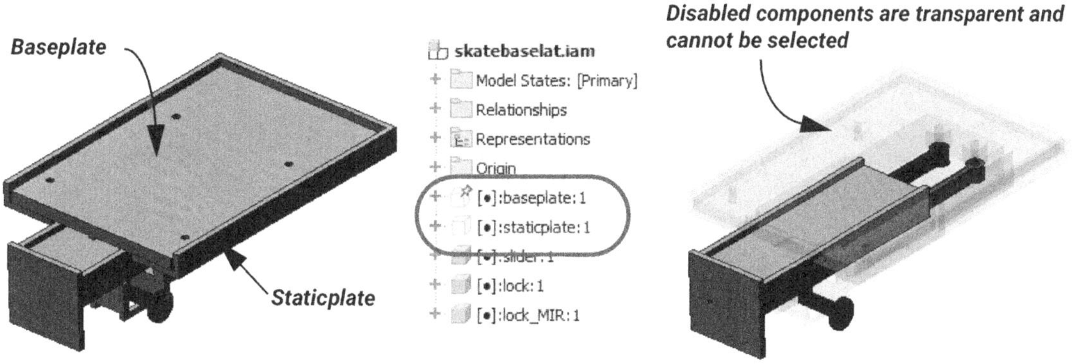

Figure 10–6

Hint: Advantages of the Visibility and Enabling Options

- Helps easily edit components inside or behind others.
- Helps in selecting geometry that might be obscured.
- Simplifies the display of the assembly.
- Enables faster opening and updating of assembly files, because components that are not required until later in the design process are toggled off.
- Enables you to make non-solid geometry (e.g., planes or axes) visible for constraining or referencing.

Isolating Components

The **Isolate** command enables you to toggle off the visibility of all of the components except the ones you need. To use the **Isolate** command, select the components in the Model browser or in the graphics window, right-click and select **Isolate**. This is useful in a large assembly to easily select references to create constraints.

To undo the **Isolate** command, right click anywhere in the window and select **Undo Isolate**. You can only use this option once.

Note: *Consider using a Design View if you isolate the same components routinely to create a working view.*

Transparent Components

The **Transparent** command enables you to set the visibility of an assembly component as transparent in an assembly view. Once set, the component can be selected and remains visible in a transparent display style, as shown in Figure 10–7. To set a component to transparent, use one of the following methods:

- Right-click on the component name in the Model browser or in the graphics window and select **Transparent**.
- In the component's iProperties dialog box, on the *Occurrence* tab, select **Transparent**.

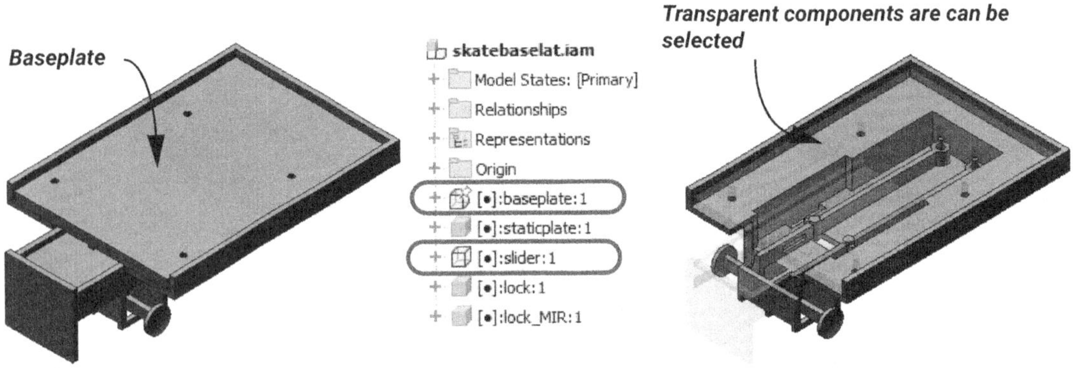

Figure 10–7

- To undo the **Transparent** command, reselect the component and clear the option.

10.4 Sectioning Assembly Models

Creating a section view enables you to work inside assemblies (or parts) while still keeping the required components visible and enabled. Section views display portions of the assembly that lie on one side or between reference planes. The three section views shown in Figure 10–8 can be created.

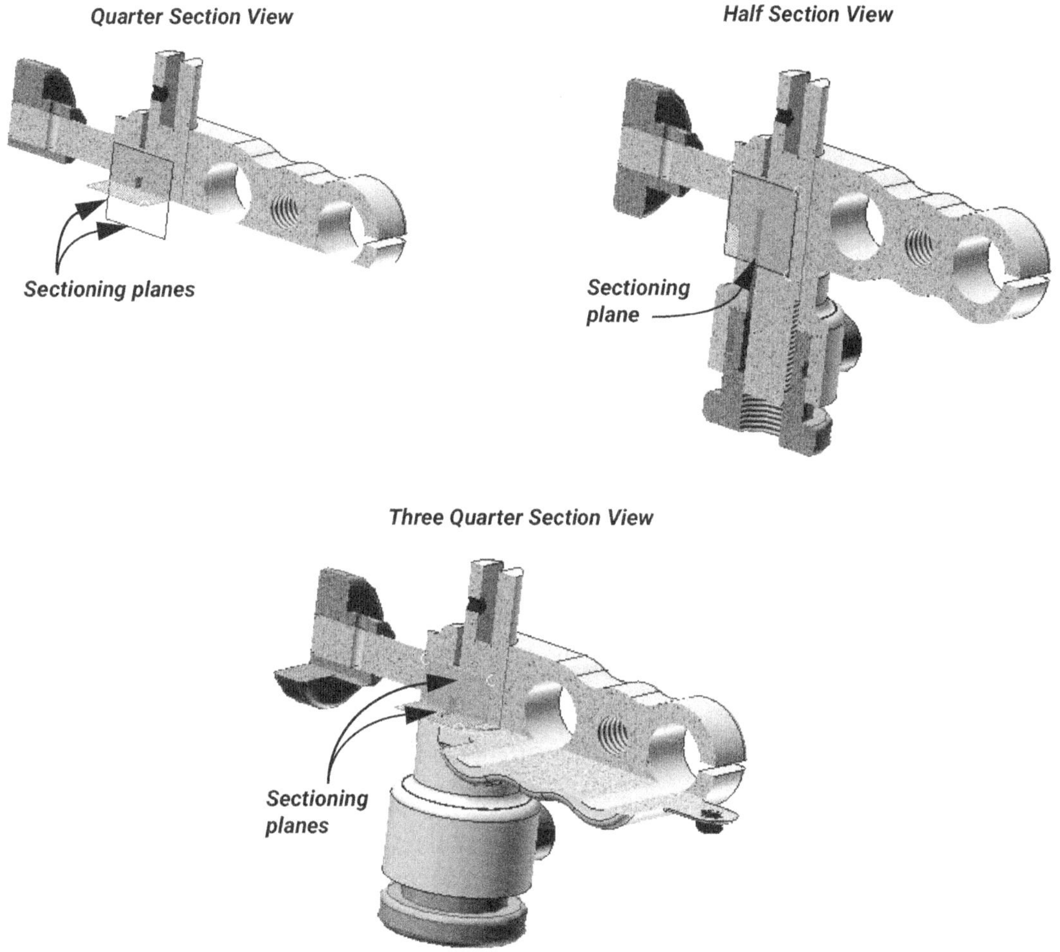

Figure 10–8

How To: Section an Assembly Model

1. In the *View* tab>Visibility panel, select the type of section view in the drop-down list, as shown in Figure 10–9.

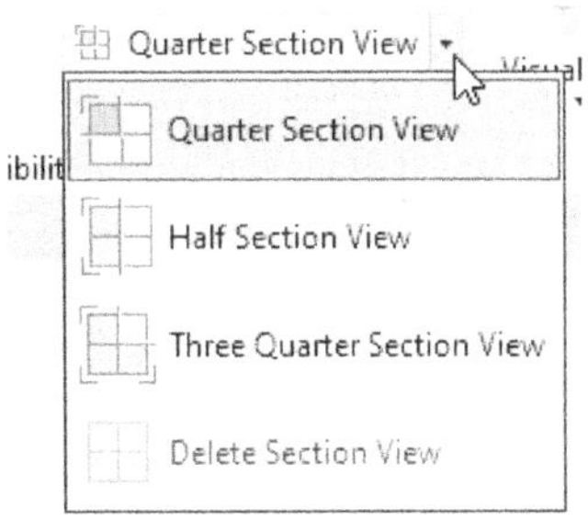

Figure 10–9

Note: The section view options on the View tab can also be used to section part models.

2. Select the plane to section about. The mini-toolbar appears in the graphics window as shown in Figure 10–10.

Figure 10–10

3. If required, move the selected plane using one of the following techniques with the  option selected.
   - In the mini-toolbar, enter a value in the *Offset* field.
   - In the graphics window, drag the arrow that appears on the section plane.
   - In the mini-toolbar, use the scroll wheel in the *Offset* field to offset incrementally. To change the scroll increments when modifying section plane placement, right-click in the graphics window and select **Scroll Step Size**, enter an increment value, and click .

   Note: To rotate the plane, select 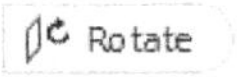 *and enter or drag the rotation handle as needed.*

4. If required, flip the section about the plane by selecting .

5. If creating a quarter or three quarter section view, click  to continue or click  to combine the section.

6. Select an additional plane to section about. If required, enter an offset value or flip the direction of the new plane using the same techniques as mentioned above. The mini-toolbar appears as shown in Figure 10–11 when a quarter or three quarter section view is being created.

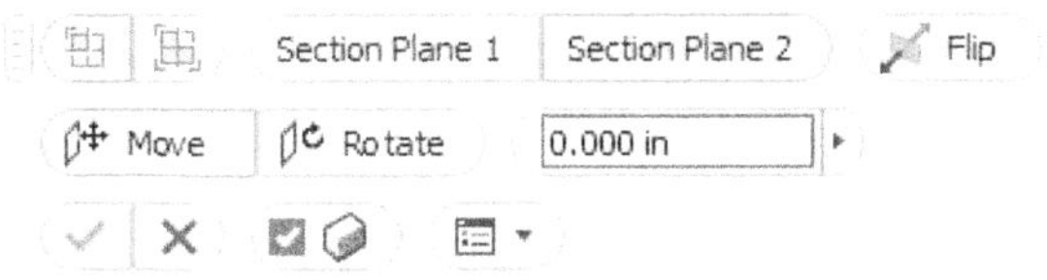

Figure 10–11

7. To further modify the offset from a selected plane, the correct plane must be active. In the mini-toolbar, select Section Plane 1 or Section Plane 2, as needed, to switch the active plane and then modify as required.

   Note: *If creating a Quarter Section or a Three Quarter Section View, you can toggle between the two. This can be done in the mini-toolbar by selecting (Three Quarter Section View) or (Quarter Section View), as needed.*

8. Right-click and select **OK (Enter)** or click ✓ to complete the view.
9. To return to a view of the entire part, select **Delete Section View** in the Section View drop-down list.

Note the following:

- Once in a section view, you can select references on cut components. Note that edges that are generated by the cut are not selectable as they are not physical edges in the model.
- Once created, a section view cannot be redefined, you would have to recreate it to make changes. However, if the section view is used in a design view, it can be modified or suppressed).

10.5 Assembly Design Views

A design view enables you to save a configuration of an assembly (or part) view that can easily be recalled for future use. Design views can store the following:

- Visibility/Isolation settings
- Enabled/disabled component settings
- Color override of components
- Assembly orientation

Saving design views has the following advantages:

- Saves a configuration where components are toggled on and off for ease of viewing or to ease selection.
- Creates different displays of your assembly for various purposes or different users.
- Reduces the loading or updating time of assemblies by displaying only the required components.

Figure 10–12 shows two saved design views of an assembly.

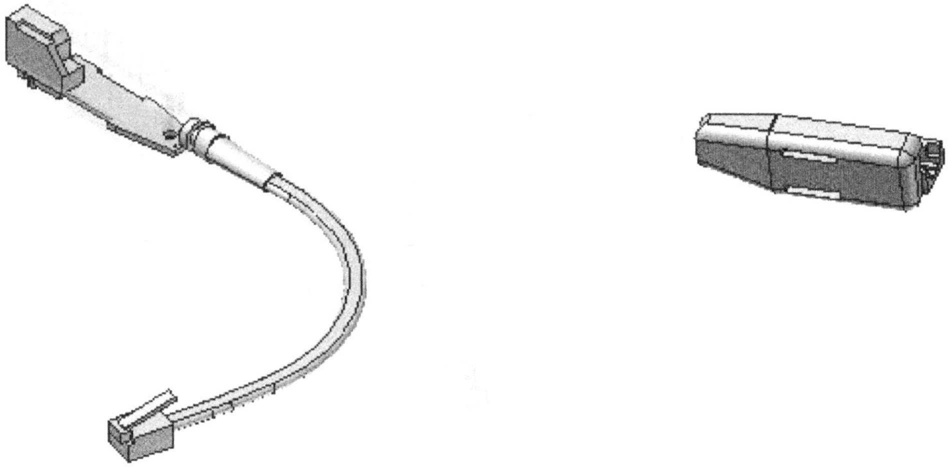

Figure 10–12

How To: Save a Design View

1. Expand the *Representations* node in the Model browser, right-click on the *View: Default* node, and select **New**, as shown in Figure 10–13.

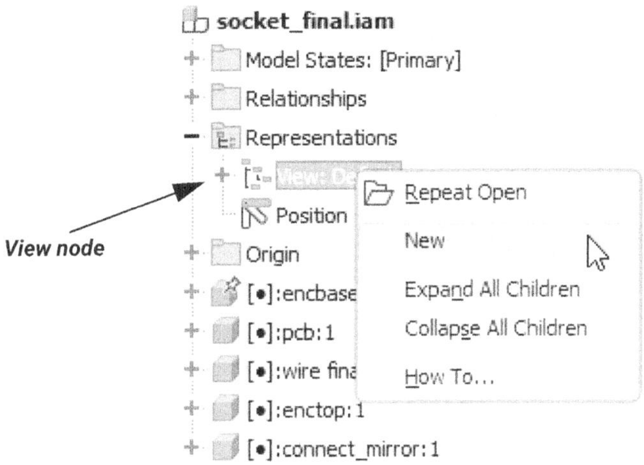

Figure 10–13

Note: *Design views can be created in the View node in part models.*

2. Configure the view display for the assembly.
3. Select the new view, left-click again (do not double-click) and enter a descriptive name (typically the same name as the assembly file) for the view.
4. To lock the design view, right-click on the view in the Model browser and select **Lock**. This restricts you or others from making changes to the design view representation at a later time and prevent newly assembled components from being included in the design view.

The newly created design view is automatically made active. To display a different design view, right-click on an existing design view in the Model browser and select **Activate**, as shown in Figure 10–14, or double-click on another view name.

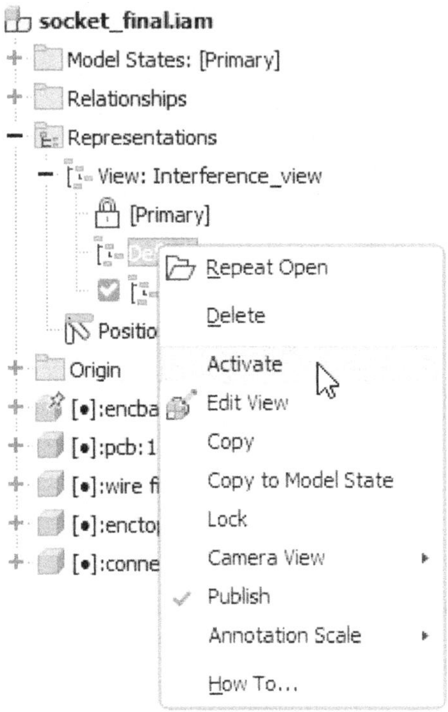

Figure 10–14

Modifying Design Views

To modify an existing design view in a model it must be unlocked. To unlock, right-click on the design view name in the Model browser and select **Unlock**. Once unlocked you can modify the design view as follows:

- Change the visibility of the components in the design view.
- If a design view has a section view, you can modify the section view or suppress it.
- Use the **Undo Isolate** command if the components were previously isolated in the design view.
- Change which components are disabled or enabled.
- Override the appearance color of components.
- Change the assembly orientation.

As an alternative to using the **Visibility**, **Enable**, and **Undo-Isolate** commands to return components to the display in a design view, you can also edit the included components by right-clicking on the design view name in the Model browser and selecting **Edit View**. Once selected the mini-toolbar opens, as shown in Figure 10–15.

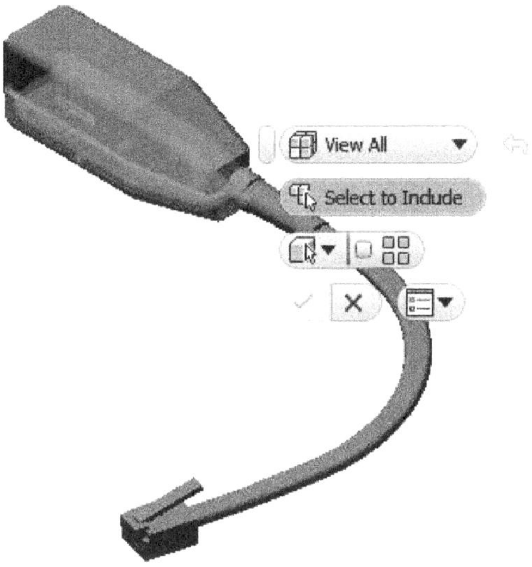

Figure 10–15

- To add additional components to the design view, ensure **View All** and **Select to Include** are active. The components highlighted in blue indicate the current components that display in the design view. Select additional components, as required, to add components to the design view.
- To remove previously included components to the design view, ensure that **View Included** and **Select to Exclude** are active. Select components in the assembly to clear them from the design view.
- Click to complete the modification.

Note: Click 

in the drop-down list to filter the display so that only those previously excluded display.

Hint: Camera Views

Right-click and use **Camera View** for the new view to control how a custom orientation is saved with the view. The options enable you to automatically save the view orientation when the design view is active (**Autosave Camera**). You can also clear this option and save the required orientations for the view. By default, the **Autosave Camera** option is enabled.

10.6 Assembly Selection Filters

Assembly selection priority options are located in the Quick Access Toolbar (), as shown in Figure 10–16. The assembly selection options can also be accessed by pressing and holding <Shift> as you right-click in an assembly.

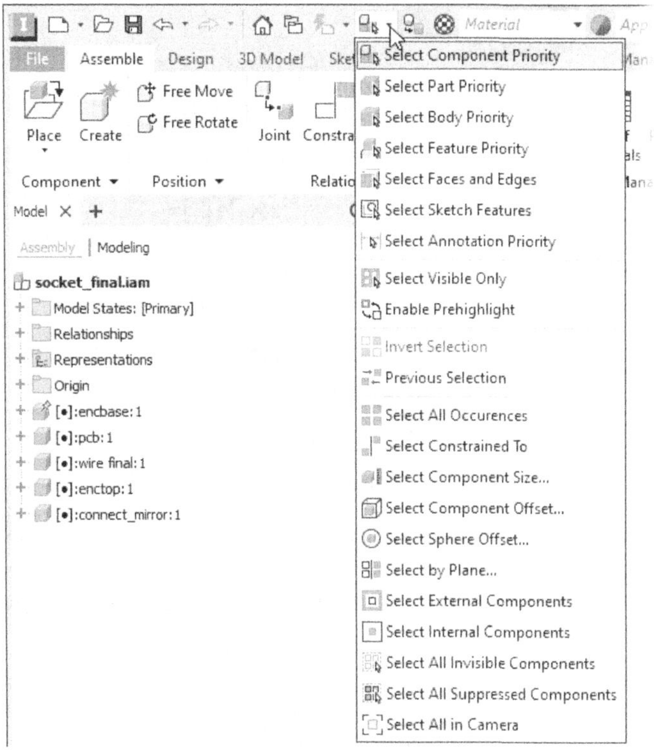

Figure 10–16

When making selections in an assembly consider enabling any one of these options to ease selection. The available options are as follows:

Option	Description
Select Component Priority	Selects an entire component, a part, or a subassembly.
Select Part Priority	Selects a part (the *leaves* in the Model browser).
Select Body Priority	Selects a Body.
Select Feature Priority	Selects a feature.
Select Faces and Edges	Selects a face or part edge.
Select Sketch Features	Selects lines, arcs, circles, splines, or other features in a sketch.

Option	Description
Select Annotation Priority	Selects 3D annotations.
Select Visible Only	Excludes invisible parts from the selection set.
Enable Prehighlight	Enables prehighlighting when you hover the cursor over an object. The option is activated by default. Toggle this off in large assemblies to improve performance.
Invert Selection	Selects all currently deselected components.
Previous Selection	Restores the previous selection set.
Select All Occurrences	Enables you to select a component and have all of its occurrences automatically selected.
Select Constrained To	Selects components constrained to the selected component.
Select Component Size	Selects components that are larger or smaller than a selected component or a specified size.
Select Component Offset	Selects components in a bounding box, based on their distance from a selected component.
Select Sphere Offset	Selects components in a sphere, based on their distance from a selected component.
Select by Plane	Selects components based on one side of a work plane or a planar face.
Select External Components	Selects external assembly components based on a set tolerance value. 100% returns all visible components and 0% returns only the most visible component.
Select Internal Components	Selects internal assembly components based on a set tolerance value. 100% returns all components that are not visible and 1% returns all the components except for the most visible.
Select All Invisible Components	Selects all components that have had their visibility cleared. This provides an easy method to select all invisible components at once to enable their visibility again.
Select All Suppressed Components	Selects all components that are suppressed. This provides an easy method to select all suppressed components at once to unsuppress them.
Select All in Camera	Selects the components in the camera view.

Practice 10a
Manipulate Components

Practice Objectives

- Create a Half Section view to display geometry through a selected work plane.
- Add a new view representation to an assembly such that it does not include any additional components that are added to the model.
- Use the **Visibility**, **Enabled**, and **Isolate** tools to control whether components are displayed and available for selection in an assembly.

In this practice, you will open a previously created vise assembly (shown in Figure 10–17) and use the tools available in Inventor to control component visibility, create a section view, and store the manipulated view in a design view.

Figure 10–17

Task 1: Create a new assembly and section it through the spindle component.

1. Open **Vise_final.iam**.

2. Select the *View* tab. In the Appearance panel, click (Half Section View). You might need to expand the Section View drop-down list to access this command.

3. Expand the **Spindle** component and its *Origin* node in the Model browser. Select **XZ Plane**. The assembly displays similarly to that shown in Figure 10–18. Note how the section is not parallel to the top or bottom of the vise. This is because the spindle rotates. A better reference plane for the section would be one that is stationary in the assembly.

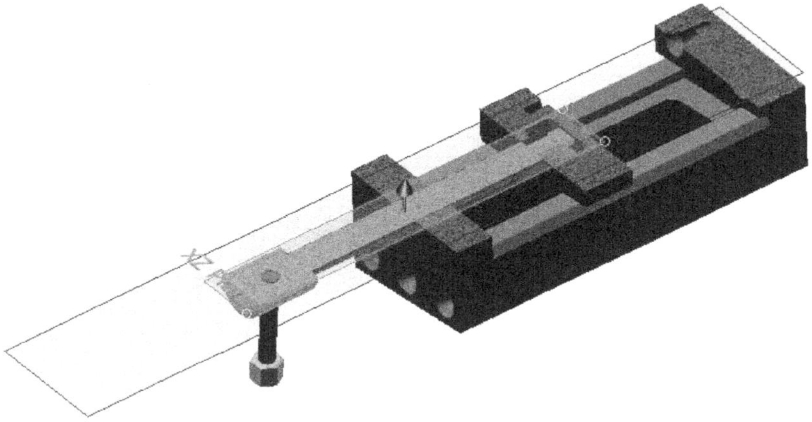

Figure 10–18

4. Click ✕ to cancel section creation.
5. Right-click on **Body** in the Model browser and select **Isolate**. This displays only the Body component, which enables you to create a new work plane by selecting references only in the Body component.
6. In the Assemble panel, click (Axis) and select the circular hole that the Spindle inserts into. Work Axis 1 is created, as shown in Figure 10–19.

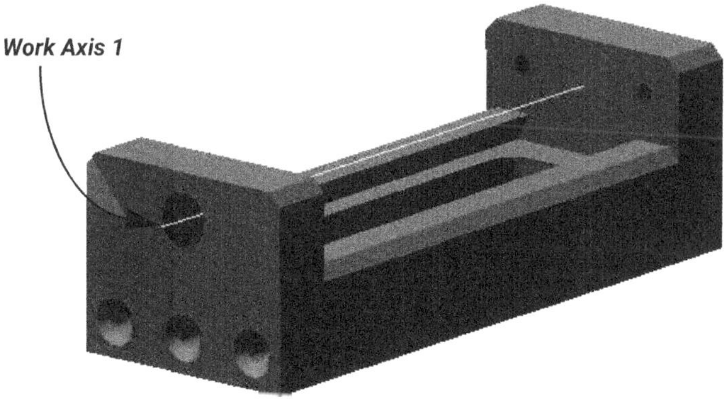

Figure 10–19

7. In the Assemble panel, click (Work Plane) and select the newly created **Work Axis 1**. As a second reference, select the top planar face of the component, as shown in Figure 10–20.

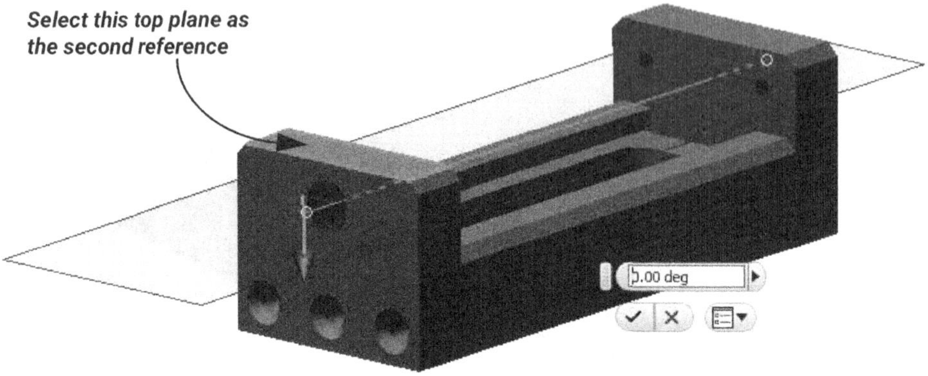

Figure 10–20

8. Enter **0.00 deg** to ensure that the new work plane is parallel with the top of the component. Click .
9. Right-click on **Body** in the Model browser and select **Undo Isolate** to return all components to the display.
10. Press and hold <Ctrl> and select **Work Axis 1** and **Work Plane 1**. Right-click and select **Visibility** to clear them both from the display.
11. Select the *View* tab. Change the *Visual Style* setting to **Shaded with Edges**. This helps with visualizing the edges of a sectioned view.
12. In the Appearance panel, click (Half Section View).
13. In the Model browser, select **Work Plane 1** that was just created. Click in the mini-toolbar to create the section view.

14. Reorient the model to the **Front** view using the ViewCube. The assembly displays similar to that shown in Figure 10–21. Note how the Spindle edge and Moving Jaw edge are connected. Disable the visibility of any remaining work planes if any are displayed.

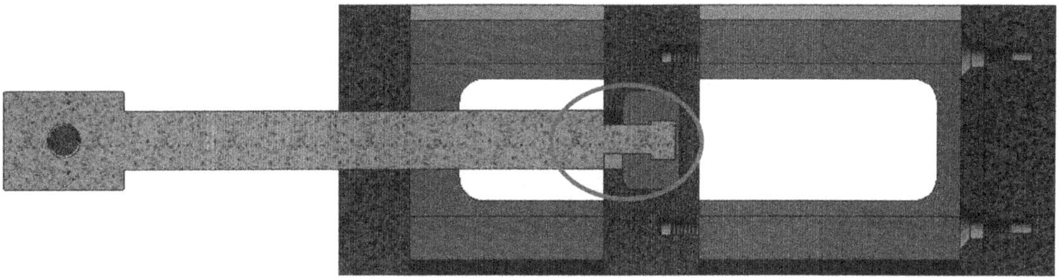

Figure 10–21

15. Expand the **MovingJaw** component in the Model browser and select the **Insert:4** constraint, as shown in Figure 10–22. The Insert constraint connects the two edges such that they align with one another.

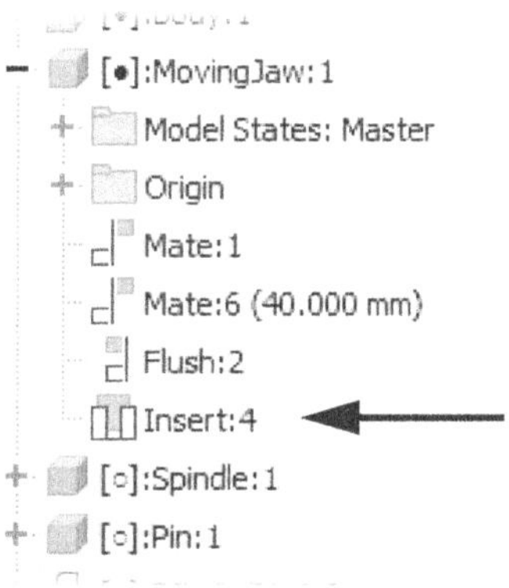

Figure 10–22

16. Right-click the **Insert:4** constraint and select **Edit**.

17. In the Edit Constraint dialog box, select  (Mate) to change the constraint type. The references do not have to be modified. Click **OK**.

18. Select the **Spindle** and drag it away from the MovingJaw component, as shown in Figure 10–23. Another constraint must be added to fully constrain the component.

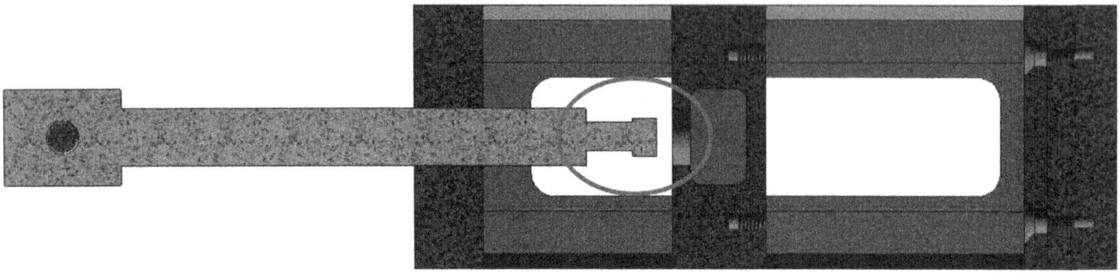

Figure 10–23

19. Add an additional **Mate** constraint that mates the end of the Spindle with the inside face of the MovingJaw component. The assembly and Model browser should appear as shown in Figure 10–24.

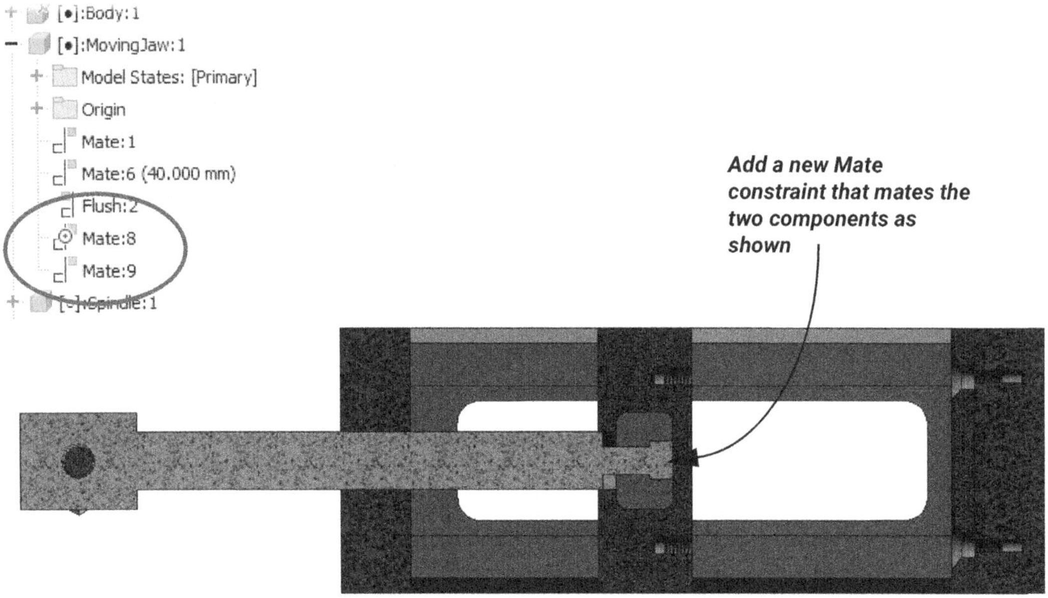

Figure 10–24

20. Select the *View* tab. In the Appearance panel, click (Delete Section View) to display the entire assembly. Note that the section view was created to help review placement and could be left displayed while defining new constraints.

21. Reorient the model to its isometric Home view.

Task 2: Create a design view representation.

1. Expand the **Representations** and **View** nodes in the Model browser. The Model browser displays as shown in Figure 10–25.

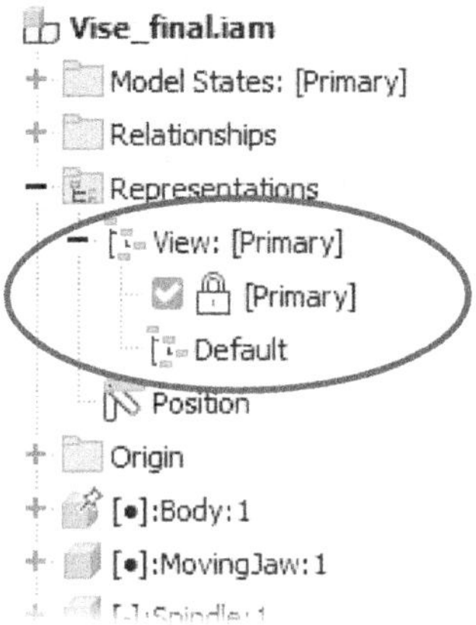

Figure 10–25

2. Right-click on **View: Primary** in the Model browser and select **New** to create a new design view.
3. Select **View1** in the Model browser. Select it again (do not double-click) and rename the view as **Sectioned_View**.
4. Recreate the Half Section view that went through Work Plane 1. Without the design view being used to save the section view, it would have to be recreated anytime it needed to be reviewed.
5. Double-click on **Default** to make it the active design view. The assembly returns to its full display.

   Note: *To lock a design view, right-click on the view name in the Model browser and select* ***Lock****. This restricts you from adding components to the design view. Any new components in the assembly will not be included in this view.*

Task 3: Modify the existing design view.

1. Double-click the **Sectioned_View** to activate it. The section view is displayed without having to recreate it.

2. Right-click on **Sectioned_View** in the Model browser and select **Edit View**. The mini-toolbar and model display as shown in Figure 10–26.

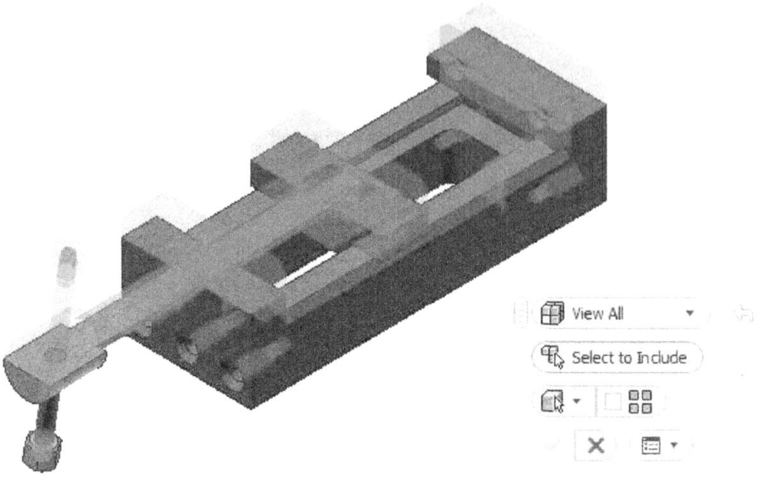

Figure 10–26

3. Ensure that **View All** is selected in the drop-down list, if it is not already active. Note that the components that are currently included are highlighted in blue.
4. Click **View Included** in the drop-down list. Note that **Select to Exclude** is now active.
5. Select **Pin** and the two **DIN 917 M6** components in the Model browser or directly in the graphics window to remove them from the design view. Note how their icon in the Model browser changes.
6. Click  to complete the modification.
7. Activate the **Default** design view. Note that all of the components are still visible.
8. Activate the **Sectioned_View** design view to verify that the components are removed and the section view is displayed.
9. Activate the **Default** design view prior to saving the assembly.
10. Save the assembly. Close the model.

End of practice

Chapter Review Questions

1. Which of the following statements are true about moving components in an assembly? (Select all that apply.)

a. Components that are partially constrained can be moved by selecting and dragging them.

b. Components that are fully constrained can be moved using the Free Move command.

c. Components that are partially constrained can be moved using the Free Move command.

d. Components that are fully constrained can be moved by selecting and dragging them.

2. If you move constrained components apart (as shown in Figure 10–27), how can you display them in their constrained positions again?

Figure 10–27

a. Use Update.

b. Use Degrees of Freedom in the View tab.

c. Use Zoom All.

d. Reapply the constraints.

3. Which of the following statements about  (Free Rotate) is true?

a. You can rotate multiple components at the same time.

b. Only unconstrained components can be rotated.

c. Grounded components cannot be rotated.

d. When you rotate a component that is constrained, the constraints change based on a new component position.

4. Which of the following statements is true regarding suppressing constraints?

a. Suppressing a constraint removes both components referenced in the constraint from the display.

b. Suppressing a constraint locks the constraint references such that they cannot be edited.

c. Suppressing a constraint removes its associated component from the display.

d. Suppressing a constraint enables you to ignore the constraint restrictions and drag the component as required in the assembly.

5. What is the purpose of a section view?

a. To simplify the display of an assembly.

b. To update an assembly more quickly.

c. To create an exploded view of an assembly.

d. To work inside an assembly while keeping the required components visible.

6. What is the purpose of a design view? (Select all that apply.)

a. To simplify the display of an assembly.

b. To update an assembly more quickly.

c. To return to a specific view of an assembly.

d. To rotate assembly components.

7. Which of the following filter options is used in the Edit View mini-toolbar to remove components from an existing design view?
   a. View All
   b. View Included
   c. View Excluded

8. When a section view is active (as shown in the Three Quarter Section View in Figure 10–28), you cannot select components or reference entities.

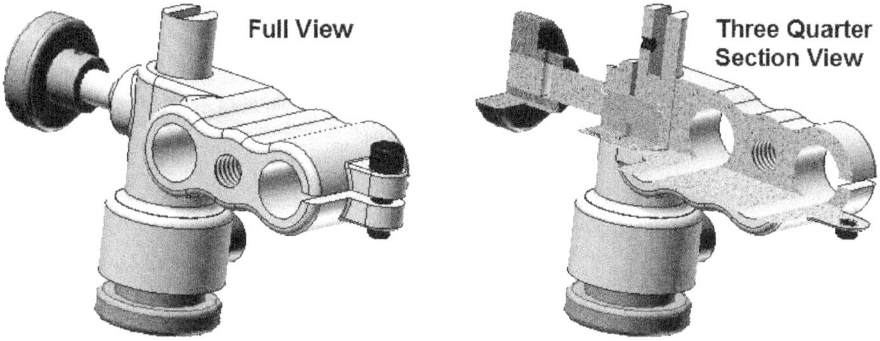

Figure 10–28

   a. True
   b. False

9. What is the difference between toggling off the visibility of a component and isolating that same component?
   a. When the visibility of a component is off, it is not displayed. However, when isolated, the visibility of all of the other components is toggled off and only the selected component is visible.
   b. No difference. Either option can be used to remove the component from the display.
   c. When the visibility of a component is off, it is not displayed; however, when isolated, the component is activated for editing.

10. Which of the following statements are true for the Model browser and assembly shown in Figure 10–29? (Select all that apply.)

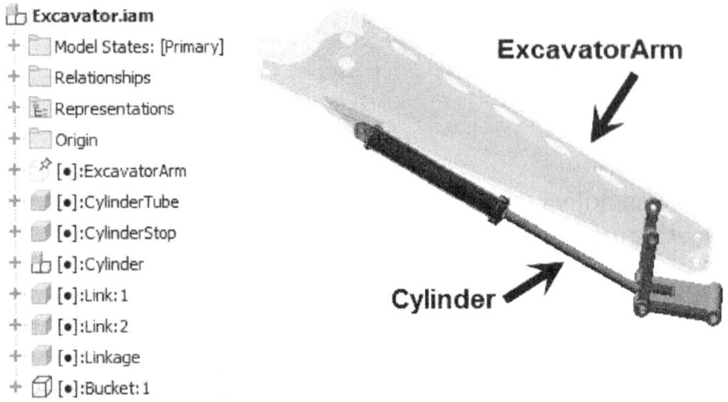

Figure 10–29

a. Bucket's visibility has been cleared.

b. Excavator Arm and Cylinder have been enabled.

c. Excavator Arm is a grounded component.

d. Excavator Arm has been isolated.

11. Which of the following statements is true of a part that is disabled (i.e., the **Enabled** option is cleared) in an assembly?

a. It is completely invisible.

b. It is completely visible but not editable.

c. It is displayed as transparent and is not selectable.

d. It is not subjected to constraints.

Command Summary

Button	Command	Location
N/A	Edit View	• **Context Menu:** In Model browser with a design view selected
N/A	Enable (component visibility control)	• **Context Menu:** In Model browser with a component selected • **Context Menu:** In the graphics window with a component selected
	Free Move (component)	• **Ribbon:** *Assemble* tab>Position panel • **Context Menu:** In Model browser with a component selected • **Context Menu:** In the graphics window with a component selected
	Free Rotate (component)	• **Ribbon:** *Assemble* tab>Position panel • **Context Menu:** In Model browser with a component selected • **Context Menu:** In the graphics window with a component selected
	Global Update (individual part or subassembly)	• **Quick Access Toolbar**
N/A	Isolate (component visibility control)	• **Context Menu:** In Model browser with a component selected • **Context Menu:** In the graphics window with a component selected
	Local Update (individual part or subassembly)	• **Quick Access Toolbar**
	Object Visibility (work features)	• **Ribbon:** *View* tab>Visibility panel
N/A	Suppress (constraint)	• **Context Menu:** In Model browser with a component selected • **Context Menu:** In the graphics window with a component selected
N/A	Undo Isolate (component visibility control)	• **Context Menu:** In Model browser with a component selected • **Context Menu:** In the graphics window with a component selected

Button	Command	Location
N/A	**Visibility (component)**	• **Context Menu:** In Model browser with a component selected • **Context Menu:** In the graphics window with a component selected

Chapter 11

Model Information

Obtaining measurements on your model is often required for entities to which explicit dimensions have not been assigned. To accomplish this, the Autodesk® Inventor® software provides a measure tool. In addition, tools are available to assign and work with model properties to capture additional information in your model.

Learning Objectives

- Use the Measure command to conduct measurements in part and assembly models.
- Calculate the area of a selected closed sketch.
- Set the physical properties for a model.
- Set material appearances and overrides.

11.1 Measurement Tools

The Autodesk Inventor software enables you to measure the distance, angle, perimeter, or area for entities in part and assembly models. To conduct a measurement, use the **Measure** command using any of the following methods.

- In the *Inspect* tab>Measure panel, click (Measure).
- In the *Tools* tab>Measure panel, click (Measure).
- Right-click in the graphics window and select **Measure** in the Marking menu.

Once the command is selected, the Properties panel and the Tool palette (assembly models only) open, as shown in Figure 11–1.

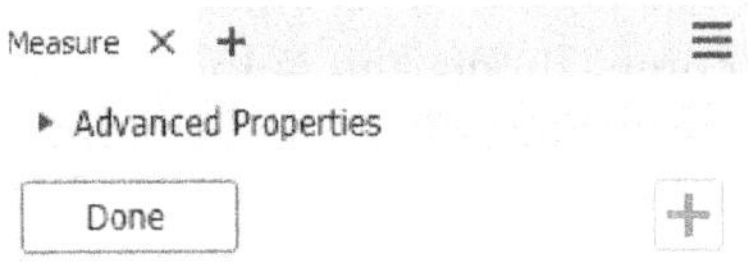

Measure panel for part models

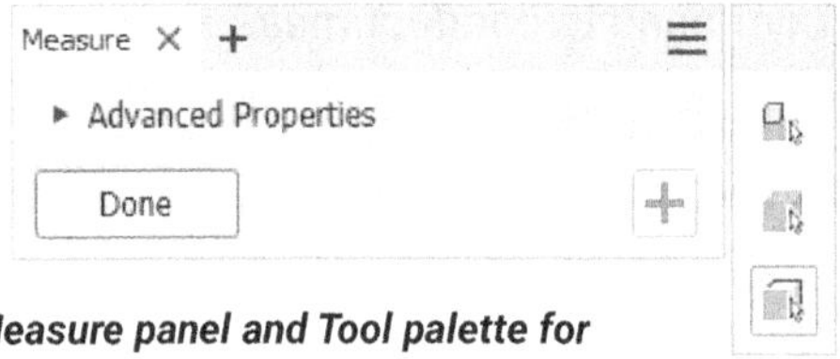

Measure panel and Tool palette for assembly models

Figure 11–1

- The Measure panel displays the measurement results as geometry is selected.
- The Tool palette is only available when measuring assembly models and provides the selection priority buttons that enable you to set whether components, parts, or faces and edges are to be selected. By default, faces and edges are set.
- The expandable *Advanced Properties* area enables you to define the precision for the results and whether to display the result in multiple unit formats when the measurement displays.

  Note: *The Measure panel can be merged with the Model browser by dragging it into the browser area so that it is docked.*

Measuring Entities and Points

To measure linear and circular entities and points, the (Select Faces and Edges) option must be active for assembly models. Depending on the type or number of entities selected, the displayed results vary as follows:

- Select an edge to measure length and two edges to measure the distance between them, as shown in Figure 11–2.

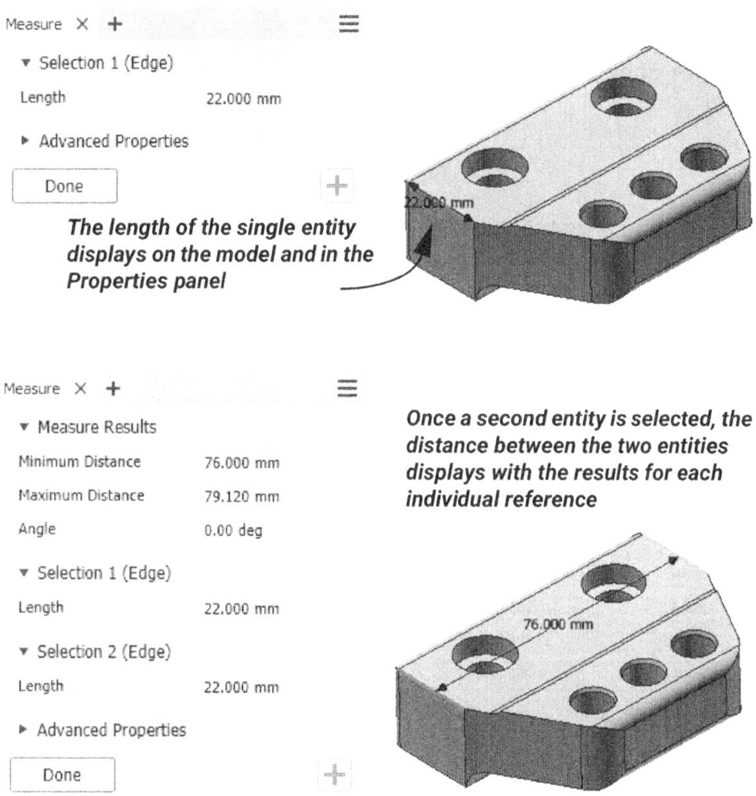

Figure 11–2

- Select a circular edge to measure its diameter, radius, length, and angle, as shown in Figure 11–3.

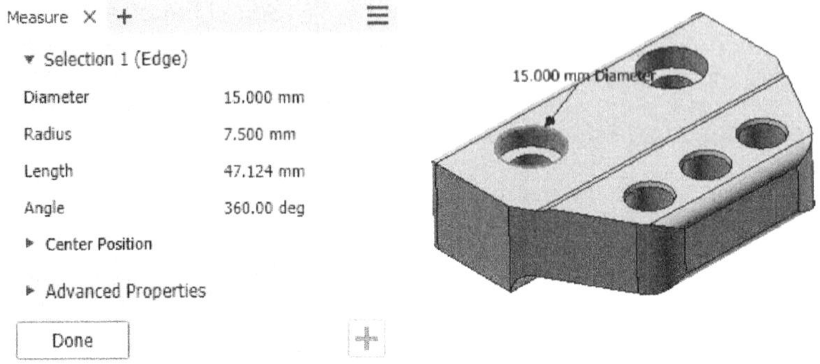

Figure 11–3

- Select a point to measure its location (X, Y, and Z) relative to the active coordinate system, as shown in Figure 11–4. Select a second point to measure the distance between them. Individual position values are also measured. The midpoints of entities can also be selected as measurement references. To select a center point on a circular entity, hover the cursor over the entity and use the **Select Other** tool to select the center point.

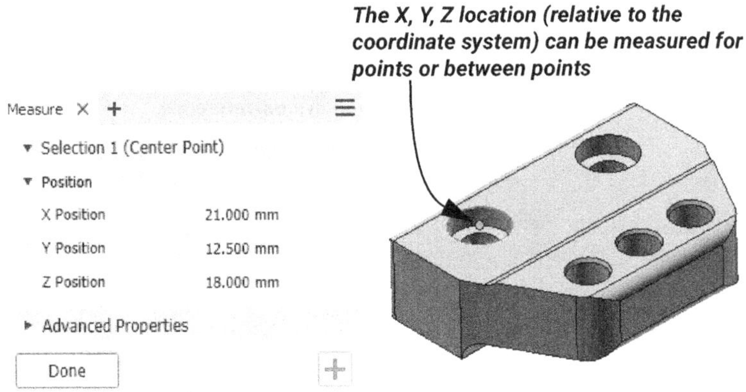

Figure 11–4

Note: *To copy a result or all results to the clip board, right-click on the value and select* ***Copy*** *or* ***Copy All***.

Measure the Distance Between Components

To measure the minimum distance between components, change the filter option to (Part Priority) or (Component Priority) and then select two components in the model. The Properties panel displays similar to that shown in Figure 11–5.

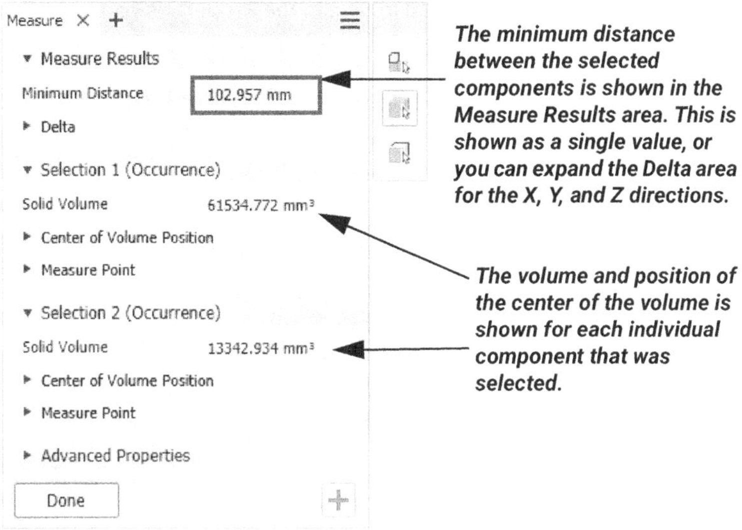

Figure 11–5

Measuring an Angle

To measure an angle, the (Select Faces and Edges) option must be active in an assembly.

- To measure the angle between two lines or faces, select the two lines or faces. Axes can also be selected. Angular measurements are shown in Figure 11–6.
- The measurement value that is highlighted in blue in the Properties panel is the value that displays on the model. To display another value, simply select it.

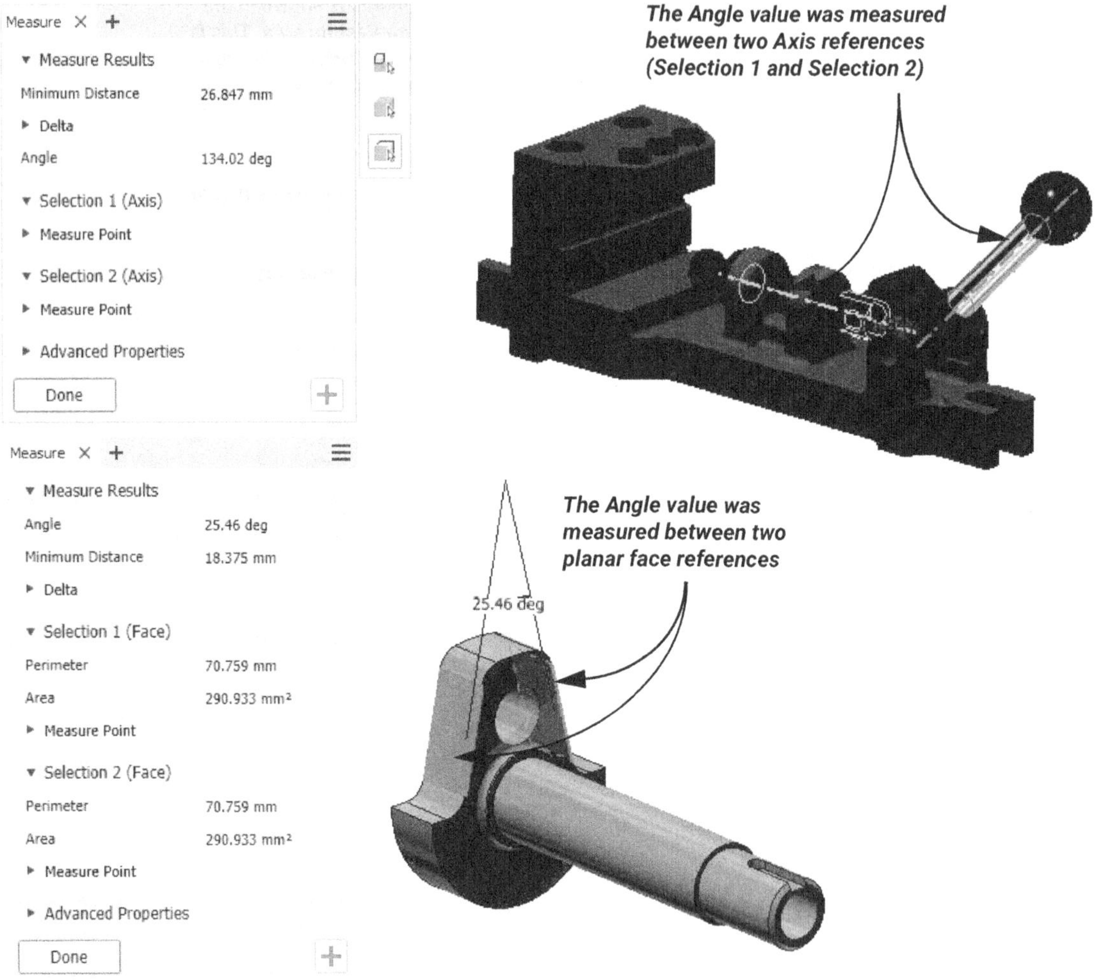

Figure 11–6

- To measure the angle created by three points, select the first two points that define a line, then hold <Shift> and select the third point that defines the angle.
- To measure the angular extent of a circular edge or arc, select it.

Measuring Planar Faces

To select a planar face for measurement, the (Select Faces and Edges) option must be active in an assembly. Once the reference is selected, the outside perimeter, the total loop perimeter (all edges that lie on the face), and the area of the face display as shown in Figure 11–7.

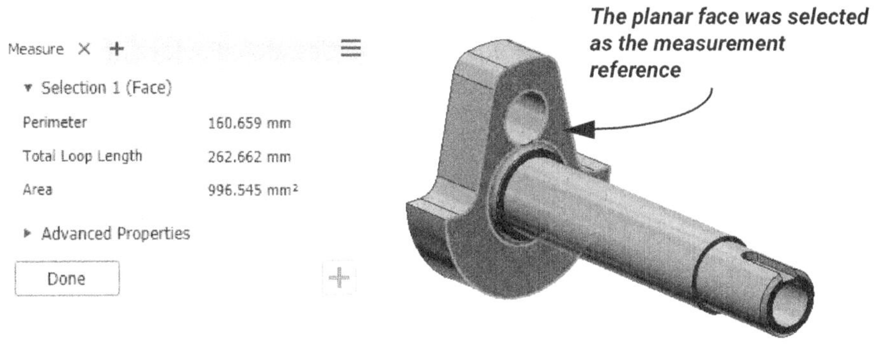

Figure 11–7

Measuring Cylindrical Faces

To select a cylindrical face for measurement, the (Select Faces and Edges) option must be active in an assembly. Once the reference is selected, the radius, diameter, total loop perimeter (all edges that lie on the face), and the area of the face are reported, as shown in Figure 11–8.

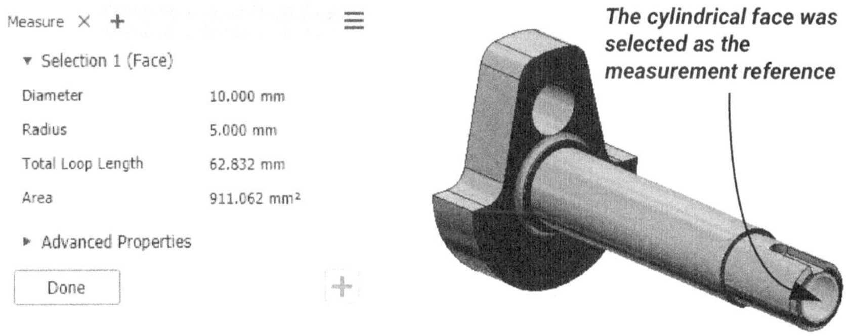

Figure 11–8

Restart a Measurement

To take a new measurement, left-click in the graphics window to clear the reference selection.

Alternatively, you can right-click and select **Restart** from the drop-down list or click (Restart Measure) at the bottom of the Properties panel.

Add to Accumulate

The sum of multiple linear measurements, as well as area, volume, and angular measurements can be determined using the **Add to Accumulate** option in the Properties panel.

How To: Use the Accumulate Function

1. Once the initial measurement is made, click **Add to Accumulate**, as shown on the left in Figure 11–9. Once selected, the *Accumulated Properties* area displays at the top of the panel, as shown on the right.

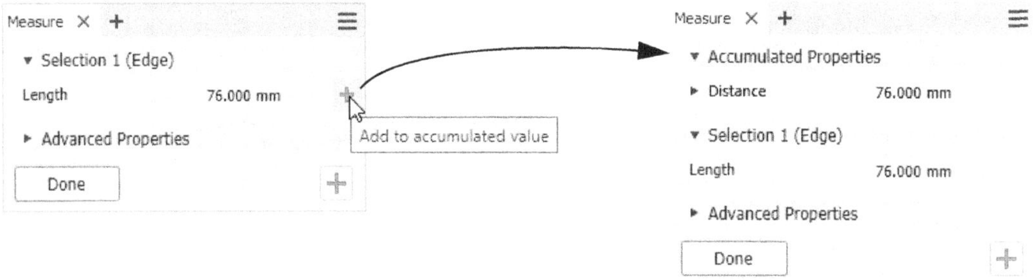

Figure 11–9

2. Select an additional entity in the graphics window. The Properties panel updates listing its values. The *Accumulated Properties* area remains at the top of the panel.

3. In the *Selection 2* area, click **Add to Accumulated Value**, as shown on the left in Figure 11–10, to add the new value to the previous one. The value updates in the *Accumulated Properties* area, as shown on the right.

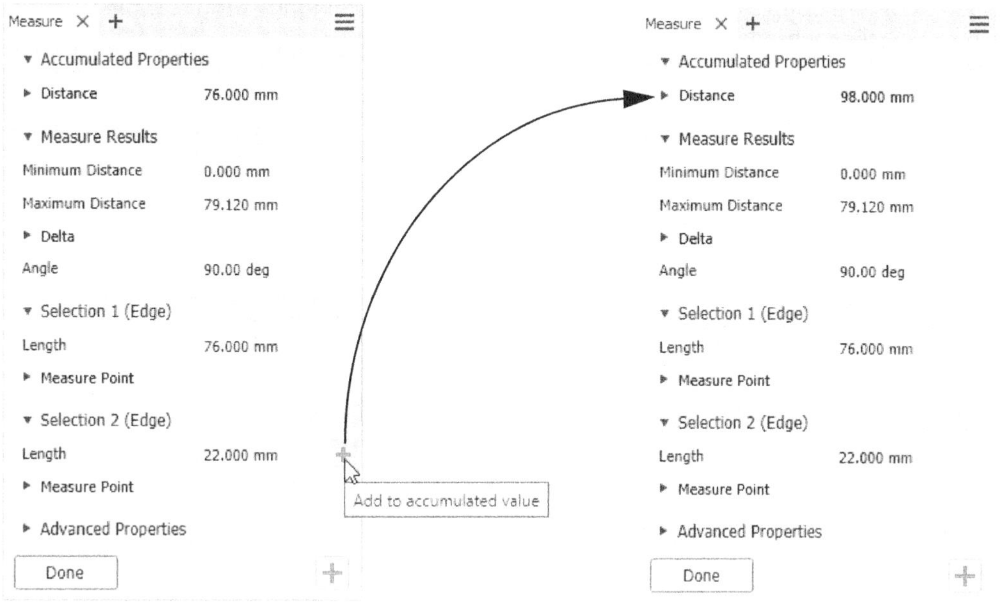

Figure 11–10

4. Continue to measure and add values as required.

Consider the following when working with accumulate values:

- To display the full list of the accumulated values, expand the **Distance** node.
- To clear a single value in the accumulate Distance node, hover over it and select (Delete) to remove it from the total.
- To clear a total accumulated Distance value, hover over it and select (Delete) to clear it.

Context Sensitive Measurements

If an object is preselected, you can right-click and select **Measure** in the marking menu, or in the expanded **Measure** options in the shortcut menu, as shown in Figure 11–11. If the preselected objects can provide a measured value, the results are displayed.

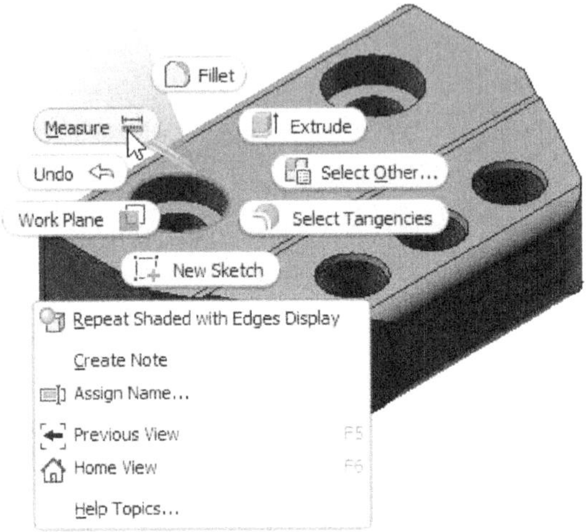

Figure 11–11

Using Measure When Entering Required Values

In most cases, if you are required to enter a value, you can use the **Measure** option (shown in Figure 11–12). This accesses the measuring tool to conduct a measurement on the model that is automatically populated into the value field. The **Measure** option is also available in Edit Dimension dialog boxes.

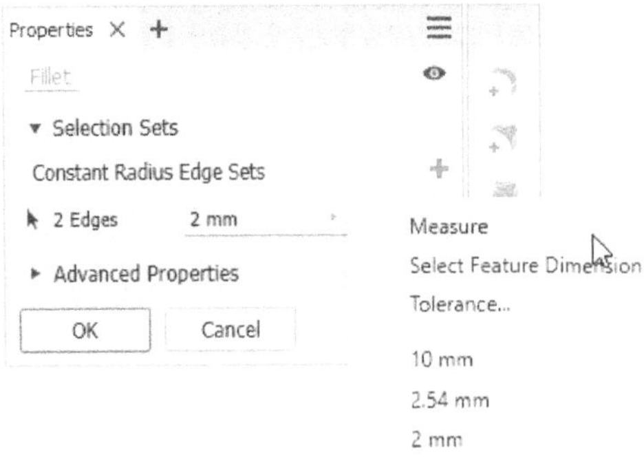

Figure 11–12

Region Properties

The **Region Properties** option calculates properties for a closed sketched area. You must be in the Sketch environment to use this command. To activate the tool, select the *Inspect* tab>Measure panel and click (Region Properties). Alternatively, the option can also be accessed in the *Tools* tab>expand Measure panel. In the Region Properties dialog box, select **Click to Add** in the *Selections* area, select a section and click **Calculate**. The calculations are completed based on the sketch coordinate system. In Figure 11–13, the results for the sketched oblong section are shown on the right.

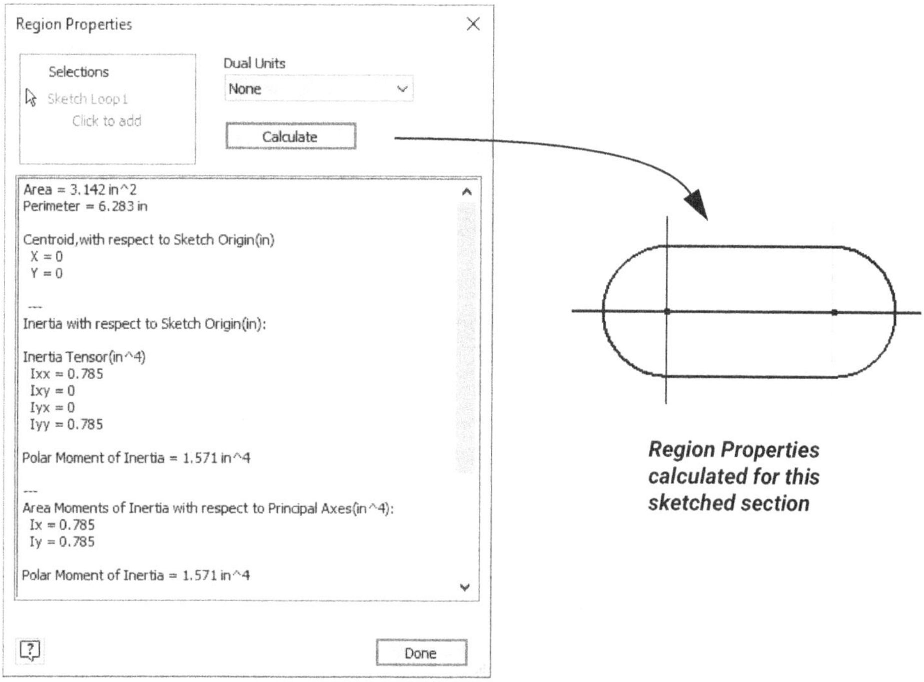

Figure 11–13

11.2 Model Material and Appearance Settings

Material

By assigning a specific material to a model, you can calculate the physical properties (e.g., volume, mass, center of gravity, etc.) of the model based on that material. The physical properties of a model are listed in the model's iProperties dialog box. To access this, right-click on the model name in the Model browser, select **iProperties**, and select the *Physical* tab. Alternatively, you can expand the **File** menu and select **iProperties** to open the iProperties dialog box. To assign material, select a type in the Material drop-down list, as shown in Figure 11–14. The values in the dialog box are automatically calculated based on the material selected.

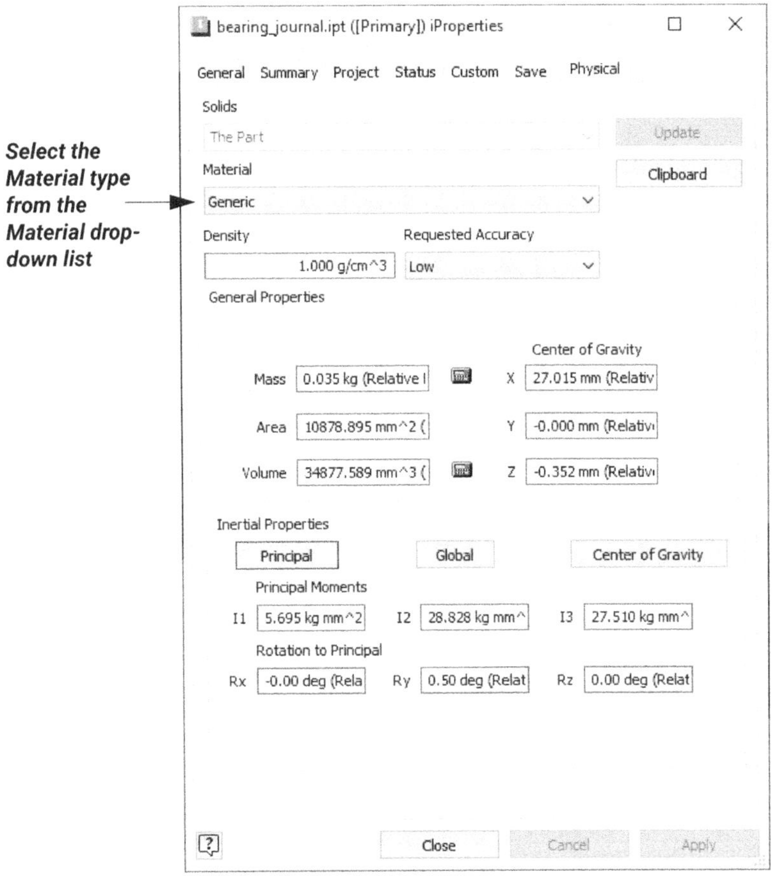

Figure 11–14

- The *Requested Accuracy* field sets the degree of accuracy for calculations. Low accuracy takes less time to calculate but is less accurate.

- Click **Update** to recalculate the physical properties of changes to part features, or to recalculate the physical properties of an assembly after changes are made to it.
- Click **Clipboard** to copy the physical property information to the Windows clipboard for pasting into a text editor.
- Mass and volume properties can be overridden by entering new values directly in their fields and clicking **Apply**. If the mass or volume properties are overridden, the other properties in the dialog box do not update to reflect the new value(s). Once overridden they are shown with the hand symbol, as shown in Figure 11–15. To remove the override, delete the contents of the field(s) and click **Apply**.

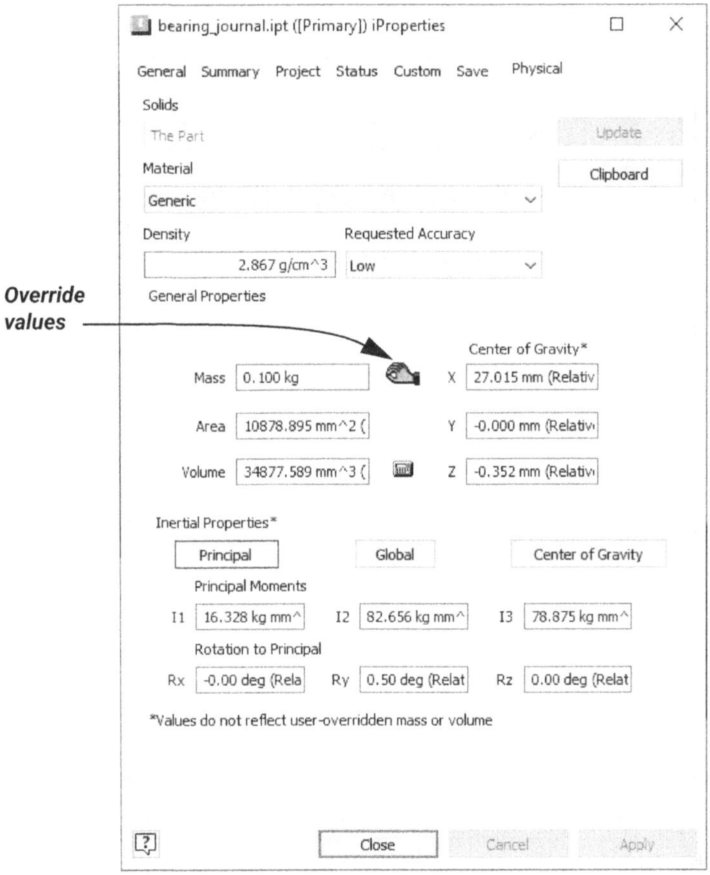

Figure 11–15

- If the material has been changed in the iProperties dialog box, the Materials drop-down list updates to reflect the change, as shown in Figure 11–16. You can use the Materials drop-down list as an alternative to changing the material in the iProperties dialog box.

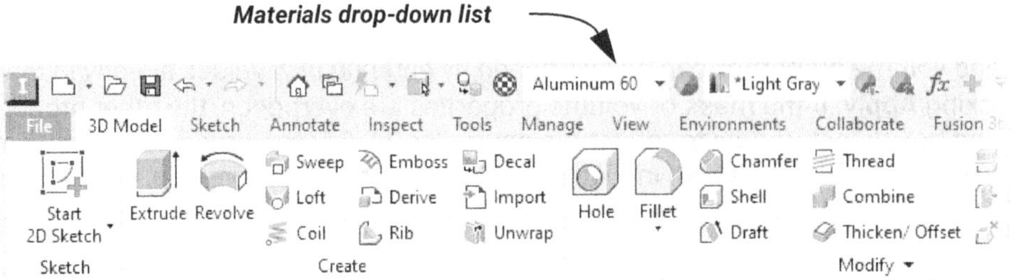

Figure 11–16

Appearance

By default, the color of a model is based on the assigned material's color. To assign a different appearance to the model while maintaining the iProperty data for the material, you can select an alternate appearance in the Appearance Override drop-down list, as shown in Figure 11–17.

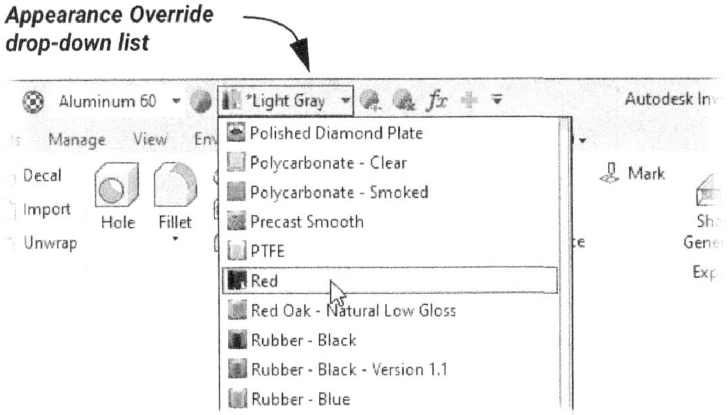

Figure 11–17

Note: By default, the materials listed in the Materials drop-down list are those from the Inventor Material Library. To switch to the Autodesk Material Library, select it at the bottom of the Materials drop-down list.

To assign an override color on specific features in the model, select the features, right-click, and select **Properties**. In the Feature Properties dialog box, select a feature appearance from the Feature Appearance drop-down list.

- Any overriden feature appearances are maintained regardless of a change to the Appearance Override.

- To clear a feature or model appearance override, in the *Tools* tab>Material and Appearance panel, click (Clear) and select the features to clear. This option is also available in the Quick Access Toolbar.

Practice 11a
Properties and Measurements

Practice Objectives

- Use the iProperties dialog box to change the material that is assigned to a component in an assembly.
- Use the **Measure** command to conduct measurements in a model

In this practice, you will apply material to components in the Bore Device assembly. You will then practice taking measurements of elements in the assembly.

Task 1: Open an assembly file.

1. Open **BoreDevice_3.iam**. The assembly displays as shown in Figure 11–18.

Figure 11–18

Task 2: Obtain and assign model properties.

1. Double-click on the **Ball Lever** component in the Model browser to activate it.
2. Right-click on **Ball Lever** in the Model browser and select **iProperties**. Select the *Physical* tab to display the physical properties of the part, as shown in Figure 11–19. Click **Update** to update the values, if required.

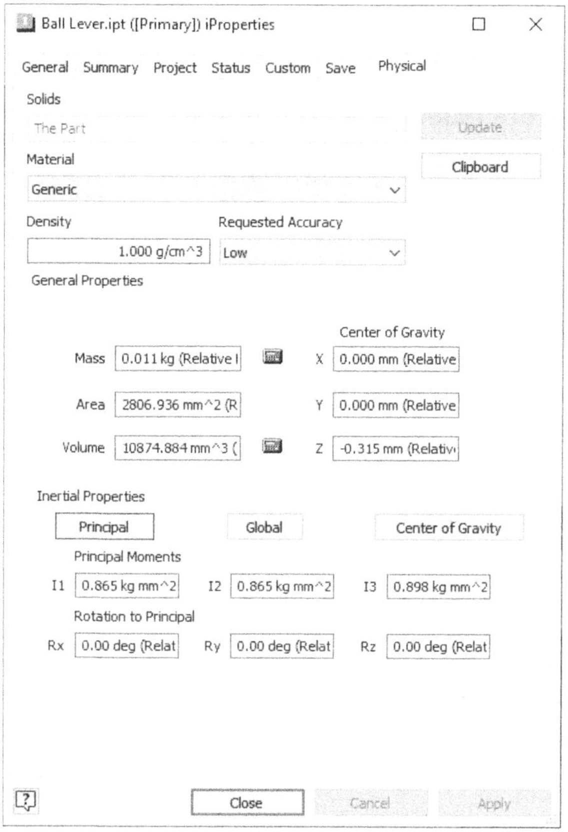

Figure 11–19

Note: *Alternatively, you can expand the **File** menu and select **iProperties** to open the iProperties dialog box.*

3. Select **ABS Plastic** in the Material drop-down list. The values in the dialog box update.
4. Click **Apply** and click **Close**. In the Quick Access Toolbar, note that the *Material* is set to **ABS Plastic** and the *Appearance Override* is set to **Smooth-White**.
5. In the Appearance Override drop-down list in the Quick Access Toolbar, select **Red**. The color of the model updates in the graphics window.
6. Double-click **Pin Seized** in the Model browser to activate it.

7. As an alternative to using the iProperties dialog box to assign the material, select **Aluminum-6061** in the Materials drop-down list in the Quick Access Toolbar.
8. Double-click **BoreDevice_3.iam** in the Model browser to activate the top-level assembly again, or in the *3D Model* tab>Return panel, click (Return).
9. Right-click **Pin Seized** in the Model browser and select **iProperties**.
10. Select the *Physical* tab when the dialog box opens. Note that the **Aluminum-6061** material has been assigned. Click **Update** to update the values, if required.
11. Close the iProperties dialog box.

Task 3: Take a series of measurements in the model.

1. In the *Inspect* tab>Measure panel, click (Measure). The Properties panel and the Tool palette open, as shown in Figure 11–20. All measurements are displayed in the Properties panel, and the Tool palette provides the selection priority buttons to define the type of entities to select.

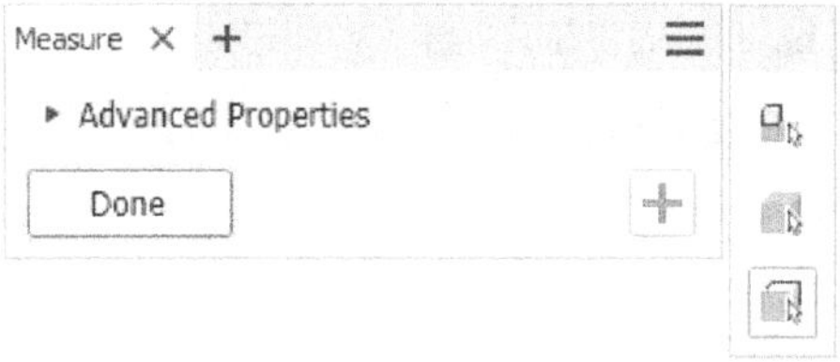

Figure 11–20

Note: The Advanced Properties area of the Properties panel enables you to define the precision and dual unit settings for the measurement.

2. Rotate the model as shown. Ensure that (Select faces and edges) is selected in the Tool palette, and select the cylindrical surface shown in Figure 11–21. The Properties panel displays the measurement values for the *Radius*, *Diameter*, *Perimeter*, and *Area* of the selected surface.

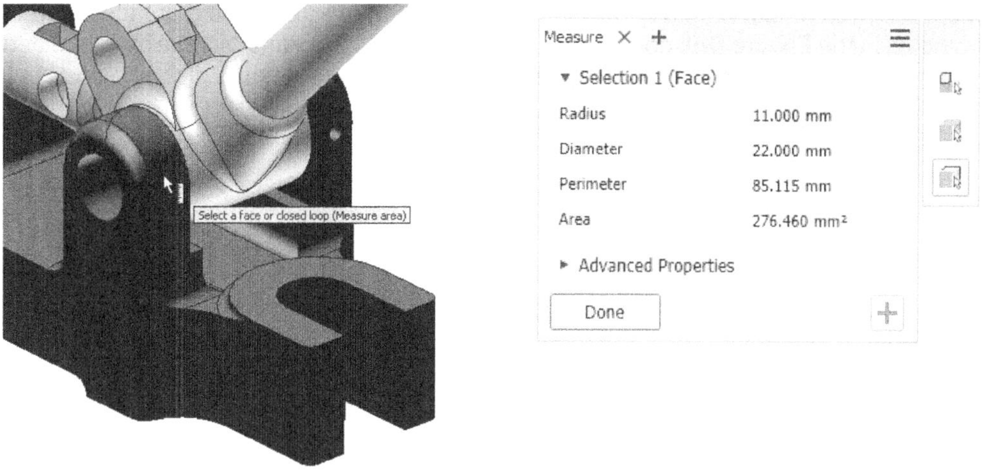

Figure 11–21

3. Left-click in the graphics window to clear the measurements. Alternatively, you can right-click in the graphics window and select **Restart** to clear the Properties panel.
4. Select the top edge of the model shown in Figure 11–22. The length displays in the Properties panel for Selection 1.
5. Select the bottom edge of the model shown in Figure 11–22. The distance between the two edges displays in the *Measure Results* area of the Properties panel. The lengths of the individual edges also display.

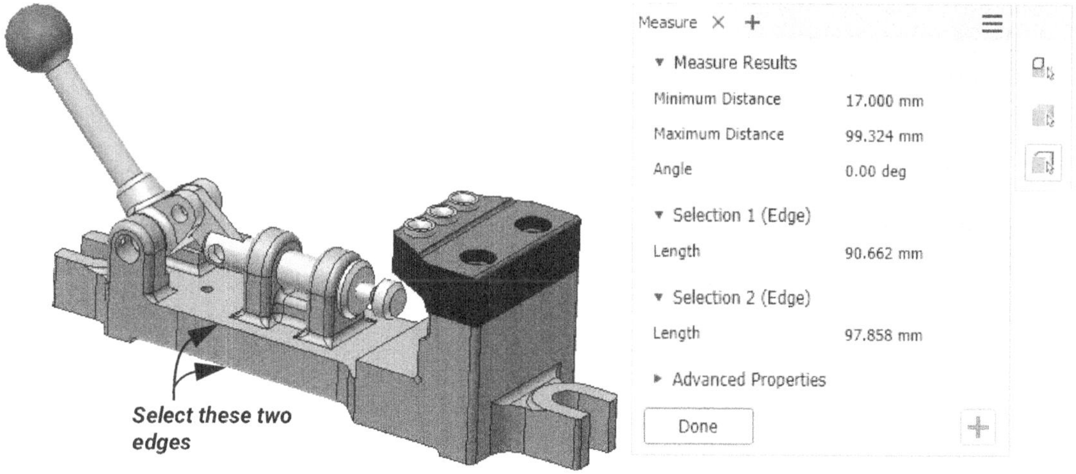

Figure 11–22

6. Left-click in the graphics window to clear the measurements.

7. Select the two circular edges shown in Figure 11–23 to measure the distance between the two holes in the **Fixture Drill** component. The Properties panel displays the distance between the centers of these edges as **40mm**. Additional measurements are also shown.

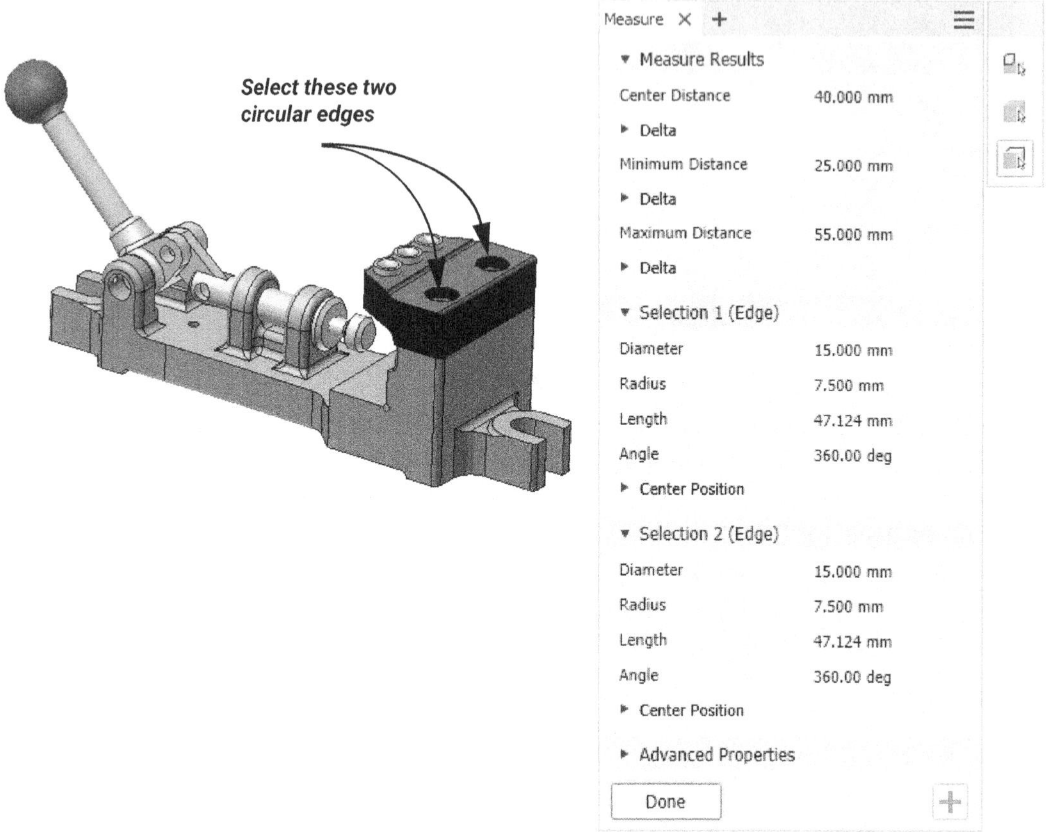

Figure 11–23

8. Left-click in the graphics window to clear the measurements.

9. Measure the distance between the surface and hole of the components shown in Figure 11–24 by first selecting the face and then selecting the circular edge. Note that the reported *Minimum Distance* is the minimum distance to the hole. Clear the measurement.

10. Select the face first and then hover the cursor over the edge of the hole. Right-click and select **Select Other** (or hover the cursor over the edge of the hole until the Select Other list displays). In the Select Other drop-down list, select the axis of the hole. The Properties panel should display a distance of **119.562mm**. As an alternative, you could have selected the surface of the hole and it would measure to the axis.

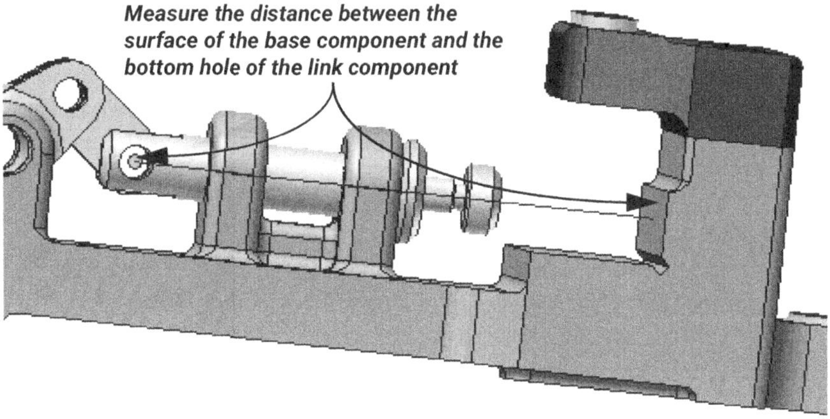

Figure 11–24

11. Practice taking additional measurements.

12. Save and close the model.

End of practice

Practice 11b (Optional) Model Measurements

Practice Objective

- Select and use the correct measurement tools to obtain values for a list of required measurements.

In this practice, you are provided with a list of required measurements. You will need to select and use any of the various measurement tools to fill in a table. Consider creating work planes tangent to surfaces and parallel to existing work planes to determine the distances between curved surfaces. The use of the **Select Other** drop-down list can help with selecting the correct references while measuring.

Task 1: Open a part file.

1. Open **bearing_journal.ipt**. The model displays as shown in Figure 11–25.

Figure 11–25

Task 2: Take a variety of measurements.

1. Use the measuring options on the *Inspect* or *Tools* tabs to take the measurements shown in Figure 11–26. Compare your results to those listed in the table to ensure that the measurement has been taken correctly.

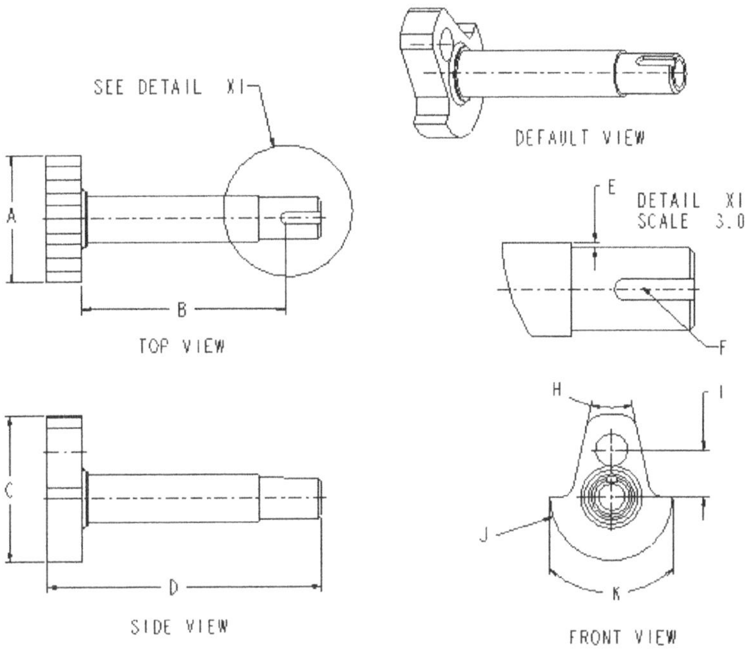

Figure 11–26

Dimension	Description	Value
A	Overall width of model	46.00
B	From face to center of arc on slot	75.00
C	Overall height of model	53.00
D	Overall length of model	101.00
E	Height of step	1.00
F	Surface area of slot	58.28
H	Angle	25.46
I	Center to center between shaft and hole	17.00
J	Diameter	46.00
K	Arc length	72.26

Chapter Review Questions

1. Which of the following measurements can be generated using the **Measure** option? (Select all that apply.)
   a. Edge Length
   b. Diameter
   c. Angle
   d. Distance between points
   e. Distance between edges
   f. Area of a sketch

2. Which of the following best describes how to use the **Measure** command to enter a required value when creating a feature?
   a. With the Properties panel, dialog box, or mini-toolbar open, in the Inspect tab>Measure panel, select Measure. Select the geometrical references to perform the required measure. This value is automatically used in the value field.
   b. In the Properties panel, dialog box, or mini-toolbar, click the arrow next to the value field you want to change and select Measure in the drop-down list. Select the geometrical references to perform the required measure. This value is automatically used in the value field.
   c. In the Inspect tab>Measure panel, select Measure. Select the geometrical references to perform the required measure. Create the feature and in the expanded menu for the required dimension value, select the value that was just measured.

3. The iProperties dialog box provides you with information about which physical properties of a part? (Select all that apply.)
   a. Mass
   b. Center of Gravity
   c. Area
   d. Volume

4. In an assembly file, the material cannot be changed using the iProperties dialog box.
   a. True
   b. False

5. Where do you find information such as the mass and volume of a part, as shown in Figure 11–27?

Figure 11–27

a. Analysis Tools (Inspect tab>Measure panel)

b. iProperties dialog box (File menu>iProperties)

c. Parameters dialog box (Manage tab>Parameters)

d. Document Settings dialog box (Tools tab>Document Settings)

6. Which of the following best describes how to change the color of a specific feature in the model?

a. Select the feature and select a material that uses the appropriate color in the Materials drop-down list.

b. Select the feature and select a material that uses the appropriate color in the *Physical* tab in the iProperties dialog box.

c. Select the feature and select a color in the Appearance Override drop-down list.

d. Select the feature and select a color in the Properties dialog box.

Command Summary

Button	Command	Location
N/A	**iProperties**	• **Context Menu:** (*from Model browser with Component name selected*) • **File Menu**
	**Measure**	• **Ribbon:** *Inspect* tab>Measure panel • **Ribbon:** *Tools* tab>Measure panel • **Context Menu:** In the graphics window with an entity selected>Measure
	**Region Properties**	• **Ribbon:** *Inspect* tab>Measure panel • **Ribbon:** *Tools* tab>expanded Measure panel

Chapter 12

Working with Projects

When working with assemblies in the Autodesk® Inventor® software, you need to access and manage multiple part, drawing, subassembly, and presentation files. If you work as part of a design team, managing access to the shared data becomes crucial. Project files enable you to organize and access these files.

Learning Objectives

- Activate a project file in an Autodesk Inventor session.
- Create new project files for use with your current working environment.
- Use the Resolve Link dialog box to locate, substitute, or ignore missing files.

12.1 Project Files

A Project file is used to organize and provide access to all files associated with a specific design project. You can create multiple project files as required to manage all of your work.

The project file (.IPJ) is a text file. It assigns a default project location for the files in the project and maintains all of the required links between files. Among other options, a project file also specifies who can access the files, and which libraries to access. When you open a model, the paths specified in the active project are searched to find all of the referenced files.

Project files are managed in the Project dialog box. Use one of the following methods to open the Project dialog box:

- On the Home page, select ⋮ (Projects and Settings) > **Settings**.
- **File** menu > **Manage**, and then select **Projects.**
- Click **Projects** in the Open or Create New File dialog boxes.

All previously loaded project files are listed at the top of the The Projects dialog box. The active project is identified with a checkmark adjacent to its name. When you select a project, its details display in the Project Tree in the lower area of the dialog box, as shown in Figure 12–1.

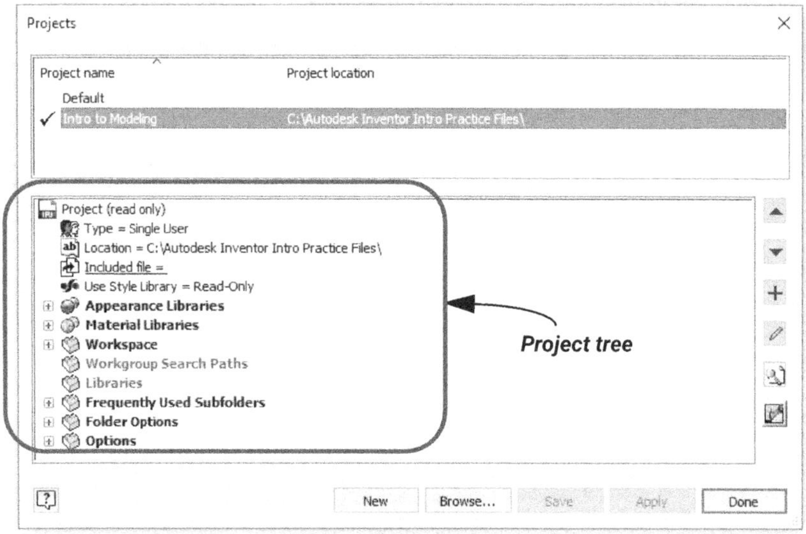

Figure 12–1

Activating a Project File

Any of the projects listed at the top of the Projects dialog box have been previously loaded and can be activated. To activate a project, ensure that all file(s) are closed and then use one of the following methods:

- Double-click on a project name at the top of the Projects dialog box.
- Select the name of the project at the top of the Projects dialog box and click **Apply**.
- Select the project name in the *Project* drop-down list on the *Home* page, as shown in Figure 12–2.

Figure 12–2

Loading a Project File

To add an existing project file to the list of available projects, in the Projects dialog box, click **Browse** at the bottom of the dialog box and navigate to and select an existing .IPJ file. Once loaded, it becomes the currently active file. Alternatively, you can right-click in the top area of the dialog box and select **Browse** on the menu.

Creating a New Project File

How To: Create a New Project File

1. Click **New** at the bottom of the Projects dialog box or right-click anywhere in the top area of the Projects dialog box and select **New**. The Inventor project wizard dialog box opens as shown in Figure 12–3.

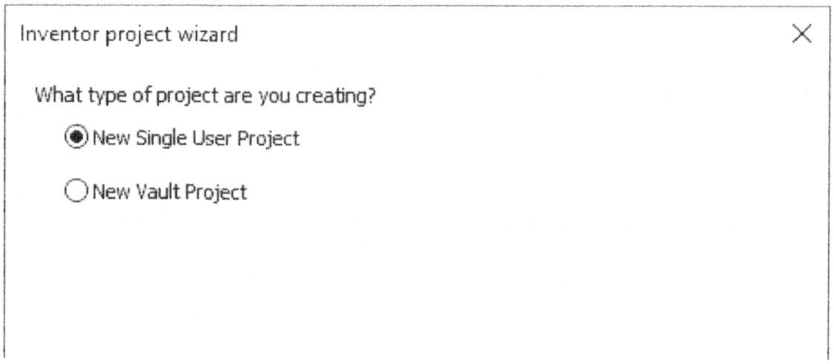

Figure 12–3

2. Select the type of project and click **Next**.
   - The **New Single User Project** type stores all design files in a personal workspace or local paths that are only accessible to the user.
   - The **New Vault Project** type ensures files are stored in a vault and are never accessed directly. They can only be accessed through an Autodesk Vault installation. The vault maintains version history and other file attributes. If Autodesk ®Vault® is not installed, only a Single User project type can be created.
3. Enter the project name and home folder (workspace), as shown in Figure 12–4. The project file (.IPJ) is stored in the assigned home folder. The project filename and path are automatically determined based on the name and folder specified. Click **Next**.

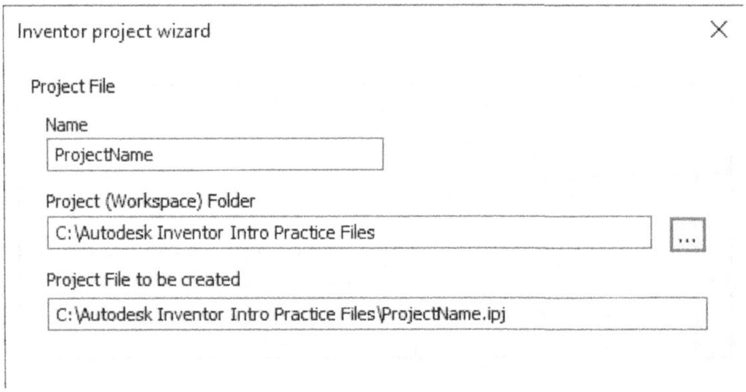

Figure 12–4

Note: *The Inventor project wizard will vary depending on the type of project you are creating.*

4. Define the library paths using the Inventor project wizard window.
   - Library paths in existing projects are listed in the *All Projects* area on the left. Library paths that are added to the new file are listed in the *New Project* area on the right. Use the **Arrow** icons to add or remove libraries from the new project. The *Library Location* field displays the path for the selected library.
5. Click **Finish** to create the project and return to the Projects dialog box.
6. Modify the Project Tree options to customize the project file, as required. These options will be described in the next topic.
7. Click **Done** to close the Projects dialog box. The new project becomes the active project.

Project Tree Customization

The project tree enables you to customize specifics on the project using the categories shown in Figure 12–5.

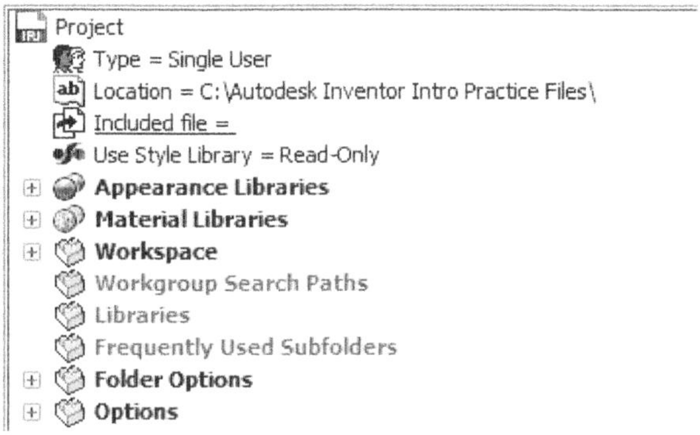

Figure 12–5

The categories that can be customized are as follows:

- The *Included File* setting enables you to add another project file so that path information in both projects can be combined. The included file typically defines the shared workgroup or library paths. To add a file, right-click on the node and select **Edit** or click  and browse to and select a file.
- The *Use Style Library* setting defines whether the style library is **Read-Only** or **Read-Write**, controlling whether a designer can make changes to the library. To set this option, right-click on its node and select the required permission setting.
- The *Appearance Libraries* and *Material Libraries* settings (shown in Figure 12–6) enable you to specify the default Appearance and Material Libraries that are initially opened. Additional libraries can be explicitly opened later. To set the default library, expand its node, right-click on the library and select **Active Library**. To load a new library, right-click on the parent node and select **Add Library** or click . The Inventor Material Library is set as default.

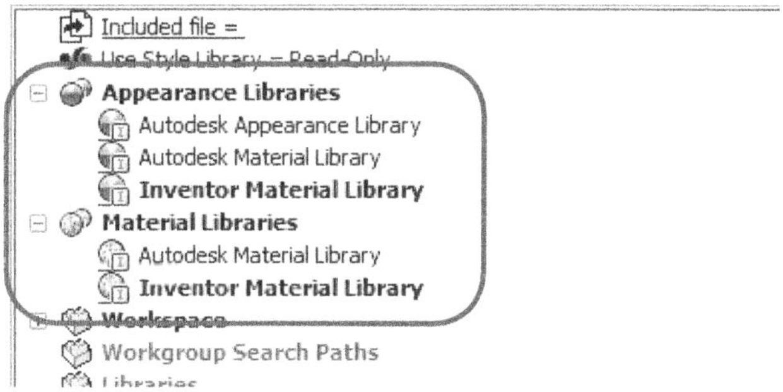

Figure 12–6

- The *Workspace*, *Workgroup Search Paths*, and *Libraries* categories specify locations for new files, files on a server/network drive, or the location of typically non-edited standard and custom parts, respectively. Additionally the *Frequently Used Subfolders* category can be used to add shortcuts to commonly used folders. To add libraries, right-click on the node and select **Add Path** or click +. Note the following when setting library paths:
  - Library paths are searched first. Use the ▲ and ▼ arrows to reorder the paths.
  - Parts placed from a library have a special tag. When searching, the software reads the tag to obtain the path. If no tag exists, the library is not searched.
  - Libraries can be added to a new project from other projects.
  - Libraries should not be renamed, to maintain existing references.
  - Since standard parts are not intended to change, parts in libraries cannot be edited.
  - Any part created or placed in a library folder is considered a library part and cannot be edited in the project.
  - Click to configure the Content Center Libraries.

  Note: *Only one Workspace can be set in a project file. Additional options for adding paths are available on the shortcut menu when selecting any of the path categories.*

- The *Folder Options* category enables you to assign locations for design data, templates, and content center files that might be required when working in a project.
- Additional customization for a project can be made using the *Options* category in the project tree, as shown in Figure 12–7. These options enable you to control such things as the number of previous versions stored in the *OldVersions* folder, whether or not files in a project have unique names, identifies the project owner, etc.

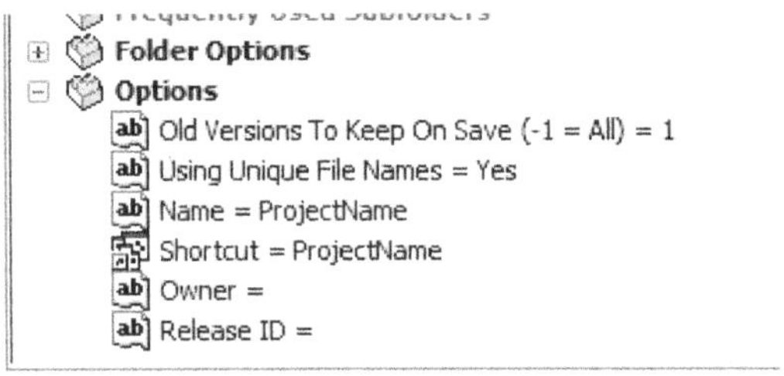

Figure 12–7

Note: *For more information on the Options, refer to the Help documentation.*

Search Sequence

When you open a file, the system searches through the project's Search Paths for referenced components in the following order: Library Paths (1), Workspace (2), Workgroup Search Paths (3), and the folder containing the file to be opened (4).

The search sequence flow chart is shown in Figure 12–8.

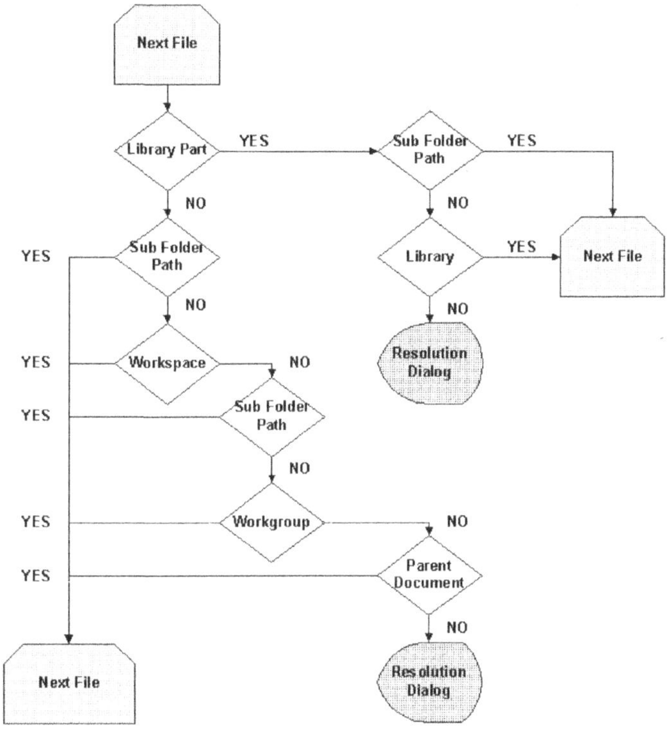

Figure 12–8

Note the following about the search sequence:

- When multiple paths are in a category, the order of listing determines the search order. Use the ▲ and ▼ arrows to reorder the paths.
- If files are found with the same name in multiple paths, the first file found is used.
- Paths can be added after a project has been started, but starting with the appropriate list helps avoid unresolved links.
- In general, the fewer search paths the better. For optimal performance, use a single workspace or workgroup location (plus libraries) per project, with relative paths (subfolders). This speeds file resolution and makes moving data easier.

Hint: Working with Subfolders

Note the following about subfolders:

- Do not define the subfolders of a project location as separate locations in the project. This causes file resolution problems that display red in the project's dialog box.
- When placing assembly components from a subfolder, the subfolder path (relative path) is saved as part of the assembly. When opening the assembly, the system combines the project's search location with this relative path to find components.
- Components moved into subfolders cannot be located because a relative subfolder path was not stored with the assembly. Use the Resolve Link dialog box to fix the failure.
- A flat directory structure (few subfolders) increases loading speed.

12.2 Resolving Links

If a referenced file cannot be found in the search paths of the active project, the Resolve Link dialog box opens as shown in Figure 12–9. Use this dialog box to find the referenced file, to substitute another file, or to ignore the missing file.

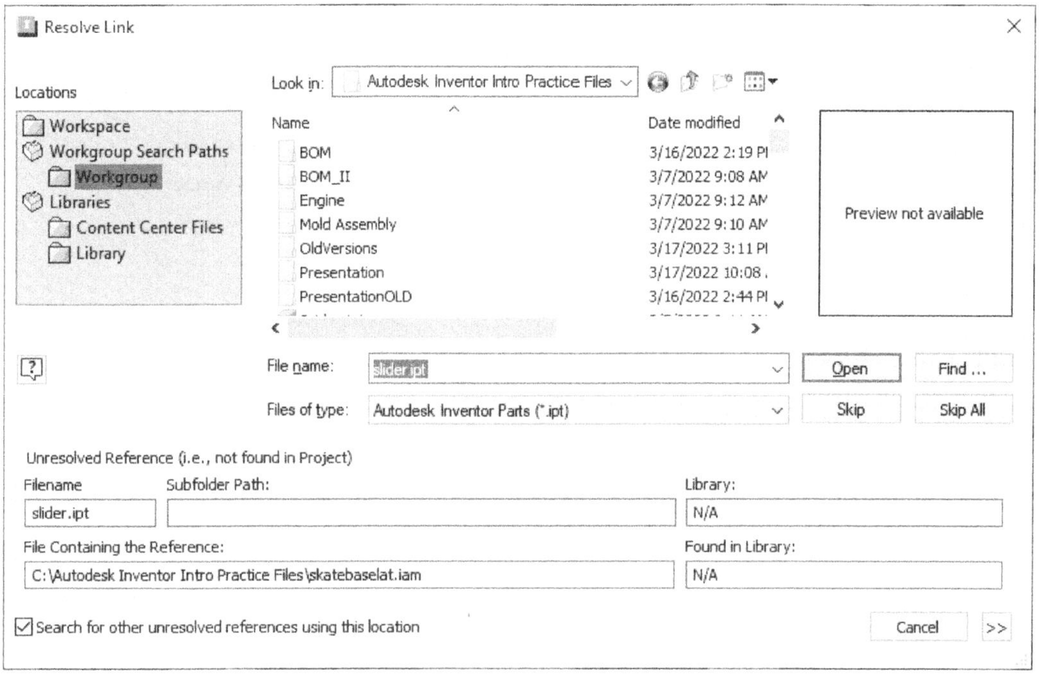

Figure 12–9

The Resolve Link dialog box displays the file location, folder, and file format. The operations on the right side of the dialog box are described as follows:

Open	Opens a selected file that will resolve the failure. You can also double-click on the name of the file to open it.
Find...	Opens the Find dialog box, which enables you to search for a file based on selected criteria. 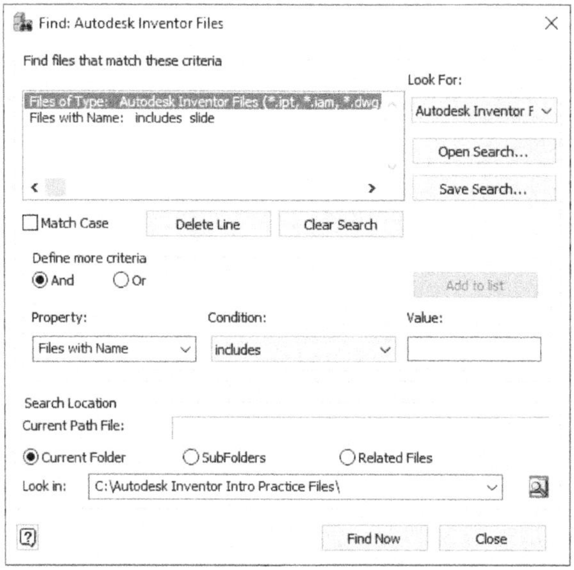
Skip	Skips the unresolved file and goes to the next file. The skipped file does not display in the assembly and any updates that depend on the unresolved component do not solve until the missing link is resolved. You can later replace the component in the assembly or resolve the link by right-clicking on the assembly name at the top of the Model browser and selecting **Resolve File**. 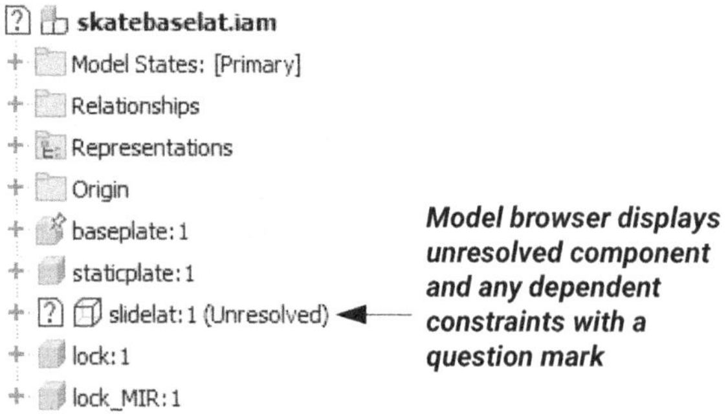
Skip All	Skips all unresolved files. All failed files display in the Model browser with a question mark icon and each should be individually resolved as described for individually skipped files.

The *Unresolved Reference* area in the Resolve Link dialog box displays information about the component that is not resolved (e.g., filename, path, etc.), as shown in Figure 12–10.

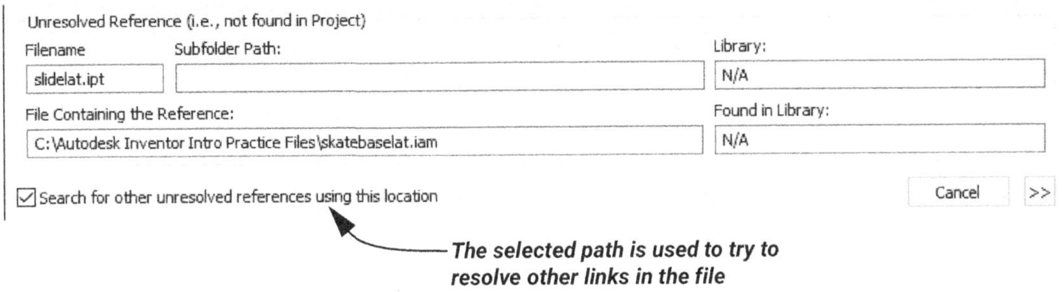

Figure 12–10

The file might be missing for the following reasons:

- The file no longer exists in the active project search paths.
- The file has been renamed outside context of its parent model.
- The file has been moved to another library or subfolder.
- There are network or server complications.

If the file that you select to resolve the link is in the project locations or their subfolders and you save the host file, the link is automatically resolved the next time you open the host file. If the file you select is not in the defined project location, you need to resolve the link each time you open the host file. To avoid this, the unresolved file(s) should be moved to one of the project search locations, or the project should be modified to include the file location.

Practice 12a
Create a Project File

Practice Objectives

- Create a new project that assigns and modifies various categories in the project file.
- Resolve a link for a file that was renamed outside the assembly and is therefore missing when the assembly is opened.

In this practice, you will create a new project file and resolve a link in the project.

Task 1: Create a project file.

1. Ensure that all files are closed in the current session prior to starting this practice. Projects cannot be set with files open.
2. Use one of the following methods to open the Projects dialog box. Once open, the active project (Intro to Modeling) displays with a checkmark to the left of its name.
   - On the Home page, click ⋮ (Projects and Settings) > **Settings**.
   - Click (Projects) in the Quick Access Toolbar at the top of the interface.
   - In the **File** menu, select **Manage>Projects**.
3. Right-click in the top section of the dialog box and select **New** or click **New** at the bottom of the dialog box. The Inventor project wizard opens.
4. Select **New Single User Project** and click **Next**.
5. Enter **Your_Name** in the *Name* field.
6. Click ... next to the *Project (Workspace) Folder* field. In the Browse For Folder dialog box, browse to the directory in which your training files are located.
7. Click **OK** to close the Browse For Folder dialog box.
8. Click **Finish** to create the project. The **<Your_Name>** project displays in the Projects dialog box and is set as the active project (as indicated by the adjacent checkmark).

Task 2: Assign workspace and libraries to the project file.

1. If a checkmark is not displaying next to the active project name. Double-click on **<Your_Name>** in the upper area of the dialog box to activate it. The lower area of the dialog box displays, as shown in Figure 12–11.
2. Expand the *Workspace* category in the project tree area.

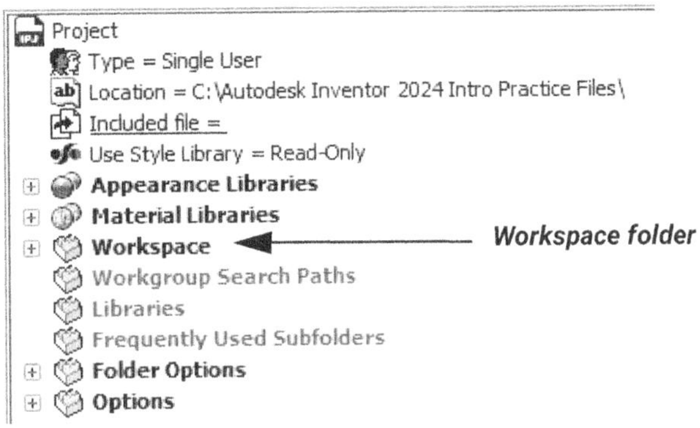

Figure 12–11

3. Select the *Workspace* node, right-click, and select **Edit**.

   Note: The temp directory is only assigned for this practice. Normally, project files would use a well-defined folder structure.

4. Click and browse to the *C:\Temp* directory, or click **Make New Folder** to create the directory if it does not already exist.
5. Click **OK** to close the Browse For Folder dialog box.
6. Press <Enter> to apply the changes.
7. Select **Workgroup Search Paths** in the project tree area, right-click and select **Add Path**.
8. Click . Browse to your practice files directory. Delete the **Workgroup** node name in the path, if displayed.
9. Click **OK** to close the Browse For Folder dialog box.
10. Press <Enter> to apply the changes.
11. Select **Libraries** in the project tree area, right-click, and select **Add Path**.
12. Click . Navigate to and select the following folder:
    - *C:\Users\Public\PublicDocuments\Autodesk\Inventor 2024\Catalog*
13. Select the software's *Catalog* folder in the Browse For Folder dialog box.
14. Click **OK** in the Browse For Folder dialog box.

15. Press <Enter> to apply the changes. The project tree should display similar to that shown in Figure 12–12.

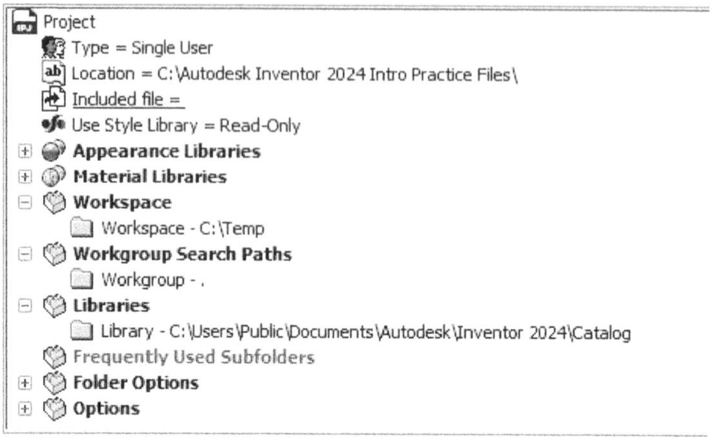

Figure 12–12

16. Expand the *Options* folder and select **Old Version To Keep On Save**.
17. Click  on the right side of the project tree. You can also select the option a second time to edit its value.
18. Enter **2** in the field that displays and press <Enter>. This option controls the number of previous versions of the file to keep after a save operation. The default is one.
19. Click **Save** at the bottom of the dialog box to save your changes to the project.
20. Click **Done** to close the Projects dialog box.
21. On the *Home* page, expand the projects list, as shown in Figure 12–13. Scroll through the list of projects. Note that the **<Your_Name>** project is listed on the Home page and has a check mark adjacent to it on the drop-down list, both indicating that this is the active project.

Figure 12–13

Task 3: Open an assembly and resolve the link.

1. Select **Open** on the Home page, **File** menu, or the Quick Access Toolbar.
2. Select **Workgroup** to switch to the *C:\Autodesk Inventor 2024 Intro Practice Files* path. The Open dialog box displays, as shown in Figure 12–14.

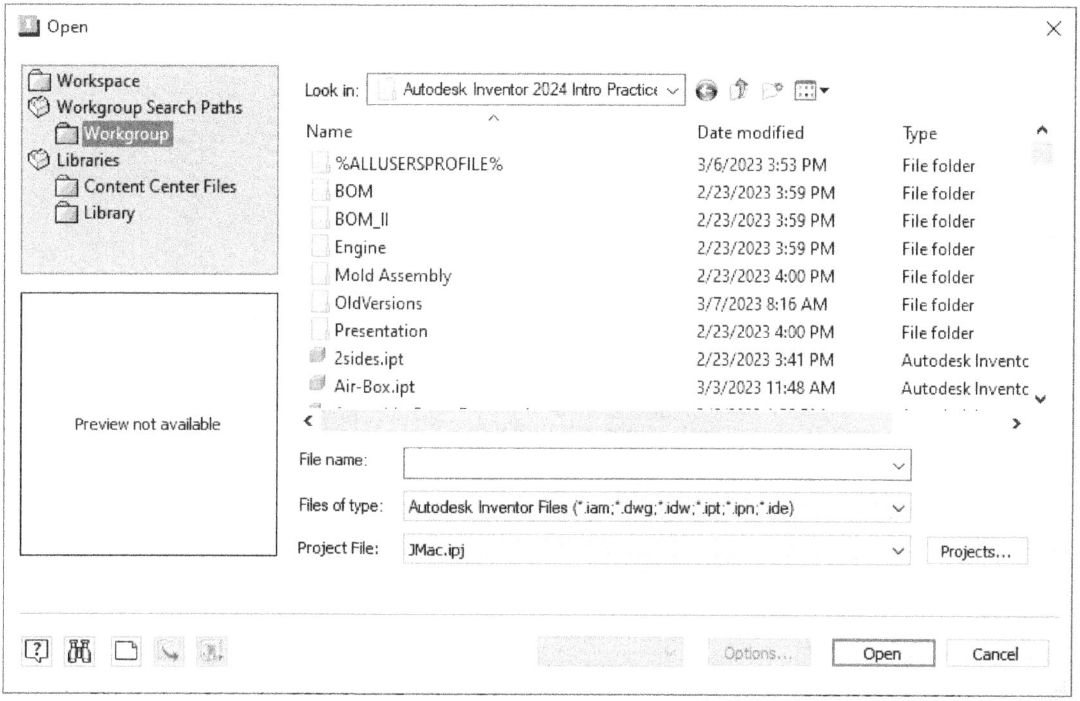

Figure 12–14

3. Select and open **skatebaselat.iam**. The Resolve Link dialog box opens and indicates that the **slidelat.ipt** part could not be found. For now, click **Skip** and continue opening the assembly.
4. A warning box displays explaining that you can work in assemblies with unresolved components. However, updates that depend on the unresolved component will not solve until components are resolved. Click **OK**.

5. The assembly displays in the graphics window. Note the missing part (**slidelat**) displays the icon, as shown in Figure 12–15, indicating that the part definition is missing.

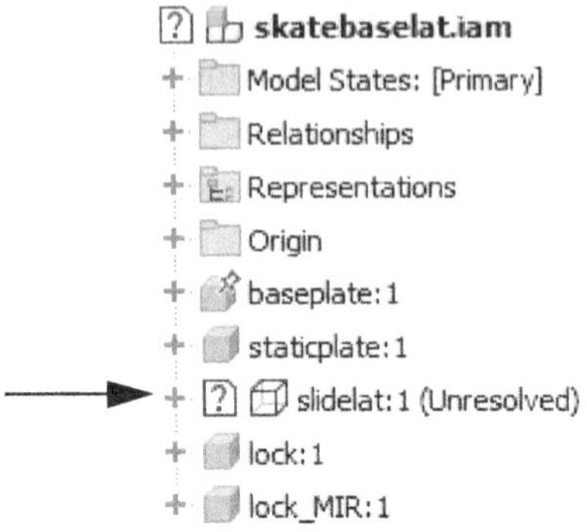

Figure 12–15

6. Right-click on **skatebaselat.iam** in the Model browser and select **Resolve File**.
7. The Resolve Link dialog box opens. Click **Find**. The Find dialog box opens.
8. Select **Files with Name** in the Property drop-down list. Select **includes** in the Condition drop-down list. Enter **slide** in the *Value* field. Click **Add to List**.
9. Set the *Look in* folder to your course directory if not already set. The Find dialog box should appear as shown in Figure 12–16.

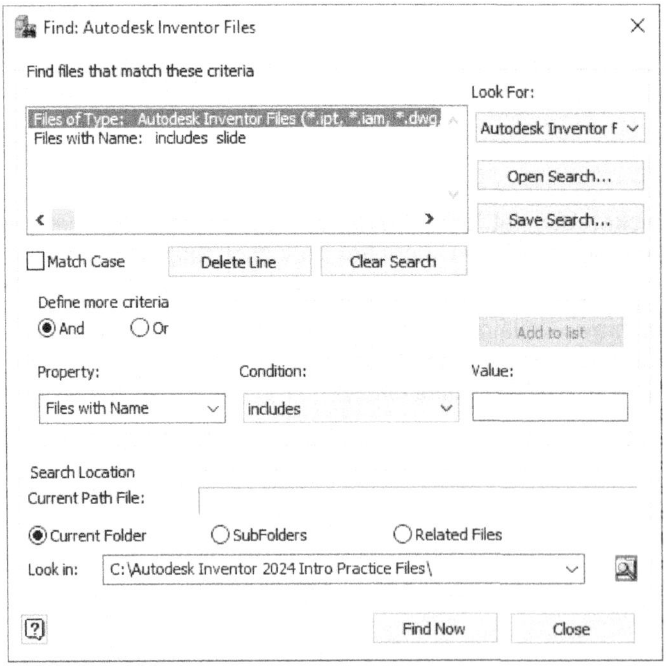

Figure 12–16

10. Click **Find Now** to perform the search. The Autodesk Inventor Files Found dialog box opens, as shown in Figure 12–17, indicating that files were found.

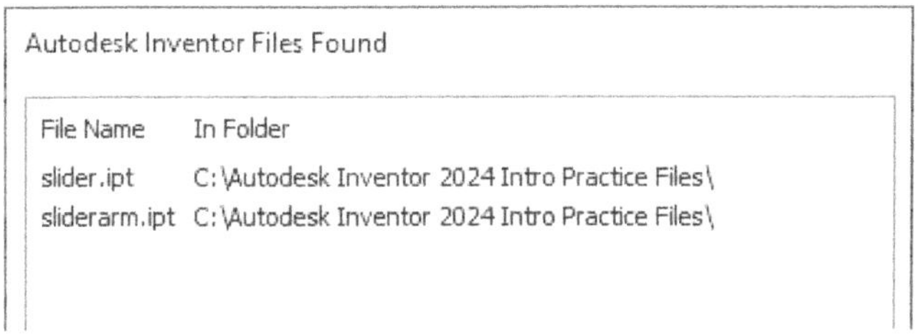

Figure 12–17

11. Select **slider.ipt** in the list and click **OK**.
12. Close the Find dialog box. The assembly displays in the graphics window, as shown in Figure 12–18. Note that the filename in the Model browser is now displayed correctly. The assembly has been reoriented for clarity.

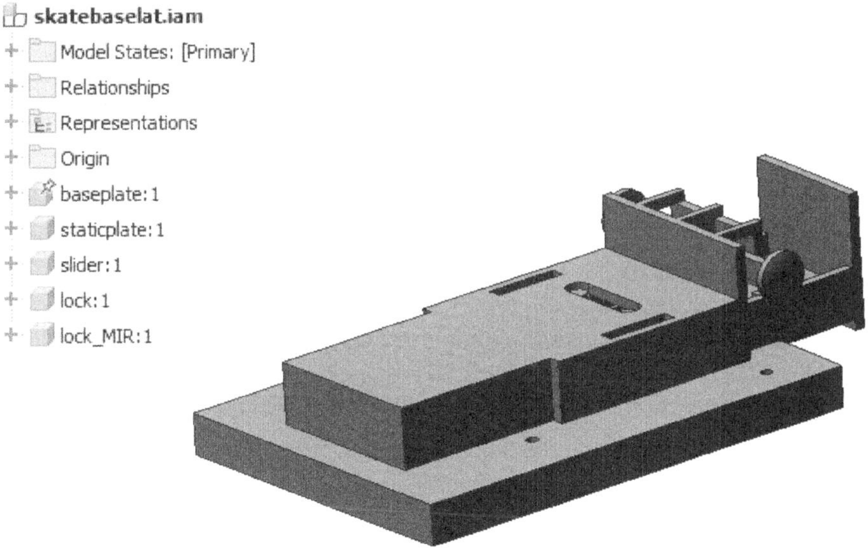

Figure 12–18

13. Save the assembly and close the window.

End of practice

Chapter Review Questions

1. What is the primary purpose of Projects in the Autodesk Inventor software? (Select all that apply.)
   a. To set default templates for new files.
   b. To manage file locations and links between related files.
   c. To control default text styles, dimension format, etc.
   d. To define a search sequence for the projects folders.

2. You can change the active project while an Autodesk Inventor file is open.
   a. True
   b. False

3. Which file extension is used to store the information in a project file?
   a. .IPT
   b. .IPN
   c. .IPJ
   d. .IPK

4. Which command sequence is used to open the Projects dialog box? (Select all that apply.)
   a. On the Home page, click ⋮ (Projects and Settings) > Settings.
   b. In the Create New File dialog box, select Projects.
   c. In the Open dialog box, select Projects.
   d. File menu>Manage and click .
   e. In the Tools tab>Options panel, click .

5. Which of the following can be customized in the Project tree to create an Autodesk Inventor Project file? (Select all that apply.)
   a. Project's directory location.
   b. Model names that reference the Project file.
   c. Library locations.
   d. Active Material library.
   e. Default Material setting.
   f. Template folder location.
   g. Number of versions to keep when saving.
   h. Content Center folder location.

6. All of the missing links must be resolved to open and edit an assembly.
   a. True
   b. False

7. When a component in an assembly is missing during retrieval, what actions can be done to resolve the failure? (Select all that apply.)
   a. Open an alternate file to replace the failed file.
   b. Skip the failed file.
   c. Delete the failed file.
   d. Find the failed file.

Command Summary

Button	Command	Location
	Projects	• **Quick Access Toolbar** • **Home Page:** Projects and Settings • **Dialog Box:** Open • **Dialog Box:** New • **File Menu:** Manage

Chapter 13

Customizing Autodesk Inventor

Customizing the software enables you to change the system's default appearance and options to tailor to specific needs or preferences. You can customize settings to affect the entire company or changes can be user-specific.

Learning Objectives

- Use the Application Options to globally customize the modeling environment.
- Use the Document Settings to customize the active part, assembly, or drawing file.
- Edit iProperty information for parts, assemblies, and drawing files.

13.1 Application Options

The Application Options dialog box contains settings that control the software's behavior and configuration. Select the *Tools* tab> Options panel and click (Application Options) to open the Application Options dialog box. Alternatively, you can also click **Options** on the **File** menu to open the Applications Options dialog box.

General Tab

The *General* tab sets operation behaviors, such as startup, tooltips, selection, etc., as shown in Figure 13–1.

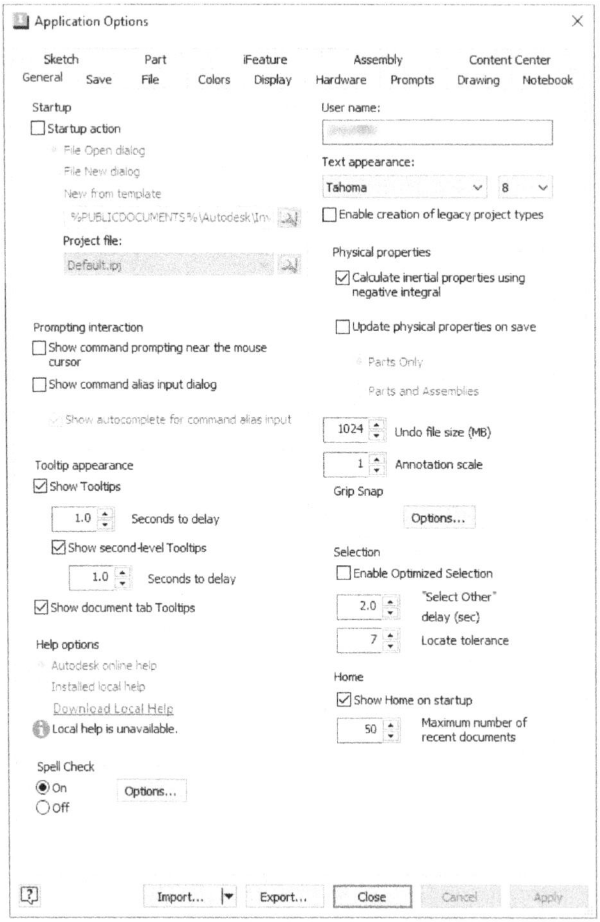

Figure 13–1

Save Tab

The *Save* tab can be used to set the default save behavior when assembly components or library files are saved, as shown in Figure 13–2.

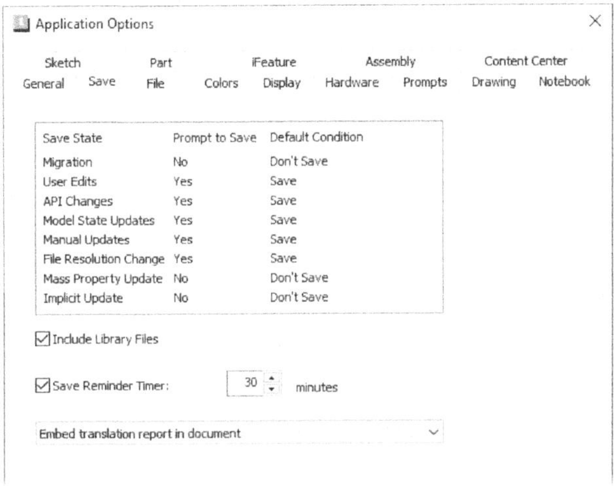

Figure 13–2

File Tab

The *File* tab controls the default locations of the files used by the software. To change a file location, click  next to the appropriate field. It also controls the default options and settings to accelerate file opening times for assemblies, and set the default templates.

Colors Tab

The *Colors* tab controls the colors used in the graphics window and the presence of reflections and textures, assigns a color scheme for objects in the graphics window or drawing files, or assigns a background color (color, gradient, or background image). The *Colors* tab also enables you to control the color theme of the user interface (UI) for software (Light or Dark) and the in-canvas color theme for the graphics window.

Display Tab

The *Display* tab controls the appearance of active and inactive components and a model's display quality. In addition, it controls the 3D Navigation controls and behavior for the software. Options on this tab also enable you to customize the middle mouse button behavior.

Drawing Tab

The *Drawing* tab (shown in Figure 13–3) sets options for the behavior of drawings.

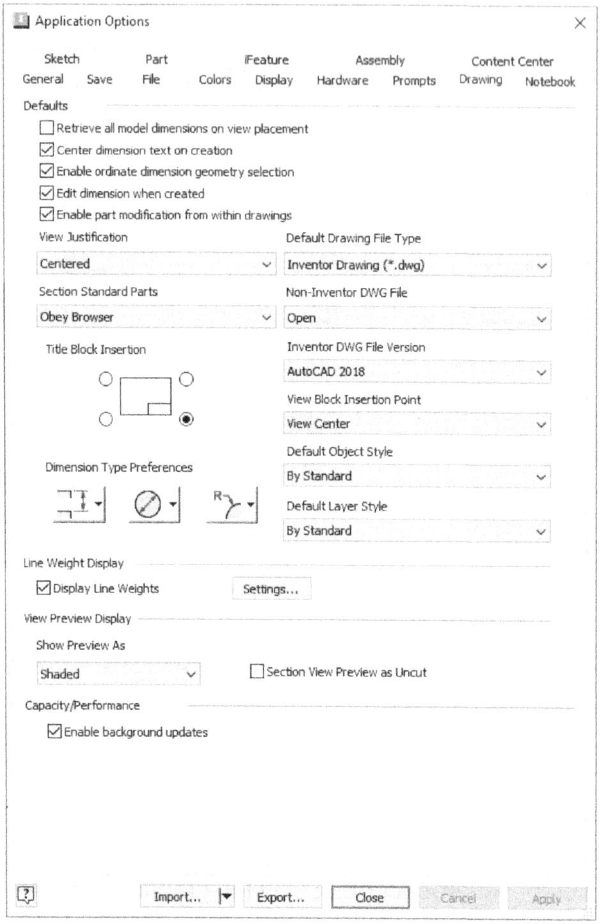

Figure 13–3

Note: *The* ***Enable part modification from in drawings*** *enables you to allow model dimension changes at the drawing level, or not.*

Prompts Tab

The *Prompts* tab enables you to select the prompts that display while working. To do so, select a prompt and right-click in their *Response* or *Prompt* columns.

Sketch Tab

The *Sketch* tab (shown in Figure 13–4) controls the sketch settings.

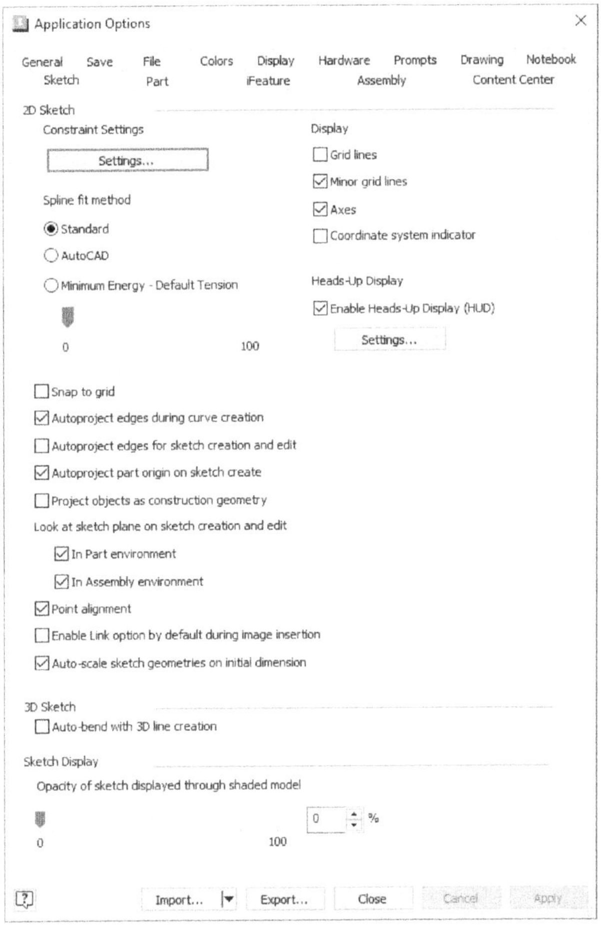

Figure 13–4

Part Tab

The *Part* tab (shown in Figure 13–5) controls the defaults for creating new parts, along with some constraint settings.

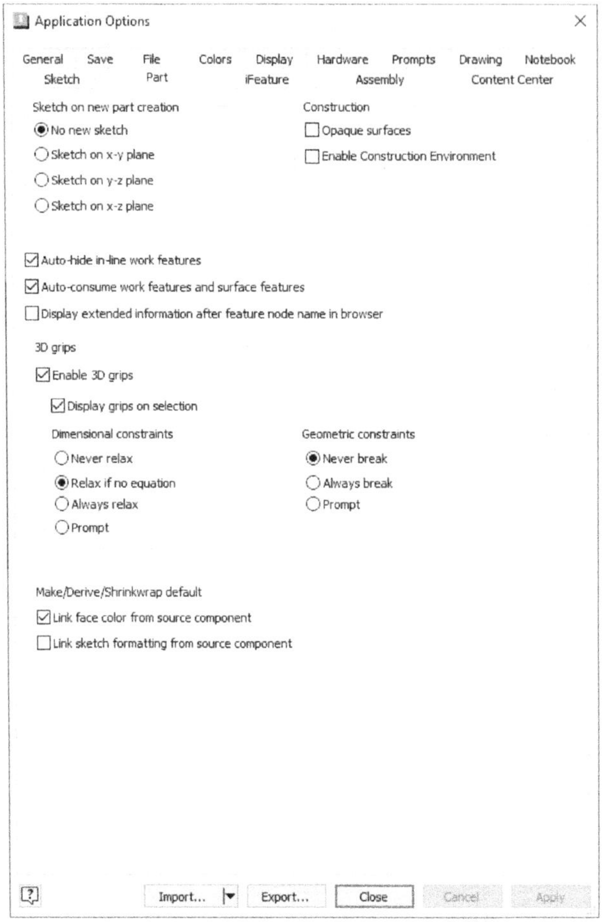

Figure 13–5

Assembly Tab

The *Assembly* tab (shown in Figure 13–6) controls the defaults for working with assemblies.

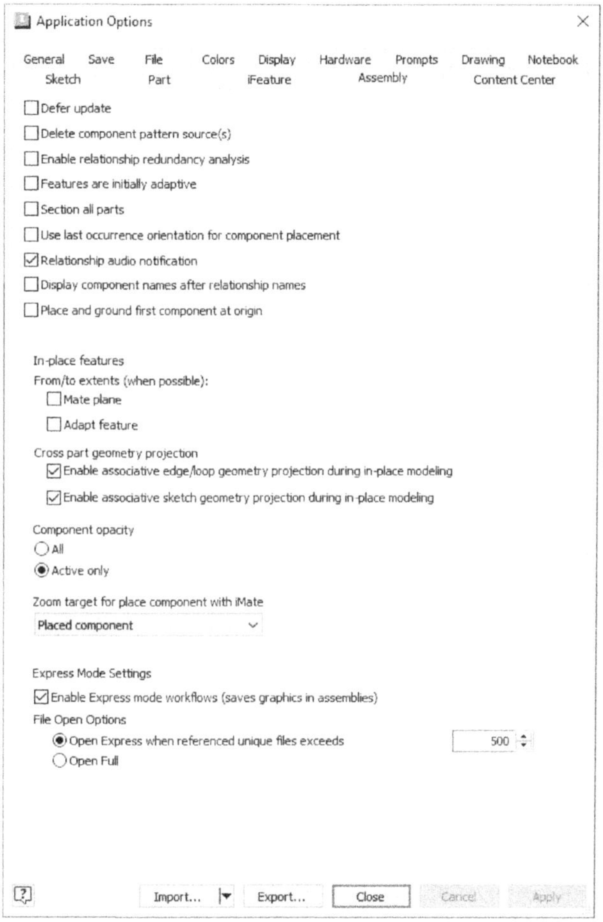

Figure 13–6

13.2 Document Settings

To control the current file settings (e.g., grid or units) you use the Document Settings. Settings made here only apply to the current file. Select the *Tools* tab>Options panel, and click (Document Settings) to open the Document Settings dialog box. The options that are available in the Document Settings dialog box are dependent on the file type that was active when document settings were opened.

Standard Tab

The *Standard* tab enables you to set the following:

- Lighting style and display appearance
- Material for the model
- Active standard for annotations in a drawing

Units Tab

The *Units* tab (shown in Figure 13–7) displays the default unit system, precision values, and display settings for model dimensions and parameters. The *Units* tab is not available in a drawing. In an assembly, the Units tab is the same as in a part.

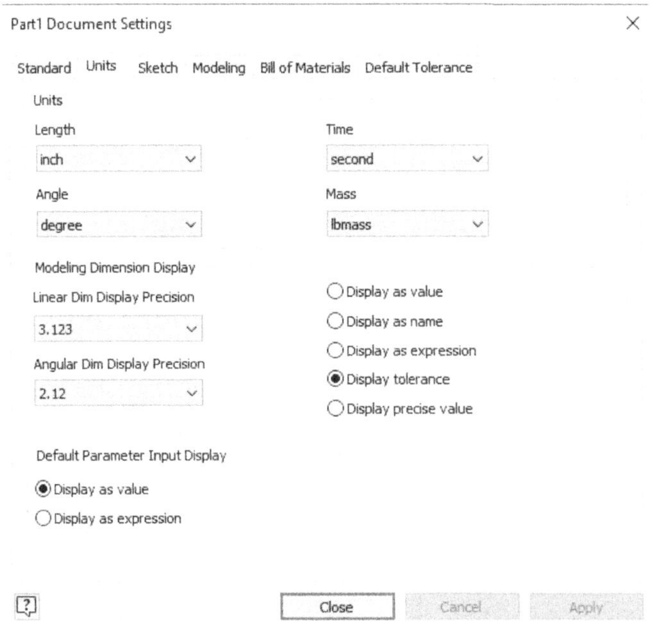

Figure 13–7

Sketch Tab

To set the sketch grid settings, select the *Sketch* tab, as shown in Figure 13–8. You can also set the radius for corner bends placed on 3D lines as you sketch them, as well as line weight display.In an assembly, the *Sketch* tab has the same options as a part, except for the 3D Sketch area. In a drawing, the *Sketch* tab only contains Snap Spacing and Grid Display areas.

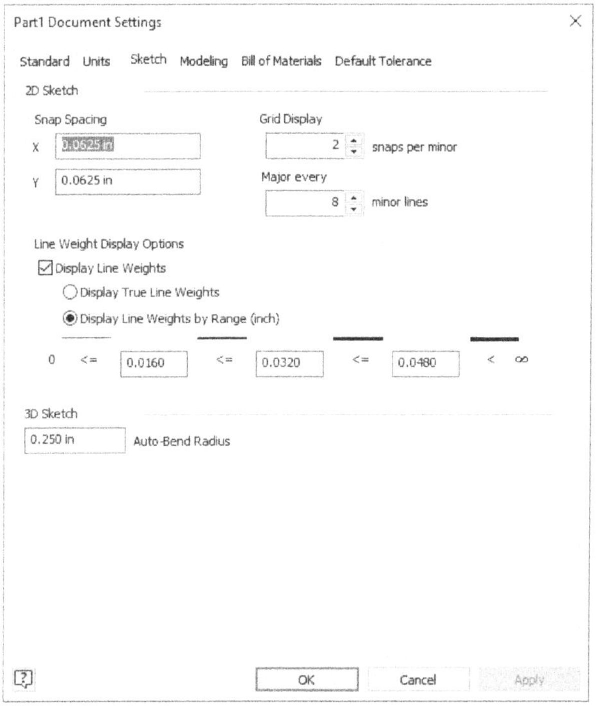

Figure 13–8

Modeling Tab

The *Modeling* tab (shown in Figure 13–9) controls whether adaptivity is available in an assembly, 3D snap spacing when you sketch in 3D in an active part, sectioning through a part, and tapped hole diameter, initial view extents. In addition, you can define naming prefixes and defaults. In an assembly, the *Modeling* tab has a reduced set of options that pertain to the assembly environment, and it also contains some additional options for Interactive Contact. The *Modeling* tab is not available in a drawing.

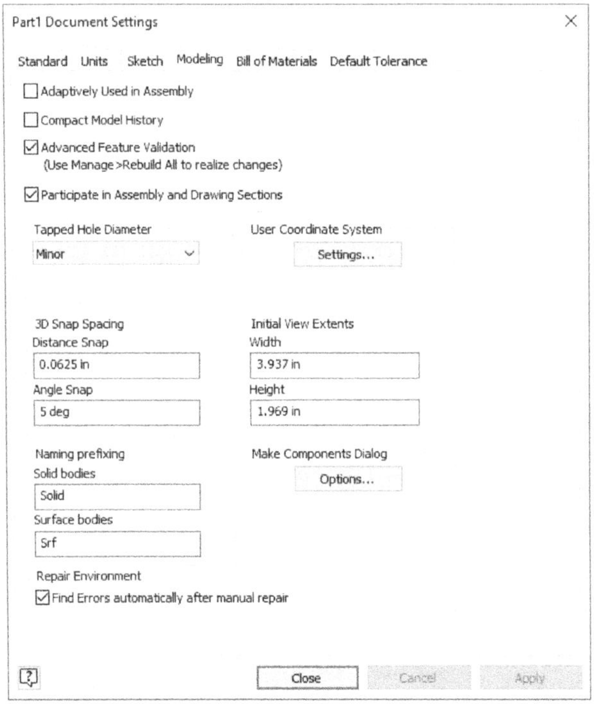

Figure 13–9

Bill of Materials Tab

The *Bill of Materials* tab (shown in Figure 13–10) controls the bill of materials settings, such as BOM structure and unit quantity. In an assembly, the *Bill of Materials* tab is the same as in a part. The *Bill of Materials* tab is not available in a drawing.

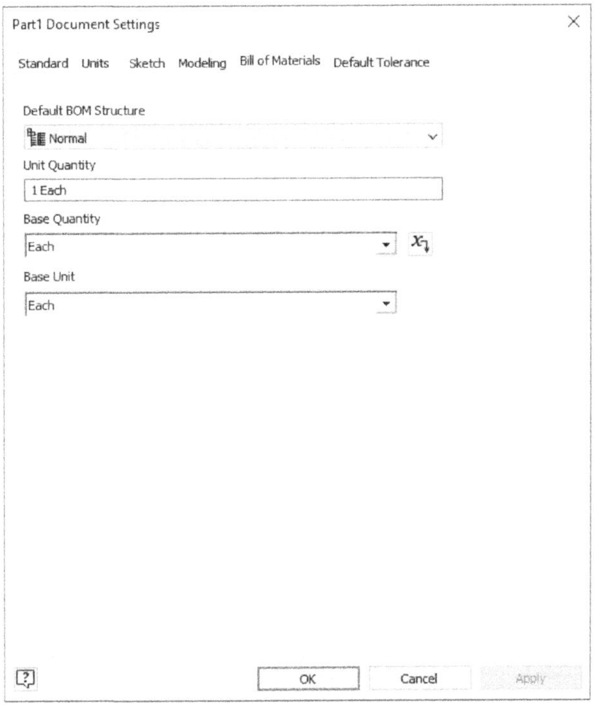

Figure 13–10

Default Tolerance Tab

The *Default Tolerance* tab controls the linear and angular part dimension tolerances and precision levels. The *Default Tolerance* tab is not available in a drawing or in an assembly.

Drawing Tab

The *Drawing* tab (shown in Figure 13–11) controls settings such as deferring updates to drawings, dimension updates, cross hatch clipping, automated centerlines, and shaded view settings. This tab is only available in a drawing.

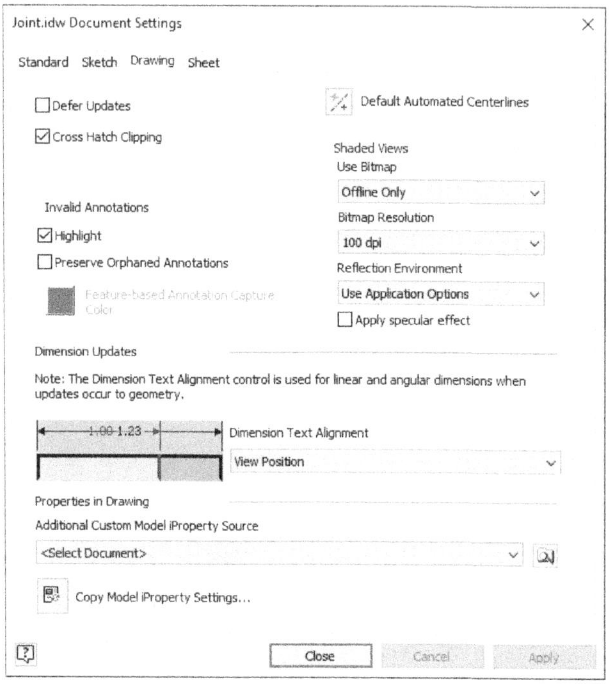

Figure 13–11

Sheet Tab

The *Sheet* tab controls colors in a drawing and the default name for each sheet (default is Sheet). This tab is only available in a drawing.

13.3 File Properties

You can store non-graphical information in a file using the iProperties dialog box. To open the iProperties dialog box, right-click on the filename at the top of the Model browser and select **iProperties**. Alternatively, in the File menu, select **iProperties** to open the iProperties dialog box. The iProperties dialog box for the current file opens, similar to that shown in Figure 13–12. Information from the iProperties dialog box is automatically entered in the drawing title block of your model.

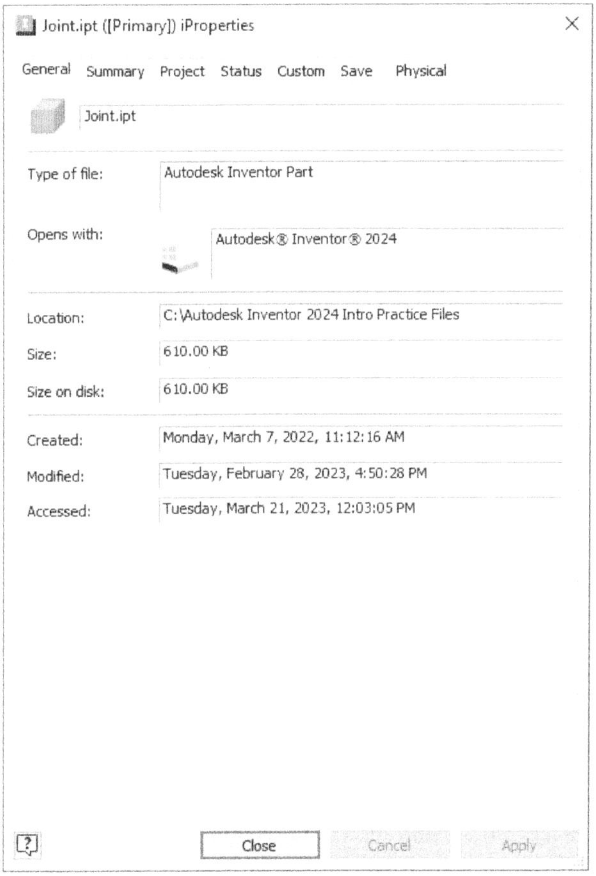

Figure 13–12

The tabs on the Properties dialog box are described as follows:

Tabs	Description
General tab	Displays basic file information, such as file format, location, and size. This information is read-only.
Summary tab	Enables you to enter information in several categories. The information can be used in a title block, or for sorting and searching for files. • In the *Author* field, the username for the user logged onto the computer is automatically entered when the file is created. You can change the name by typing over it. • The **Save Preview Picture** option at the bottom of the dialog box is grayed out and is no longer used.
Project tab	Enables you to enter information for tracking the design. • **Location:** Entered automatically when you assign the filename. It contains the path where the file is located. • **File Subtype:** Entered automatically and describes the type of file, such as **Modeling**, **Assembly**, or **Drawing**. • If you do not enter a *Part Number*, the name of the file is automatically entered in that field. • The *Designer* field populates with the username for the user logged onto the computer when the file is created. You can change the name by typing over it. • The *Creation Date* field populates with the date on which the file was created. You can change the date by selecting the calendar on the right and selecting a new date.
Status tab	Enables you to track the status of the file.
Custom tab	Enables you to define your own properties. The properties display in the lower area of the dialog box. • You can set the type to **Text**, **Date**, **Number**, or **Yes/No**. • Custom properties can be used to search/sort files and create reports.
Save tab	Enables you to create a thumbnail image of the file that displays in the File Open dialog box and to determine which image is used.
Physical tab	Enables you to display the physical properties of the part or assembly. It is not available in presentation or drawing files. In a part file, you can change the material of the part to change the properties.

Some information in the iProperties dialog box can also be accessed from outside of the Autodesk Inventor software. Right-click on the name of the file in Windows Explorer and select **iProperties** to open the Properties dialog box for that file.

Chapter Review Questions

1. Which of the following statements is true about the Application Options or Document Settings dialog boxes?
   a. The options set in the Document Settings dialog box only apply to the current file.
   b. The color scheme for the software is applied only to the current file using the Document Settings dialog box.
   c. The Document Settings dialog box is only accessible when working in a drawing file.
   d. Any Application Option settings are maintained for the entire session that the Autodesk Inventor software is open. The option must be reset in any future sessions, even if using the same model file.

2. Which of the following describe how to access the iProperties dialog box? (Select all that apply.)
   a. File menu>iProperties.
   b. Right-click on the filename in the Model browser and select iProperties.
   c. Right-click on the feature name in the Model browser and select Properties.
   d. Using the Select Bodies selection priority, right-click on the model in the graphics window and select Properties.

3. Which tabs in the iProperties dialog box (shown in Figure 13–13) are used to add non-geometrical information to the model? (Select all that apply.)

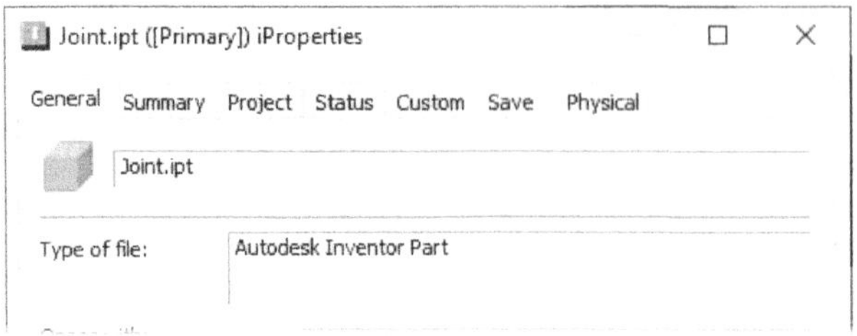

Figure 13–13

a. Summary
b. Project
c. Status
d. Custom
e. Save
f. Physical

Command Summary

Button	Command	Location
	**Application Options**	• **Ribbon:** *Tools* tab>Options panel • **File** menu>Options
	**Document Settings**	• **Ribbon:** *Tools* tab>Options panel
N/A	**iProperties**	• **File** menu • **Context Menu**: In Model browser with model name selected • **Windows Explorer**: right-click on the model name and select **iProperties**

Appendix

A

Feature Relationships

Feature relationships are defined as a dependency between features. They are established as you add each additional feature to the model. If the parent feature is modified or deleted, the child features are affected. Learning how to use feature relationships to your advantage and how to make changes to unwanted relationships is a valuable tool in designing models.

Learning Objectives

- Understand the parent/child relationships that are established when creating pick and place features.
- Understand the parent/child relationships that are established when creating sketched features.
- Use the Model browser and Parameters dialog box to recognize the possible relationships between features in the model.
- Use editing tools to change an existing parent/child relationship in a model.

A.1 Establishing Feature Relationships

Feature relationships are the result of a dependency between features. The independent feature is referred to as the parent and the dependent feature is called the child. When such a dependency exists, the parent feature is used to place or locate the child feature. Feature relationships can be created when pick and place or sketched features are used.

Pick and Place Features

For pick and place features (e.g., holes, fillets, chamfers) you are only required to select placement references to locate a feature. The placement references establish feature relationships between the new feature and the existing features that were used for placement.

- In Figure A–1, the hole shown on the right was created by referencing the indicated face and the center of the cylindrical extrusion. A feature relationship has now been established between the hole (child) an the cylindrical extrusion (parent).

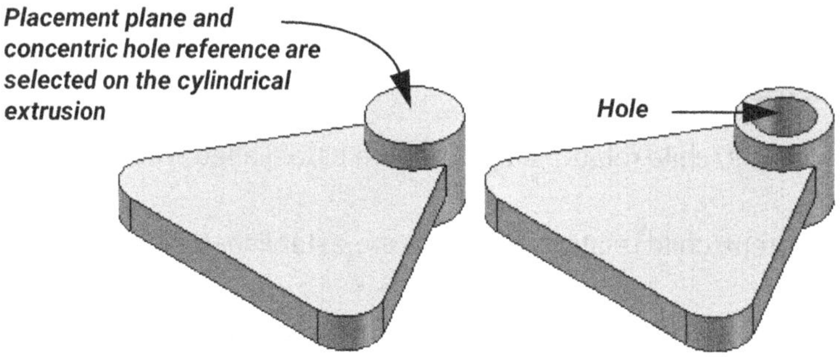

Figure A–1

- In Figure A–2, the fillet shown on the right was created by referencing the edge shown. The edge reference establishes a feature relationship with the cylindrical extrusion. A feature relationship has now been established between the fillet (child) an the cylindrical extrusion (parent).

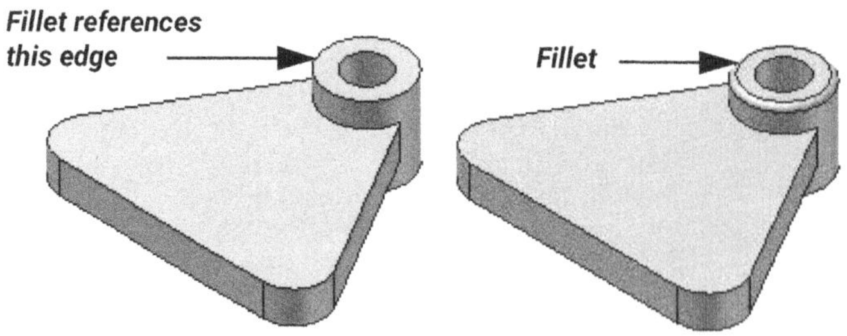

Figure A–2

- In Figure A–3, the chamfer shown on the right was created by referencing the edge shown. The edge reference establishes a feature relationship with the cylindrical extrusion. A feature relationship has now been established between the chamfer (child) an the cylindrical extrusion (parent).

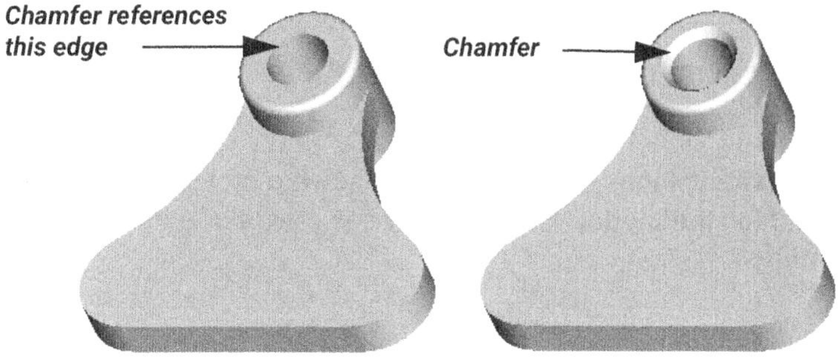

Figure A–3

Sketched Features

The process of creating a sketched feature results in the creation of feature relationships when the sketch plane and sketch references are selected. Additionally, references might be required for using some of the available depth options.

Sketch Planes

The sketch plane defines a planar reference on which a 2D section is sketched. The sketch plane is then established as a parent of the 2D sketch and any features that are subsequently created from that sketch.

- In Figure A–4, the sketch plane for a new sketched feature is a face belonging to an extrusion. This makes the new sketch and any feature created from the sketch a child of the extrusion.

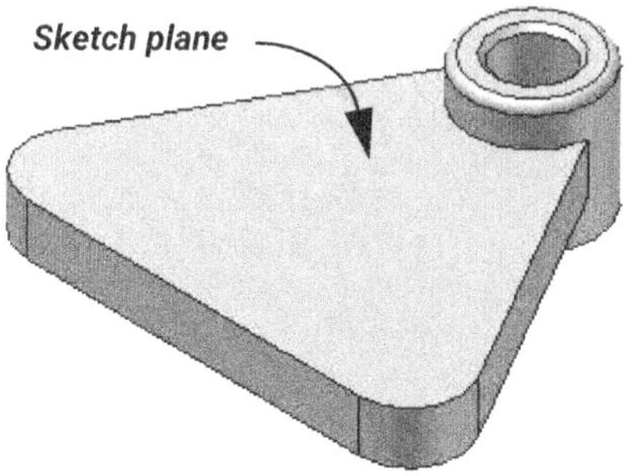

Figure A–4

Sketching References

Sketching references are used to locate sketched geometry. When you select sketching references, feature relationships are established. The sketched geometry is located with respect to these entities using dimensions and constraints. Sketching references can be projected origin or work features, or existing model edges and faces.

> **Note:** *Origin work features provide robust sketching references because they can never be moved or deleted.*

- In Figure A–5, the origin planes (YZ and XZ planes) were projected onto the sketch plane for locating the sketch on the model. These references create a feature relationship with the origin plane features.

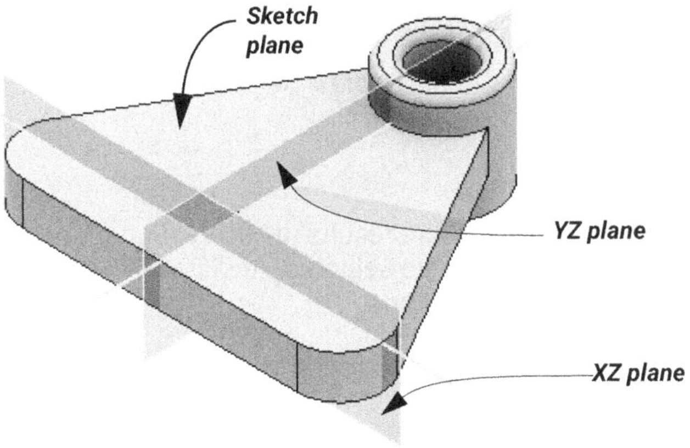

Figure A–5

- In Figure A–6, the cut was located relative to the edge of the square extrusion by assigning a dimension and vertical constraint. The cut is a child of the extrusion and remains in alignment. Additionally, the bottom edge of the base feature was also selected to locate the cut so the base feature is also a parent.

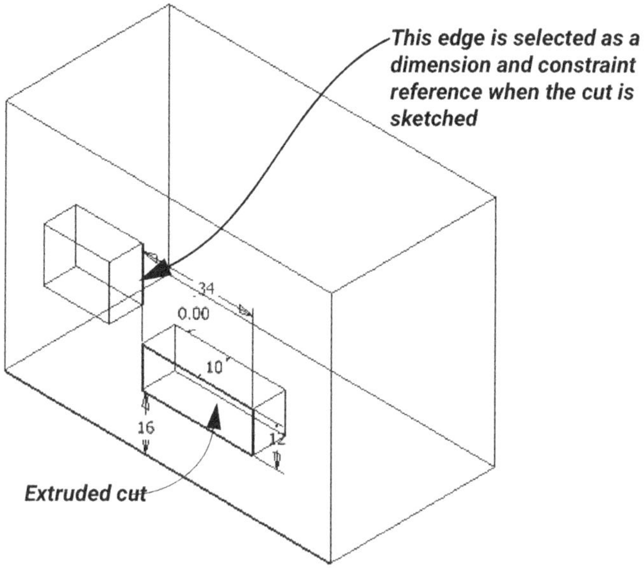

Figure A–6

- In Figure A–7, the rectangular sketch was located by dimensioning it to the hole and the chamfer. The features created with this sketch are now a child of both the hole and the chamfer.

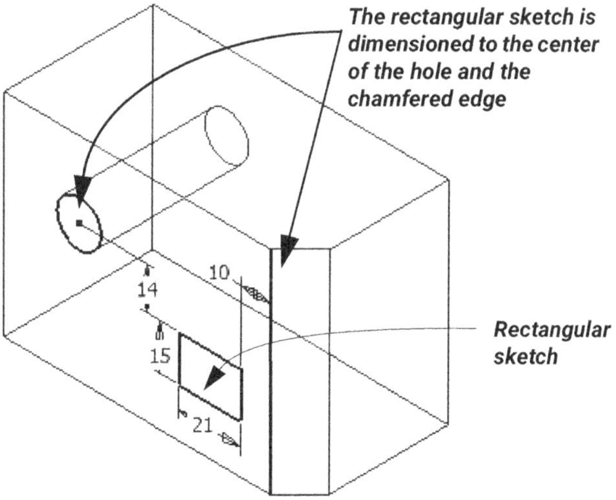

Figure A–7

Note: *It is not recommended that you dimension a feature to another feature that might change later in the design (e.g., fillets or chamfers). If the reference feature is changed or deleted, the new feature might no longer be positioned correctly, or it might fail because it has lost its reference.*

- Certain geometry creation tools, such as offsetting an existing edge, create an implicit alignment and therefore establish feature relationships. In Figure A–8, the entities at the bottom of the base extrusion are selected as edge references for offsetting. As a result, the new feature is a child of the base feature.

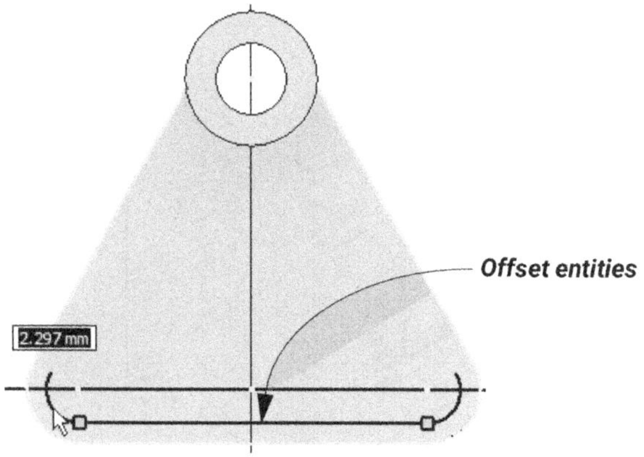

Figure A–8

Note: A feature relationship would also have been established if concentric arcs were used to create the feature.

Depth Options

Some From and Distance options establish feature relationships. The (To) and (To Next) options shown in Figure A–9 establish feature relationships because a plane or face must be selected as a reference to define the depth.

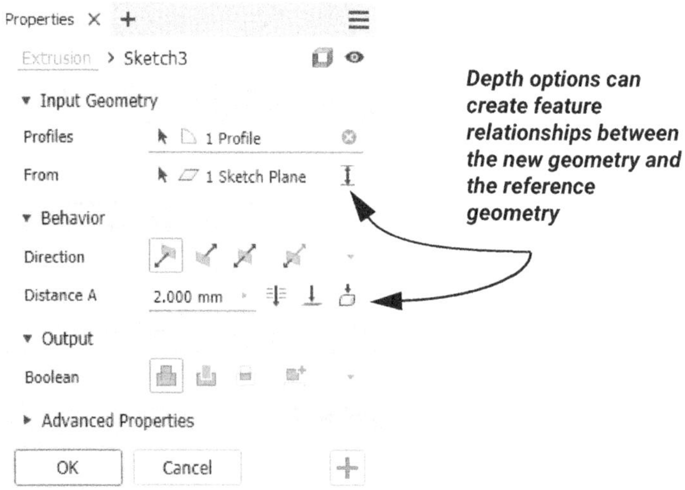

Figure A–9

A.2 Controlling Feature Relationships

Feature relationships can make models more robust and powerful. Use the following tips to control feature relationships:

- Use the origin features. Since they are never deleted, origin features are useful as sketch planes and sketching references. This establishes the origin feature, rather than a geometry feature, as parents of future features.
- Consider a face carefully before selecting it as a sketch plane. Is it the best selection as a parent for this feature?
- When in the Sketch environment, select references and project from the model in a 3D orientation to ensure that you are selecting the correct references.
- When in the Sketch environment, consider using and offsetting edges, as well as sketching concentric arcs and circles to establish relationships.
- Carefully consider the references before using the **To Next**, **To**, or **Between** depth options. Is this reference the best selection as a parent for this feature?
- Once a pick and place or sketched feature has been created, you can also establish a feature relationship using equations.

A.3 Investigating Feature Relationships

In many cases, you might be required to continue someone else's design or make modifications to a completed model. In such cases, it is important to know how to investigate the model to help understand the existing design and feature relationships. You can use the Model browser and Parameters dialog box to accomplish this.

Model Browser

The Model browser displays all of the features in the model. By reviewing the Model browser, you can understand the hierarchy of the model and understand which features can possibly reference others.

To provide a better overview of the relationships between features, you can right-click on a feature name in the Model browser and select **Relationships**. The Relationships dialog box displays, similar to that shown in Figure A–10. This dialog box can quickly reveal the relationships between features and enable you to make changes, if required.

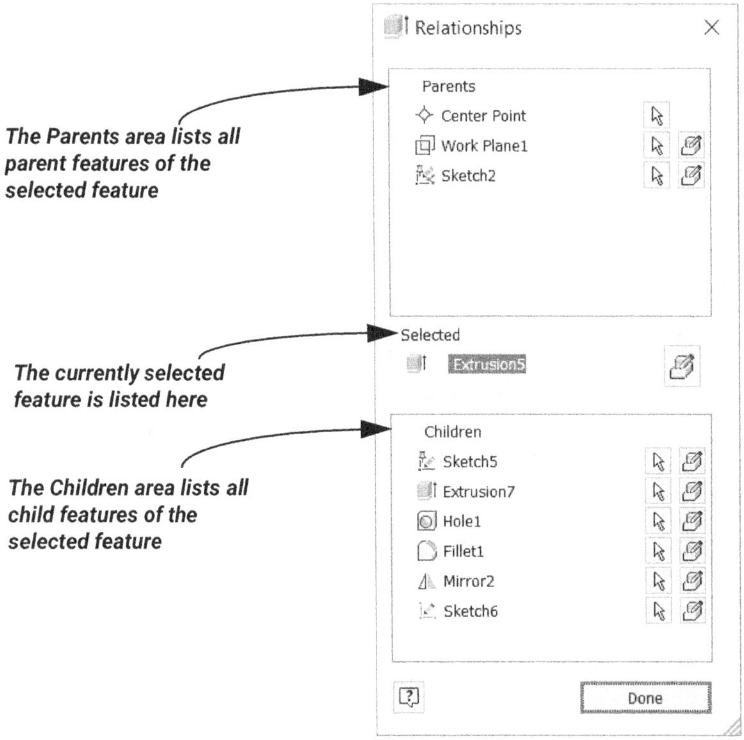

Figure A–10

Note: *To select features directly in the graphics window, ensure that* ***Select Features*** *is the active option in the selection filter list.*

- **(Make Selected):** Enables you to sets any of the parent or child features as the new selected item.
- **(Edit Feature):** Enables you to access the Edit Feature dialog box for any of the parent or child features.

Equations

Equations are used in models to control design intent. In doing so, they establish feature relationships. You can use the Parameters dialog box to investigate if equations exist in the model. To open the dialog box, in the *Manage* tab>Parameters panel, click f_x (Parameters) or click f_x in the Quick Access Toolbar. Any existing relationships display in the *Equation* column, as shown in Figure A–11.

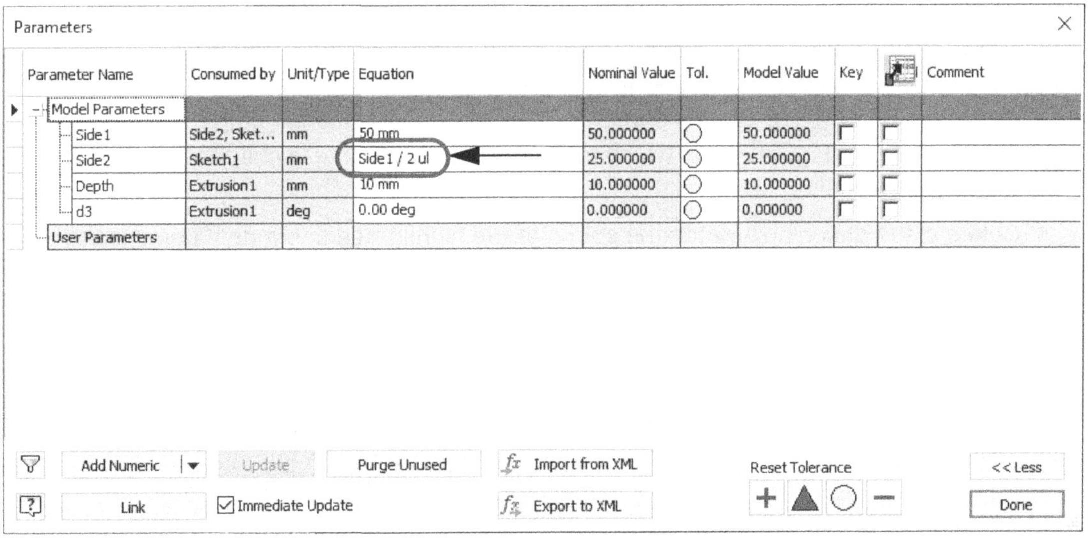

Figure A–11

Hint: Displaying Equations in a Model

To display equations when dimensions are shown, right-click and select **Dimension Display>Expression**. To display sketch dimensions as an expression, click in the Status Bar and select **Expression**.

A.4 Changing Feature Relationships

When the design intent of the model changes, unwanted relationships might occur as a result of modifying or deleting a parent feature. The goal of making a design change is to ensure that not only the feature being changed is modified, but that any children update as expected. Consider using the following editing tools when changes to parent/child dependency are required: **Edit Sketch**, **Redefine**, **Show Dimensions**, **Dimension Display**, **Edit Feature**, and **Delete**.

- **Edit Sketch:** Enables you to access the Sketch environment to define new references or sketch elements.
- **Redefine:** Enables you to change the sketch plane of an existing sketch.
- **Show Dimensions** and **Dimension Display:** Enable you to display feature dimensions and equation relationships in the graphics window. Double-click on the dimensions to change dimensional values or equations in the Edit Dimension dialog box.
- **Edit Feature:** Enables you to access the dialog box or Properties panel that was used when the feature was created where you can define new references or elements.
- **Delete:** Enables you to delete a selected feature by pressing <Delete> or right-clicking and selecting **Delete**. When deleting a feature with children, the Delete Features dialog box opens (as shown in Figure A–12) which requires you to decide how child features should be handled during deletion.
    - Colors in the dialog box match the colors of the highlighted dependent items in the graphics window.
    - You can clear the options in the Delete Features dialog box (e.g., **consumed sketches and features**, **dependent sketches and features**, etc.) to maintain dependent features and preserve sketches in the model after deletion.
    - Ensure that missing child references (identified by ⓘ in the Model browser) are fixed after a feature is deleted.

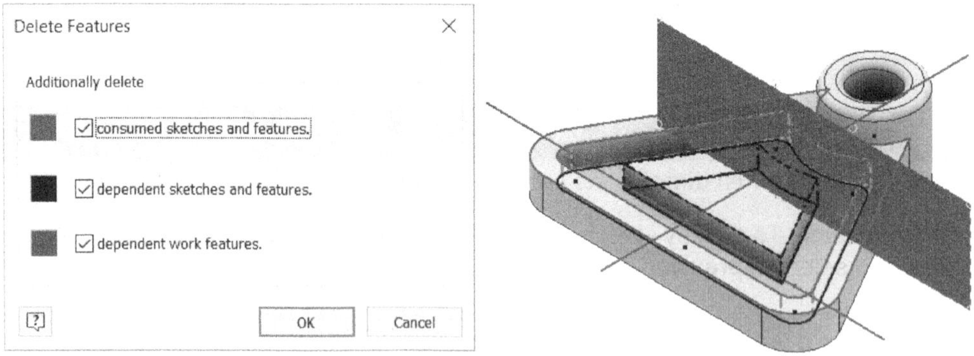

Figure A–12

Hint: Missing Sketch Planes

When deleting a feature that also removes the sketch plane of another feature, a work plane is automatically created in the model to replace the deleted sketch plane. The new work plane is fixed relative to the coordinate system. It is recommended that you replace the work plane and redefine the sketch plane to a reference that is relative to the model geometry.

Practice A1
Change Feature Relationships

Practice Objective

- Use editing tools to efficiently change existing parent/child relationships in a model.

In this practice, you will open the model shown on the left in Figure A–13 and delete the hole and chamfer. In deleting these features, the Delete Features dialog box opens, indicating any relationships to these features. You will deal with these relationships to create the model shown on the right.

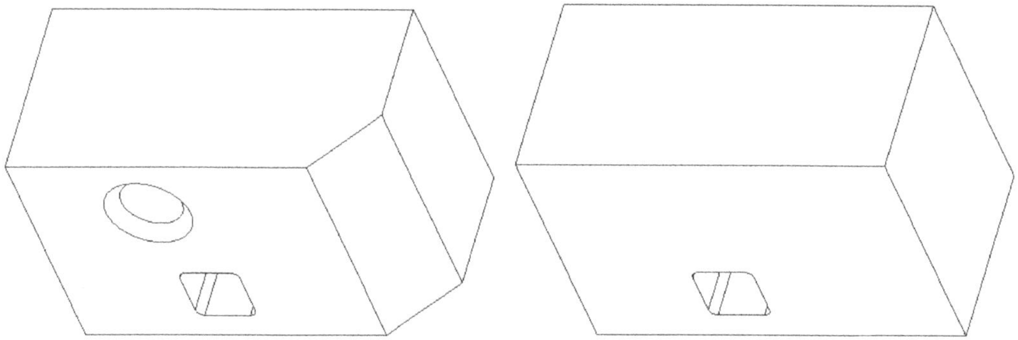

Figure A–13

Task 1: Open and investigate a part.

1. Open **pc01.ipt**.
2. Review the Model browser to understand the hierarchy of the model and understand which features can reference others.
3. Display the dimensions associated with **Extrusion2** (square cut) to review its dimensioning scheme. The square cut is located with respect to **Chamfer1** and **Hole1** (dimensioned to the center of the hole and the edge of the chamfer).

4. Modify the **Chamfer1** dimension to **5.00**. The model before the chamfer dimensions are modified is shown on the left in Figure A–14, and the model after modifications are finished is shown on the right. The cut has moved to the right as a result of modifying the chamfer. Is this the design intent? Why is it generally not a good idea to dimension the edges created by features, such as fillets and chamfers?

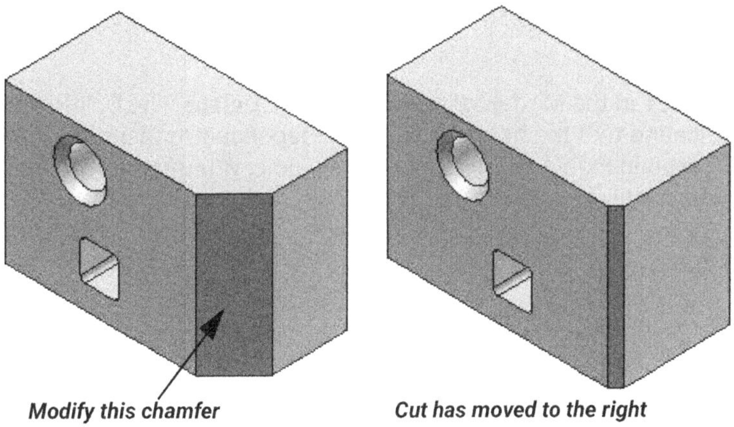

Figure A–14

Task 2: Redefine the location of the cut.

1. Edit the sketch for **Extrusion2**. You need to re-dimension the cut so that it does not reference the chamfer.
2. Delete the **50** dimension that locates the cut to the chamfer. Additionally, delete the projected edge that was projected from the chamfer.
3. The cut is now under-constrained and needs one dimension added. Add a dimension from the cut to the vertical edge on the left side of the model, as shown in Figure A–15.

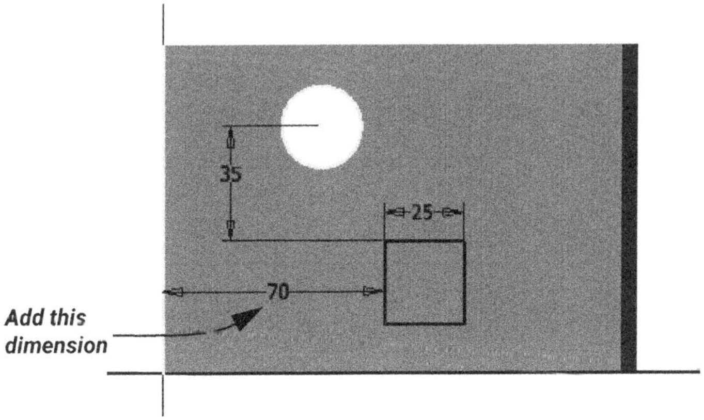

Figure A–15

4. Finish the sketch.
5. Delete **Chamfer1**. The Delete Features dialog box opens, indicating features are dependent on the chamfer. The Model browser indicates that **Hole1** and **Extrusion2** are placed on the face that is affected by a chamfer. This face still exists after the chamfer is deleted so deleting it will not cause a failure. Click **OK**. Is the square cut or hole affected?

Task 3: Delete the hole.

1. Right-click on **Hole1** in the Model browser and select **Delete**. The Delete Features dialog box opens, indicating that the hole has children (dependent/consumed sketches and features), as shown in Figure A–16. To delete the hole, you must fix the references for the dependent feature (square cut).

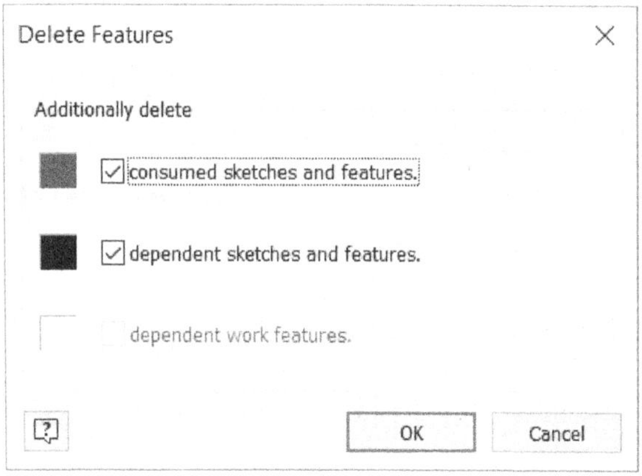

Figure A–16

2. Click **Cancel** to close the Delete Features dialog box and cancel the delete action.
3. Edit the sketch for **Extrusion2**. Re-dimension the cut from the top edge of the base feature instead of from the center of the hole.
4. Finish the sketch.
5. Right-click on **Hole1** in the Model browser and select **Delete**. The Delete Feature dialog box opens, indicating that the hole has referenced consumed sketches and features.
6. The sketch and chamfer do not need to exist without the hole. Click **OK** to delete both features.
7. Save the part and close the window.

End of practice

Practice A2
Delete a Sketch Plane

Practice Objective

- Use the Delete Features dialog box such that the dependent sketches and features are not deleted with their parent geometry.

In this practice, you will open a model that has been provided for you, delete a feature, and observe how it affects the sketch plane of another feature. The original and final models are shown on the left and right in Figure A–17 respectively.

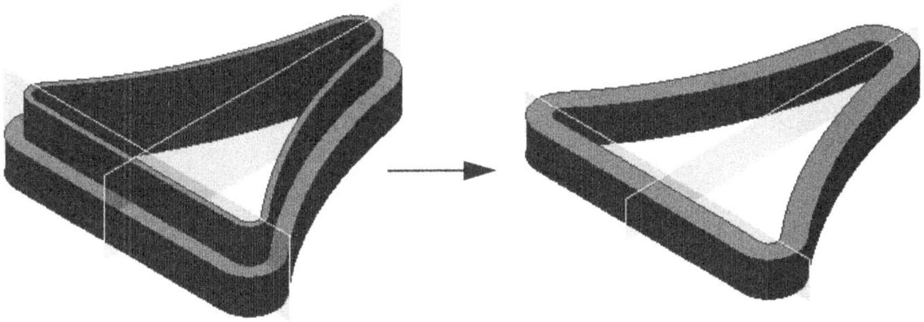

Figure A–17

Task 1: Open a part file.

1. Open **redefine.ipt**. The model displays as shown in Figure A–18.

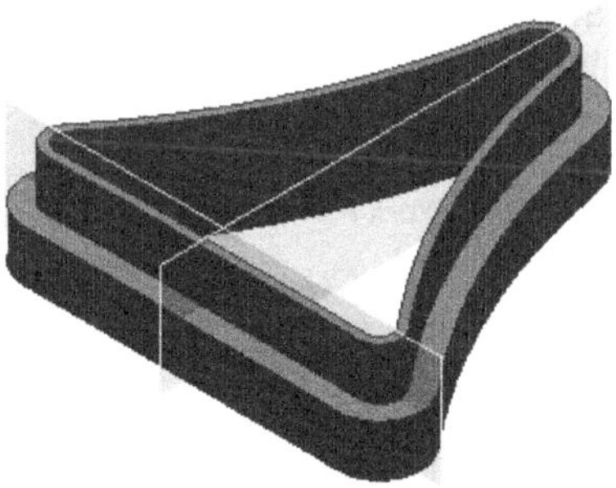

Figure A–18

2. Edit the sketch for **Extrusion3**. Note that the sketch for the cut is placed on the top face of **Extrusion2**.

3. Finish the sketch. As an alternative, you can also right-click on the sketch associated with Extrusion3 in the Model browser and select **Show Input** to highlight its sketch plane.

Task 2: Delete Extrusion2.

1. Select **Extrusion2** in the Model browser and press <Delete>. The Delete Features dialog box opens as shown in Figure A–19, indicating that the highlighted features (**Extrusion2**, **Extrusion3**, and **Sketch3**) will also be deleted. However, the design intent is to maintain the cut.

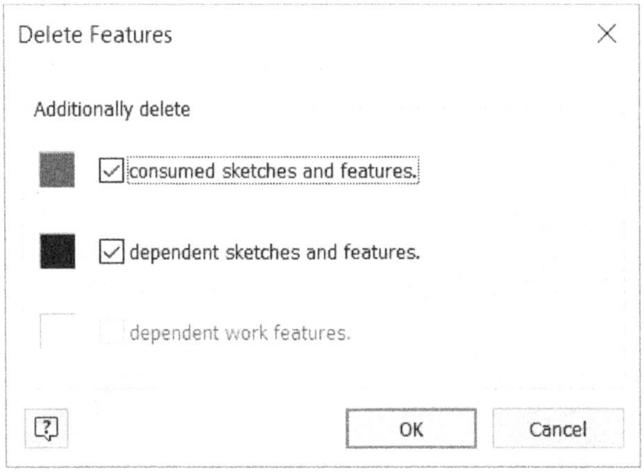

Figure A–19

Note: The colors in the dialog box match the highlighted dependent sketches and feature colors in the graphics window.

2. Clear the **dependent sketches and features** option.
3. Click **OK** to delete the **Extrusion2** sketch. The model displays as shown in Figure A–20 with **Work Plane1** created automatically in place of the deleted face. The sketch was automatically transferred to **Work Plane1** when the original sketch plane was deleted.

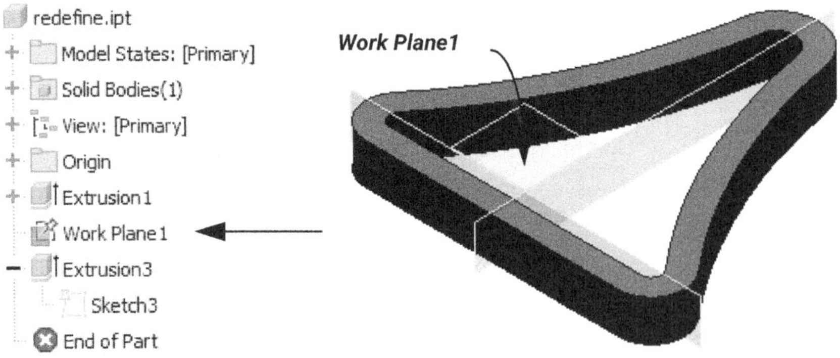

Figure A–20

4. It is recommended that you redefine the placement plane of the sketch to select a more stable reference that will truly reflect the geometry. Right-click on **Sketch3** and select **Redefine**. Select the face of **Extrusion1** as the new sketch plane.
5. Delete **Work Plane1**.
6. Save the model and close the window.

End of practice

Chapter Review Questions

1. A pick and place feature can be the parent of another pick and place feature.

a. True

b. False

2. Which of the following actions create a feature relationship when sketching a feature? (Select all that apply.)

a. Selecting the sketching plane.

b. Selecting sketching references.

c. Creating an offset entity.

d. Using an existing edge to create a new entity.

e. Dimensioning the length of a line.

f. Aligning a new entity with an existing entity.

g. Extruding to a Blind depth.

h. Extruding through all surfaces.

i. Extruding to intersect with a selected face or plane.

3. Which of the following features create a parent/child relationship when created in a model? (Select all that apply.)

a. Origin Planes

b. Work Planes

c. Extrude

d. Hole

e. Chamfer

f. Fillet

g. Shell

4. Which of the following processes of creating a sketched cut feature result in the creation of feature relationships? (Select all that apply.)

a. Selecting sketch planes.

b. Selecting sketching references.

c. Cutting through all geometry.

5. If a parent feature is deleted, which of the following options can be used to change the references to the child feature? (Select all that apply.)

a. Edit Sketch

b. .Share Sketch

c. .Redefine

d. .Edit Feature

6. The Delete Features dialog box opens if you select and delete the hole shown in Figure A–21. Which of the following best describes why this dialog box becomes available?

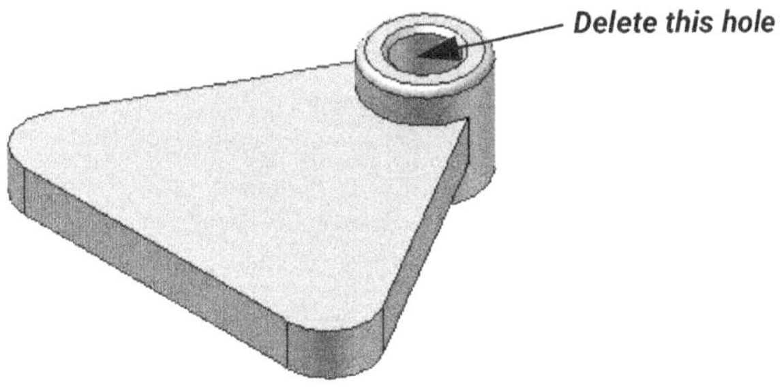

Figure A–21

a. Because the Delete Features dialog box opens when deleting all of the pick and place feature types.

b. Because a chamfer was placed on the edge generated by the creation of the hole.

c. Because there are other pick and place features in the model and you need to select the other ones to delete at the same time.

d. Because the hole was placed as a Coaxial hole and is a child to the extruded cylinder.

7. The (Make Selected) icon in the Relationships dialog box only enables you to change the active feature to a listed parent feature. You cannot use it to activate a child.

   a. True

   b. False

Appendix B

Sketching Options

This appendix provides a detailed summary of the options that you can use on the Sketch Ribbon to create a sketch.

Learning Objective

- Understand the available sketching options.

B.1 Summary of the Sketch Geometry Creation Options

All of the sketch geometry creation options are located in the *Sketch* tab>Create panel. Expand the commands to locate all of the options. A summarized list of the available sketch creation options is as follows.

(Line)	Creates straight lines or arced segments. Select two points to create a line. Selecting a third point creates a line between the second and third point. To sketch an arc, press and drag an arced entity from the end point of a line. 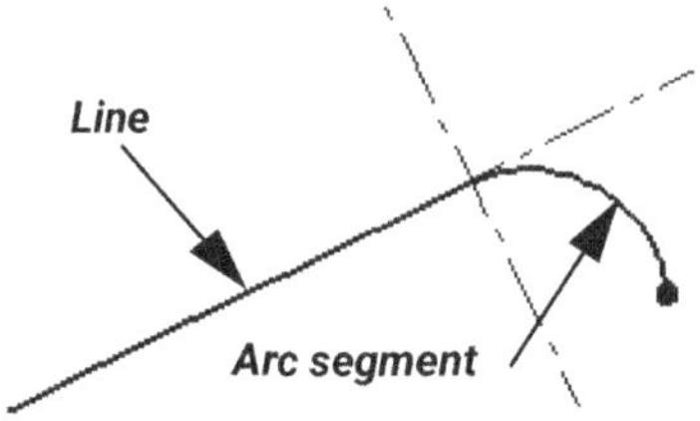
(Spline (Control Vertex))	Enables you to sketch a free-form curve. Select multiple points to create the spline. Each point that is placed defines the vertices of the control frame.
(Spline (Interpolation))	Enables you to sketch a free-form curve. Select multiple points to create the spline. The spline is drawn through each point.
(Equation Curve)	Draws a curve based on the entry of an equation.
(Bridge Curve)	Draws a smooth G2 curve between two selected entities.
(Circle (Center Point))	Creates a circle by selecting its center point and a point on its perimeter.
(Circle (Tangent))	Creates a circle based on three lines that you select. The circle is tangent to all three lines. There might be more than one circle that can be drawn for any three given lines. You can control which circle displays, based on where you select the lines. Select the line near the locations at which the circle should touch.
(Ellipse)	Creates an ellipse based on its center, and one point on each of its major and minor axes.
(Arc (Three Point))	Draws an arc based on three points that you select. First select the two end points, then select a point on the arc. The last point determines the center, radius, and included angle of the arc.

(Arc (Tangent))	Draws an arc tangent to an existing line or an arc. Select the end of the line or arc as the start point. The arc is drawn tangent to the selected object. Complete the arc by selecting a second point. When the first point is selected, the object to which the arc is tangent is highlighted in red, and a green dot displays at its end point.
(Arc (Center Point))	Enables you to select three points to draw the arc. The first point determines the center of the arc and the other two points determine the ends of the arc. You can select the end points in either order. After selecting the first point, move the mouse in the direction in which the arc should be drawn.
(Rectangle (Two Point))	Creates a rectangle with its sides parallel to the X- and Y-axes. Select two opposite corners to create the rectangle.
(Rectangle (Three Point))	Creates a rectangle at any angle. Select three points to create the rectangle. The first two points that you select define one side and the third point locates the opposite side.
(Rectangle (Two Point Center))	Creates a rectangle along the X and Y axis. Select two points to create the rectangle. The first point defines the center of the rectangle and the second point defines the outer corner.
(Rectangle (Three Point Center))	Creates a rectangle at any angle. Select three points to create the rectangle. The first two points define one side and the third point locates the center.
(Slot (Center to Center))	Draws a slot by selecting three points. The first two points define the entire length of the slot between its centers, and the third selection defines the slot's thickness.
(Slot (Overall))	Draws a slot by selecting three points. The first two points define the entire length of the slot and the third selection defines the slot's thickness.
(Slot (Center Point))	Draws a slot by selecting three points. Select the center point of the slot, followed by the center point of one arc and finally select a point to define the slot's thickness.
(Slot (Three Point Arc))	Draws a slot by selecting four points. The first three points define the arc length and radius of the slot and the fourth selection defines the slot's thickness.
(Slot (Center Point Arc))	Draws a slot by selecting four points. The first three points define the center point of the arc, its arc length and radius of the slot. The fourth selection defines the slot's thickness.

(Polygon)	Draws regular polygons, where all sides and all angles are the same. Like rectangles, polygons can be drawn with a series of lines, but it is easier to draw using this specialized command. There are two options for drawing polygons: **Inscribed** and **Circumscribed**. **Inscribed** uses a vertex between the two edges to determine the size and orientation of the polygon. **Circumscribed** uses the midpoint of an edge to determine the size and orientation of the polygon. 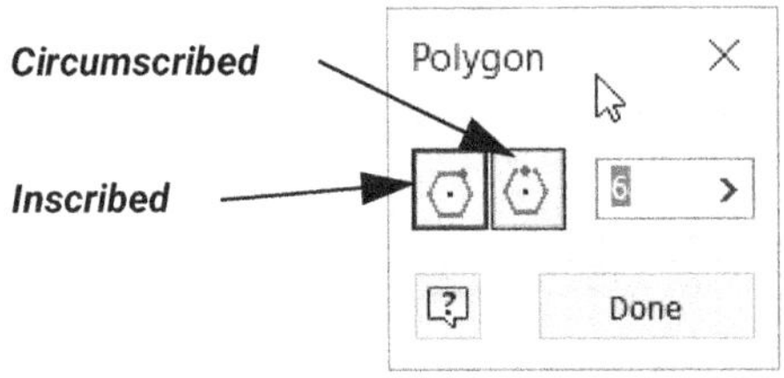
(Chamfer)	Adds an angled corner. The size of the chamfer is determined by distances along each line from their intersection, or by a distance and an angle.
(Fillet)	Adds an arc to create a rounded corner, and dimensions the arc. The 2D Fillet dialog box enables you to specify the radius of the fillet.
(Point)	Adds points to the sketch.

B.2 Summary of the Sketch Editing Options

All of the sketch editing options are located in the *Sketch* tab> Modify and Pattern panels. A summarized list of the available options is as follows.

(Move)	Moves objects more precisely and enables you to copy sketch entities.
(Trim)	Removes the segment to the nearest intersection in each direction from the point selected. If an intersection only occurs in one direction, the end of an object is removed. If intersections occur in both directions, the center of the object is removed.
(Scale)	Enlarges or reduces the size of sketched entities by entering a scale factor as a multiplier.
(Copy)	Copies source entities to one or more new locations in the sketch. No relationship is established between the newly copied entities and the source.
(Extend)	Continues an object to meet the next object in its path or to close an open sketch.
(Stretch)	Stretches sketched entities. It enables you to stretch constrained geometry while maintaining its constraints. The select-and-drag technique cannot be used to manipulate constrained geometry.
(Rotate)	Rotates objects at a specified angle. You have the option of making a copy of the objects while rotating them.
(Split)	Splits an entity (line, arc, or spline) based on an intersecting entity (entity, work plane, or surface).
(Offset)	Creates parallel shapes with another object tool.
(Rectangular Pattern)	Creates copies of entities in two directions. The directions do not need to be perpendicular to each other.
(Circular Pattern)	Creates copies of entities about an axis.
(Mirror)	Copies entities across a center line.

B.3 Summary of the Sketch Constraint Options

All of the sketch constraint options are located in the *Sketch* tab>
Constrain panel. A summarized list of the available constraints that is as follows.

(Coincident)	Makes two selected points coincident. If the centers of two circles, arcs, or ellipses are selected, the objects become concentric. If a point and an object are selected, the point lies on the object or along the extension of the object.
(Collinear)	Makes selected entities lie on the same line.
(Concentric)	Makes selected arcs, circles, or ellipses have the same center point.
(Fix)	Fixes a selected point or object relative to the default coordinate system (Sketch environment 0,0,0).
(Parallel)	Makes two selected entities parallel to each other. This constraint can be applied between two lines or ellipse axes.
(Perpendicular)	Makes two selected entities perpendicular to each other. This constraint can be applied between two lines or ellipse axes.
(Horizontal)	Makes a line horizontal or aligns two selected points horizontally.
(Vertical)	Makes a line vertical or aligns two selected points vertically.
(Tangent)	Makes the selected items tangent. The objects do not need to touch to be tangent.
(Smooth (G2))	Makes selected entities continuous in curvature.
(Symmetric)	Makes selected lines or points symmetric about a reference line. To apply this constraint, select the first line or point, select the second line or point, and select the line of symmetry.
(Equal)	Makes selected lines the same length or all of the selected circles and arcs the same radius.
(Edit Coordinate System) (Constrain panel drop-down list)	Moves or rotates the coordinate system to any location on the sketch plane.

B.4 Dimension Type Options

A summarized list of the dimensioning types that can be used to constrain a sketch is as follows.

Linear: Select the entities to dimension. Move the cursor to the required location for the dimension and place the dimension using the left mouse button.

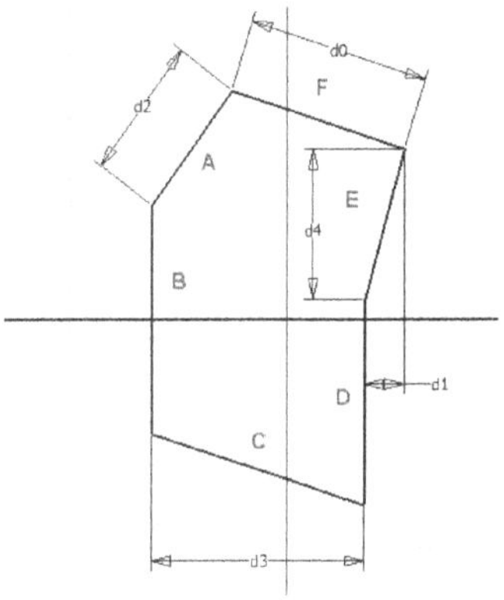

Center: Select two entities. Move the cursor to the required location and place the dimension using the left mouse button. To place an aligned dimension, place the dimension at a point along a line that joins the two entities that are being dimensioned. An aligned icon ( ) displays. Click the left mouse button, move the cursor to the required location, and click the left mouse button again. An aligned dimension displays. You can also right-click and select the location for the dimension when you are placing it.

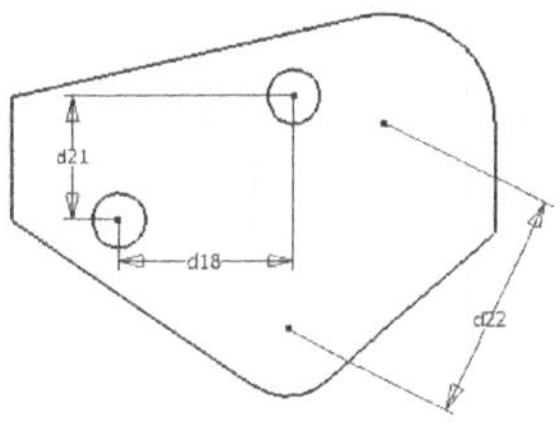

Arc Length: Select the arc, right-click, and select **Dimension Type>Arc Length** and then place the dimension.

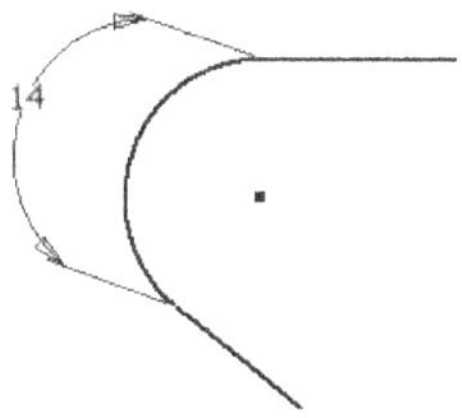

Radius/Diameter: Circles default to a diameter dimension. An arc defaults to a radius dimension.

To dimension a circle with a radial dimension, right-click and select **Radius**. Move the cursor to the required location and place the dimension using the left mouse button.

Use the same technique to dimension an arc with a diameter dimension. Right-click and select **Diameter**.

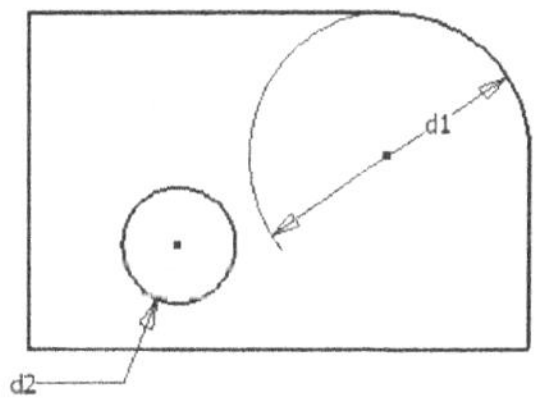

Angular: Select lines **A** and **B** and place the dimension using the left mouse button. The resulting angle depends on the placement location of the dimension.

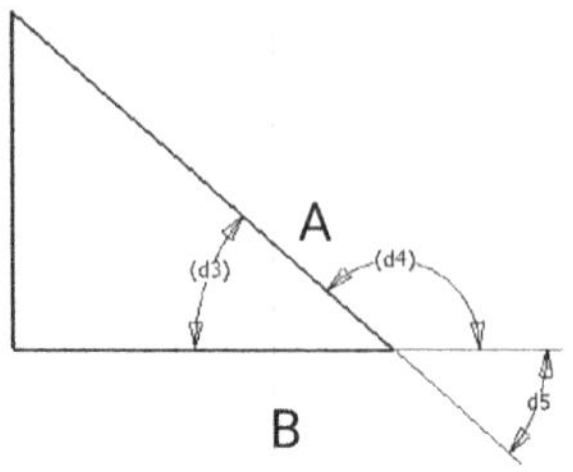

Tangent: Select arc **A** and move the cursor onto arc **B** so that  displays. Select arc **B** and place the dimension using the left mouse button.

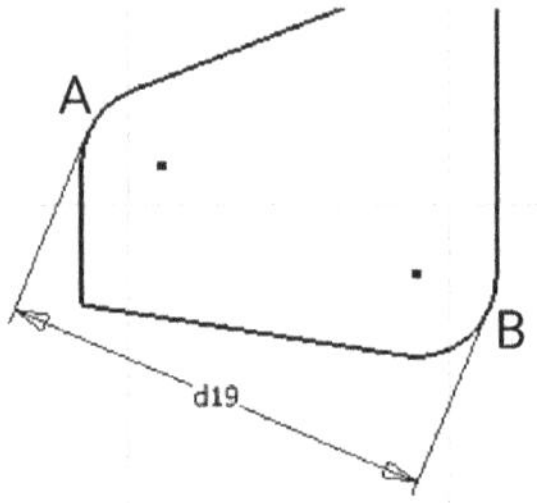

Revolved: Sketch half of the cross-section of a revolved feature. The diameter dimensions are created by selecting the center line of the revolved cross-section and then selecting the geometry, right-clicking, and selecting **Linear Diameter**.

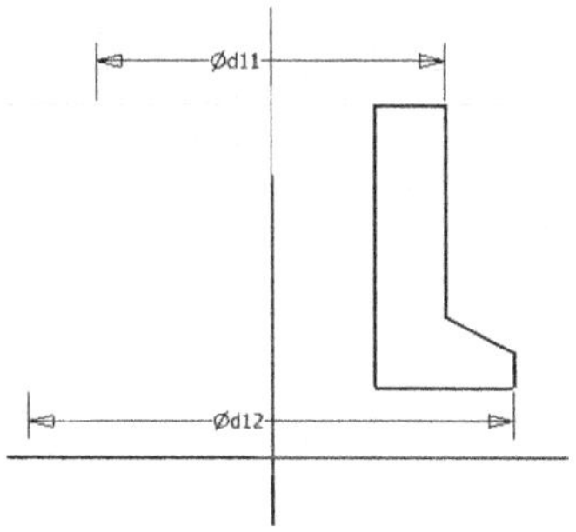

Index

S

T

U

V

W

Z

Made in the USA
Coppell, TX
04 November 2026

11207033R00269